STRATEGIES AND TECHNOLOGIES FOR GREENHOUSE GAS MITIGATION

Strategies and Technologies for Greenhouse Gas Mitigation

An Indo-German contribution to global efforts

Edited by
JÜRGEN-FRIEDRICH HAKE
Research Centre Juelich
NARENDRA BANSAL
Indian Institute of Technology, New Delhi
MANFRED KLEEMANN
Research Centre Juelich

*Studies
in
Green Research*

LONDON AND NEW YORK

First published 1999 by Ashgate Publishing

Reissued 2018 by Routledge
2 Park Square, Milton Park, Abingdon, Oxon OX14 4RN
711 Third Avenue, New York, NY 10017, USA

Routledge is an imprint of the Taylor & Francis Group, an informa business

Notice:
Product or corporate names may be trademarks or registered trademarks, and are used only for identification and explanation without intent to infringe.

Publisher's Note
The publisher has gone to great lengths to ensure the quality of this reprint but points out that some imperfections in the original copies may be apparent.

Disclaimer
The publisher has made every effort to trace copyright holders and welcomes correspondence from those they have been unable to contact.

A Library of Congress record exists under LC control number : 98074511

ISBN 13: 978-1-138-34418-1 (hbk)
ISBN 13: 978-1-138-34421-1 (pbk)
ISBN 13: 978-0-429-43865-3 (ebk)

Contents

v

PART II: RENEWABLE ENERGIES FOR CLIMATE
            PROTECTION

List of Contributors

Indian Contributors

Dr. Mahabir Singh Bhandari
Centre for Energy Studies, Indian Institute of Technology, New Delhi

Prof. Narendra Bansal
Centre for Energy Studies, Indian Institute of Technology, New Delhi

Dr. Bharat Bhargava
Ministry of Non-Conventional Energy Sources, New Delhi

Dr. Viresh Dutta
Centre for Energy Studies, Indian Institute of Technology, New Delhi

Prof. Hari Prakash Garg
Centre for Energy Studies, Indian Institute of Technology, New Delhi

Dr. Ajit Gupta
Ministry of Non-Conventional Energy Sources, New Delhi

Sujata Gupta
Tata Energy Research Institute, New Delhi

Dr. Prabhat Kumar Koner
Centre for Energy Studies, Indian Institute of Technology, New Delhi

Dr. Murari Lal
Indian Institute of Technology, New Delhi

Ritu Mathur
Tata Energy Research Institute, New Delhi

Dr. Jayant Ramakrishna Meshram
Ministry of Non-Conventional Energy Sources, New Delhi

Dr. Sudhir Mohan
Ministry of Non-Conventional Energy Sources, New Delhi

Thotuvelil Krishna Pillai Ayyappankutty Nair
Ministry of Environment and Forests, New Delhi

Dr. Leena Srivastava
Tata Energy Research Institute, New Delhi

German Contributors

Dr. Witta Ebel
Passive Building Institute Darmstadt

Frank Elbe
German Ambassador to India, New Delhi

Dr. Wolfgang Feist
Passive Building Institute Darmstadt

Dipl.-Math. Jürgen-Friedrich Hake
*Programme Group Systems Analysis and Technology Evaluation,
Research Centre Juelich*

Dipl.-Phys. Rainer Heckler
*Programme Group Systems Analysis and Technology Evaluation,
Research Centre Juelich*

Dr. Martin Kaltschmitt
*Institute of Energy Economics and the Rational Use of Energy,
University of Stuttgart*

Dr. Manfred Kleemann
*Programme Group Systems Analysis and Technology Evaluation,
Research Centre Juelich*

Dr. Wilhelm Kuckshinrichs
*Programme Group Systems Analysis and Technology Evaluation,
Research Centre Juelich*

Dr. Peter Markewitz
*Programme Group Systems Analysis and Technology Evaluation,
Research Centre Juelich*

Dr. Dag Martinsen
*Programme Group Systems Analysis and Technology Evaluation,
Research Centre Juelich*

Dr. Jens Simon
Institute of Solid State Research, Research Centre Juelich

Prof. Heribert Wagner
Institute of Thin Film and Ion Technology, Research Centre Juelich

Prof. Hermann-Josef Wagner
Department of Energy Economics and Environment, University of Essen

Preface

Effective climate protection can be achieved only through co-ordinated national and international efforts. It is a matter of great urgency that industrialized countries and developing countries act hand in hand. Therefore the Systems Analysis and Technology Evaluation Group (STE) of the Research Centre Juelich and the Centre for Energy Studies (CES) of the Indian Institute of Technology (IIT) Delhi performed a joint workshop on "Strategies and Technologies for Greenhouse Gas Mitigation" in December 1996 in New Delhi. The purpose of this seminar was to discuss national strategies and technological options to reduce climate-relevant emissions in Germany and India. The meeting was opened by the Indian Secretary of State of the Ministry of Environment and Forest and the German Ambassador to India.

The papers and discussions at the workshop and the material subsequently submitted form the basis of this volume. Chapter I deals with national strategies and reduction potentials in Germany and India. Chapter II outlines the utilization of solar, wind and biomass energy for climate protection in the two countries. Chapter III focuses on the various reduction options and potentials in the residential sector. A German and an Indian contribution is provided for each topic addressed in the book.

The authors of this book and the organizations that sponsored the seminar hope that the data and information contained in the papers will provide a useful contribution to global CO_2 mitigation.

Acknowledgements

This study was sponsored by four organizations. Max Mueller Bhavan (Goethe Institute, New Delhi), the Indian Institute of Technology Delhi (IITD), the International Bureau (INT) of the German Ministry of Education and Research (BMBF) and the Research Centre Juelich. All of them deserve special thanks.

The authors gratefully acknowledge the generous hospitality of Prof. Raju, Director of IIT, and host of the workshop. Special thanks are due to Prof. J. Treusch, Director of the Board of the Research Centre Juelich for his encouragement. The authors are especially indebted to Dr. Waldraff, Head of Max Mueller Bhavan, Mrs. P. Matusche of Max Mueller Bhavan and Dr. Staehle, Head of INT, for their support.

Finally, thanks are extended to Dipl.-Ing. S. Koenig and Mrs. U. Seele for editorial assistance, to Mrs. S. Roethel and Mr. E. Stute for word and image processing and to Mrs. J. Carter-Sigglow, who helped to improve the language of the final text.

Presidential Address
THOTUVELIL KRISHNA PILLAI AYYAPPANKUTTY NAIR

Ladies and Gentlemen - Human induced climate change is not a fiction. Since the late 19th century the global mean surface temperature has increased by about 0.5 degree Celsius. Recent years have been amongst the warmest, and global sea levels have risen by 10 to 25 cm over the past 100 years. We are all aware of the erratic 1990-95 persistent warm phase of the El Niño-Southern Oscillation which caused droughts and floods worldwide. By the year 2100 there will be a 2 degree Celsius mean global temperature escalation and an average sea level rise of half a metre. The number of extremely hot days will increase. The brunt of these adverse impacts will be in the tropics and subtropics, which will experience substantial agricultural productivity losses, delayed forest regeneration, irreversible desertification, coastal flooding and wide-ranging deleterious effects on human health. We, in India, are specially concerned because India's population is predominantly dependent on the health of its agriculture, and about 8 million of our population live in the coastal areas.

Hence the relevance of this seminar. It is very satisfying to note that this seminar has a strong representation from Germany. Germany is not only forcing the pace of greenhouse emission reduction globally through its own exemplary domestic efforts, it has also taken the lead in the ongoing international negotiations presently underway, wherein the existing U.N. Framework Convention on Climate Change will be buttressed by a protocol, expectedly by the end of 1997, when the commitments of the industrialized countries to mitigating greenhouse gases will be further strengthened.

I should have mentioned that the developing countries do not have an obligation to reduce greenhouse gases under the Convention. The Convention, founded on the doctrine of "common but differentiated responsibilities", explicitly recognizes that the paramount priority of developing countries is economic development and poverty eradication consequent to which emissions of greenhouse gases will grow. Even though the developing countries do not have mitigation commitments, yet they have an obligation to invent sinks and sources of the greenhouse gases (GHGs), and communicate this to the Climate Change Secretariat, along with a general description of proposed "no-regrets" response strategies.

The commitment of developing countries under the Convention is conditional on the availability of finances from the industrialized countries. Implicit in the responsibility assigned to developed countries by the Convention are conspicuous North-South differentials in respective contributions to greenhouse gas atmospheric concentrations and the means at their disposal for responding to the problem. However, the expected transfer of technology and financial resources to developing countries has not commenced in any meaningful manner. The Convention is explicit and I quote, *The extent to which developing country parties will effectively implement their commitments under the Convention will depend on the effective implementation by developed country Parties of their commitments under the Convention related to financial resources and transfer of technology...*

The Convention acknowledges that the industrialized countries are responsible for the human-induced greenhouse effect. The profligacy of the industrialized countries, consuming far more than their entitlement of environmental goods has resulted in a 28 per cent increase of carbon dioxide since the industrial revolution, a 59 per cent increase of methane, and a 13 per cent increase of nitrous oxide. About 80 per cent of the human-induced climate change is due to carbon dioxide increase. The objective of the Convention to stabilize the atmospheric concentrations of GHGs at safe levels takes into account the life spans of past emissions - 50 to 200 years for carbon dioxide, 12 to 17 for methane, and 120 years for nitrous oxide.

Delays in reducing emissions by developed countries will make adaptation even more difficult and diminish significantly the options and opportunities available to developing countries. However, over 1,000 policies and measures have been identified in the industrialized countries which are appropriate for the purpose of greenhouse gas reduction. The range of sectors are: (a) energy and transformation, (b) industry, (c) residential, commercial and institutional, (d) transport, (e) agriculture, (f) land use change and forestry, (g) waste management and sewage treatment, (h) cross-sectoral economic instruments. This seminar will be addressing some of these sectors, as I notice from the programme. The current international discussions on policies and measures have only recently moved from the analysis and assessment phase to the negotiating phase. It is expected that some of these policies and measures will be implemented jointly by developed countries, and some nationally.

The concept of Activities Implemented Jointly (AIJ) which came to be engendered last year in Berlin is basically about implementing policies and measures in joint ventures between industrialized countries and developing countries; the rationale being lower marginal costs in the developing country, which would also be the recipient of the investment. This AIJ (Activities Implemented Jointly) is in a pilot phase and reflects a lack of agreement about availability of credits and other issues. The concept needs to be further refined. Also, a more thorough division of labour between the GEF (Global Environment Facility) and AIJ needs to be established with implications for technology transfer and related issues.

The discipline as regards AIJ, decided through negotiations, is as follows:

- No credits shall accrue to any party as a result of GHG emissions reduced or sequestered during the pilot phase from AIJ;
- AIJ between industrialized and developing countries will not be seen as a fulfilment of current commitments by developed parties;
- Financing of AIJ shall be additional to financial obligations of industrialized country parties under current ODA (Overseas Development Agency) flow;
- AIJ projects under the pilot phase require acceptance by governments.

We have stressed that the terms of transfer of technology pursuant to the Convention be accorded clarity and greater content. Evaluation of technologies and options has to be given more drive. The experts gathered for this 3-day seminar could also explore the potential for South-South transfer of technologies which would be cheaper and more adaptable.

It is clear that sectors like energy and transport will grow in developing countries like India. Demand for power in the agricultural sector is growing at the rate of 12 per cent per annum. And I believe that the Power Ministry has projected a growth in generation capacity of 57,000 MW in the Ninth Plan period. Also, there is tremendous scope for energy efficiencies in energy-intensive industries like aluminum, steel, fertilizers, paper, cement, and some others.

In this respect, the report of the Intergovernmental Panel on Climate Change (IPCC) Working Group 2 is technologically promising, which discusses the supply and demand side management of energy systems, industry, transportation, renewable energy technologies, etc. The scope for funding some demonstration projects, or even an effort of a preparatory or facilitative character would be a well-directed step. The seminar should discuss this aspect. As I see from the programme, the seminar will be examining some frontline technologies.

The IPCC report has indicated several technologies and processes that could substantially reduce GHG emissions: gas turbine technology; coal and biomass gasification technology; production of transportation fuels from biomass; wind energy utilization; electricity generation with photovoltaic and solar thermal electric technologies; approaches to handling intermittent generation of electricity, fuel cells for transportation and power generation, hydrogen as a major new energy carrier - produced first from natural gas and later from biomass, coal and electrolysis.

India fully supports the Framework Convention on Climate Change and is committed to its prompt start and continues to participate in the international efforts to find a coordinated, equitable and effective set of actions to combat the threat of climate change. The Government of India recognizes the need to reduce greenhouse gas emissions firmly but believes that countries should share the burden of abatement in a way that reflects their relative levels of development and differential capacities. The Climate Change Convention is not merely about the control of greenhouse gases. Eradication of poverty, avoiding risk to food production and sustainable development are three principles quite explicit in the Convention. The alleviation of poverty and the prospect of sustained and sustainable growth by themselves would serve to qualitatively improve the environment in developing countries and, by implication, the global environment. Poverty remains the central issue and the challenge is to find a development path that is not only sustainable but also socially just and culturally acceptable.

Let me conclude now on this note and in the hope that the seminar will provide an opportunity for assessing, channelling and facilitating the transfer of state-of-the-art technology to reduce greenhouse gas emissions. We attach great significance to the fact that Germany has taken this initiative and is participating in good strength. Germany and India have been consulting each other in the international climate change negotiations. The two countries have also been cooperating in various pollution control programmes.

We have large scientific capabilities in India which could be used for probing and monitoring the atmosphere. Various organizations like the CSIR (Centre for Scientific and Industrial Research), ISRO (Indian Space Research Organisation), ICAR (Indian Council for Agricultural Research) and MOEF (Ministry of Environment and Forests) actively participate in the endeavours to achieve the objectives of the Framework Convention.

The Indian Institutes of Technology (IIT), which are our centre of technological excellence, could spearhead the research activities in this area and also provide the required scientific manpower. The initiative taken by IIT Delhi in organizing this Seminar is most welcome and let us hope it will be the beginning of greater participation by the IITs in our national endeavours for the protection and preservation of our environment in consonance with our developmental objectives.

Ambassador's Address

FRANK ELBE

Ladies and Gentlemen, it is a great pleasure for me to address you today in this "temple" of science and technology, as IIT Delhi is known throughout the world.

I am indeed proud of the fact that my country has been able to contribute to the establishment of this worldwide reputation of IIT.

I am aware that you, Dr. Raju, as the Director of this famous institution - I should rather say "Dr.-Ing." Raju, because I understand that you earned your doctoral degree at one of our prestigious scientific and engineering institutions, namely the Technical University of Karlsruhe, I am very well aware that you have always maintained close and often personal contacts with the science community in Germany and in particular in Karlsruhe.

By your recent appointment as a member of the Indo-German Consultative Group as well as of the Indo-German Committee on Science and Technology, the Indian Government has indeed recognized your role as one of the most active and instrumental personalities in Indo-German cooperation in science, education, research and technology.

We are living today in an era of globalisation: globalisation of politics, globalisation of industry, globalisation of communication, globalisation of science and technology. These are key words in today's world. The subject of this Indo-German Seminar on Greenhouse Gas Emissions is also a global one: namely the global change of our earth's climate by man-made interferences, especially by the emission of greenhouse gases into the atmosphere. The damaging impact of this climate change on a local or regional level is not yet known in detail. What we know, however, for sure is that it will not only affect India and Germany, it will affect the entire globe. The threat to the climate which we are currently witnessing is, therefore, a global threat. The challenge of coping with it is a global challenge.

During this seminar, you will discuss national strategies and policies to reduce climate-relevant gas emissions in Germany and India, and the implementation of these strategies by technical means in both our countries.

Permit me to share with you briefly some ideas on international strategies and efforts to cope with this global challenge.

A first step in this direction was made when the UN Conference on Environment and Development - the so called Rio Conference - passed the Framework Convention on Climate Change in 1992. The industrialized countries committed themselves to reduce their greenhouse gas emissions to 1990 levels. However, they did so without specifying a time limit for these reductions.

During the first Conference of the Parties to the Framework Convention in Berlin in April 1995, the so-called "Berlin Mandate" was adopted. It calls for the widest possible cooperation by all countries - industrialized and developing countries - in order to protect the climate system for the benefit of present and future generations.

With this in mind, the Conference decided to initiate a negotiation process to quantify target limitations and reduction objectives within specified time frames, such as 2005, 2010 or 2020. This internationally agreed process is still under way. It is not an easy one, due to divergencies of interests not only between industrialized and developing countries, but also among industrialized countries. However, we do hope that the international community will succeed in concluding an ambitious climate protocol during the next Conference of the Parties to the Convention in Kyoto, Japan.

In this context, I should mention that a large part of German industry has already committed itself to a 20 per cent reduction in specific greenhouse gas emissions by the year 2005. It would be a major step on the way to internationally supported time frames if the Kyoto-Conference were to agree on reductions of up to 10 per cent by the year 2005. Let me assure you that my Government will do its utmost to achieve this objective.

Another important result of the Berlin Conference was the decision to establish a pilot plan for activities implemented jointly between industrialized and developing countries. The basic idea of this new and innovative instrument to limit and stabilize greenhouse gas emissions is to jointly implement activities in countries where costs are relatively low, in order to gain the highest possible global effect. Industrialized countries are to be encouraged to invest in countries where a higher reduction of emissions may be achieved for the same amount of money. In other words: this new concept aims at creating a market where no market exists so far, by introducing a worldwide system of tradable emission certificates.

My Government has actively supported and continues to support this innovative instrument, which mobilizes the creativity and dynamism of market forces. It has accepted the idea of testing this new instrument within the framework of a pilot plan, and has already initiated joint activities of this kind - together with industrial partners - in several countries, such as Indonesia, Jordan or Zimbabwe.

We would also like to see such joint implementation acitivities taken up with partners in India.

With this in mind, my Government has suggested to the Indian Ministry of Environment and Forests that such joint activities should be initiated within the framework of ongoing negotiations on a Memorandum of Understanding between the German Ministry for the Environment and the Ministry of Environment and Forests.

And - to become more concrete - we have initiated joint project proposals with the Tata Energy Research Institute in Delhi on energy efficiency improvement of thermal power plants and on cogeneration to reduce energy inputs. These projects could perhaps be implemented and tested during the joint implementation pilot phase.

I am convinced that by reciprocal information on national environmental policies - as intended during this Indo-German Seminar - and by acting together in a spirit of responsability for the protection of our global environment both Germany and India can effectively contribute to coping with the global challenge of climate change.

Thank you very much.

PART I
National Strategies and Programmes

1 Greenhouse Gas Mitigation Strategies in Germany and the European Community

JÜRGEN-FRIEDRICH HAKE AND WILHELM KUCKSHINRICHS

Introduction

Climate change refers to the observation that human activities have come to influence natural processes in the atmosphere. Presently, climate change is one of the major concerns of all nations. As a result of the Rio Conference, Article 2 of the UN Framework Convention on Climate Change (FCCC) requires the

> stabilization of greenhouse gas concentrations in the atmosphere at a level that would prevent dangerous anthropogenic interference with the climate system. Such a level should be achieved within a time-frame sufficient to allow the ecosystems to adapt naturally to climate change, to ensure that food production is not threatened and to enable economic development to proceed in a sustainable manner.

Following the assessment of the Intergovernmental Panel on Climate Change (IPCC) the most dominant greenhouse gases (GHGs) are carbon dioxide, methane, and nitrous oxide. These gases contributed 75 per cent to the anthropogenic greenhouse effect during the 1980s. Other greenhouse gases are ozone (O_3), chlorofluorocarbons (CFCs) and water (H_2O) vapour.

Carbon dioxide (CO_2) is responsible for 55 per cent of the human contribution to the greenhouse effect. The main emissions result from burning fossil fuels. Each year human beings shift 22 billion tonnes of carbon dioxide from the earth to the air. Half of the global emissions remains in the atmosphere leading to an increase in the gas's atmospheric concentration of about 0.5 per cent annually.

Anthropogenic sources of methane (CH_4) are e. g. the extraction and distribution of crude oil and natural gas, coal mining and waste dumps, where inorganic material is depleted under anaerobic conditions. Methane accounts for 15 per cent of the human-induced intensification of the greenhouse effect. Because it is relatively rapidly removed from the atmosphere

11

by chemical reactions in the air, emission reductions of about 15 to 20 per cent would be required to stabilize methane at its current high concentrations.

Nitrous oxide (N_2O) is produced by a variety of biological and chemical processes in soils and water. Two recently identified major sources are the production of nylon and nitrogen fertilizers. Scientists estimated that a 70 to 80 per cent reduction in human-induced emissions would be needed in order to stabilize concentrations at their present high level.

The contribution of different gases to the greenhouse effect can be compared with the concept of global warming potential (GWP). Carbon dioxide is used as a reference (GWP = 1). For the GHGs under consideration here and with an expected lifetime of 100 years, GWP equals: $GWP_{100}(CH_4) = 11$, $GWP_{100}(N_2O) = 270$. Though the relative weight of CH_4 and N_2O increases using the concept of GWP, carbon dioxide still dominates due to its tremendous amount.

Population growth and economic development directly represent the main driving forces for increased use of fossil fuels and indirectly for climate change. Obviously, the situation differs for individual geographical regions or countries. For an OECD country like Germany, an increase in GDP has been accompanied by a decline of primary energy consumption while the population has remained on a stable level over the past 5 years. For other countries like India, a transition from a less developed country to a fast developing country with high growth rates for population and economic development can be observed. In addition, multinational organizations like the European Community have become more important in facing a wide range of new problems, because policy making is increasingly being transferred to multinational organizations.

Economic development needs an adequate energy supply. Regarding greenhouse gas mitigation strategies, the dependence of any economy on a sufficient supply of energy services cannot be left out of consideration.

Present Situation in Germany

Since the beginning of the nineties, German society has had to face three major challenges:

1. Harmonization of internal development after the unification of East and West Germany: After 6 years of harmonization, economic and social structures still differ. Though many policy measures have been taken up to increase the speed of harmonization, overall policy has not been as successful as expected. One of the sectors where the harmoni-

zation process was most successful is the energy sector, mainly the electricity sector.

2. Further integration into the European Community which is developing towards a single market: As one of the 15 EC states Germany plays a very important role with regard to economic and technological development. Further integration in the EC towards a single market is an ongoing challenge.

3. Globalization of environment and economy: For a variety of goods and services, globalization processes create worldwide competition. This development is accompanied by severe structural changes in the industrialized countries, especially in Europe. Additionally, globalization refers to environmental aspects. In the case of CO_2, the increase of emissions is a global problem, which cannot be solved on a national level.

Any strategy to mitigate GHG emissions in Germany has to be embedded into the complex system of interdependent policy responses to these challenging developments.

GHG Emissions

Emissions of GHGs in Germany do not show a uniform picture (Table 1.1). Regarding the emission of carbon dioxide, the official statistics report a decrease from 1,014 million tonnes of CO_2 in 1990 to 895 million tonnes in 1995. Energy-related emissions are dominant. Their contribution decreased from 987 million tonnes in 1990 to 869 million tonnes in 1995. It seems that the observed reduction of CO_2 emissions has slowed down and probably reached a stable level of approximately 870 million tonnes.

Table 1.1 GHG emissions in Germany from 1990 to 1995

		1990	1991	1992	1993	1994	1995
CO_2 (total)	10^6 t	1,014	975	927	918	905	895
Energy-related	10^6 t	987	951	901	893	879	869
CH_4 (total)	10^3 t	5,682	5,250	5,194	5,013	4,849	4,788
Energy-related	10^3 t	1,768	1,631	1,594	1,430	1,289	n.a.
N_2O (total)	10^3 t	226	220	226	218	219	210
Energy-related	10^3 t	37	39	40	41	42	n.a.

Source: BMU 1997.

In 1990, the emissions of methane and nitrous oxide were 5.7 and 0.2 million tonnes, respectively. The energy-related fractions are much lower. Even when one takes into account the global warming potentials of these substances, CO_2 remains the dominant substance.

Demographic and Economic Development

The main demographic and economic data for Germany are given in Table 1.2. The population has slightly increased to 81.6 million over the last six years because of net immigration. The number of households increased at a higher annual rate from 34.9 million to 36.7 million over four years.

From 1991 to 1995, the German gross domestic product (GDP) grew from 1,719 billion US $[1] to 1,821 billion US $. The structure of GDP and sectoral production shows a shift from energy-intensive towards service-oriented (and labour-intensive) sectors. This development is accompanied by further capitalization of production, which results partly in the replacement of other factor inputs by capital goods (in the the form of equipment and buildings).

The most dominant industrial sector with respect to energy use is the iron and steel sector, which is expected to decline in Germany within the next 25 years. The energy demand in 2005 is expected to decrease by 30-40 per cent compared to 1989. Another energy-intensive sector is aluminium production. The production of primary aluminium is expected to decrease by 30-50 per cent between 1989 and 2005. In contrast, recycling of aluminium scrap to secondary aluminium shows large growth rates. But in total, due to the expected rise of aluminium demand accompanied by the decrease of domestic primary aluminium smelting capacity, Germany turns out to be a large importer (Jochem, 1996).

German Energy Sector

Since unification of West and East Germany, the energy sector can be characterized by a decreasing consumption of primary energy towards a level of approximately 14,100 PJ (Table 1.3). Fossil energy carriers dominate and covered 87 per cent of the primary energy sources in 1995. The contribution of lignite, the dominant primary energy carrier in East Germany, has been reduced, while oil and particularly gas now have increased shares. Nuclear energy remains stable. In contrast to public discussion, renewable energy does not play a major role in Germany due to unfavourable natural and economic conditions.

Table 1.2 Main demographic and economic data for Germany

	1990	1991	1992	1993	1994	1995
Population (million)	79.3	80.0	80.6	81.1	81.5	81.6
Households (million)	34.9	35.3	35.7	36.2	36.7	n.a.
GDP (billion US$$_{1991}$)	-	1,719	1,757	1,737	1,787	1,821

Source: Federal Ministry of Economics 1996.

Table 1.3 Primary energy balance of Germany in PJ

	1990	1991	1992	1993	1994	1995
Primary energy	14,795	14,466	14,150	14,185	14,071	14,165
Sectors						
Industry	2,977	2,693	2,562	2,435	2,468	2,477
Household	2,380	2,500	2,394	2,611	2,538	2,702
Small consumers	1,704	1,694	1,597	1,521	1,486	1,433
Transport	2,379	2,430	2,520	2,594	2,535	2,585
Non-energetic	958	888	911	888	964	979
Conversion	4,396	4,253	4,165	4,135	4,080	3,989
Energy carriers						
Oil	5,234	5,548	5,627	5,744	5,697	5,700
Coal	2,307	2,330	2,195	2,139	2,139	2,057
Lignite	3,200	2,506	2,178	1,984	1,864	1,732
Gas	2,315	2,433	2,406	2,547	2,591	2,837
Nuclear	1,448	1,386	1,498	1,439	1,424	1,436
Water	164	129	111	173	199	243
Other	126	135	135	158	155	158

Source: BMWi, 1996.

For the end-use sectors one can draw the following picture: The energy demand of the industrial sector fell by 17 per cent from 1990 to 1995, while demand for the transport sector grew by 9 per cent. Demand in the sectors of household and small industrial consumers rose slightly by 0.8 per cent per year to 4,135 PJ.

Data on specific energy consumption and specific GHG emissions are given in Table 1.4. In 1995, primary energy consumption per capita was 174 GJ. The energy-related emissions of CO_2 per capita reached a level of 11 tonnes. The corresponding data for methane and nitrous oxide are less certain.

The structural change in the economy is indicated by the consumption of primary energy per GDP or CO_2 emissions per GDP (Table 1.4). The trend towards less energy- and less CO_2-intensive production has not yet stopped.

Table 1.4 Specific energy consumption and specific GHG emissions in Germany

	1990	1991	1992	1993	1994	1995
Primary energy						
per capita (GJ)	181	176	174	174	172	174
per GDP (GJ/1,000 US $\$_{1991}$)	8.85	8.42	8.05	8.17	7.88	7.78
CO_2 per capita (t)	12.8	12.2	11.5	11.3	11.1	11.0
CO_2 per GDP (kg/1,000 US $\$_{1991}$)	604	568	528	528	506	491
CH_4 per capita (kg)	71.7	65.6	64.4	61.8	59.5	58.7
N_2O per capita (kg)	2.85	2.75	2.83	2.69	2.69	2.57

Source: BMU, 1997; BMWi, 1996.

West and East Germany

Six years after the unification of Germany many differences still exist between West and East Germany (former GDR). Although a process of convergence can be observed in some areas of the economy, experts expect it will take at least another decade to overcome the differences. Table 1.5 shows some of the main indicators.

The large difference in specific domestic production refers to non-homogeneous economic conditions and activity levels in West and East Gemany. Though production is increasing in East Germany at a much higher level, production per capita will not reach comparable West German levels within the next few years.

Primary energy use per capita in East Germany is nearly 30 per cent lower than in West Germany. On the one hand this is due to lower economic activity levels, on the other hand due to the different modal split in transport, supporting public transport in East Germany. Additionally, e.g. provision with household appliances still has not reached the West German level.

Specific CO_2 emissions are slightly higher in East Germany. Electricity production basically depends on the use of lignite. The average age of the car fleet is still higher in East Germany. The carbon intensity of production in East Germany is twice as high as in West Germany. This reflects

Table 1.5 West and East Germany 1993

	West Germany	East Germany
Population (million)	65.4	15.7
Gross domestic product (US $\$_{1991}$ per cap.)	24,000	8,100
Primary energy (GJ per cap.)	184	135
Energy-related CO_2 emissions (t per cap.)	10.9	11.2
Energy intensity (GJ per 1,000 US $\$_{1991}$ GDP)	7.6	16.6
Intensity of energy-related CO_2 emissions (kg per 1,000 US $\$_{1991}$ GDP)	450	1,370

Source: BMWi, 1995.

differing regional intensities of production as well as differing carbon intensities of the regional primary energy mix. Therefore, the energy system in East Germany still shows considerable potential for reduction in specific CO_2 emissions. Obviously, the West German energy system offers similar possibilities, too, e.g. in the electricity-generating sector or some end-use sectors.

Specific data on the energy sector of East Germany are given by Table 1.6. Between 1990 and 1995 final energy demand in East Germany decreased by 33 per cent to 1,345 PJ. As industrial production partly collapsed after 1990, this sector mainly contributed to the reduction of final energy demand. Its demand decreased radically by 60 per cent. Additionally, final energy demand by households and small consumers was reduced by 33 per cent.

Only in the transport sector did final energy demand increase. Although greater use is made of public transport in East Germany than in West Germany, private transport is dominating more and more. In total, final energy demand for transport increased by 30 per cent (Walbeck and Martinsen, 1996).

Accordingly, this development was accompanied by an increase of 45 per cent for oil demand. Due to the restructuring of the energy supply, especially for electricity, lignite has lost its dominance as the most important energy carrier in the former GDR. Lignite use decreased sharply by 64 per cent to 803 PJ. To a certain extent natural gas has become more important. Its use increased by 68 per cent to 472 PJ. Nuclear power plants were closed in East Germany after unification.

Table 1.6 Primary energy balance of East Germany in PJ

	1990	1991	1992	1993	1994	1995
Primary energy	3,300	2,477	2,233	2,172	2,110	2,122
Sectors						
Industry	725	431	331	296	281	296
Household	522	384	331	384	390	422
Small consumers	477	381	317	255	255	252
Transport	288	293	328	349	363	375
Non-energetic	168	126	123	111	129	138
Conversion	1,121	853	803	759	692	639
Energy carriers						
Oil	528	607	695	730	750	768
Coal	138	91	85	76	70	73
Lignite	2,260	1,545	1,202	1,061	935	803
Gas	281	246	255	302	360	472
Nuclear	64	0	0	0	0	0
Hydro*)	23	-23	-15	-9	-15	-6
Other	6	12	12	12	9	12

Source: BMWi, 1996.

*) Including exports of electricity

The Goal for CO_2 Reduction

In 1990, the German Government pledged itself to make a 25-30 per cent reduction in national CO_2 emissions by 2005 on the basis of 1987 CO_2 emissions. This decision is mainly based on results obtained by two Study Commissions of the German parliament also recommending a reduction of 50 per cent by 2020. In 1995, the emission reduction goal was reformulated: a 25 per cent reduction of CO_2 emissions is to be achieved in 2005 with respect to 1990 emissions. Since unification of the two German states, the reduction target is now valid for Germany as a whole.

The Government maintains that its climate-protection policy is beginning to have an effect. It calls attention to the measures it has been implementing since 1990. This package demonstrates the intention of integrating economic instruments, regulatory approaches and supporting measures. In the first report of the German Government pursuant to the UN FCCC, a list of 88 measures is given that have been approved and implemented, another 30 measures are currently being approved or approval is currently being prepared. These measures refer to:

- Energy supply: For the supply side this includes for example the Act on the Sale of Electricity to the Grid ("Einspeisegesetz"), the Federal Government district heating modernization programme for the area of the former GDR, funding for renewables, the 4th Ordinance on the Execution of the Federal Immissions Control Act ("4. BimSchV"), the amendment to the Energy Management Act ("Energiewirtschaftsgesetz"), etc.
- Traffic and transport: These measures comprise for example the emission-oriented motor-vehicle tax, the Federal Traffic Infrastructure Plan, German railways' site concept, etc.
- Buildings and structures: Important measures include the amendment of the Thermal Insulation Ordinance ("WSchV"), the amendment of the Heating Systems Ordinance ("HeizAnlV"), the Ordinance on Small Combustion Plants ("1. BimSchV"), etc.
- New technologies: This programme comprises for example research into, and technical refinement of, power plant and firing plant technology, especially cleaner coal-firing technology, research and development concerning gas and steam turbine power plants and use of renewable energies and fusion research.
- Overarching measures: This programme includes for example systems analysis within the Instruments for Climate Gas Reduction Strategies project (IKARUS), support for provision of information concerning third-party financing models and support for advice to small and medium-sized companies concerning environmental protection and energy use.

In addition to the German Government, federal institutions are preparing climate protection programmes as well. Numerous communities have begun to develop and implement community CO_2 reduction concepts. German industry emphasizes that it is willing to reduce GHG emissions on the basis of self-commitment declarations and compensation solutions.

Outlook for Germany: Options and Trends

Several institutions are participating in the discussion on future trends in the German economy. With respect to climate change, much attention is paid to the energy sector. Prominent institutions in this field are the PROGNOS Institute, Esso, Shell, etc. The latest study carried out on behalf of the German Federal Ministry of Economics was written by the PROGNOS Institute providing an energy outlook for Germany (BMWi, 1996).

Demographic and Political Background

Population development depends on birth, death rates and net immigration. In 2020, the German population will reach a level of 80.9 million people.

Economic growth is expected to reach approximately 2.5 per cent per year until 2005. After the year 2005, the growth rate is expected to decrease approximately by 2.1 per cent annually.

The development in East Germany will be different for the next 25 years. Until 2005, growth rates of 7 to 8 per cent are expected for East Germany. After 2005, the growth rate will decline to 2.9 per cent per year.

Presently, German energy policy focuses on the following topics:

- Adjustment of mining capacities for German hard coal: Mining costs for domestic hard coal are 3-4 times higher than the price on the world market. For domestic hard coal mining, a steady decrease can be expected.
- Deregulation in the electricity and gas sectors: The amendment to the Energy Management Act will accompany the energy law reform, aiming at the introduction of an effective competition within the electricity and gas industries.
- Nuclear and renewable capacities: Several German nuclear power stations will have to be closed within the next 25 years. Presently, no new nuclear power plant is under construction or planned for construction within the next few years. Existing plants are expected to be phased out. In case of renewables, capacity expansion for wind energy has been very successful in Germany. Due to components of the German energy law, e.g. the "Act on the Sale of Electricity to the Grid", and measures like the "250 MW Wind Energy Programme", private investment in wind energy has grown considerably during the last few years (see Part II, Chapter 8).

Prices for fossil energy carriers depend on the oil price. Until 2020, the real oil price is expected to rise to approximately 26 $/b. Until 2005, the real oil price is expected to remain stable at the present level. Moreover, assumptions for the oil price in DM are strongly speculative because one also has to estimate the exchange rate between DM or Euro and $.

Energy Outlook

Since unification of the two German states, power generation capacity in East Germany has been restructured. One remarkable example of investment in a new power plant is the lignite power plant in Schkopau. Its capacity of 900 MW serves to supply electricity to the public grid, the chemical production plants of the "Buna Dow Leuna Olefinverbund" and the German Federal Railways. With its net efficiency of 40 per cent, the new plant is one of the leading lignite power plants worldwide. Compared to the old "Buna" power plant considerable reductions of emissions have been achieved: for SO_2 from 9,000 mg/m^3 to 400 mg/m^3, for NO_x from 400 mg/m^3 to 200 mg/m^3, and for dust from 900 mg/m^3 to 50 mg/m^3. Additionally, according to the increase of net efficiency, CO_2 emissions per unit of electricity have decreased. Therefore, this new power plant contributes to an efficient and economic structure of the energy supply. Moreover, it helps to protect the environment and to stabilize the mining industry in East Germany.

At Lippendorf, near Leipzig, another lignite power plant is planned. Its capacity of 1,600 MW will serve to supply electricity to the Eastern part of Germany and to Bavaria and Baden-Wuerttemberg. Roughly 60 per cent of the heat demand of Leipzig will be met by this plant. The investment costs amount to DM 5 billion.

In West Germany, an advanced steam power plant is planned for construction near Duesseldorf. This new capacity of 900 MW will replace old units. Its investment costs are expected to amount to DM 3.1 billion.

Obviously, in the next millenium there will be a gap between existing and required capacities in West Germany (Figure 1.1). This gap depends on several factors as for example required capacities, technical lifetime of existing capacities, retrofitting, etc. According to statements by German power companies, capacity construction may be based to a large extent on gas power plants due to the favourable economic and ecological conditions of this technology. Liberalization of the German energy market may support this development, as can be seen in the UK.

Based on the assumptions and remarks of the previous chapter, the PROGNOS Institute has performed an energy outlook for Germany.

Table 1.7 shows that the consumption of primary energy will stay around 14,500 PJ until 2005, thereafter the demand will decrease slightly to 14,231 PJ. The energy mix will probably change towards less lignite and hard coal. The share of crude oil will show a peak around 2005. The share of gas will increase steadily.

The energy-related CO_2 emissions can be derived from the structure of the energy demand. Table 1.8 shows that Germany will not reach the emission target in 2005, unless additional measures to reduce CO_2 are introduced. Mainly, the development of the transport sector overcompensates successful efforts in other sectors to reduce energy-related emissions. Further measures have to be considered.

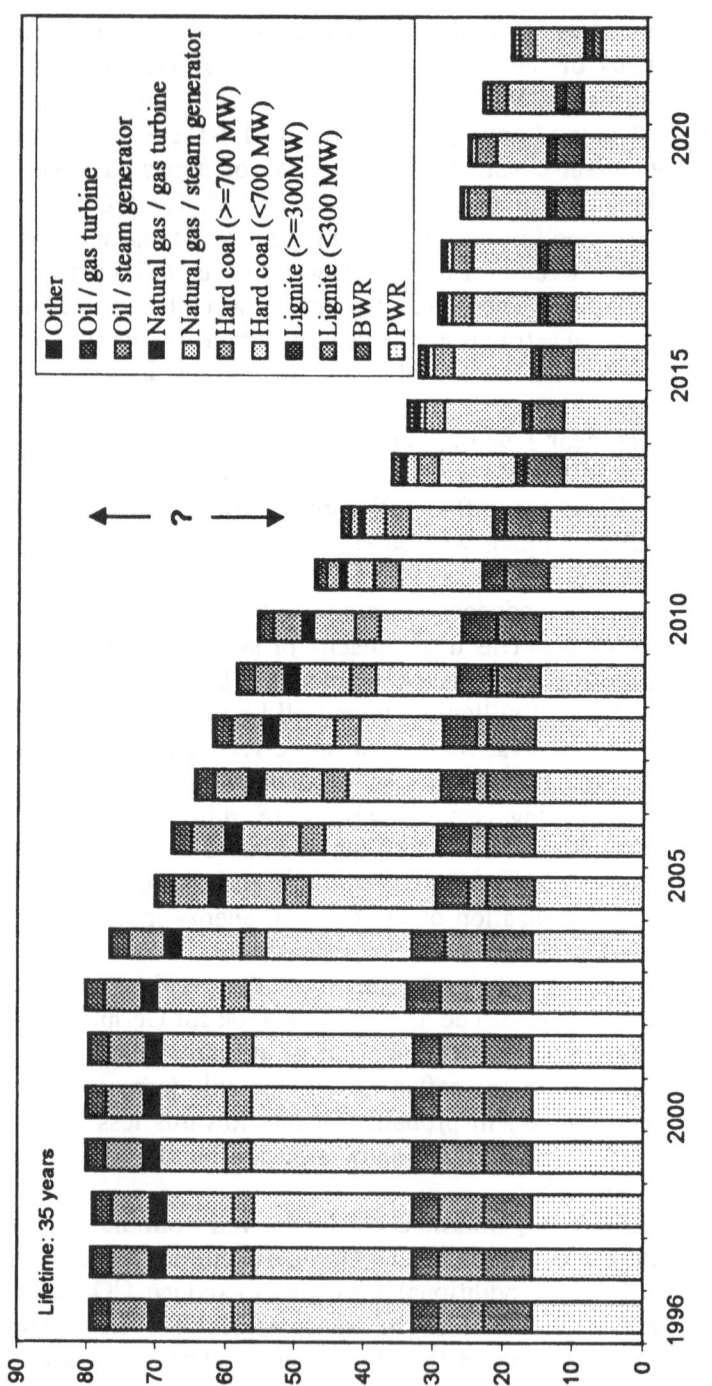

Source: P. Markewitz, 1996.

Figure 1.1 Expected shutdown of existing West German power plants

Table 1.7 Consumption of primary energy till 2020 in Germany (PJ)

	1990	1995	2000	2005	2010	2015	2020
Hard coal	2,306	2,060	2,154	2,118	2,076	2,036	2,020
Lignite	3,201	1,732	1,610	1,563	1,532	1,525	1,521
Other solid fuels	-	-	160	188	215	224	233
Crude oil, oil products	5,238	5,690	6,055	5,970	5,807	5,629	5,464
Gas	2,293	2,814	2,917	3,062	3,181	3,279	3,396
Electricity (import balance)		38	20	95	157	196	190
Renewables	312	426	172	174	175	174	170
Nuclear	1,446	1,470	1,430	1,332	1,299	1,271	1,237
Total	14,796	14,230	14,517	14,502	14,442	14,334	14,231

Source: BMWi, 1995; BMWi, 1996; BMU 1997.

Table 1.8 Emission of energy-related CO_2 till 2020 in Germany (million tonnes)

	1990	1995	2000	2005	2010	2015	2020
Power plants	354	318	327	331	333	335	338
District heat	43	32	30	27	26	25	24
Industry	170	127	131	128	126	126	128
Transport	185	196	223	224	221	215	209
Households, small consumers, military	204	187	185	179	173	169	164
Other conversion sectors	43	24	21	19	18	17	16
Total	999	884	917	908	897	887	879

Source: BMWi, 1995; BMU, 1997.

Science and Research

Climate change represents a great challenge for politicians and scientists. Measures have been taken on several levels.

In 1995, there was an update to the German Energy Research Programme which intends to support continuous reduction of the environmental and climate burden, and modernization of the economy to stabilize the German position regarding technological competitiveness. This 4th German Energy Research Programme focuses on four topics:

- Reduction of energy use: To reduce energy use, improvements in energy conversion and the introduction of new secondary energy carriers have to be promoted. Additionally, measures to improve efficient energy use and to reduce the use of fossil energy carriers in the end-use sectors have to be introduced.
- Energy supply with reduced emissions inclusive of CO_2: This refers to the use of renewable and nuclear energy.
- Long-term options for the energy supply: Fusion is expected to be a long-term option for the energy supply.
- Interdisciplinary topics: This topic refers to the use of systems analysis concepts including the generation of data bases to support systems-oriented projects.

This federal programme is intended to serve two strategic goals: mitigation of climate change and competitiveness of German energy-related R&D. The programme has an annual budget of DM 749 to 834 million from 1996 to 2000.

The IKARUS project represents one element of the German Energy Research Programme. The goal of the project is to develop and implement PC-based tools for the analysis of GHG mitigation strategies in Germany. Presently, the set of tools consists of:

- A data base containing data for emission factors, costs of all technologies for the German energy system, information on housing structures, industrial processes and transport systems;
- A macroeconomic simulation model to demonstrate macroeconomic consequences of strategies in terms of GDP growth, development of sectoral capital stocks and employment, etc;
- An energy-economy model to optimize the German energy system;
- Three sectoral simulation models for (1) transport, (2) electricity and district heat and (3) space heat for private households;
- A model to visualize energy chains, which are based on the energy-economy model.

These tools support comprehensive analyses of GHG mitigation strategies on various levels (Hake et al., 1994).

For a business-as-usual scenario, both the IKARUS project team and

PROGNOS conclude that though remarkable progress can be expected with regard to autonomous energy efficiency increase, carbon dioxide emissions will be higher than stated in the government reduction goal. As calculated by the IKARUS model (Kleemann et al., 1996), the reduction goal can be achieved with respect to several technical measures (Wagner, 1996). But to reach the reduction goal within the remaining time until 2005, a variety of political measures have to be introduced (see Part I, Chapter 2).

The European Perspective

Climate change represents a global problem. Hence, measures initiated by individual countries have to be analysed with respect to their contribution to a global solution. The European Community has become a supranational unit of increasing importance. On the other hand, individualism of the member states has remained a non-negligible element. For this reason, the European Community can serve as a model to detect many problems occurring in other multinational units or multicultural countries.

European Community

The European Community (EC) consists of 15 member states: Belgium, Denmark, Germany, Greece, Spain, France, Ireland, Italy, Luxembourg, the Netherlands, Austria, Portugal, Finland, Sweden, and the United Kingdom. For a contrast, data for India are also given in Table 1.9. Although Austria, Finland, and Sweden only became members in 1995, data of the EC for previous years include data for these countries in order to give a consistent picture.

With 3.24 million km^2 the land area of the EC nearly equals that of India. Germany roughly accounts for 11 per cent of the EC land area, but around 22 per cent of its population. India's population is more than twice that of the EC. Population density equals about 112 capita/km^2 in the EC (228 in Germany), but 277 in India. A comparison of GNP per capita figures reflects different levels of economic activity for the EC and India. But even inside the EC large differences exist, as shown by the figures for Germany and the EC. A comparison of commercial energy use shows similar facts. On average, in the EC energy consumed per capita is considerably higher than in India. Accordingly, specific CO_2 emissions are ten times higher in the EC than in India. For Germany, this figure even is around 25 per cent higher than the EC average.

Table 1.9 Basic demographic, economic and environmental data for Germany, the EC and India

1994	Germany	EC	India
Area (1000 km^2)	357	3,240	3,288
Population (million)	81.5	371	913.6
GNP per capita ($_{1991}$)	23,500	18,800	300
Commercial energy per capita (GJ)	172	150	10
CO_2 emissions (1992) per capita (t)	10.77	8.19	0.84

Source: World Bank, 1996; EC DG XVII, 1996.

Energy Sector

The energy consumption of the European Community and its relation to the global situation is outlined in Table 1.10. The EC consumes 16 per cent of the world's primary energy. In 1990, the consumption per capita of primary energy compared to the world level was more than twice as high. As a consequence of the different economic and technical standards, the world's energy intensity was approximately 1.5 times as high as in the EC. The EC's share in global CO_2 emissions amounts to 15 per cent.

The energy sector of the European Community is described by Table 1.11. The gross domestic consumption has increased to approximately 57,000 PJ. The share is 24 per cent for solids, 41 per cent for oil, 17 per cent for gas. The industrial sector consumes 11,000 PJ, transportation 11,000 PJ, and the residential/tertiary sectors 15,000 PJ.

Table 1.12 shows the resulting CO_2 emissions. At the level of member states the EC does not show a uniform picture. The reduction in countries like France, Germany, the UK and Italy is nearly compensated by a volume increase in the rest of the EC.

Emission Goal of the European Community

As outlined in the Green Paper *For a European Energy Policy* and by a *Commission White Paper*, European energy policy is based on three key objectives:

- Competitiveness of the economy,
- Security of energy supplies,
- Protection of the environment.

Table 1.10 World and European energy consumption and CO_2 emissions

	1990	2000	2010	2020
Primary energy (PJ)				
World	343,000	388,000	459,000	528,000
European Community	55,000	61,000	66,000	65,000
Primary energy per capita (GJ)				
World	67	64	66	67
European Community	152	162	172	179
Energy intensity (GJ/1000 US $_{1991}$)				
World	12.1	10.1	9.1	8.0
European Community	8.5	7.6	6.5	5.7
CO_2 emissions (million tonnes)				
World	21,716	24,074	28,258	32,283
European Community	3,248	3,366	3,555	3,721

Source: EC DG XVII 1996.

Table 1.11 Primary energy balance of the European Community (PJ)

	1990	1995	2000	2005	2010	2015	2020
Gross domestic consumption	55,482	57,332	61,224	63,686	65,765	67,094	68,557
Sectors							
Industry	11,216	11,044	11,773	12,315	12,865	13,347	13,834
Transport	10,623	11,289	12,290	13,149	13,951	14,627	15,261
Domestic & tertiary	14,340	14,976	15,596	16,007	16,512	16,935	17,334
Conversion	19,304	20,022	21,565	22,214	22,437	22,185	22,128
Energy carriers							
Solids	13,036	10,022	10,354	9,919	9,078	8,489	8,415
Oil	22,891	24,041	25,040	25,434	25,682	25,966	26,072
Natural gas	9,309	11,600	13,197	15,176	17,626	19,165	21,008
Nuclear	7,591	8,592	9,131	8,891	8,261	7,417	6,105
Electricity (import balance)	98	52	26	82	53	82	72
Renewables	2,556	3,025	3,477	4,184	5,065	5,974	6,886

Source: EC DG XVII 1996.

Table 1.12 Energy-related CO_2 emissions of the EC

	CO_2 emissions million tonnes		Change %
	1990	1994	1990 – 1994
Austria	56	57	1.8
Belgium	111	117	5.4
Denmark	52	63	21.2
Finland	52	61	17.3
France	368	349	-5.2
Germany	978	897	-8.3
UK	579	550	-5.0
Greece	72	78	8.3
Ireland	30	32	6.7
Italy	402	393	-2.2
Luxembourg	10	12	20.0
Netherlands	157	164	4.5
Portugal	40	45	12.5
Spain	208	229	10.1
Sweden	50	56	12.0
EC	3,165	3,103	-2.0

Source: EC DG XVII 1996, Eurostat (et 9/96, 571).

Mitigation of climate change refers to the third item. The European Community is called upon to return to its 1990 level of anthropogenic emissions of carbon dioxide and other greenhouse gases. For the near term this requirement is in line with the target to stabilize CO_2 emissions in the Community as a whole by the year 2000 at the 1990 level. There remains a need for harmonization because individual member states have different reduction goals as outlined for Germany (Enquete, 1995; IEA, 1994).

Outlook

The study *European Energy to 2020* by the European Commission (DG XVII) looks to 2020 by exploring four different socio-political scenarios. Subsequently, only the scenario called *Conventional Wisdom* is used. Like the PROGNOS study, this scenario denotes the business-as-usual case representing a conventional wisdom view of events. Economic growth gradually weakens as demographic changes mean slower growth in the labour force. Although some progress is made, many of the world's structural and economic problems remain.

Table 1.13 contains demographic data for the EC Conventional Wisdom scenario. The population remains approximately stable after 2005. The GDP is expected to increase to $\$_{1991}$ 12,144. The gross domestic consumption of energy grows from 55,482 PJ to 68,557 PJ over 30 years. The right-hand part of Table 1.13 gives more details on the future development of the EC as result of the Conventional Wisdom scenario. The results can be summarized:

- Primary energy grows slowly because energy intensity can be improved in the range between 1.1 per cent to 1.8 per cent per year.
- The structure by fuels changes: natural gas grows most, oil consumption grows very slowly, coal consumption declines, renewables grow fast, and nuclear energy supply declines rapidly.
- Electricity supply is increasingly generated by gas. Electricity demand continues to grow to a share of 21 per cent of final demand.
- The transport sector is the major contributor to incremental growth in the EC final energy demand. Although efficiency gains were assumed, final energy demand for transport increases by 44 per cent.

Table 1.13 Demographic data and energy-related CO_2 emissions of the EC

	1990	1995	2000	2005	2010	2015	2020
Population (million)	365	373	378	381	383	384	384
GDP (billion $\$_{1991}$)	6,540	6,994	8,078	9,107	10,132	11,127	12,144
Gross domestic consumption (PJ)	55,482	57,332	61,224	63,686	65,765	67,094	68,557
CO_2 emissions (million tonnes)	3,166	3,119	3,299	3,390	3,457	3,502	3,608

Source: EC DG XVII, 1996.

The last row of Table 1.13 shows the resulting CO_2 emissions. By 2020, European Community CO_2 emissions could be 14 per cent above the 1990 level as a result of increasing electricity demand and transport growth. Power generation accounts for half of the rise in CO_2 while transport accounts for the bulk of the increase in the sectors of final energy consumption, almost matching the volume increase of power generation.

For methane and nitrous oxide, the EC study expects that the volume of emissions will increase, too.

Conclusions

For Germany and the European Community, it will be difficult to achieve the GHG emission goals. As pointed out, a business-as-usual path would not lead to a reduction or a stabilization of GHG emissions.

After unification of the two German states, harmonizing of internal development is an ongoing process. Due to unfavourable economic conditions and the introduction of new technologies, for example in the conversion sector, CO_2 emissions in East Germany have been reduced. West Germany has not been that successful in reducing energy-related emissions. In total, developments in Germany result in a decrease of CO_2 emissions.

For Germany, a list of measures has been considered and partly already implemented in order to reach the goal of a 25 per cent reduction of energy-related CO_2 emissions. This list comprises technical measures, as well as regulatory approaches and market-based instruments. A study carried out with the energy system optimization model of the IKARUS project shows that in principle CO_2 emissions can be reduced according to the reduction goal by introducing a variety of measures. A detailed quantification of the various measures is given in Part I, Chapter 2. For the EC, the emission goal is less ambitious.

As pointed out for the EC, progress in individual countries as for example France, Germany, the UK and Italy, will be overcompensated by other countries. Individual reduction goals show that the expected emission paths will increase for some countries.

The IPCC studies have shown that stabilization or even a 25 per cent reduction of CO_2 and of other GHG emissions will probably not be sufficient to stabilize concentrations of GHG in the atmosphere. Hence, other measures have to be considered in order to go beyond the present status. Here, science can point out potentials and available options. But political initiatives are still necessary to realize these potentials and options.

Acknowledgements

The authors are grateful to Joachim Müller-Kirchenbauer for supporting the data collection.

Note

1   Base year 1991. Some useful relationships:
    US $\$_{1991}$ = DM$_{1991}$ 1.66
    US $\$_{1991}$ = US $\$_{1996}$ 1.13
    PJ = 10^6 GJ = 23,870 toe

References

BMBF (1996): 4. Programm Energieforschung und Energietechnologien, Bonn.

BMU (1994): Umweltpolitik - Klimaschutz in Deutschland: Erster Bericht der Regierung der Bundesrepublik Deutschland nach dem Rahmenübereinkommen der Vereinten Nationen über Klimaänderungen, Bonn.

BMU (1997): Umweltpolitik - Klimaschutz in Deutschland: Zweiter Bericht der Regierung der Bundesrepublik Deutschland nach dem Rahmenübereinkommen der Vereinten Nationen über Klimaänderungen, Bonn.

BMWi (1995): Die Energiemärkte Deutschlands im zusammenwachsenden Europa - Perspektiven bis zum Jahr 2020, Bonn.

BMWi (1996): Energiedaten '96, Bonn.

EC - DG XVII (1996): Energy in Europe: European Energy to 2020, Brussels.

Enquete-Kommission (1995): Mehr Zukunft für die Erde: Nachhaltige Energiepolitik für dauerhaften Klimaschutz, Bonn.

Forschungszentrum Jülich (1997): Politikszenarien für den Klimaschutz – Untersuchungen im Auftrag des Umweltbundesamtes, Jülich.

Hake, J.-Fr., Jagodzinski, P., Kuckshinrichs, W., Markewitz, P., Martinsen, D., Walbeck, M. (1994): "IKARUS: A Model System to Reduce Energy-Related GHG Emissions in Germany", J.-Fr. Hake et al. (eds.), Advances in Systems Analysis: Modelling Energy-Related Emissions, Forschungsgszentrum Jülich, pp. 213-238.

IEA (1994): Climate Change Policy Initiatives, 1994 Update, Paris.

IPCC (1996): Climate Change 1995. Cambridge University Press.

Jochem, E., Bradke, H. (1996): "Energieeffizienz, Strukturwandel und Produktionsentwicklung der deutschen Industrie", Monographien des Forschungszentrums Jülich, Vol. 19.

Kleemann, M., Markewitz, P., Martinsen, D. (1996): "IKARUS - Szenarien für eine klimaverträgliche Energieversorgung", Draft, Jülich.

Markewitz, P. (1995): "Approach of the IKARUS models in the context of R&D Assessment", IEA Experts Group on Technology Assessment and Methodologies for Priority Setting and Evaluation, Juelich.

Schiffer, H.-W. (1996): "Deutscher Energiemarkt '95", *Energiewirtschaftliche Tagesfragen*, Vol. 46, No. 3, pp. 150-163.

Walbeck, M., Martinsen, D. (1996): "The Role of Transport Sector within the German Energy System under Greenhouse Gas Reduction Constraints and Effects on Other Exhaust Gases", Draft, Jülich.

Wagner, H.-F. (1996): "Das vierte deutsche Energieforschungsprogramm", *Energiewirtschaftliche Tagesfragen*, Vol. 46, No. 9, pp. 558-563.

World Bank (1996): World Development Report 1996. Oxford University Press.

2 Programme of Measures to Reduce CO_2 Emissions in Germany

MANFRED KLEEMANN

Types of Measures to Reach the 25 Per Cent Reduction Goal of the German Government

At the first Conference of the Parties to the Framework Convention on Climate Change in Berlin, 1995, the German Chancellor declared the national CO_2 reduction goal to be 25 per cent by the year 2005, relative to the internationally defined base year 1990 (see Part I, Chapter 1). The relative reduction rate of 25 per cent means a reduction of about 250 million tonnes in absolute terms (see Table 2.1).

Table 2.1 CO_2 reduction goal by 2005

	Emission 1990 10^6 t	Emission 1995 10^6t	Goal 2005 10^6 t	Change 1990-2005 10^6 t %
CO_2 (energy-related)	986*	869*	740	246 25

* *Sources*: UBA, 1997 and BMU, 1997.

Reduction and/or limitation of non-CO_2 climate-relevant emissions, such as methane (CH_4), nitrous oxide (N_2O), nitrogen oxides (NO_x), carbon monoxide (CO), non-methane volatile organic compounds (NMVOC), hydrofluorcarbons (HFC), perfluorcarbons (PFC) and sulphur hexafluoride (SF_6), have also been included in the German climate protection programme. However, these kinds of greenhouse gases are not considered in this chapter.

Since market forces alone are unlikely to produce a response of the energy economy towards a 25 per cent CO_2 reduction, there is a need for government intervention. To reach the 25 per cent reduction goal a variety of policy measures have been already applied and further measures are proposed. The following types of measures are included in the programme:

- Regulatory measures,
- Economic measures,
- Voluntary agreements,
- Information and education,
- Research and development.

Each type of measure offers advantages and drawbacks and has a different effect on CO_2 reduction. Measures often interact and function in combination.

Regulatory measures aim at the minimization of administrative constraints or prescribe the technology standard to be applied. An example of the latter is the German Thermal Insulation Ordinance for buildings. The ordinance is expected to reduce the heating requirements for buildings due to improved thermal insulation.

The range of economic measures varies from taxes to subsidies. Examples of taxes are the "mineral oil tax" or the "emission-oriented motor vehicle tax". Often economic measures are intended to provide incentives to reduce energy consumption and hence CO_2 emissions. Examples are the various funding programmes for modernization of old and energy-wasting buildings.

Voluntary agreements with industry aim at avoiding government interventions such as regulatory measures. In 1991 several important German industrial associations issued a declaration committing themselves to reducing CO_2 emissions. In this connection, the German Government has stated its willingness to postpone additional regulatory measures in order to give priority to industry's own initiative.

Information campaigns are directed at the general public and at more specific groups in order to motivate people and to disseminate technical know-how for energy conservation.

Research and development activities include climate system research and research on prevention of climate changes.

Scenarios for CO_2 Emissions

Four scenarios describing possible developments from 1990 to 2005 under various conditions are considered in this study:
- Scenario I, worst case (frozen state of the art)
- Scenario II, no reduction measures (business as usual)
- Scenario III, with implemented measures
- Scenario IV, with additional measures (reduction goal).

Scenario I is defined as a fictitious worst case scenario on the assumption that no CO_2-reduction measures are taken after 1990. Additionally it is based on the assumption of a frozen state of the art at the 1990 level. This scenario can answer the following question: Which level of CO_2 emissions caused by economic and population growth would be reached in 2005 under worst case conditions? This serves as a reference or baseline for the following scenarios.

Scenario II includes structural changes in the energy economy and autonomous efficiency improvements. But active reduction measures as defined in the typology above are not included. This scenario can be defined as a e.g. "business as usual scenario".

The third scenario refers to developments on the assumption that only those measures become effective by 2005 which have been implemented from 1990 to 1995. Structural changes in the energy economy and autonomous efficiency improvements are also included as in Scenario II. Scenario III provides information about the effectiveness of the implemented CO_2 reduction measures and it indicates the need for additional measures to reach the CO_2 reduction goal.

Scenario IV identifies supplementary measures which are necessary to reach the 25 per cent reduction goal in 2005. Table 2.2 summarizes the impacts of the four scenarios on CO_2 emissions.

In the case of the Scenario I the CO_2 emissions will increase from 986 to 1,258 million tonnes by the year 2005. This increase is caused by the growth of the various sectoral demands as shown in Table 2.3. These growth rates are applied for each of the four scenarios.

Scenario II with no measures ends up with CO_2 emissions of 938 million tonnes in 2005. Compared to Scenario I the CO_2 emissions are 320 million tonnes lower by the year 2005. This is due to structural changes in industrial production, to shifts from high-carbon-containing coal to low-carbon-containing natural gas and last but not least to autonomous efficiency improvements.

Table 2.2 Development of CO_2 emissions in Germany by the year 2005

Scenario	1990 10^6t	2005 10^6t	Change (1990 –2005) 10^6t	%
I	986	1,258	+272	+28
II	986	938	-48	-2
III	986	852	-134	-13
IV	986	740	-246	-25

Table 2.3 Growth rates of sectoral demands in the period 1990 – 2005

End use sector	Growth rate in %
Industry	35
Commerce, military	16
Transport	
Passenger	26
Goods	55
Residential sector	17
Weighted average	27

In comparison to 1990 Scenario III is expected to lead to a reduction of 134 million tonnes by the year 2005, which is equal to a reduction rate of about 13 per cent. This shows very clearly that the implemented measures are not sufficient to reach the ambitious 25 per cent reduction goal. The efforts must be nearly doubled.

Implemented Policy Measures

Autonomous Developments and Policy Measures

The following analyses distinguish two types of measures which result in a reduction of CO_2 emissions:

1. *Autonomous measures* (autonomous development). These measures or developments are induced by regular market forces. CO_2 reduction is not their main purpose but it is a welcome side effect. These measures or effects are not a result of an active CO_2 reduction policy. Typical examples are the regular improvements of the state of the art and structural changes in the economy such as reduction of steel production and phasing out of East German lignite production etc. Another important measure of this kind is the liberalization of the electricity market in Germany. A consequence of this development is that power plants, using expensive German coal, will be replaced by efficient gas-fired combined cycle plants. This results in a considerable decrease of CO_2 emissions in the conversion sector.
2. *Policy measures* (implemented measures). This includes all policy measures by the government or other authorities which are taken with the sole objective of reducing CO_2 emissions in Germany. Typical examples are regulations, taxes, subsidies, voluntary agreements, information and motivation programmes etc.

The sectoral CO_2 reduction effects of the policy measures implemented in the period 1990 – 1995 are summarized in Table 2.4. The total net reduction of autonomous and policy measures amounts to 134 million tonnes of CO_2. About two thirds or 86 million tonnes are brought about by the implemented policy measures. This average relation differs considerably in the respective subsectors.

Table 2.4 Development of sectoral CO_2 emissions for scenario III with implemented measures

	1990[1]	Scenario III 2005	Overall	Autonomous development	Implemented measures
	10^6 t	10^6 t	10^6 t/yr	10^6 t/yr	10^6 t/yr
Conversion sector	439	365	-74	-60	-14
Industrial sector	170	107	-63	-47	-16
Commercial sector	70	51	-19	-3	-16
Transport sector	179[2]	218	+39	+51	-12
Residential sector	128	111	-17	+11	-28
Total	986	852	-134	-48	-86

1) *Source:* UBA, 1997 and BMU, 1997
2) Inclusive vehicles of industry, commerce and military

The overall CO_2 reduction in the conversion sector is expected to reach 74 million tonnes. This is the highest contribution to the total net reduction in comparison to the other sectors. More than 80 per cent or 60 million tonnes are achieved by autonomous measures. The second highest contribution to total net reduction takes place in the industrial sector. Due to structural changes the share of autonomous measures reaches 47 million tonnes or 75 per cent. The situation is reversed in the commercial sector because autonomous measures here only bring about 16 per cent of the overall sectoral reduction. Compared to the conversion and the industrial sector, the overall reduction level of the commercial sector is low.

Developments in the transport sector are quite different. The total sectoral CO_2 emissions will increase drastically, due to the fast increasing transport demand (see Table 2.3) and the persistent trend towards bigger cars. The emissions increase in Scenario II from 179 million tonnes in 1990 to 230 million tonnes (179 + 51 = 230) by the year 2005. Since the implemented policy measures cause a reduction of 12 million tonnes, the sectoral emissions in Scenario III decline to 218 million tonnes (see Table 2.4).

The residential sector displays a similar development. As a consequence of the increasing number of buildings the CO_2 emissions of Scenario II reach the amount of 139 million tonnes in 2005 (autonomous development: $128 + 11 = 139$). Due to the high reduction rate of the implemented policy measures the emissions of the residential sector in Scenario III decline to 111 million tonnes by the year 2005 ($139 - 28 = 111$).

The implemented policy measures are of main interest in this chapter. Table 2.5 presents a summary of these measures. They are discussed in the following paragraphs.

Voluntary Commitment by German Industry

The declaration by German industry was issued in 1995 and updated and considerably expanded in 1996. The Federation of German Industries and 19 individual industrial associations declared their willingness to make special efforts to reduce their specific CO_2 emissions by 20 per cent in 2005, based on the 1990 levels. Most of the associations, namely 12, also made a commitment regarding absolute reduction of CO_2 emissions. German industry's voluntary commitment covers more than 70 per cent of industrial final energy consumption, over 99 per cent of the public power supply and parts of the residential and commercial sector. Compliance with the commitments will be monitored by an independent agency.

Since voluntary commitments on the one hand and certain autonomous and policy measures on the other overlap, it is necessary to separate them. Therefore Table 2.5 only shows the net effects of voluntary commitments after deduction of the overlapping parts.

Conversion Sector

According to Table 2.4 CO_2 emissions from the conversion sector accounted for 44 per cent of total German CO_2 emissions in 1990. The conversion sector is the sector with by far the highest emissions. Despite this fact the broad catalogue of policy measures of the German Government does not include actions aimed directly at the reduction of CO_2 emissions from fossil-fired power plants. There are some R+D projects sponsored by the Government which are developing enhanced conversion efficiency technologies, but their contribution to CO_2 reduction by the year 2005 is difficult to quantify at present.

Table 2.5 Implemented policy measures (CO_2 reduction in 2005)

	10^6 t/yr
Conversion sector	
Voluntary agreement (net)	7
Renewable energy utilization	7
Industrial sector	
Voluntary agreement (net)	11
Regulations	1
Other measures	4
Commercial, military sector	
Voluntary agreement (net)	6
Regulations	4
Other measures	6
Residential sector	
Regulations	12
Funding programmes	11
Voluntary agreement (net)	2
Other measures	3
Transport sector	
Mineral oil tax	5
Increasing use of public transport	3
Other measures	4
Total	86

The net reduction of the voluntary commitments in the conversion sector amounts to 7 million tonnes of CO_2. This includes efficiency improvements in conventional power plants (5 million tonnes) and capacity improvements in existing nuclear power plants (2 million tonnes).

There is a comprehensive programme supporting the utilization of renewable energy in Germany. The total number of policy measures amounts to 41. But most of the measures are difficult or even impossible to quantify. It is beyond the scope of this book to discuss all 41 measures in detail. About 98 per cent of the quantifiable CO_2 reduction potential of 7 million tonnes is achieved by two measures:

- "The 250 MW Wind Programme" (0.6 million tonnes)
- "Act on the Sale of Electricity to the Grid" (6.4 million tonnes)

Both programmes are described in detail in Part II, Chapter 8.

Industrial Sector

The CO_2 reduction based on the expected net savings of the voluntary commitment refers to measures which aim at higher energy efficiencies. According to Table 2.5, about 70 per cent or 11 million tonnes of the expected savings are due to voluntary commitments by the industrial associations. A reduction of nearly 1 million tonnes is achieved by the Thermal Insulation Ordinance and the Heating System Ordinance (see residential sector). The remaining CO_2 savings of 4 million tonnes, summarized under "other measures", are caused by the following activities:

• ERP environmental and energy-saving programme, which supports the installation and modernization of facilities and machinery (ERP = European Recovery Programme).
• Various research programmes concerning the promotion of new technologies for the efficient use of energy.
• Climate protection programmes by states, towns and local authorities. There are various activities which aim at energy conservation mainly in buildings and in small and medium-sized industries.

Commercial and Military Sector

In this sector the estimated net effect of the voluntary commitment amounts to 6 million tonnes. These savings can be assigned to the following associations: Association of Gas and Water Industries (BGW), Association of Municipal Enterprises (VKU) and Association of Oil Industries (MWV). The regulations in the building sector achieved a CO_2 reduction level of 4 million tonnes. The considerable amount of 6 million tonnes summarized under "other measures" is saved by ERP, research and municipal programmes (see *Industrial Sector*).

Residential Sector

The residential sector provides by far the highest sectoral contribution to the total CO_2 reduction by policy measures. It reaches 28 million tonnes or 33 per cent. The largest fraction of 12 million tonnes is achieved by the following three regulations:

• Amendment of the Heat Insulation Ordinance (WSchV). The new ordinance, which came into force in 1995, is expected to reduce the annual heating demand for new buildings by 30 per cent in comparison to previous regulations. For measures in existing buildings the amendment sets forth certain requirements. If the renovation of an existing building exceeds a certain limit, then the insulation measures must be equivalent to those customarily found in new buildings.

- Amendment of the Heating System Ordinance (HeizAnlV): The amended version of this ordinance came into force in 1994. This ordinance sets forth requirements for minimum efficiencies of oil- and gas-fired boilers used to heat buildings. After the beginning of 1998 new heating system boilers must be certified as low-temperature boilers or as condensing boilers.

- Amendment of the Ordinance on Small Firing Systems (1. BImSchV): It contains a mandate for adapting the standard for the maximum permissible exhaust gas losses to the current state of the art. Over 30 per cent of the some 12 million boilers in Germany are over 15 years old. These installations have poor energy efficiencies and contribute significantly to the residential CO_2 emissions. Therefore old systems must be brought in line with the new standard for exhaust gas losses within the next few years.

A considerable CO_2 reduction of 11 million tonnes is reached with the aid of funding programmes. There are mainly three KfW (Reconstruction Loan Corporation) programmes:

- Housing modernization in East Germany. The programme provides low interest loans for renovation and modernization of housing. A considerable part of this money has been invested in energy-saving measures. It is expected to contribute 6 to 7 million tonnes to CO_2 reduction.

- The joint programme "Economic Recovery in East Germany". This special programme provides subsidies in the range of 20 per cent for the modernization of heating systems, thermal insulations and other housing-related energy-saving measures. The resulting CO_2 reductions are in the range of 1 to 2 million tonnes.

- Programme for CO_2 emission reduction in existing buildings in West Germany. Financing is provided in the form of low interest loans. Support is provided for the modernization of thermal insulations, subject to the condition that the requirements of the "Heat Insulation Ordinance" are met. Installation of low-temperature boilers and condensing boilers is also being financed. The estimated CO_2 savings of this programme amount to about 2 million tonnes.

According to Table 2.5 the amount of 2 million tonnes remains for the net CO_2 savings of the voluntary commitment. Mainly the BGW, VKU and

MWV associations are involved (see *Commercial, military sector*).

The CO_2 reduction of 3 million tonnes, summarized under "Other measures" in Table 2.5 (see *Residential sector*) can be assigned to the following two programmes:

- Subsidies for "low-energy" houses. Financial support is provided in addition to the standard subsidy for owner-occupied houses, if heat pumps, solar systems or heat recovery systems are installed. Additional subsidies are provided for improved thermal insulations. The government made it a condition that the annual heat requirement is at least 25 per cent less than prescribed in the "Heat Insulation Ordinance". Due to the limited overall amount of funding, the reduction in CO_2 emissions thus achieved is not expected to exceed 0.5 million tonnes.
- Climate protection and energy saving programmes by states, towns and local authorities: There are various activities for the building sector which can achieve CO_2 savings in the range of 2 to 3 million tonnes.

Transport Sector

The amendment of the mineral oil tax on gasoline and diesel oil fuels will lead to a CO_2 reduction of 5 million tonnes. The added tax revenue resulting from the increase of the mineral oil tax is to be used to finance urgent tasks in the transport sector and to reduce the debt of German Rail (DB). This action makes a vital contribution to strengthening the railway as an environmentally compatible mode of transportation.

About 3 million tonnes of CO_2 emissions are saved by an increasing use of local public transport. Support has been provided for measures such as construction and expansion of underground railways and city trams, of central bus stations and maintenance facilities and of traffic-control systems for municipal roads; financing has also been provided for "park and ride" facilities and for the procurement of new buses with reduced emissions. Since 1992 other types of vehicles for local public transport as well as construction of attractive bus and tram stops and installation of equipment to speed up local public transport have also been supported.

About 4 million tonnes of CO_2 are saved by the following "other measures" in the transport sector:

- Research programme on city traffic. These projects aim at increasing the use of environmentally compatible forms of mobility.
- Improving continuity of traffic flow. Equipping roads with traffic control systems helps to reduce environmental pollution, because these systems are also used in connection with speed limits.

- Construction and expansion of public traffic areas of freight centres. Within local transport systems, these centres provide the basis for an efficient organization of distribution traffic.
- German rails development concept for an improved combined road/rail transport.
- Shifting of international transit traffic from roads to railways and waterways. This traffic concept has been introduced in order to reduce road traffic.

Proposed Additional Measures and Constraints

In Scenario III with implemented measures a CO_2 reduction of 134 million tonnes is achieved (see Table 2.4). To reach the 25 per cent (246 million tonnes) reduction goal another 112 million tonnes have to be saved. Since autonomous developments have been exhausted in Scenario III, the 115 million tonnes of CO_2 have to be saved completely by additional policy measures. Table 2.6 shows the potential range of these measures due to various analyses and computer-supported calculations. In the traffic sector, a figure near the lower bound is likely to be realized and in the other sectors figures near the upper bounds.

Table 2.6 CO₂ reduction potential of additional policy measures by the year 2005

	10^6 t/yr
Conversion sector	40 – 55
Industrial sector	5 – 10
Commercial, military	10 – 15
Transport sector	10 – 25
Residential sector	20 – 30
Total (average)	112

Source: UBA, 1997.

Conversion Sector

The high additional CO_2 savings of 40 to 55 million tonnes require an extensive replacement of coal-fired power plants by gas combined cycle power plants. At least 5 GW have to be installed by 2005. Apart from the short time span for the installation of a suitable gas supply infrastructure and the construction of the power plants, there is no policy measure which could enforce the introduction of such plants. At present it does not seem to be clear whether this proposed development can be reached fully through market forces alone.

The second supply side option to reach the CO_2 reduction goal is the increased utilization of renewable energies. Especially the contribution of wind, biomass and to a certain extent of hydropower have to be expanded. To realize these proposals, additional subsidies are necessary due to the still high electricity generation costs of these options. New programmes to provide incentives are being discussed but they have not yet been put into force.

Industrial Sector

The additional contribution of the industrial sector amounts to 5 to 10 million tonnes and is relatively low. This is due to the fact that this sector has already implemented far-reaching energy and CO_2 saving measures. To realize the proposed additional reduction level it is necessary to extend voluntary commitment by industry. This has already been discussed by various environmentalists but it seems difficult to realize due to the resistance of the industrial associations. Other proposals are:

- The introduction of an Ordinance on Heat Use, which provides an energy analysis and a bench mark for each industrial company.
- Improvement of funding programmes for energy and CO_2 savings.
- Intensification of research programmes on more efficient technologies and production processes.
- Additional programmes by states, towns and local authorities.

Transport Sector

Various studies and model calculations have shown that additional CO_2 reductions in the traffic sector are difficult to achieve. This is due to the fact that fuel-saving cars, which are assumed to offer the same standards as conventional cars, are more expensive. As a result, the CO_2 reduction costs increase in comparison to other sectors of the energy economy. But 10 million tonnes seem to be achievable in Scenario IV in comparison to Scenario III. However, one must not forget that even under these conditions the total amount of CO_2 emissions from the traffic sector will increase in comparison to 1990.

Some environmentalists demand stricter speed limits, tripling of fuel prices, road pricing and limitations for CO_2 emissions from new cars. All these measures are a matter of controversy in the public environmental discussion, and it seems difficult or even impossible to realize such measures in the foreseeable future.

Commercial and Military Sector

In this sector the same additional measures are proposed as in the industrial sector. Apart from this, considerable CO_2 reductions are expected from the new amendment of the Thermal Insulation Ordinance, which is planned to come into force by the year 2000 (see *Residential Sector*).

Residential Sector

Since most of the reduction potential is present in old buildings, about two thirds of the amount shown in Table 2.6 must be realized by the renovation and modernization of existing buildings. Experience in the past has shown that this requires extended motivation and funding programmes. But according to official statements it is difficult to provide such large volumes of money at present.

In the year 2000 the existing Thermal Insulation Ordinance will be replaced by a new, stricter Energy Saving Ordinance. The new ordinance will reduce the heat demand of buildings per sqare metre by 25 to 30 percent (see Table 2.7). This new Energy Saving Ordinance is expected to result in a CO_2 reduction of about 4 million tonnes by 2005 (see Kleemann et.al., 1997).

Table 2.7 Improvement of thermal insulation standards and annual heat demand for buildings per m² in Germany

		kWh/m²
1970	Average utilization	425
1970	DIN 4108	250 - 350
1977	1st Thermal Insulation Ordinance	180 - 250
1982	2nd Thermal Insulation Ordinance	120 - 180
1995	3rd Thermal Insulation Ordinance	60 - 100
2000	Energy Saving Ordinance	45 - 70

To reach the CO_2 reduction goal in the residential sector the following additional measures must be taken:

- Further replacement of oil-fired boilers by gas-fired boilers (3–4 million tonnes of CO_2 reduction potential).
- Further extension of the building sector programmes by states, towns and local authorities (1–3 million tonnes).
- Further measures and instruments are described in detail in Part III, Chapter 15.

Conclusion

The 25 per cent CO_2 reduction goal of the German Government means a mitigation of 246 million tonnes per year in absolute terms by the year 2005. This goal can in principle be reached in three steps:

- Autonomous developments:　　　　　　　48×10^6 t
- Already implemented policy measures:　　86×10^6 t
- Additional policy measures:　　　　　　112×10^6 t
- Total:　　　　　　　　　　　　　　　　246×10^6 t

With the autonomous development and the already implemented measures a reduction of 134 million tonnes will be reached by 2005. But it seems difficult to realize another 112 million tonnes. A further reduction of electricity demand could support efforts at achieving the reduction goal. But this seems unlikely under the circumstances of a liberalized electricity market. In the industrial sector the negotiations showed that it is difficult or even impossible to extend voluntary commitments by the industrial associations. Especially in the traffic sector additional CO_2 saving measures are difficult to establish. This is due to the high growth rates in the traffic sector. Moreover, the customer is obviously not yet willing to use small cars with a low fuel consumption rate. The reduction potential is high in the residential sector, especially for old buildings. But the number of renovations is still too low. This is due to insufficient financial incentives which are caused by a lack of budget funds. Therefore extraordinary efforts are necessary to reach the 25 per cent reduction goal in 2005.

References

BMU (1994): First Report of the Government on Climate Protection in Germany, Federal Republic of Germany, Pursuant to the United Nations Framework Convention on Climate Change, An Information Paper from the Federal Ministry for Environment, Bonn, Germany.

BMU (1997): "Climate Protection in Germany", Second Report of the Government of the Federal Republic of Germany, Pursuant to the United Nations Framework Convention on Climate Change, Federal Ministry for the Environment, Bonn, Germany.

Enquete (1995): "Mehr Zukunft für die Erde: Nachhaltige Energiepolitik für dauerhaften Klimaschutz", Schlußbericht der Enquete-Kommission "Schutz der Erdatmosphäre" des 12. Deutschen Bundestages, Bonn 1995, Economica Verlag, ISBN 3-87081-464-0.

Kleemann, M. and Kolb, G. (1997): "Maßnahmen zur Minderung der energiebedingten CO₂-Emissionen bei den privaten Haushalten", In: UBA (1997): Politikszenarien für den Klimaschutz. Published by Forschungszentrum Jülich GmbH, ISSN 1433-5530, ISBN3-89336-215-0.

UBA (1997): "Politikszenarien für den Klimaschutz", (Policy Scenarios for Climate Protection), Study carried out by German Institute for Economic Research (DIW), Research Centre Juelich (FZJ), Fraunhofer Institute (ISI), Öko-Institute (ÖKO), published by Forschungszentrum Juelich GmbH, ISSN 1433-5530, ISBN 3-89336-215-0.

3 Development of Carbon Dioxide Emissions in India

NARENDRA BANSAL

Introduction

Energy planning in India has so far shown little concern for the environmental effects of energy production, conversion, transportation and use. Burning fossil fuels and biomass-based fuels introduces large quantities of CO_2 into the atmosphere, which is a potential contributor to the warming of the global atmosphere by infrared radiation absorption. The major energy and environment issue facing the international community is the possibility of global climate change. This has been acknowledged internationally at the highest level by the Framework Convention on Climate Change (FCCC), which has been signed by over 150 countries including India. The convention recognizes the close relationship between energy use and economic growth and that, while the energy sector is not the only contributor to greenhouse gas emissions, it is a major one. The main driving forces of the future CO_2 emissions in India are summarized in the following Table 3.1.

Table 3.1 Important demographic and economic parameters 1970-2010

		1970	1980	1990	1993	2000	2010
1. Population	(10^6)	541	679	837	890	1,000	1,140
2. GDP	$(10^{12}$ US $)$	110	149	256	296	420	700
Rate of growth	(%)	3.5	3.1	5.6	5.0	5.1	5.2
3. GDP per capita	(US $)	203	219	306	333	420	631
Rate of growth	(%)	1.0	1.0	3.4	3.2	3.2	4.2
4. Primary commercial energy supply	(mtoe)	59	96	175	210	310	510
Rate of growth	(%)	5.0	5.0	6.2	6.3	5.7	5.1
kgoe/capita		109	141	209	236	310	447
kgoe/US $ GDP		0.54	0.64	0.68	0.71	0.74	0.73
5. Electricity generation	(TWh)	61	119	289	355	540	986
Rate of growth	(%)	11.6	6.9	9.3	7.1	6.2	6.2
kWh/capita		113	175	346	400	540	865

Overall Carbon Dioxide Emissions in India

Figure 3.1 summarizes the C of CO_2 emissions along with the values given by US EPA (1986) and Oak Ridge Laboratory for 1986-90. The differences in the values arise essentially in estimates from coal. Predicted values for 1999 - 2000 are 289×10^6 tonnes per year – 89 per cent higher than the values for the year 1990. The share of emissions from coal, petroleum and natural gas are given in Table 3.2 (ratio $CO_2 / C = 3.7$).

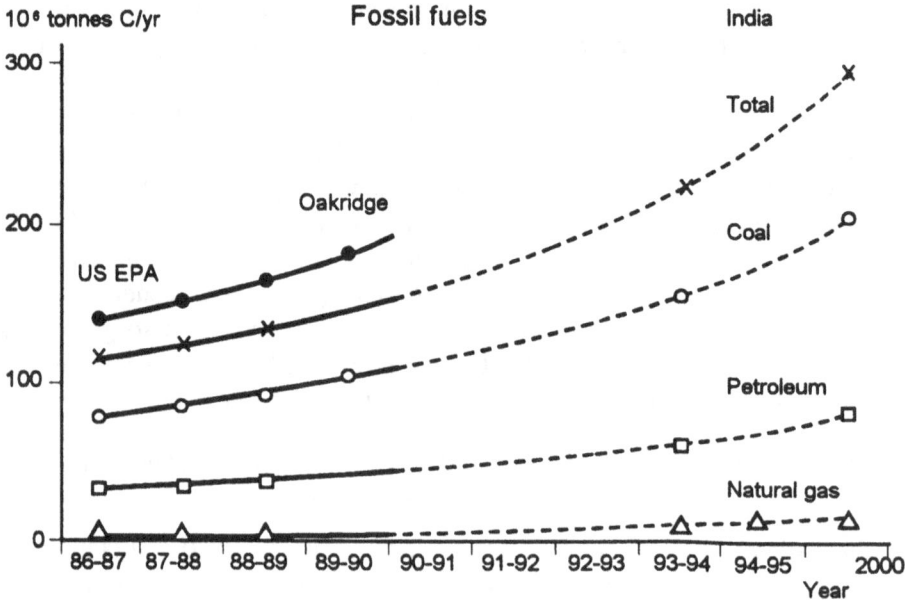

Figure 3.1 Estimates of C in CO_2 emissions for India from various fossil fuels

Table 3.2 Emissions from coal, petroleum and natural gas (in 10^6 tonnes C/yr)

	Coal		Petroleum		Natural gas	
1986-1987	80	(68 %)	34	(29 %)	3	(2.6 %)
1989-1990	105	(69 %)	41	(27 %)	7	(4.6 %)
1999-2000	200	(69 %)	75	(26 %)	14	(4.8 %)

Carbon Dioxide Emissions from Coal

Coal is the largest single source of CO_2 emissions in India. According to current trends, about 60 per cent of commercial energy consumption in India is derived from coal. Although utilization is such that the end product is CO_2, direct use of coal in combustion processes is about 60 per cent. Consumption of coal in the power sector alone shows a steady increase from 49 per cent in 1986-87 to 88 per cent in 1996-97. Unlike petroleum, the use of coal in industry is governed by its quality, which is highly inconsistent. Thus the apportioning of coal is achieved through the intermediate operation of coal beneficiation wherever needed, say, in the steel sector. In the steel sector, coals of three categories, namely cleans from coal washery, raw coal and domed imported coal are used. In the power sector, on the other hand, the middlings from the washery and raw coal are burnt. The rejects from the washery do not find any such utilization and are, therefore, excluded from the total coal consumption. A small amount of coal is also exported and is thus not included in the calculation for CO_2 emission.

Coal may be broadly classified according to the rank, i. e., maturity (the higher the rank, the higher the carbon content) and also according to the grade, i. e., organic matter content (the higher the mineral matter and moisture, the lower the carbon content). The total carbon available in a given coal, depending on its rank and grade, is ultimately converted to carbon dioxide through combustion or related processes, subject to the efficiency of operation, unless it is converted to hydrocarbons or other gaseous constituents and liquid products like tar or liquor, as in by-products of coke ovens of steel plants.

The overall spectrum of bituminous coal (carbon 75-92 per cent, dry mineral free (dmf) basis) can be broadly grouped into coking (carbon 85-91 per cent) and non-coking (carbon 75-85 per cent and above 91 per cent) types, besides lignite which is of still lower rank (carbon 50-75 per cent). The non-coking coals and lignites are used in various industries, whereas coking type coals are used in iron and steel making after conversion to metallurgical coke or to beehive coke for foundries. The by-products, both gaseous and liquid, from coke-making operations are also used to a varying extent as fuels and are thus converted to carbon dioxide. A precise estimate of the ultimate yield of carbon dioxide for coking-type coals would, thus, need a more detailed calculation. For a general consideration, however, the complete combustion of carbon dioxide from the utilization of coal in other sectors of industry like power, railways, cement etc. has been estimated on the basis of the general characteristics of coals normally deployed for the respective uses. In arriving at the estimate, the average moisture, ash and carbon content (dmf) of the coals used in the specific industrial sectors have been taken into consideration. The data concerning these characteristics are given in Table 3.3. Ultimately, however, a general factor of 90 per cent conversion of carbon to carbon dioxide has been assumed in the estimates.

Table 3.3 General characteristics of coal used in coal-based industries

Sector	Average		Organic coal	Carbon
	Moist.	*Ash*	*Subs.*	
	%	%	%	% (dmf)
Steel	2.0	17.0	79.0	88.0
Power	6.0	33.0	58.0	82.0
Railways	8.0	20.0	70.0	82.0
Cement	6.0	25.0	66.0	82.0
Sponge	6.0	25.0	66.0	82.0
Fertilizer	8.0	20.0	70.0	80.0
Soft coke	1.0	40.0	55.0	89.0
Soft coke and ITC	4.0	40.0	65.0	89.0
Others	6.0	30.0	61.0 (dmf)	80.0
Lignite	15.0	10.0	75.0	70.0

Table 3.4a presents the year-wise consumption of coal and the related emissions of CO_2 from 1986 to 1989. According to the consuming industries and total production of coal and at the end of the subsequent three five-year plans based on the projected figures (Table 3.4b), it is seen that both coal consumption and CO_2 in million tonnes per year increased steadily. Emission of CO_2 is also represented graphically in Figure 3.2. It is noted that the emission of CO_2 in million tonnes per year increased steadily between 1986-87 to 1988-89 and attained a higher rate in the following year, namely between 1988-89 and 1989-90. The amount of CO_2 emission from coal is also projected to increase at an almost steady rate over the 15-year period between 1990-91 and 2004-05. The apparent decreasing tendency of CO_2 emission over the years 1999-2000 and 2004-05 is not due to any technological impact on coal utilization but is caused by the decreasing trend in coal consumption according to the available information. The tables also show that the ratio between total coal consumption and total CO_2 emission remains within the range of 1.86 to 1.87.

Table 3.4a Estimated emissions of carbon dioxide from coal-based industries based on the consumption pattern of coal

Sector	1986-1987		1987-1988		1988-1989	
	Coal consumption	CO_2 emissions	Coal consumption	CO_2 emissions	Coal consumption	CO_2 emissions
	10^6 tonnes		10^6 tonnes		10^6 tonnes	
Steel[4]	15.4[2]	39.3[1]	18.0[2]	46.0[1]	20.5[2]	52.2[1]
Power	83.8[3]	146.1	97.4[3]	169.9	102.5[3]	178.7
Railways	8.1	17.1	7.6	15.9	6.7	14.2
Cement	8.9	17.6	8.8	17.4	9.3	18.4
Fertilizer	4.5	9.2	4.0	8.2	4.1	9.4
Soft coke	2.0	3.6[1]	1.7	3.1[1]	1.8	3.1
Others	40.6	72.7	38.7	69.2	42.9	76.8
Lignite	9.6	18.5	11.3	21.7	8.3	16.1
Total[5]	172.9	324.1	187.5	351.4	196.1	368.9
Assuming conversion of 90 % carbon to CO_2	291.7		316.3		332.0	

[1] Complete conversion of carbon to carbon dioxide has been assumed.
[2] Cleans + raw feed + imported coal
[3] Raw + washery middlings
[4] Coal consumption for beehive hard coke, which constitutes a negligible quantity (0.23 to 0.4 mt from 1986-1987 to 1988-1989), is included in the steel sector
[5] The total coal consumption excludes washery rejects (3 to 4 mt) and export (0.16 to 0.2 mt) during the period

The reason behind this phenomenon is the uniform pattern of coal utilization leading to the ultimate release of CO_2 as already mentioned earlier. On the other hand, the observation implies that coal does not find significant use in, say, carbo-chemicals and other non-fuel uses. As pointed out before, even the coal tar produced in the carbonization process is largely consumed as fuel leading to CO_2 emission.

Emission of CO_2 will follow the general trend of industrialization and coal, being the most abundantly available fossil fuel, will remain the major contributor in India. On a calorie basis, production of CO_2 from carbon-rich and hydrogen-deficient coal is greater than from petroleum. Although it would be difficult to arrest CO_2 emission till alternative fuels or energy have been deployed, the utilization of waste CO_2 may have some significance in specific areas of industrial application. Thinking in this direction has already been initiated and some in-house research projects are in progress at the Central Fuel Research Institute.

Table 3.4b Estimated emission of carbon dioxide from coal-based industries in the successive 5 year periods based on the patterns of coal consumption

Sector	1989-1990		1994-1995		1999-2000		2004-2005	
	Coal consumption 10^6 tonnes	CO_2-emissions 10^6 tonnes	Coal consumption 10^6 tonnes	CO_2-emissions 10^6 tonnes	Coal consumption 10^6 tonnes	CO_2-emissions 10^6 tonnes	Coal consumption 10^6 tonnes	CO_2-emissions 10^6 tonnes
Steel[4]	22.3[2]	56.9[1]	30.0[2]	76.4[1]				
Power	135.0[3]	236.7	206.1[3]	359.4				
Railways	6.5	13.7	3.5	7.4				
Cement	11.5	22.8	15.1	30.0	(breakdown not available)			
Sponge	1.0	2.0	2.8	5.6				
Fertilizer	5.5	11.3	6.2	12.7				
Soft coke and ITC	3.5	6.3	5.5	9.8				
Others	31.7	56.7	37.3	66.7				
Lignite	11.0	21.2	23.5	45.2	35	67.4	45	86.6
Total[5]	228.0	427.6	330.0	613.2	438	813.4	485	902.1
Assuming 90 % conversion of carbon to CO_2		384.8		551.9		732.1		811.9

[1] Complete conversion of carbon to carbon dioxide has been assumed
[2] Cleans + raw feed + imported coal
[3] Raw + washery middlings
[4] Coal consumption for beehive hard coke which constitutes a negligible quantity is included in the steel sector
[5] The total coal consumption excludes washery rejects (4 to 9 mt) and export (2.3 mt) during the period

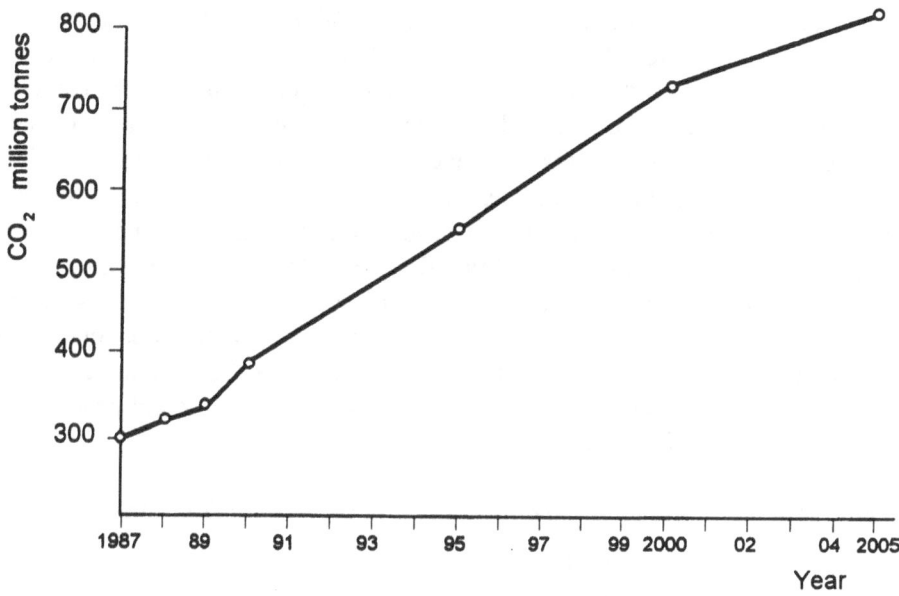

Figure 3.2 Estimated CO$_2$ emissions from coal-based industries

Carbon Dioxide Emissions from Petroleum

Petroleum refinery products are broadly classified into three categories, namely light distillates (LPG, mogas, naphtha, etc), middle distillates (light fuel oils, kerosene, etc.) and heavy ends (fuel oils, greases, lubricant oils, asphalts). The latter are used for non-energy applications and as such do not yield carbon dioxide. The present product distribution and consumption pattern indicates that over 80 per cent of the petroleum applications ultimately contribute to carbon dioxide. The consumption of petroleum products is experiencing a steady increase. It increased from 8.29 million tonnes in 1960-61 to 56.78 million tonnes in 1989-90, i.e. more than sixfold in about three decades. Consumption is expected to touch about 100 million tonnes by the turn of the century. As indicated earlier, petroleum products cater to a large variety of industries and thus it would be difficult to present sector-wise consumption patterns. But the exception to this is the transport sector, which accounts for over 42 per cent of the petroleum demand in the country.

While computing the yield of CO$_2$ from the petroleum sector, only such products which ultimately result in carbon dioxide have been considered. The carbon content for each of the petroleum products varies marginally.

The figures employed in the present exercise (Table 3.5) are provided by the Indian Oil Corporation (based on their actual chemical analyses). The degree of combustion would depend upon the type of application and efficiency of equipment. However, as these details are not readily available, complete combustion of products is assumed except for gasoline and diesel. Gasoline is completely used in automobiles such as passenger cars and two/three wheelers. A ratio of 2:3 distribution of gasoline is considered between passenger cars (4-stroke engines) and two/three wheelers (2-stroke engines) and the unburnt fuel in these cases is assumed to be 2 per cent and 25 per cent, respectively. About 90 per cent of diesel is consumed by the transport sector for vehicles such as buses, trucks, railways etc. and the remaining 10 per cent is used in other energy applications. A flat 1 per cent of unburnt fuel is assumed for diesel engines.

Table 3.5 Percentage of carbon in various petroleum fractions

LPG	82.46
Gasoline	84.85
ATF	85.91
Kerosene	86.15
HSD	86.11
LDO	87.35
FO	88.04
LSHS	88.23
Natural gas	75.00

The CO_2 contribution to the atmosphere from the petroleum sector including refinery fuel as calculated is presented in Table 3.6. The specific contributions from the transport sector as a whole are given in Table 3.7. In 1993-1994 the total consumption reached 61 million tonnes. It is expected that the consumption in 2015 can reach 120-180 million tonnes. The consumption of various petroleum products for the years 1985-86 to 1989-90 is presented in Table 3.8. At present, the gap between indigenous petroleum production and consumption is quite significant and it is being filled by imports. To add to this, the consumption of petroleum products is increasing at a faster rate (about 15 per cent) than the indigenous production of petroleum. The trend, if it continues in this way, would warrant drastic measures to curb the petroleum projections. It is expected that the actual CO_2 contribution would be lower than the estimates.

Table 3.6 Carbon dioxide emission into the atmosphere from the petroleum and natural gas sectors

Year	Petroleum sector[1]		Natural gas sector		Total	
	Volume $10^9\,m^3$	Weight $10^6\,t$	Volume $10^9\,m^3$	Weight $10^6\,t$	Volume $10^9\,m^3$	Weight $10^6\,t$
1985-86	59.29	116.47	5.53	10.86	64.83	127.33
1986-87	62.95	123.65	6.43	12.62	69.38	136.27
1987-88	67.59	132.78	7.90	15.50	75.50	148.28
1988-89	71.45	140.34	8.96	17.59	80.40	157.93
1989-90	77.27	151.78	12.2^2	23.95^2	89.47	175.75

[1] Only petroleum products such as gasoline, kerosene, light fuel oils, heavy fuel oils and refinery fuel have been considered for CO_2 contributions.

[2] The actual consumption data of natural gas subdivided between energy and non-energy applications for the year 1989-90 are not available and hence the ratio of 1988-89 is also used for 1989-90.

Table 3.7 Carbon dioxide emission into the atmosphere from the transport sector

Year	Volume $10^9\,m^3$	Weight $10^6\,t$
1988-89	33.426	65.658
1987-88	31.556	61.985
1986-87	28.712	56.398

About 42 per cent of the petroleum products are consumed by the transport sector, of which 35 per cent is accounted for by automobiles and the remaining 7 per cent by other modes of transport. The automobile sector recorded an increase of over 28 per cent between 1985-86 and 1988-89 and on the other hand the transport sector as a whole including automobiles accounted for 26 per cent growth for the same period. Thus it is apparent that automobiles, particularly individual transport, show higher growth rates. The trend is likely to continue in the future.

About 82 per cent of the LPG is used as domestic fuel and thinly distributed over the entire country. Similarly, kerosene accounts for 15 per cent of the petroleum consumption and is largely distributed in the rural sector, spread all over the country. In the absence of any alternative modes of energy, petroleum consumption is likely to grow. However, there is a good scope for improving the efficiency and thereby effectively reducing the contribution of CO_2 per unit of energy.

Table 3.8 Consumption of petroleum products (10³ tonnes)

Product	1985-86	1986-87	1987-88	1988-89	1989-90
1 Light distillates	*6,776*	*7,412*	*7,542*	*8,546*	*9,412*
LPG*	1,241	1,497	1,686	1,961	2,268
Mogas	2,275	2,505	2,810	3,015	3,491
Naphtha	3,106	3,249	2,852	3,333	3,350
SBS/Hexane	54	64	66	85	112
Others	100	97	128	152	191
2 Middle distillates	*23,948*	*25,656*	*27,998*	*29,714*	*32,484*
Kerosene	6,229	6,645	7,231	7,710	8,239
ATF/Jet A-1	1,453	1,603	1,654	1,700	1,775
HSD	14,886	16,009	17,657	18,704	20,706
LDO	1,123	1,156	1,245	1,400	1,486
MTO	100	102	104	110	118
JBO	85	70	60	70	77
Others	72	71	47	50	83
3 Heavy ends	*10,148*	*10,594*	*10,829*	*11,440*	*12,199*
FO/TDO**	3,806	3,793	4,191	4,527	4,490
LSHS**	4,094	4,254	3,953	3,849	4,330
Lube oils	658	721	756	836	926
Greases	42	34	35	38	-
Bitumen/asphalt	1,126	1,309	1,379	1,481	1,695
Petroleum coke	163	208	244	310	383
Wax	76	82	78	91	116
Other misc.	183	193	193	308	259
Total 1 + 2 + 3	*40,872*	*43,662*	*46,369*	*49,700*	*54,095*
Refinery fuel	2,491	2,612	2,643	2,790	2,684
Grand total	*43,363*	*46,274*	*49,012*	*52,490*	*56,779*

*   Includes LPG recovered from natural gas
**   Fuel oils

Carbon Dioxide and Other Pollutants Released from the Road Transport Sector

The stock of motor vehicles in the world is currently around 600 million of which 80-85 per cent are accounted for by cars, goods vehicles, buses and vans and 10-12 per cent by two wheelers. India has around 20 million vehicles, of which 66 per cent are two wheelers, 14 per cent are cars, jeeps and taxis and 9 per cent are buses and goods vehicles. For Southeast Asian countries the growth rate of motor vehicles each year is about 6-16 per cent with India having the highest growth rate (15 per cent) compared to the developed countries (0.4-4.4 per cent).

The diesel and gasoline consumption of motor vehicles in some of the developed and developing countries including India is shown in Table 3.9. It can be seen here that gasoline and diesel consumption in the developed countries, especially in the USA and Japan, is much higher than in India, but the ratio of diesel and gasoline consumption is 9-11 times higher in the case of India.

Table 3.9   Diesel and gasoline consumption (10^6 tonnes)

Country	Year	Gasoline	Diesel	Ratio of Diesel/Gasoline
USA	1989	305.2	154.9	0.51
Japan	1990	29.6	20.8	0.70
Germany	1989	26.0	17.1	0.66
U.K.	1985	20.2	6.7	0.33
Australia	1989	12.6	8.5	0.68
India	1990	3.4	20.7	6.10
Brazil	1985	5.5	12.4	2.26

Carbon dioxide and emission data for other pollutants in India for the past decade pertaining to the road transport sector for 100 per cent utilization of gasoline and diesel are shown in Table 3.10.

It is interesting to note that other than CO_2, substantial amounts of other pollutants like particulates, HC, NOx, and CO are also emitted through the road transport sector. From Table 3.10 it can be seen that the total emission of these pollutants in India over the past decade has increased by twice the amount from the beginning to the end of the decade. It is important to measure the emission amount of these pollutants because some of them are chemically transformed in the atmosphere and produce secondary pollutants causing warming of the atmosphere through OH quenching and also deteriorate air quality. The degradation of air quality is of tremendous importance in the Indian context as it leads to various human health disorders.

Table 3.10 Road transport: total pollutant emissions in India (10³ tonnes)

Year	Particulates	NO₂	HC	CO	CO₂
1980-81	20.4	96	41	889	23,205
1981-82	21.4	100	43	933	24,309
1982-83	23.6	111	47	1,015	26,837
1983-84	24.9	117	50	1,097	28,352
1984-85	27.2	128	55	1,203	30,887
1985-86	29.5	138	60	1,311	33,594
1986-87	31.9	146	65	1,431	36,269
1987-88	35.3	165	73	1,597	40,115
1988-89	37.7	176	78	1,722	42,847
1989-90	41.8	195	89	1,947	47,512

Carbon Dioxide Emissions from Natural Gas

Natural gas largely contains CH_4. Its utilization started rather late in the century, i.e. in 1970-71. Like the other two sectors, natural gas production as well as consumption is growing in the country, as expected. Gross production increased from 1.445 billion m³ in 1970-71 to 13.217 billion m³ in 1988-89, i.e. more than ninefold in two decades. Thus this sector is growing at a much faster rate than the petroleum sector. In order to reduce dependence on petroleum imports, natural gas has to be increasingly deployed for energy applications and thereby decreases the consumption of petroleum applications. Figure 3.3 shows the production of natural gas since 1970-71 (total gross production = energy application + non-energy application). The growth rate was very low in the first decade, only increasing about 1.7 fold by the end of the decade. But it increased exponentially in the second decade and registered an over sixfold increase. This growth was largely due to the availability of gas from Bombay High, which is the largest gas field in the country. Currently, the gas output from this field alone accounts for about 75 per cent of the country's production.

The consumption reached a level of 16.1 billion m³ in 1992-1993. It is estimated that the natural gas consumption in the country will grow at a yearly rate of between 9.8 and 12.3 per cent resulting in an annual natural gas consumption of between 126 and 206 billion cubic metres by 2015.

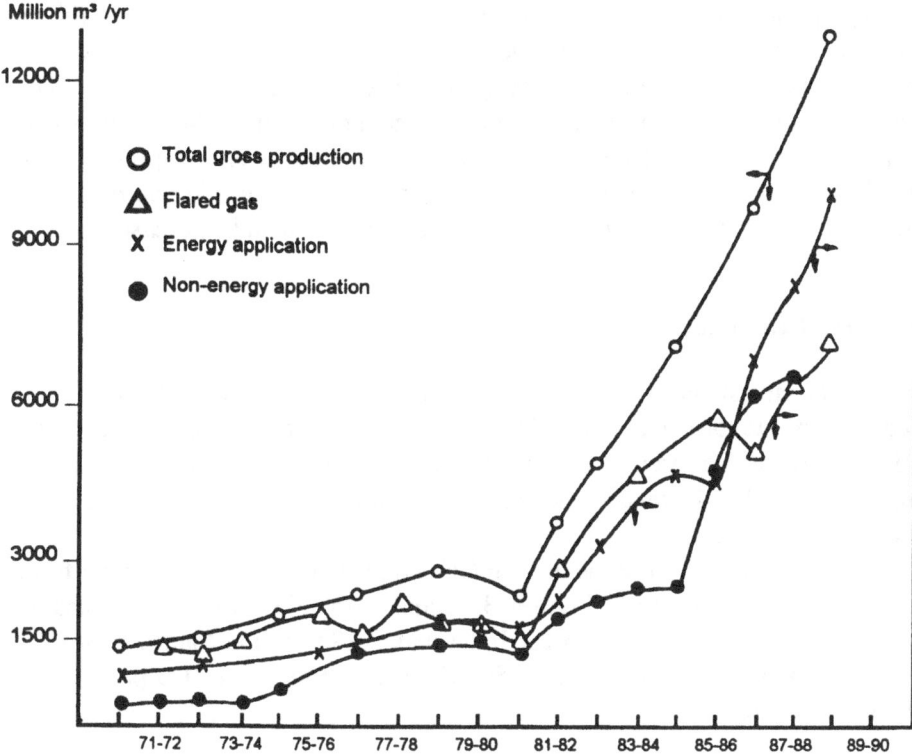

Figure 3.3 Production of natural gas (1971 – 1990)

Natural gas applications overlap with those in the coal and petroleum sector. Thus it is used as a fertilizer as well as for power generation. Consumption for petrochemical applications in non-energy segments does not yield carbon dioxide. Non-energy applications accounted for about 32 per cent of gross production in the year 1988-89, whereas the energy applications accounted for 38 per cent and the rest was flared. Thus about 68 per cent of gross production contributed to carbon dioxide in 1988-89. Gas was flared due to a lack of infrastructural facilities such as pipelines etc. to transport gas from the production site to the utilization points. Nevertheless, present plans for flaring gas have been more or less stopped.

The pattern of gas distribution among its chief applications, namely energy, non-energy, and flaring, has been examined for the last two decades. It is seen that the flaring of gas was higher in the initial period, steadily decreased over the years and was overtaken by energy and non-energy applications. This trend will continue in the future. Among the energy and non-energy applications, the former has a higher share then the latter and this is likely to continue. According to the present projection, the ratio of distributions between energy and non-energy applications will be about 3:2. The natural gas contribution to carbon dioxide including that of flared gas is calculated on the basis of the actual consumption figures and is presented in Table 3.6. Natural gas consumption and thus the carbon dioxide contribution will continue to grow in the country as energy demands increase.

Historical Emissions

Historical emissions of CO_2 from India arising from fossil fuels (including cement production) are available from the inventories published by Oak Ridge National Laboratory and are based on statistics from the United Nations and the US Bureau of Mines. The data are available from 1950 onwards.

The historical emissions of C in CO_2 from India, Brazil and China from 1950 onwards are given in Figures 3.4a and 3.4b. The cumulative emission over the periods 1950 to 1986 for India was 2,183 million tonnes C in CO_2 vis-à-vis the world emission of 1.35×10^5 million tonnes, i. e. 1.6 per cent of the world value.

Carbon Dioxide Released from Forests in India

The forests play a crucial role in the global cycling of carbon and forestry may rescue humanity from the lurking dangers of global warming. When trees are cleared or harvested, the carbon they contain, as well as the fraction of carbon in the underlying soil, is oxidized and released into the air. This release occurs rapidly if the trees are burned, but slowly if they decay naturally. Trees and plants also act as carbon sinks as they sequester atmospheric carbon and thereby initiate its building up. Of the estimated annual global carbon fixation of 100 billion tonnes, 40 billion tonnes are fixed by forest ecosystems. Tropical forests account for as much as 73 per cent of the total carbon fixation by forest ecosystems.

Reforestation, however, withdraws carbon from the atmosphere for only as long as the forests are gaining mass. After maturity, forests are approximately in balance with respect to carbon, neither accumulating nor releasing it. On the other hand, reforestation could reduce the emission of CO_2 into the atmosphere indefinitely if wood fuels were to replace fossil fuels.

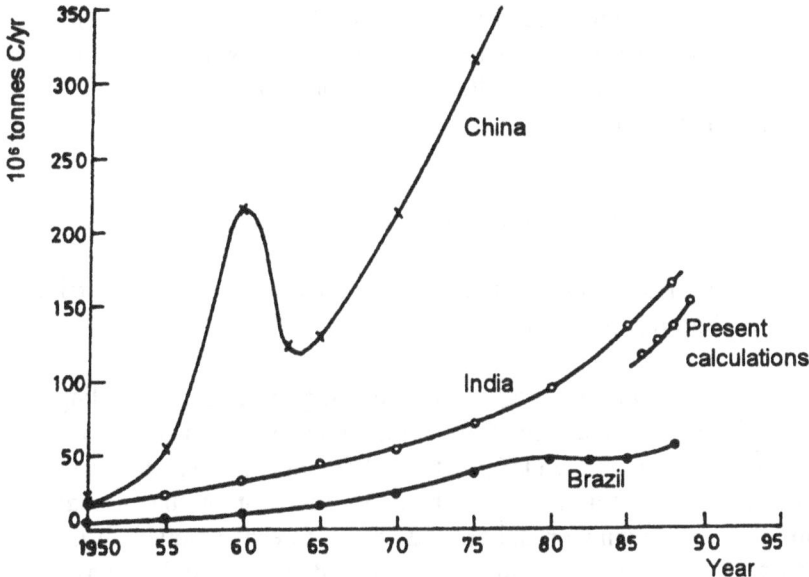

Figure 3.4a Historical C in CO₂ emissions of selected countries

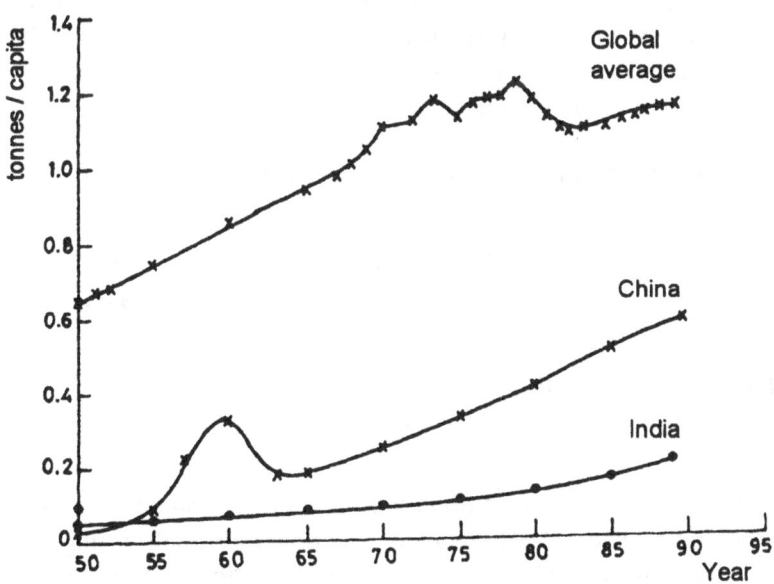

Figure 3.4b Historical C in CO₂ emissions per capita

An attempt has recently been made by the Forest Research Institute, India, to estimate the carbon emissions from different uses of forests in India such as forest clearing, shifting cultivation, accidental fires, extraction of firewood, controlled burning, etc.

Forest Uses Contributing to Carbon Release

There are various forest-related activities and product uses, which contribute to sources of carbon release in India.

Forest Clearing Clearing of forest for non-forestry purposes, including development projects or conversion to cropland or pasture, is usually accomplished by initial cutting of undergrowth and felling of trees, followed by burning. As a result of this process, about 35 per cent of the biomass is burned, and the rest remains on the ground where it decays slowly. It can be assumed that 20 per cent of the area is converted to cropland or pastures, where the biomass build-up helps in sequestrating carbon.

The net changes of forest-covered areas between 1983 and 1987 are depicted in Table 3.11. It can be seen that the tree cover was lost at the rate of 475 km²/yr. Considering biomass from this tree cover as being lost by burning, the carbon emission from this source may be estimated. Under Indian conditions a biomass of on average 70 t/ha for closed forests and 50 t/ha for open forests has been assumed.

Table 3.11 Comparison of forest cover between 1983 and 1987

Class	1983 km²	1987 km²	Net change km²
Closed forest	361,412	378,470	+ 7,058
Open forest	276,583	257,439	- 9,144
Mangrove forest	4,046	4,225	+ 179
Total	642,041	640,134	- 1,907

Shifting Cultivation This type of cultivation is common practice in northeastern parts of India. The process includes clearing by initial cutting and felling followed by burning. The cultivation only lasts for a short period, usually 3 to 5 years alternating with longer periods of fallow, about 5 to 10 years. The broad differences from the previous land use, i. e. forest clearing, are that the whole area is not cleared for crop raising and besides the forests are mostly open forests. The latest available estimates by a task force on shifting cultivation are shown in Table 3.12.

Table 3.12 Area under shifting cultivation by state

State/Union territory	Total area km²	Annual area km²
Andhra Pradesh	1,500	500
Arunachal Pradesh	2,100	700
Assam	1,392	696
Bihar	810	162
Madhya Pradesh	1,250	125
Manipur	3,600	100
Meghalaya	2,650	530
Mizoram	1,890	630
Nagaland	768	192
Orissa	26,490	5,298
Tripura	1,115	223
Total	43,565	9,156

Accidental Fires The forest types prone to accidental forest fires are tropical dry deciduous forests, thorn forests, sub-tropical pine forests, Himalayan moist temperate forests, tropical dry evergreen forests, sub-tropical broad-leaved hill forests, and sub-tropical dry evergreen forests. Fires in such forests are generally intentional with the motive of increasing the availability of minor forest products and grasses or accidental as a result of human activity.

Nearly 635,000 km² of forest in India (excluding mangrove forests) are prone to accidental fires. It is estimated that one-fifth of the closed forests and half of the open forests are accidentally burnt every year. Thus 75,600 km² of the closed forests and 128,500 km² of open forests can be accepted as forests affected by fires annually. In accidental fires, carbon is released due to the burning of litter, twigs and branches.

Seth et al. (1963) studied litter production in the New Forest, FRI plantations at Dehradun and found it to vary from 4.6 t/ha/yr for bamboo, 5.9 t/ha/yr for teak, 7.2 t/ha/yr for sal. The average litter production in closed forests in full density may be taken as 6 t/ha/yr. 70 per cent of density is in closed forests and 25 per cent in open forests. The weighted average of litter biomass accumulation on the forest floor for closed forests may be accepted as 4.5 t/ha/yr and for open forests as 1.5 t/ha/yr.

Considering 20 per cent and 50 per cent of closed and open forests, respectively, to be affected by fires we may alternatively assume such forests to be accidentally burnt at intervals of every 5 and 2 years, respectively. Thus it can be safely presumed that on an average 22.5 t/ha of litter (4.5 tonnes x 5 years) in closed forests and 3 t/ha (1.5 tonnes x 2 years) will accumulate in the open forests and would be burnt in case of accidental fires.

Controlled Burning This method is used to reduce the accumulation of combustible plant debris to prevent accidental forest fires. As carbon is allowed to reaccumulate on the land after burning, no net carbon dioxide emission occurs over time, although emissions of CH_4 and carbon monoxide result from biomass combustion. The precise area of fire lines drawn in the forests all over the country are not available. However, Ahuja (1989) approximately estimates the areas under fire lines and forest paths to be 1 per cent of the total forest area. From Table 3.11 the total forest area excluding the mangrove forest (where fires are imponderable) is 635,909 km² and 1 per cent of this area is 6,359 km². The fire lines are cleared and burnt every year and mostly contain leaf litter and twigs.

Extraction of Firewood In India logging and firewood extraction operations are generally combined. However, some forests are exclusively used for firewood production under coppice systems of sorts; such areas are subsequently soon regenerated. Harvested wood contributes to carbon releases at rates dependent upon its end-use; waste wood is burned immediately or within a couple of years, and lumber decays in up to 100 or more years.

In addition to timber, 20 million tonnes of firewood are also extracted from the forests. When the firewood is burnt a net emission of carbon takes place. Firewood is also obtained from litter accumulation on the forest floor, areas under shifting cultivation, areas deforested, controlled burning, etc.

Summary of Forest Uses The estimates of carbon emissions and sequestration of total carbon from the forest are based on the following :
- Calculations of total carbon emissions due to deforestation, shifting cultivation, controlled burning, accidental fires and extraction of firewood.
- Calculations of total carbon sequestration in areas which were near past forests by biomass build-up such as agri-crops, grasses or forest plantation depending on land use.

The estimates of carbon released by various sources of biomass burning are summarized in Table 3.13. The results show that 67 per cent of carbon released into the atmosphere is due to shifting cultivation and accidental fires. Accidental fires alone contribute about 64 per cent to total emissions. The methodology for estimating these figures is summarized in the appendix.

Human interference is the main reason for the disturbed carbon cycle, which otherwise would have been in a state of equilibrium. Shifting cultivation and accidental burning have been the biggest determent to the growth and development of forests apart from carbon released in the atmosphere. Therefore, these two major factors of carbon emission need to be controlled on a priority basis. Other factors contributing to carbon emission are part of the carbon cycle and regulated by self-correction, i.e. homeostasis.

Table 3.13 Carbon released by various forest-related activities

Sources	10^6 tonnes
Deforestation	0.25
Shifting cultivation	5.35
Accidental fires	27.23
Controlled burning	0.69
Firewood burning	9.00
Total	42.52

Stabilization of Atmospheric CO_2 Concentrations

The stabilization of atmospheric CO_2 concentrations requires eventual emission reductions to well below half the current levels. A number of different stabilization levels is investigated. An important conclusion is that the eventual stabilization level is, as a first approximation, proportional to the accumulated emissions and is much less dependent on the actual emission trajectories. This means that alternative emission profiles can in principle lead to the same atmospheric concentrations. For example, a trajectory with high emissions would initially require higher future reductions compared with a trajectory that curbs emissions immediately, assuming that both trajectories have the same cumulative emissions.

The new findings have caused a debate in the literature. Some have argued that large reductions later would be more economical compared with immediate reductions (Wigely et al., 1996). Others have argued that because of the large inertia in the energy systems, dedicated PAMs (Primary Action

Methodologies) are required immediately, in addition to research, development and demonstration (RD&D) efforts, if a substantial shift away from fossil energy sources is to be achieved before the second half of the next century (Grubb, 1996; Nakicenovic, 1996).

Another important finding is that the lower the eventual stabilization levels, the sooner the emission profiles have to decline. For example, for the stabilization level of 550 ppmv (about twice the pre-industrial level estimated at 280 ppmv), global CO_2 emissions would need to decrease to below current levels in about a century from now to achieve atmospheric stabilization in 2150, while, for 450 ppmv, this reduction would need to occur by about 2050.

The dynamics of technological and structural change is a cumulative process of learning by doing so that the early introduction of CO_2 abatement measures and policies might be a prerequisite for achieving eventual reductions of global CO_2 emission by the end of the next century. Should reductions come considerably later, it may no longer be possible to achieve a transition to the post-fossil era before a more drastic increase in atmospheric CO_2 concentrations. The historical dynamics of energy systems indicates that such a transition is unlikely to occur before about 2050 even in conjunction with appropriate PAMs. Therefore, stabilization at levels below 450 ppmv does not appear probable without unprecedented and radical change. According to the climate models, the middle course of achieving stabilization at some 550 ppmv might turn out to be the best that can be done. Despite the fact that there are many different emission trajectories leading to stabilization at about 550 ppmv, they are all constrained by some 100 GtC of accumulated emissions by 2100, or about four times the cumulative historical emissions.

In view of the increasing needs for energy services in the world, especially in the developing countries, the required emission reductions are associated with further stabilization of the world's emissions. Several proposals for "no regret" reduction measures in India are summarized in Part I, Chapter 4. Even earlier, sulphur emissions are likely to be curbed because of the regional environmental impacts, necessitating a reduction in CO_2 emissions even sooner, which in turn implies a larger future role for new technologies with lower CO_2 emissions. Thus, there is an increasing recognition in the literature that the abatement of CO_2 emissions requires a sustained commitment to RD&D and actual diffusion of these technologies today.

References

Ahuja, Dilip, R. (1989): "Regional Anthropogenic Emissions of Greenhouse Gases", Office of Policy Analysis, Environmental Protection Agency, Washington D.C.

Agarwal, A. (1996): "All for a Change", Down to Earth, New Delhi.

Bazilevich, N. O., Rodin, L. and Rozoo, N. M. (1971): "Geographical Aspect of Biological Productivity", Sou. Geogr. Transel 12; pp. 293-317.

Broun, and Lugo, A. E. (1984): "Biomass of Tropical Forest: A New Estimate Based on Forest Volumes", Science 223; pp. 1290 – 1293.

Fearnside, P. M. (1990): "Deforestation in Brazilian Amazonia as a Source of Greenhouse Gases", Paper presented at the Regional Conference on Global Warming and Sustainable Development Perspectives from Developing Countries, June 18-20, Sao Paulo.

FSI (1989): "The State of Forest Report 1989", Govt. of India, Forest Survey of India, Ministry of Environment and Forests, New Delhi.

Grubb, M. (1996): "Technologies, Energy Systems, and the Timing of CO_2 Emission Abatement: An Overview of Economic Issues", In Nakicenovic N., Nordhans W. D., Richels R., Toth, F. R. (eds). Climate Change: Integrating Science, Economics, and Policy, CP. 96-1, Laxenburg, International Institute for Applied Systems Analysis.

Hao, W. M., Liu, M. H. and Crutzen, P. J. (1990): "Estimates of Annual and Regional Release of Carbon Dioxide and Other Trace Gases to the Atmosphere from Fires in the Tropics, based on the FAO Statistics for the Period of 1975-1980", In: Fire in the Tropical Biota, Ecosystem Processes and Global Changes, Springer-Verlag, Berlin, pp. 440-462.

Houghton, R. A. (1991): "Tropical Deforestation and Atmospheric Carbon Dioxide", Climatic Change Press.

Houghton, R. A., Hobbie, J. H., Milillo, J. M., Moore, B., Peterson, B. J., Shaver, G. R. and Woodwell, G. M. (1996): "Changes in the Carbon Content of Terrestrial Biota and Solids between 1860 and 1980. A Net Release of CO_2 to the Atmosphere", Ecological Monographs 53(3), pp. 235-262.

Houghton, R. A., Bonnie, R. D., Hobbie, J. M., Palm, C. A., Peterson, B. J., Shaver, G. R., Woodwell, G. M. (1987): "The Flux of Carbon from Terrestrial Ecosystems to the Atmosphere in 1980 due to Changes in Land Use: Geographic Distribution of Global Flux", Tellus 39b, pp. 122-129.

Madhavan, Unni N. V. (1990): "Space and Forest Management in India", Special Current Event Session, IAF, Germany.

Nakicenovic, N. (1996): "Technological Change and Learning", In: Nakicenovic N., Nordhans, W. D., Richels, R., Toth, F. R. (eds.); Climate Change: Integrating Science, Economics, and Policy, CP-96-1, Laxenburg, International Institute for Applied Systems Analysis.

Rao, U. R. (1990): "Space Technology and Forest Management with Specific

Relevance to Developing Nations; Space and Forest Management in India", Special Current Event Session, IAF, Germany.

Rodin, L., Ye and Bazilevich, N. I. (1966): "Production and Mineral Cycling in Terrestrial Vegetation", Oliver and Boyd, Edinburgh.

Rodin, L., Ye, Bazilevich, N. I. and Rozon, N. (1975): "Production of World's Main Ecosystem", In: Productivity and World Ecosystem, National Academy of Science, Washington D.C., USA.

Sedjo, R. A. (1989): "Forest to Offset the Greenhouse Effect", Journal of Forestry 1987 (7), pp. 12-17.

Seiler, W. and Crutzen, P. J. (1980): "Estimates of Gross and Net Fluxes of Carbon between the Biosphere and the Atmosphere from Biomass Burning", Climate Change 2, pp. 207-247.

Seth, S. K., Kaul, O. N. and Gupta, A. C. (1963): "Observation on the Nutrition Cycle and Return of Nutrients in Pantaloons at New Forest", Indian Forester 89(2), pp. 90-98.

Whittaker, R. H. and Likens, G. E. (1975): "The Biosphere and Man", In: Lieth, H. and Whittaker, R.H. (eds.), Primary Productivity of Biosphere, Springer-Verlag, New York, pp. 305-328.

Wigely, T. M. L., Richels, R., Edmonds, J. A. (1996): "Economic and Environmental Choices in the Stabilization of Atmospheric CO_2 Concentrations", Nature 379, pp. 249-273.

UNU (1997): "The UNU-TERI Protocol on Climate Change: A Blue Print for Kyoto", TERI, New Delhi.

Appendix

Methodology for Estimating Forest Uses

Seiler and Crutzen (1980) have recommended the following formula for calculating the amount of biomass burnt per year as a result of clearing of vegetation:

$$M = A * B * a * b$$

where

M = biomass burnt per year (tonnes)

A = area of land cleared per year (ha)

B = biomass density (tonnes per ha)

a = fraction of biomass aboveground

b = fraction of aboveground biomass that is burnt

A representative value for a is 81 ± 5 per cent for closed forests and 71

± 5 per cent for open forests derived empirically from field measurements (Rodin and Bazilevich, 1966; Bazilevich et al., 1971; Whittaker and Likens, 1975; Rodin et al., 1975). Hao et al. (1990) suggested the value of b, fraction of aboveground biomass that is burnt, as 0.3 for primary (non-fallow) and 0.4 for secondary (fallow) forests. However, in the calculations these values are assumed on the basis of experience.

Further, for estimating the final amount of total aboveground carbon released it has been assumed that the aboveground biomass lying on the floor after cleaning decays over an average of about 25 years, so the average annual release of carbon is one twenty-fifth of the quantity (1-b).

Emissions of carbon resulting from soil disturbance have been estimated by using the method as follows. On an average, approximately 25-38 per cent of the carbon in surface soils is lost when tropical forests are cleared (Houghton, 1991; Fearnside, 1990), about 50 per cent is lost when temperate or boreal forests are cleared (Houghton et al., 1987). Therefore, the annual forest area converted to pasture or crop may be multiplied by the carbon content of the land's soil and a factor of 0.30 (the approximate average of 25 and 38 per cent) and finally divided by 25 years to estimate the average annual release of carbon from the soils. Carbon contents of Asian soils have been estimated by Houghton et al. (1987) as 80 t/ha and used for the calculations.

The deforestation of an area is generally followed by its conversion to pastures or agri-lands. On this assumption, the new stock of carbon that builds up due to sequestration may be estimated by multiplying the figures for the converted area by 5, i. e. the biomass carbon in tonnes per hectare sequestered by cultivation (Houghton et al., 1987).

Forest Clearing (Deforestation) The emission of carbon from forest areas put to other uses is calculated in two stages; aboveground and soil.

Aboveground emission: M = 590,188 tonnes, where A = 47,500 ha, B = 50 t/ha, a = 0.71 (taking the forest converted as open) and b = 0.35.

The annual aboveground biomass decayed: M = 43,843 tonnes, where A = 47,500 ha, B = 50 t/ha, a = 0.71 and b = 0.65 (figures divided by 25).

Thus the total amount of carbon released by the aboveground biomass is C(1) = 285,314 tonnes.

Subsoil emission: Due to soil disturbance the emitted carbon content amounts to (947,500 x 0.20 x 80 x 0.30)/25 or C(2) = 9,120 tonnes assuming 20 per cent area of forest converted being utilized for agriculture or horticulture.

Carbon sequestration by the biomass that regrows on these converted lands results as C(3) = 47,500 tonnes. The remaining 80 per cent of such converted areas is generally left for use as grazing lands or lie fallow over time.

Thus the net carbon released is C(1) + C(2) - C(3) = 246,934 tonnes.

Shifting Cultivation Aboveground emission: The biomass burnt above-ground per year M(1) = 9,012,669 tonnes, where A = 995,600 ha, B = 25.5 t/ha (as the forests are generally very open), a = 0.71 and b = 0.50 (as-sumed).

The annual aboveground biomass decay M(2) = 360,507 tonnes, where A = 995,600 ha, B = 25.5 t/ha, a = 0.71 and b = 0.50 (figures divided by 25).

Thus the total amount of carbon released by the aboveground biomass C(1) = 9,373,176 tonnes.

Subsoil emission: Due to soil disturbance the carbon content emitted C(2) = 955,776 tonnes.

Carbon sequestration by the biomass that regrows on the converted land C(3) = 4,978,000 tonnes.

Thus the net carbon released is C(1) + C(2) - C(3) = 5,350,952 tonnes.

Accidental Fires In this case the value of b is assumed to be 30 per cent. On an average, 10 per cent of the biomass accumulated is presumed to decay per year (10 years taken as time for decay), therefore the value of b for closed and open forests will differ, as the biomass accumulation before likely fires is about a period of five years or two years, respectively. The value of b thus is calculated to be 20 per cent and 26 per cent for closed and open forests, respectively.

For closed forests M(1) = 34,020,000 tonnes, where A = 7,560,000 tonnes, B = 22.5 t/ha, a = 1 and b = 0.20.

For open forests M(2) = 10,023,000 tonnes, where A = 12,850,000 tonnes, B = 3 t/ha, a = 1 and b = 0.26.

Therefore carbon released due to accidental burning amounts to C(1) = (M(1)+M(2)) * 0.45 = 19,820,000 tonnes.

Per year the biomass decay M = 16,460,000 tonnes (considering that the rest of the biomass decays in 10 years). Carbon released to decay is therefore C(2) = 7,407,000 tonnes.

Thus the net carbon released is C = C(1) + C(2) = 27,230,000 tonnes.

Controlled Burning The total litter in closed forests will be 378,470 * 600 tonnes (6 t/ha x 100 = 600 t/km²) and in open forests 257,409 * 214 tonnes (2.14 t/ha x 100 = 214 t/km²). 1 per cent of the forest area will have 1 per cent of the total litter biomass, which is calculated to be M = 2,821,675 tonnes.

The biomass burnt due to controlled burning M = 1,410,838 tonnes, where A * B = 2,821,675 tonnes, a = 1 and b = 0.50 (assumed).

The carbon released due to burning C(1) = 634,877 tonnes.

The carbon released due to decaying C(2) = 63,488 tonnes (assuming that the remaining 50 per cent decays in 10 years).

The total carbon released is C = C(1) + C(2) = 698,365 tonnes.

Extraction of Firewood The release of carbon into the atmosphere due to burning of firewood C = 20,000,000 * 0.45 = 9,000,000 tonnes.

4 Global Emission Aspects and Proposals for "No Regret" Measures in India

MURARI LAL

GHG Emissions and Carbon Budget of the Atmosphere

Currently the release of carbon into the atmosphere from combustion of fossil fuel is estimated to be about 5×10^9 tonnes per year (t/yr). The release of carbon into the atmosphere due to deforestation (tropical land use) is between 1.0 and 2.0×10^9 t/yr. Thus, a sum total of about 6 to 7×10^9 tonnes of carbon is released into the earth's atmosphere per year. The atmospheric concentration of CO_2 is currently rising at the rate of about 1.6 ppm, i.e. 3.3×10^9 t/yr. Hence it is believed that the balance amount of carbon released into the atmosphere is being absorbed by oceans, terrestrial biota and soil. It is likely that the role of carbon sinks may be influenced by climate feedbacks through physical, chemical and biological processes in the future.

The main greenhouse gases with currently growing surface emission are listed in Table 4.1. In the absence of mitigation policies or significant technological advances that reduce emissions and/or enhance sinks, concentrations of GHGs and aerosols are expected to grow throughout the next century.

By the year 2100, CO_2 emissions are projected to be in the range of 6 to 36×10^9 t/yr (assuming low population and economic growth). Methane emissions are projected to be in the range of 540 to $1,170 \times 10^6$ t CH_4 per year (1990 emissions were about 500×10^6 t CH_4); nitrous oxide emissions are projected to be in the range of 14 to 19×10^6 t N per year (1990 emissions reached about 13×10^6 t N).

For the best estimate of climate sensitivity and including the effect of future increases in GHGs and aerosols, climate models project an increase in global mean temperature of about 2 °C by the year 2100. A rise in sea level of about 50 cm is also projected in this time period. The average rate of warming would probably be greater than any observed during the last 10,000 years. Also, regional temperature changes could differ substantially from the global mean value.

If carbon dioxide emissions were maintained at near current levels, they would lead to a nearly constant rate of increase in atmospheric concentrations for at least two centuries, reaching about 500 ppm (approaching twice the pre-industrial concentration of 280 ppm) by the end of the 21st century. A range of carbon cycle models indicates that stabilization of atmospheric CO_2 concentrations at 450, 650 or 1,000 ppm could be achieved only if global anthropogenic emissions drop to 1990 level by, respectively, 40, 140 and 240 years from now, and drop substantially below 1990 level subsequently.

Table 4.1 Summary of important trace gases with growing surface emissions

Gas	Surface concentrations	Atmospheric trends	Atmospheric lifetime	Primary man-made sources
CO_2	355 ppmv	0.4 % per yr	~50-200 yrs	Fossil-fuel-burning, land-use-conversion
CH_4	1714 ppbv	0.8 % per yr	~11 yrs	Domestic animals, rice paddies, mining leaks
CO	120 ppbv	1-2 % per yr	~0.4 yrs	Energy use, agriculture, forest clearing
N_2O	311 ppbv	0.25 % per yr	120 yrs	Fossil-fuel burning, fertilization of soils
NO_x	10-200 pptv	unknown	<0.02 yrs	Fossil-fuel burning, biomass burning
$CF Cl_3$	280 pptv	~5 % per yr	55 yrs	Chemical industry produced
$CF_2 Cl_2$	503 pptv	~5 % per yr	102 yrs	Chemical industry produced
$C_2Cl_3F_3$	320 pptv	~10 per yr	85 yrs	Chemical industry produced
CH_3CCl_3	120 pptv	~5 % per yr	~6 yrs	Chemical industry projected
CF_2ClBr	1 pptv	0-30 % per yr	~12-15 yrs	Fire extinguishers
CF_3Br	1 pptv	unknown	~110 yrs	Fire extinguishers
SO_2	10-200 pptv	unknown	~0.02 yrs	Coal and petroleum burning
COS	500 pptv	<3 % per yr	2-2.5 yrs	Biomass burning, fossil-fuel burning

Stabilization of CH_4 and N_2O concentrations at today's levels would involve reductions in anthropogenic emission of 8 per cent and more than 50 per cent, respectively.

The increasing concentration of carbon dioxide, largely as a result of fossil fuel combustion, has received most attention in the global warming issue. The percent contribution of GHGs to global warming for the decade of the 1980s is depicted in Figure 4.1. While no other single gas is likely to have the direct impact on climate close to the magnitude of that expected from CO_2, studies suggest that the sum of radiative effects from other trace gases, such as CH_4, N_2O and the CFCs, could effectively double the climatic impact of model-projected increases in CO_2 if current trends in the atmospheric concentrations of these gases continue. For atmospheric concentrations of interest, the radiative forcings from these individual gases are nearly additive with respect to their impact on the surface-troposphere climate system.

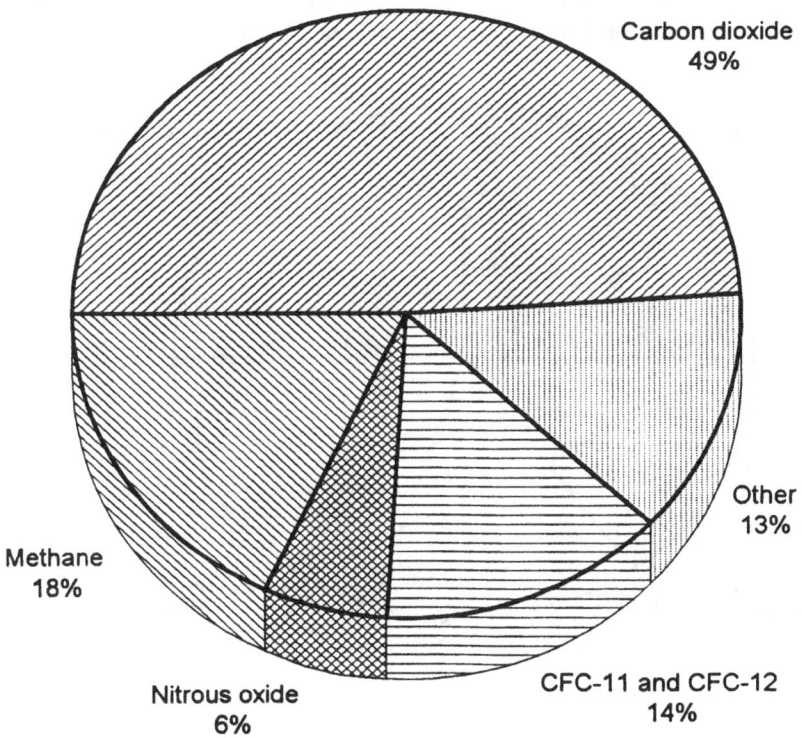

Figure 4.1 Per cent contribution of various GHGs to global warming

Human Activities and GHGs

As the greenhouse gas emissions are related to fundamental human needs (energy, comfort and food), there is a clear link between the emission of GHGs and the growth of population, production and consumption. Energy-related emissions slowed down during 1973-1980 due to the energy crisis but have begun rising again since 1985 due to the low energy prices and the continuing growth of production and consumption. The exploitation and use of fossil fuels causes emissions of CO_2, CO (plays an essential role in the CH_4-CO-OH cycle), hydrocarbons and nitrogen compounds. Currently, the global emission due to coal is about twice that due to natural gas of the same amount of energy (oil-related emission is about one and half times as much). Methane from fossil origins is released by the exploitation of coal and oil, if it cannot be used or flared, and also by the distribution of natural gas. Methane, as a product of the anaerobic digestion of organic material, is also released from landfills, wetlands, rice paddies and due to fermentation by ruminants. Nitrous oxide is mostly produced by denitrification processes in environments with a high nitrogen load such as soil and polluted water.

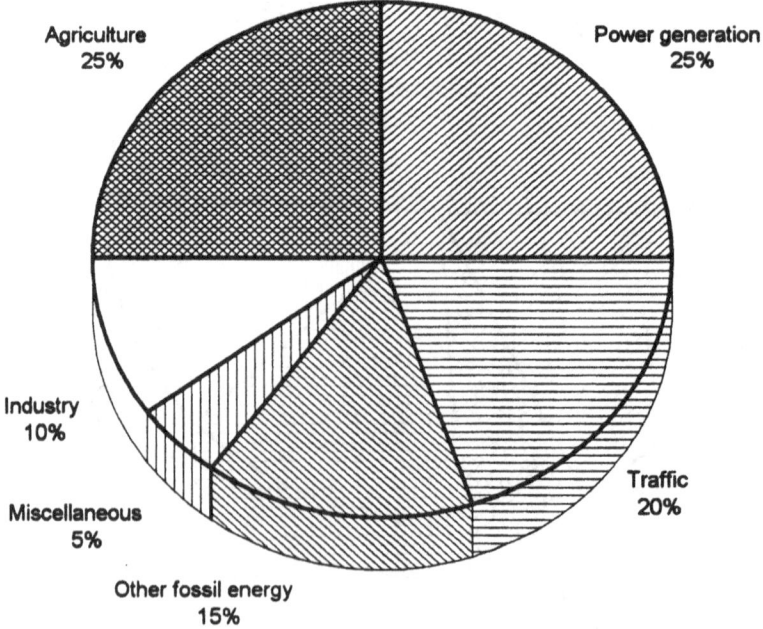

Figure 4.2 Relative contribution of various sectors to global warming

Nitrogen oxides and non-methane hydrocarbons are precursors of the tropospheric ozone, which also acts as a greenhouse gas. Depending on the assumption and definitions, it can generally be said that the combined agriculture and industrial sectors cause 35 per cent of the problem, while 65 per cent is caused by the energy sector (Figure 4.2). Within the energy sector, transportation, power generation and other combustion processes play an equal role. The carbonaceous fuels (about 86 per cent) dominate the energy system of the world. The second important source is biomass (about 15 per cent).

Direct and Indirect Radiative Effects of GHGs

The direct radiative forcing on the atmosphere that results from any given amounts of CO_2 and other trace gases is generally well understood and is not in question. However, the magnitude of climate change that could result is still uncertain. In particular, there are many uncertainties in the climatic feedback processes that will determine the eventual change in temperature and other climatic variables. The extent of future climate change will depend on complex interactions between atmospheric radiative, dynamic and chemical processes as well as the climatic feedback mechanisms. In addition to direct radiative effects of surface-emitted gases, there are indirect radiative effects on climate that also need to be considered. Atmospheric chemistry plays a key role in the determination of many of these effects. Finally, the actual atmospheric composition of the greenhouse gases will depend not only on natural and anthropogenic surface emissions, but also on any atmospheric chemical processes affecting their concentrations and distributions. Unlike the direct radiative effects, photochemical processes affecting atmospheric composition are generally coupled and non-linear. Because of this, the estimation of net radiative impact of changes mediated by photochemistry tends to be specific to the detailed scenario assumed for trace gas abundance and emission trends.

Recent studies on chemical interactions involving hydroxyl (OH) and ozone (O_3) in the troposphere and involving ozone and water vapour in the stratosphere have amply demonstrated the important role of atmospheric chemical processes in the climate change issue. The hydroxyl radical, OH, is not itself a greenhouse gas with a direct radiative effect on climate, but it is extremely important as a chemical scavenger of many trace gases in the troposphere. OH is the primary tropospheric scavenger of CH_4, CO, CH_3CCl_3, CH_3Cl, CH_3Br, H_2S, SO_2, DMS (di-methyl sulphide) and many other hydrocarbons and hydrogen-containing halocarbons. Some of these species such as CH_4 do have direct radiative effects on climate. Therefore, a change in global OH concentration can impact the atmospheric lifetimes of these species and thereby modify their abundances and climate. Reactions with OH in the troposphere also limit the amount of CH_4 and halocarbons reaching the stratosphere, where these species can lead to changes in the ozone distribution. In addition, OH and other closely related species in the HO_x family play a central role in the production of tropospheric ozone by oxidizing NO to NO_2 by removing the active form of NO_x and, in the lower troposphere, by initiating the oxidation of hydrocarbons. Table 4.2 indicates, for the same gases described previously in Table 4.1, that OH is closely coupled, both in its formation and destruction, with gases important to the chemistry - climate interaction. The net effect of these interactions on OH is still largely unknown. To fully understand and integrate these effects will require three-dimensional global tropospheric chemical models.

Any prediction of future changes in global average tropospheric OH abundances depends on accounting for the simultaneous action of many coupled HO_x-controlling processes outlined above. Significant uncertainties are encountered even in the investigation of implied trends of OH in the re-

Table 4.2 Direct radiative effects and indirect trace gas interactions affecting climate

Gas	GHG	Tropospheric concentrations affected by chemistry	Indirect effects on tropospheric chemistry	Indirect effects on stratospheric chemistry
CO_2	yes	no	no	affects O_3
CH_4	yes	reacts with OH	affects OH, and O_3	affects H_2, O_3
CO	no	reacts with OH	affects OH, and O_3	not significantly
N_2O	yes	no	no	affects O_3
NOx	no	reacts with OH, O_3	affects OH, and O_3	affects O_3
$CFCl_3$	yes	no	no	affects O_3
CF_2Cl_2	yes	no	no	affects O_3
$C_2Cl_3F_3$	yes	no	no	affects O_3
CH_3CCl_3	yes	reacts with OH	no	affects O_3
CF_2ClBr	?	photolysis	no	affects O_3
CF_3Br	yes	no	no	affects O_3
SO_2	weak	reacts with OH	not significant	increases aerosols
COS	weak	reacts with OH	no	increases aerosols

cent past. In studies of the CH_4 abundance, 20 to 80 per cent of the CH_4 increases has been ascribed to OH decreases. But unresolved uncertainties in CO, NO_x and NMHC (non-methane hydrocarbons) trends, as well as the global distribution of NO_x sources, lifetimes and abundances contribute to the wide range of possible recent change. Considering the troposphere as a whole, it is thought that the current situation is NO_x-poor with respect to net HO_x production in CO, CH_4 and NMHC oxidation. Projected increases in these compounds are thus likely to lead to continued decreases in total tropospheric OH abundance. This average conclusion includes, however, significant regional diversity, in which some areas of the troposphere may be characterized by OH increases.

The connection between average tropospheric OH abundance, CO and CH_4 lifetimes and climate has been discussed above. If, as seems likely, CO and CH_4 emissions continue to increase, the average OH abundance could decrease, subsequently enhancing the tropospheric concentrations of CH_4 beyond that expected from the direct increases in emission, and leading to a larger climate impact. Other species of radiative or stratospheric photochemical importance (e.g., hydrogen-containing halocarbons), that are primarily destroyed by reaction with OH, would similarly be affected by such a feedback mechanism. Calculation suggests that an increase in methane emissions in the atmosphere at the 1 per cent per year level could decrease tropospheric OH by as much as 0.25 per cent per year, assuming that all other trace gas emissions remain at current levels.

Because water vapour is the parent compound for OH and other HO_x species, changes to its concentration should alter the concentration of tropospheric OH. Tropospheric water vapour is in balance with an evaporation and transpiration source from the oceans, soils, plants and the precipitation sinks. Global increases in temperature, driven by a climate change, are expected to lead to changes in the tropospheric water budget. If the sources of water vapour are not perturbed by changes in vegetative cover and if circulation patterns do not lead to more frequent precipitation events, then the concentration of H_2O might be expected to increase, noting that global average relative humidity tends to remain almost constant with warming in global climate model experiments. As a simple estimate, a 2 °C increase in temperature could be associated with a 10 to 30 per cent increase in tropospheric H_2O level, implying a few per cent increase in OH and other HO_x family members.

Thus, it is clear that the chemical interaction of greenhouse gases is quite complex and to precisely evaluate their role in climate change with the current scientific understanding more elaborate investigations are warranted for confident predictions of climate change in the future. Unambiguous detection of climate-induced changes to most ecological and social systems will, thus, prove extremely difficult in the coming decades. Nevertheless, because of the potential for irreversible damage due to climate change (as a result of long time lags between GHG emissions and their effects), global cooperation and joint action has to be taken right away for effective protection of the earth's climate system. A prudent strategy to deal with climate change would be to collectively reduce the emission levels of GHGs through a portfolio of actions aimed at mitigation and adaptation measures.

Global Energy-Related CO_2-Emissions by Major World Regions

Since most GHG emissions have originated from the industrialized nations, the responsibilities for the initial mitigation efforts are placed on these countries. In the Toronto Agreement, these countries consented to control their emissions to within the 1990 emission levels by 2000. Due to their very low emissions, no specific mitigation target was required from the developing countries (see Table 4.3). The need for serious mitigation efforts from developing countries, however, is now being increasingly acknowledged since (a) their future emissions are set to grow very rapidly, and (b) there are many low cost (or even negative cost, i.e. "no regret") mitigation opportunities available in the developing countries. India has climbed from 13th to 6th place as a national contributor of CO_2 emissions from 1950 to 1990. Its total emission has increased by 10.4 times over this 40-year interval and per capita emission has increased almost four times. Any GHG mitigation regime for achieving the aims of the Framework Convention cannot be feasible nor economically efficient without the participation of the developing countries.

Table 4.3 **Contribution of developed and developing countries to historical GHG emissions in per cent (period: 1880-1988)**

	Industrial CO_2	Total CO_2	$CO_2 + CH_4$
Developed countries	83.8	67.8	66.9
Developing countries	16.2	32.2	33.1
India	1.6	4.5	4.8

The parties to the FCCC are committed to protecting the climate system for the benefit of present and future generations of mankind on the basis of equity and in accordance with their common but differentiated responsibilities and respective capabilities (Article 3.1 of UNFCCC). The stabilization of the GHG concentration must be achieved in a manner conducive to enabling economic development to proceed in a sustainable manner. Account must also be taken of the differences in starting points and approaches, economic structures and resource bases, the need to maintain strong and sustained economic growth, available technologies and other circumstances as well as the need for equitable and appropriate contributions by each of the parties.

Global energy demand has grown at an average annual rate of approximately 2 per cent for almost two centuries. Based on aggregated national energy balances, 385 EJ of primary energy was consumed in the world in 1990, resulting in a release of 6 Gt C of CO_2. Figure 4.3 depicts

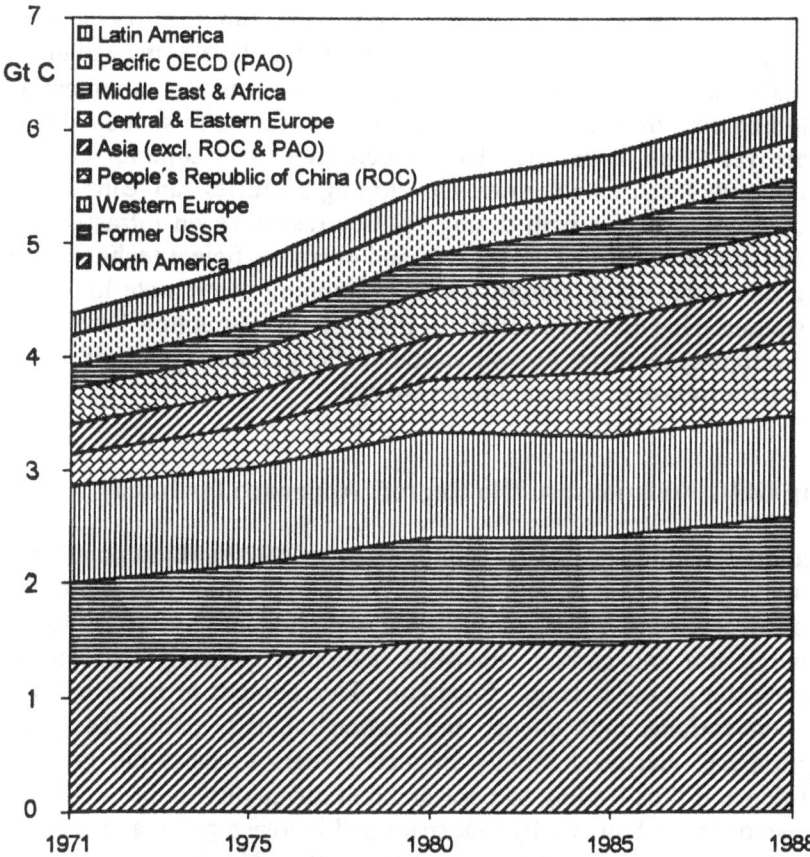

Figure 4.3 Global energy-related CO_2 emissions by major world region in Gt C per year

total energy-related emissions by major world region. The Organization for Economic Cooperation and Development (OECD) nations have been and remain major energy users and fossil-fuel CO_2 emitters, although their share of global fossil-fuel carbon emission has been declining in recent years. Developing nations, taken as a group, still account for only a small portion of total CO_2 emissions in comparison to industrialized nations. Future energy demand is anticipated to continue to grow, at least through the first half of the next century. This essentially calls for linking the energy and environment policies with economic development.

Significant reductions in net GHG emissions are technically possible and can be economically feasible. These reductions can be achieved by utilizing an extensive array of technologies and policy measures that accelerate technology development, diffusion and transfer in all sectors, including the energy, industry, transportation and agriculture/forestry sectors. Future energy use and emission intensities from the developing countries will invariably be decided by their development patterns. As in almost all the developing countries major infrastructure investments to support development are yet to be made, they have much wider and superior choices compared to industrialized countries. Developing countries can leapfrog the conventional development path through policy decisions on infrastructure like rail and communications, renewable and energy-efficient technologies, managing the urbanization pattern, location planning to promote lower logistic costs and educating consumers to influence consumption behaviour. Today, developing countries present varied challenges and opportunities for the least-cost response to global climate change.

Reducing GHG Emissions: A "No Regret" Approach for India

India is a fast growing developing economy. India's 920 million population is expected to grow to 1,400 million in the year 2025. Three quarters of the population live in rural areas with a traditional economy system. The per capita energy use and carbon emissions, although growing, still remain much below the global average. Economic development in India has followed a conventional high energy and carbon intensity path. Fossil fuel consumption has increased rapidly in recent years to meet the growing transport demand thus leading to poor ambient air quality in cities. Unsustainable use of forest biomass by industries and increasing demand for land contributed to severe deforestation until the 1980s. Nearly 40 per cent of carbon emissions from anthropogenic sources in India are attributed to land-use change. Domestic coal has continued to be the dominant energy source for electricity and industry. Power generation in India will continue to be dominated by coal, although the share of coal-based power generation will decline to half of generation capacity in the year 2035 compared to the present share of two thirds. The contribution of gas-based power increases to 20 per cent in the year 2035. In the same year, hydropower generation capacity will increase nearly threefold. In recent years, several renewable energy technologies have penetrated decentralized and rural applications as well as centralized electricity generation. These technologies are currently at a take-off stage and can penetrate rapidly if a level playing field is provided by subsidizing the renewables or by taxing fossil fuels. Perhaps it might be necessary for India to impose a carbon tax to stabilize the atmospheric GHG concentration in the long run.

Assuming the observed international cost trend on renewable technologies, if basic macroeconomic intervention in terms of both carbon taxes and subsidies are allowed in India, a remarkable acceleration in the penetration of renewables is feasible. For example, with no tax or subsidy policy, the renewable electricity-generating technologies should reach the penetration level of 20,000 megawatts in the year 2035. Under high subsidy and tax levels, the penetration could more than triple (Figures 4.4 and 4.5). The subsidy (absolute value declines with time) prompts early penetration of renewables, while the carbon tax (with increasing trajectory in time) accelerates penetration.

Future penetration of wind power systems under a subsidy and carbon tax regime are depicted in Figures 4.6 and 4.7. It is evident that the penetration of renewable technologies is profoundly influenced by the subsidy and carbon tax levels. Electricity generation from renewable technologies has the capacity to replace up to 150 million tons of coal annually in the year 2035. Perhaps, a practical proposition can be made to impose a mild carbon tax and recycle the revenue to subsidize renewable technologies.

In India, transport is among the fastest growing sectors. In the past two decades, the share of road transport has increased from 59 to 77 per cent for passenger movement and 35 to 56 per cent for freight movement. Future infrastructure improvements in terms of increased electrified track length, additional locomotives, increased wagon capacity and the resulting shift from road to rail could contribute to 2 per cent energy savings and 0.5 per cent savings in carbon emission in the year 2035. Additional gains include reduced oil consumption and better air quality in metropolitan areas.

There is considerable scope for adapting to better management practices in India as regards the aerosol and SO_2 emissions from coal burning and the problem of ash disposal. Coal washing capacity has stagnated at the

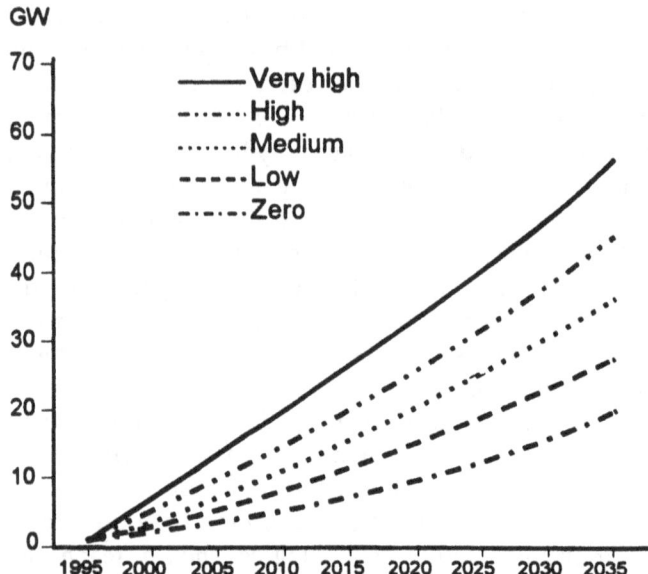

Figure 4.4 Renewable electricity generation capacity (subsidy scenarios)

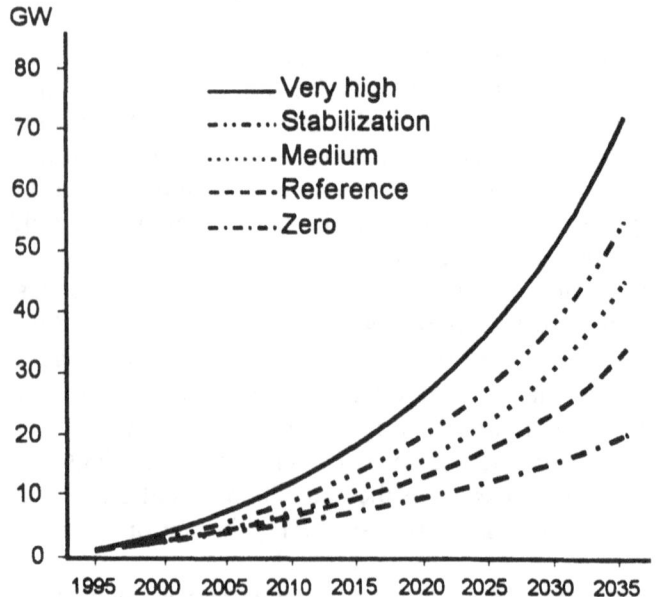

Figure 4.5 Renewable electricity generation capacity (carbon tax scenarios)

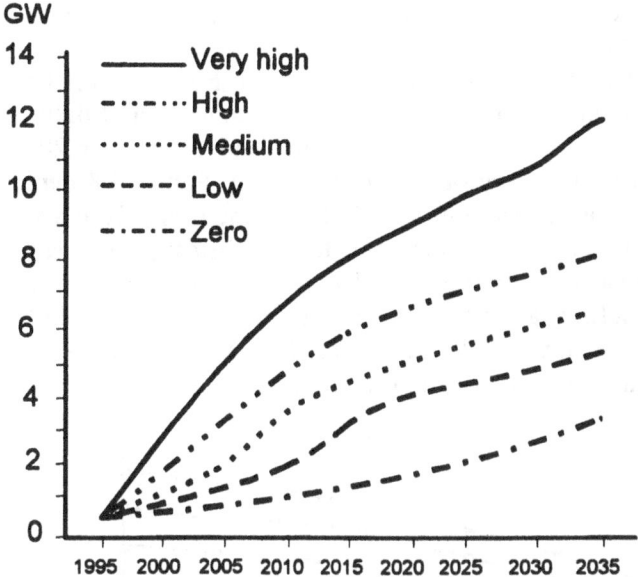

Figure 4.6 Wind power capacity (subsidy scenarios)

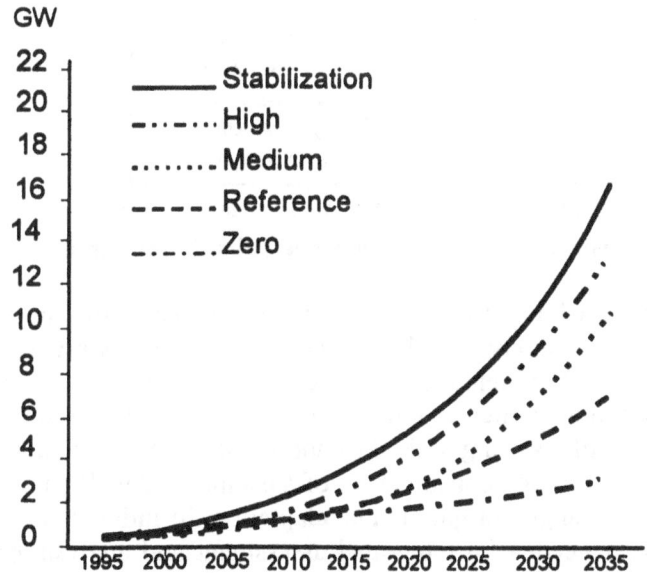

Figure 4.7 Wind power capacity (carbon tax scenarios)

10 per cent level for the last two decades. Enhanced washing capabilities should also provide better combustion efficiency.

In India, careful targeting of subsidies is essential. For example, kerosene is used by low income and rural households for cooking and lighting. It enjoys a high subsidy which, if removed, could lead to an over 20 per cent increase in biomass consumption in the year 2035. Figure 4.8 depicts the future trends in biomass consumption in India for the range from a very high Kerosene Subsidy Scenario (60 per cent) to no subsidy (at successive reductions of 15 per cent over other cases). The removal of subsidy would, thus, lead not only to deforestation but also to high indoor pollution. In this respect, the kerosene subsidy should be regarded as a developmental instrument rather than an energy policy intervention.

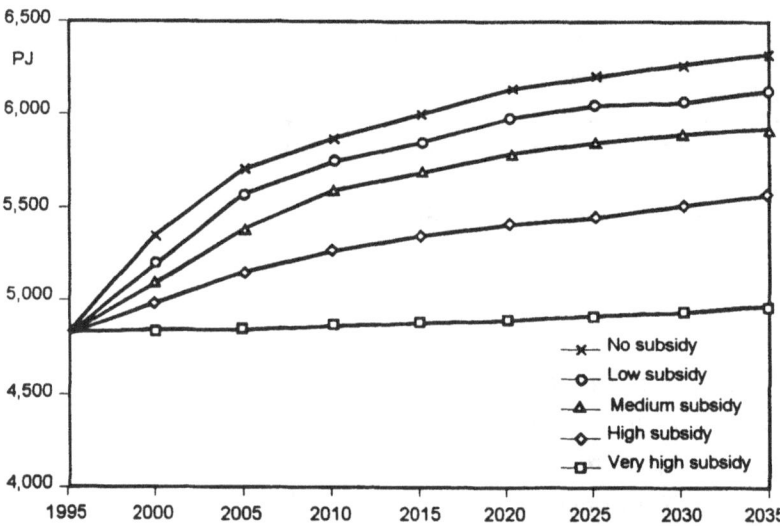

Figure 4.8 Biomass consumption in PJ (kerosene subsidy scenarios)

India requires support for institutional and indigenous capacity building to effectively participate in climate change decision making. A prudent way to deal with the issue of reducing greenhouse gas emissions in India is through a portfolio of actions aimed at mitigation and adaptation based on precautionary principles of averting risk. Promotion of public education and training for optimal resource consumption of sustainable development should facilitate climate change mitigation and adaptation. In India, a coordinated research effort is needed on integrated assessment and analysis of decision making related to climate change. Research and development related to energy efficiency technologies and non-fossil commercial energy options offer high potential in India. Figure 4.9 depicts various possible

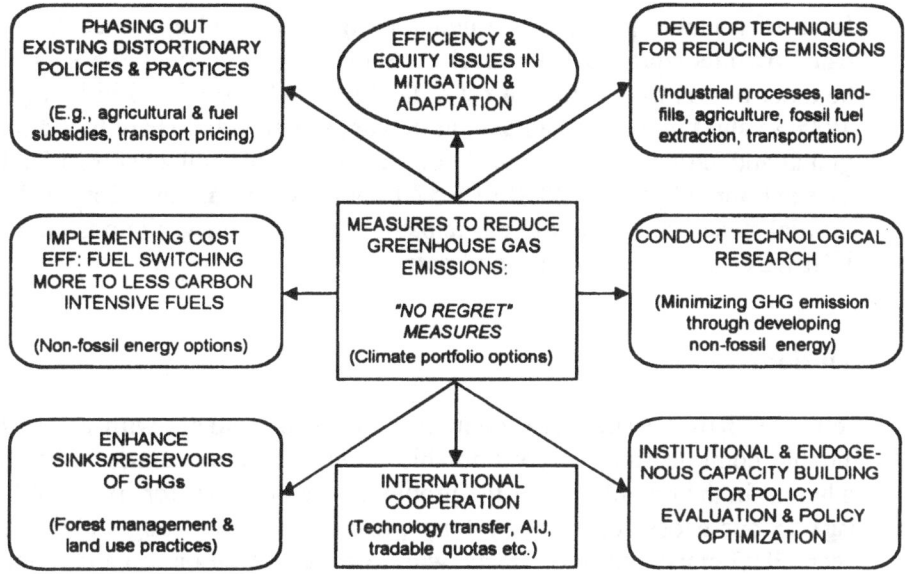

Figure 4.9 Principal measures for reducing GHG emissions in India

actions that policy makers in India may consider, in accordance with applicable international agreements, to implement cost-effective measures to reduce emissions of greenhouse gases and to adapt to climate change.

Some of the issues that require immediate attention by policy makers in India with reference to various sectors as effective measures to reduce our contribution to the global build-up of greenhouse gas are:

1. Transport: Switch to alternate fuels/mobility patterns, shift traffic from road to rail.
2. Land use: Massive afforestation (60 to 90 Gt C could be sequestered in the forestry sector alone in the next 50 years), wasteland reclaimation, eco-conservation/regeneration, improving fertilizer use efficiency.
3. Electricity generation: Shift towards coastal sites, use of combined-cycle gas turbines, clean coal usage (additional washing facility), promote wind/solar PV power generation, efficiency in power generation, transmission and distribution (10-30 per cent gain with only improved management practice, 50-60 per cent feasible with relevant technology/finances availability).
4. Future energy options: Conservation and efficiency improvements, nuclear and synthetic biomass fuel switching, use of GHG benign energy technologies, penetration of renewable technologies (subsidy cum tax policy), choice of policy instruments (regulatory vs. market-based).

5. Issue of tradable permits: "Grandfathering Emission" approach (allocated permits equal to 1990 level emission by a country; India should be a net buyer) may lead to a net annual loss in 2030 of $50 billion (at 1985 $ value) while per capita emission approach (equal share based on global and national population; India should be a net seller) should lead to a net annual gain in 2030 of $ 57 billion. India has, therefore, substantial stakes in agreeing to participate in the global negotiations under UNFCCC for initial allocation of permits.

Conclusions

The climate change issue has presented the decision makers with a set of formidable complications: a considerable number of uncertainties (which are inherent in the complexity of the problem), the potential for irreversible damage to our ecosystem, a very long planning horizon, long time lags between GHG emissions and effects, wide regional variation in causes and effects, global scope of the problem and the need to consider multiple greenhouse gases and aerosols. The value of better information about climate change processes and impacts and our response to arrest these risks are likely to be great. We, the Indian scientists, firmly believe that the principle of sustainable development must guide all our future development strategies. It is, therefore, our responsibility to undertake innovative research on technology options, contribute to creative environmental literacy and convince the decision makers to adopt new environmental policies and programmes.

References

Chattopadhyay, D. and Parikh, J. K. (1992): "CO_2 Emissions Reduction from Power System in India", IGIDR Discussion Paper No. 79, p. 21.

IPCC (1995a): "Climate Change 1995 - A Synthesis Report of the Intergovernmental Panel on Climate Change", p. 64.

IPCC (1995b): "Climate Change 1995 - The Economic and Social Dimensions of Climate Change" (Eds. J. P. Bruce, H. Lee and E. Haites), Cambridge University Press, UK, p. 448.

Loulou, R., Shuka, P. R. and Kanudia, A. (1996): "Energy and Environment Strategies for a Sustainable Future: Analysis with the Indian MARKAL Model", Allied Publishers, New Delhi.

Parikh, J. and Gokarn, S. (1992): "Climate Change and India's Energy Policy Options", IGIDR Discussion Paper No. 76, p. 33.

PART II
Renewable Energies for Climate Protection

5 Status of Renewable Energy Utilization in the Federal Republic of Germany

HERMANN-JOSEF WAGNER

Motivation for the Utilization of Renewable Energies

Considerable efforts have been made in the Federal Republic of Germany since the two oil-price crises in 1973 and 1978 to develop renewable energy technologies and to establish them on the market. The motivation for these efforts was the fear of rising costs for fossil fuels due to the international political situation, as well as the concern about the long-term depletion of the reserves of fossil energy. Fortunately, the development of energy prices has levelled off during the last 15 years. There is now a sufficient supply of oil on the world market, making an increase of costs or physical shortage unlikely at present.

At the same time environmental aspects of power generation, especially concerning the generation-related emissions (e. g. CO_2, SO_x, NO_x, etc.), have become relevant. An international discussion of measures for reducing CO_2 emissions was initiated at the Rio Conference in 1992. In this debate the renewable energies with their lower emissions are becoming more important. For increased utilization renewable energies have to be adapted to the existing consumption structures and they have to compete with the established technologies. At the moment, alternative energies play a major part in neither the structure of power generation nor the heat supply in Germany.

Table 5.1 presents the structure of electricity generation in Germany. Obviously, the nuclear power plants and the fossil power plants (lignite- and hard-coal-fired) produce the main part of the required electric energy. Hydroelectric power generation has a share of four per cent. Oil, natural gas and pumped-storage power stations are only used for peak load. Other power plants, e.g. waste combustion and wind converters, amount to about three per cent. The total generation of 121 GW capacity is 530 TWh (352×10^6 t CO_2).

Table 5.1   Structure of electricity generation in Germany 1995 (industry and public suppliers) and CO_2 emissions

Operation mode	Type of power station	Share of electricity generation
Base load > 6,000 h/yr	Nuclear	29 %
	Lignite	28 %
	Water	5 %
Medium load 2,000 - 5,000 h/yr	Hard coal	27 %
Peak load < 2,000 h/yr	Natural gas	7 %
	Oil	1 %
	Pumped storage, others	2.6 %
No load management	Wind	0.4 %
	Photovoltaic	
	Total 121 GW	100 %

Source: Energiedaten, 1996.

Forms of Renewable Energies Used in Germany

Although the availability of renewable energies in Central Europe is very low, various forms of renewable energies, e.g. water in rivers, wind, solar radiation, biomass and organic gas, are used. Normally, in Germany biogas occurs only in sewage farms and waste dumps, where it is used in cogeneration. The motivation to do this is not to support renewable energies, but to destroy the gases. In the following we will not discuss this option further.

The thermal use of solar energy in large plants with more than 350 MW installed capacity, as in California, is not possible because the level of direct solar radiation in Central Europe is too low. In the following the forms of renewable energies used in Germany are described.

The largest portion of renewably generated power is produced in approximately 5,000 hydroelectric power plants amounting to about 5 per cent of total electricity generation. Only 7 per cent of these 5,000 hydroelectric installations generate 90 per cent of the electricity. This figure illustrates that only large plants generate the major fraction.

The second most important source of renewable energy is the generation of electricity by wind-electric generators. The electricity produced has a share of slightly less than one per cent of total generation. In order to establish this technology the market-pertinent legislation and special funds provided by the Government were created to support the operation of wind mills (see Part II, Chapter 8). At the same time development focused on bigger units. The average capacity load of wind converters currently in operation amounts to approximately 370 kW (Table 5.2). However, units installed in the first half of 1997 have a rated output of 600 kW. Plants with ratings of up to 1,5 MW capacity have been introduced into the market in 1997 as prototype engines.

Table 5.2 Status of the utilization of wind energy in Germany (as of: 30th July 1997) (DEWI, 1997)

	Classification [kW]					Total
	5 – 80	81 - 200	201 - 400	401 - 750	> 750	
Number	742	600	829	2,451	83	4,705
Installed capacity (MW)	42	92	221	1,321	88	1,764
Annual electricity (GWh)*	52	165	443	2,590	146	3,396

* Assuming that all wind mills operate during the whole year

Up to now most facilities have been located near the coast due to better wind-conditions. But meanwhile the number of inland wind converters is also increasing. Further efforts are being undertaken to optimize inland operation. Replacing small wind converters by bigger units will slightly increase the share of wind energy in electricity generation.

Using photovoltaic energy comes third in the renewable energy ranking a long way behind wind energy. Generally, three forms of developments are distinguished:
1. decentralized installations, in particular installations from 1 up to 3 kW_p for detached houses,
2. central facilities, i.e. 300 kW_p installations, linked operation,
3. combination of photovoltaically generated power and storage by means of water electrolysis.

The decentralized installations were supported by a special Government programme (roof-PV programme), which resulted in a total of about 2,200 installations in linked operation on the roofs of houses. The programme was designed to collect and disseminate practical experience and to investigate technical reliability and energy gain of the installed photovoltaic facilities. It led to a number of technical developments and improvements of the units. The energetic evaluation can be integrated to a characteristic value, the so-called facility output. The facility output is defined as the generated energy (in kWh and measured at an inverter output at 230 voltage level) per installed capacity (kW_p) of a photovoltaic system.

The average facility output of the supported installations is about 700 kWh per kW_p and does not differ over the years (1000-Dächer, 1997). But there is a widespread distribution of particular installations: on the one hand there are facilities with a facility output of more than 800 kWh/kW_p and on the other hand there are installations which produce less than 600 kWh/kW_p. The specific investment costs for installations amount to 24,000 DM per kW_p (1DM $\cong$ 0.6 US $ (1997)).

In the early eighties the first central facility with a capacity of 300 kW_p was built. This installation was promoted by the Government, further units were supported by energy supply companies, for instance installations with a capacity of 300 kW_p and, in cooperation with a Spanish partner, a 1 MW_p facility in Toledo, Spain. These bigger plants which operate smoothly generate about 850 kWh per kW_p installed.

The combination of a hydrogen back-up system and photovoltaic power represents another possibility for the further development of photovoltaic systems: hydrogen is produced with surplus photovoltaic power in an electrolytic process. If required, in poor weather, the hydrogen can be combusted using the thermal energy or it can be transformed directly back to electricity by a fuel cell. As yet there are, however, only demonstration plants.

To sum up we can say that the market for photovoltaic systems measured in economic quantities is very small. The estimated share of these systems of power generation is less than 1 per thousand. This is mainly caused by the high investment costs. Therefore photovoltaic producers have concentrated their production facilities. Currently, photovoltaic systems are only economically viable for special applications, e.g. parking meters and stand-alone converter stations for telecommunications (see Part II, Chapter 7).

Energy supplied by solar heating systems is negligible, in the same way as photovoltaic, due to the low insulation in Germany, too. The area of installed solar-thermal facilities amounts to 349 thousand square metres with a heat gain of 85,500 MWh/yr. Average energy densities are about 250 kWh per square metre of collector area. Normally, solar heating systems are operated in addition to conventional heating systems, for instance a gas- or oil-fired boiler. Therefore they only can save fuel but not replace conventional units.

Potentials

There are different definitions of the potential of renewable energies. Frequently, the maximum potential of a future utilization is expressed by the technical potential. This is defined as the physical supply of energy and the possible space for utilizing it, considering the availability of the location, the utilization rates of technical systems and other technical conditions. The technical potential takes into account neither the costs, nor the aspects of integrating the energy in an existing system, nor the transient (non-static) development of consumer demand. In accordance with (Kaltschmitt, 1993) Table 5.3 presents the technical potentials. The wind potential given here is considerably higher than in Part II, Chapter 8 (14-80 TWh). The lower values seem to be more realistic, due to the various constraints, which limit wind energy utilization.

To illustrate the difficulties in using the potentials, Table 5.4 presents some examples.

Today the technical potential of hydroelectricity has been almost fully exploited. The technical potential of photovoltaic, wind-energy and solar systems used today is still very low. For biomass, which is not included here, see Part II, Chapter 9.

Table 5.3 Technical potentials of renewable energies

Technology	Potential in TWh/yr
Hydroelectricity	26
Wind energy (average speed < 5m/s)	90
Wind energy (average speed > 5m/s)	25
Photovoltaic on roofs	approx. 98
Photovoltaic on additional free space	410
Solar heating systems[1]	8 – 550

[1] Space needed for solar heating systems cannot be used for photovoltaic facilities. Therefore, the potentials of photovoltaic and solar heating cannot be added up.

Table 5.4 Number of units to be installed to fully exploit the technical potentials

Technology	Example	
Hydroelectricity	5,300	units (1 MW; duration load 5,000 h/yr)
Wind energy	560,000	units (80 kW; 2,000 h/yr)
	29,000	units (300 kW; 2,200 h/yr)
	and 2,000	units (1.2 MW; 2,400 h/yr)
Photovoltaic	24.5 million	units (4 kW; 1,000 h/yr)
		3,900 m^2 space (efficiency 13 %, space-exploitation 80 %, radiation 1,000 kWh/m^{2}yr)
Solar heating	270 - 1,800 million	m^2 collector-area (300 kWh/m^2)

Renewable Energies and Environmental Aspects

The utilization of renewable energy replaces part of the required fossil energy which would be used in a conventional system, for instance an oil-fired heating system. Therefore, emissions of pollution and climate-relevant gases are reduced. In return, to build facilities using renewable energy, a lot of energy is required, too, because there is an immense need for materials to build the big plants due to the low energy-density of solar and wind energy. The emissions linked with this energy requirement must be included in a life cycle analysis. The resulting question is whether an overall balance of emissions for a renewable energy system is positive. In order to find an answer, all the steps of a process-chain must be analysed, from the cradle to the grave. To do this, all the materials of a facility and their associated emissions have to be considered during the processes of producing, operating and decomposing or recycling a system. The same question arises for the energy requirements.

Figure 5.1 illustrates a life cycle analysis for the production of a solar collector: to manufacture a collector, raw materials, ancillary requirements, energy, fuels and machines are needed. However, to employ machines and factories, these so-called investment goods also have to be produced and a proportion of the required energies for this must be taken into account, too. The same method has to be applied to all materials and services used.

In order to compare one energy system with another, some characteristic values are defined. The energy payback time of a system states the op-

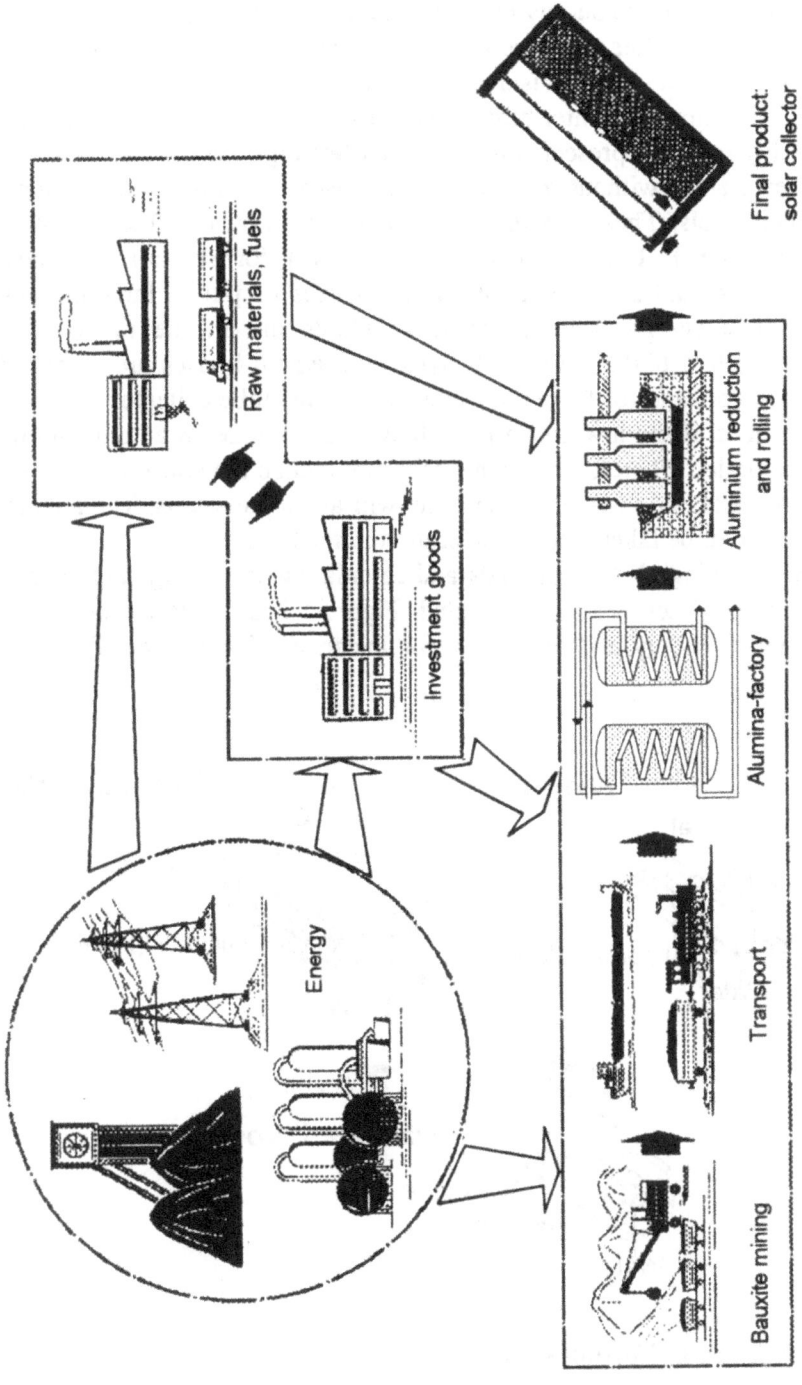

Figure 5.1 Example of a process–chain-analysis

eration time needed to supply the same amount of primary energy as used to produce it. Only after this time does the system really save primary energy. The return time of emission is defined similarly.

In the following, water heating systems recovering solar energy are discussed. Figure 5.2 represents different solar heating systems.

Absorber plants (without glass cover) are used to supply warm water for swimming pools. These plants have energy densities of 200 kWh/(m²yr) to 350 kWh/(m²yr). Further plants are discussed for single-family houses (small plants) and such for multi-family houses or public buildings (large plants). The energy densities of these plants are in the range of 900 kWh/(m²yr) to 1,620 kWh/(m²yr). Systems used for houses are various flat plate collectors and for large plants also evacuated tube collectors.

Because of the low insulation, all systems include an additional oil- or gas-fired boiler. Therefore, systems can only reduce the consumption of fuel but not investment costs. Reducing fuel will avoid emissions. The additional boilers have to be taken into consideration in the balances.

After listing all the materials and calculating the energy and emissions the energy payback time is calculated. Figure 5.3 presents the energy payback time of energy and emissions, for instance CO_2 for the different systems.

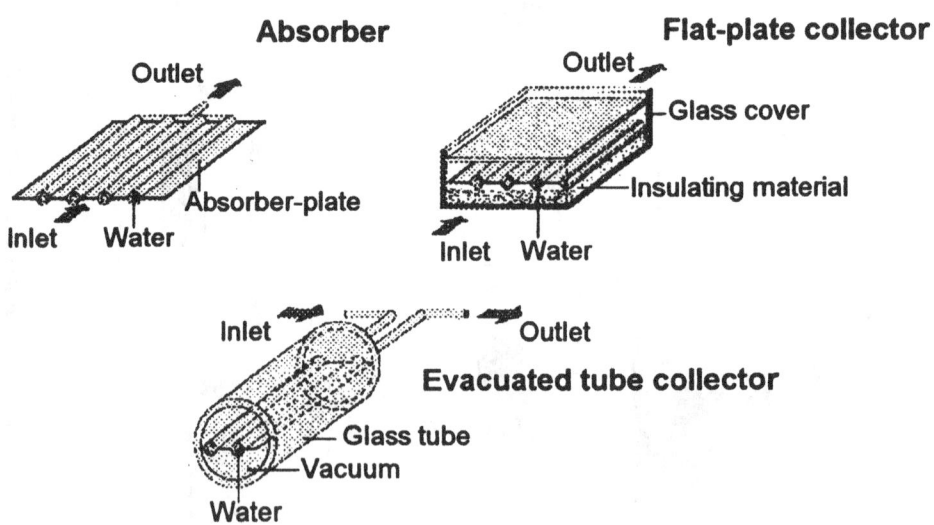

Figure 5.2 Solar heating systems

In comparison with the lifetime of the systems amounting to about 20 years, payback times for energy and CO_2 are very low. However, the range of energy payback times for the plants are half a year to 2 years, due to the different materials applied in the various plants. Generally, payback times for CO_2 are less than payback times for energy. Large plants have the longest and absorber plants for swimming pools the shortest payback times. Although the material requirements are very high, these plants save energy and emissions.

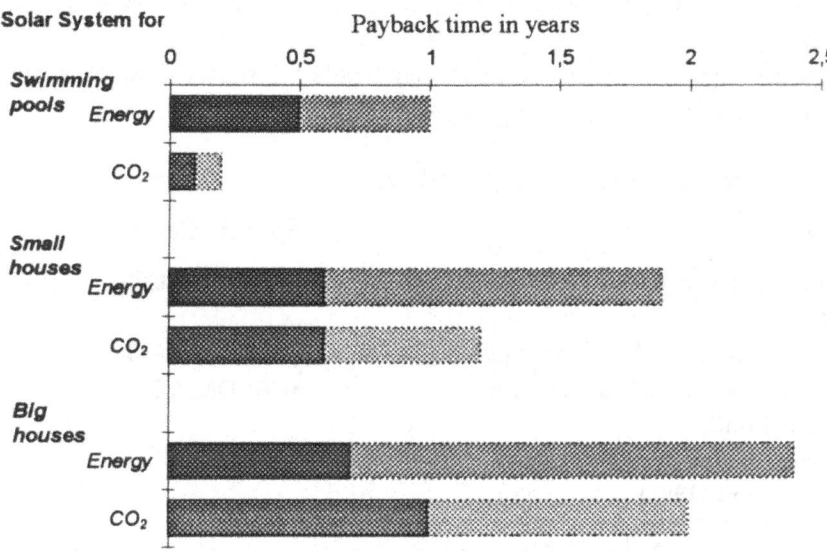

Figure 5.3 Energy and CO_2 payback times (Wagner, 1997)

Renewable Energies in Competition

The reduction of environmentally relevant gases motivates the utilization of renewable energies. Nevertheless, the question is whether renewable energies can compete with the costs of improving existing technologies and with the costs of more efficient fossil energy utilization. The reduction of CO_2 by improvements or utilization of renewable energy illustrates the problem: CO_2 emissions from power generation and heat supply in 1995 amounted to approximately 350 million tonnes (Energiedaten, 1996). The aim of the Government is to reduce them to 75 per cent of the 1990 level. From 1993 to

1995 alone the reduction was about 7 million tonnes of CO_2 due to 186 different measures in the field of efficiency improvements in fossil fired power plants. The major fraction was achieved by replacing turbine blades. From 1995 to 1996 an additional 2 million tonnes was avoided by a further 42 measures. This quantity seems to be low in comparison with the total amount of CO_2. However, the potential of renewable energies to reduce CO_2 emissions is lower. For instance, to avoid 10 million tonnes of CO_2 14,000 wind converters would have to be installed with rated capacities of 500 kW and 2,200 h/yr full use of the capacity. In Part II, Chapter 6 various CO_2 reduction scenarios and the respective contribution of renewable energies are analysed.

Another aspect is the investment costs. Table 5.5 shows some examples of specific costs for avoiding CO_2.

Table 5.5 Specific costs for CO_2 avoidance

Measure	Specific Costs[*]
Replacing turbine blades (coal power plants)	30 DM/t CO_2
Electricity generated by photovoltaic	$\approx$ 3,000 DM/t CO_2
Replacing electric bulb by modern fluorescent bulb	$\approx$ 70 DM/t CO_2
Improved insulation of houses	$\approx$ 150 - 800 DM/t CO_2

[*] 1 DM $\cong$ 0.6 US \$ (1997)

According to Table 5.5 the cheapest measure is to replace turbine blades. The utilization of photovoltaic to reduce CO_2 cannot compete with conventional technologies. Using a modern fluorescent bulb costs only up to 70 DM per tonne of CO_2.

An analysis like this makes it clear that the reduction of emissions cannot be the sole motivation for the utilization and support of renewable energies. They have to compete with conventional technologies to deal with environmental problems.

Conclusions

In order to enlarge the energy reserves and to protect the environment, the development of renewable energies and their establishment on the market has been started. In the last 10 years the share of renewable energies in the total amount of generated power has risen. A severe problem is that renewable energy technologies, however, do not supply firm power and most of them are not economically viable.

Renewable energies can reduce the consumption of fossil fuels and at the same time emissions of pollution and climate-relevant gases. Nevertheless, they have to compete economically with improvements of conventional energy systems, e.g. the improvement of turbine blades.

Because there is sufficient cheap energy available in the short and medium term, from the viewpoint of economics it is not meaningful to maximize the share of renewable energies for power generation, but to most efficiently reduce the emissions of CO_2.

It is not a question of whether renewable energies should participate in the system of power generation, but the question of the right time.

References

Bundesministerium für Wirtschaft (1996): *Energiedaten 1996*, Bonn.

DEWI (1997): *Zeitschrift des Deutschen Windenergie-Instituts*, Wilhelmshaven, No.11, August 1997, pp.12-23.

Fraunhofer Institut für Solare Energiesysteme (1997): "100-Dächer Meß- und Auswerteprogramm", Jahresjournal 1996, Freiburg.

Kaltschmitt, M., Wiese, A. (1993): *Brennstoff Wärme Kraft BWK*, No. 3, pp. 79-85.

Wagner, H.-J. (1997): "Emissionsbilanz von Solaranlagen", *VDI-Fortschritts-berichte*, Series 6, No. 366, pp. 20 - 39, Düsseldorf, VDI-Verlag.

6 Renewable Energy for Power Generation Under Changing Conditions in Germany

JÜRGEN-FRIEDRICH HAKE, PETER MARKEWITZ
AND DAG MARTINSEN

Introduction

In Germany the share of renewables in primary energy consumption is slightly more than 2 per cent today. In 1994, approximately 19 TWh of electricity was produced from hydropower, biomass, wind and photovoltaics. This corresponds to a fraction of approximately 4.3 per cent of total German electricity consumption (incl. grid losses) and is comparable to the electricity production of five to six state-of-the-art hard coal power plants.

Energy policy discussions attribute great significance to the future use of renewable energy sources. Typical examples are discussions on the greenhouse gas problem or the conservation of resources. The energy memorandum of the Deutsche Physikalische Gesellschaft (German Physical Society) (DPG, 1995), for example, calls for a share of power generation from renewables of 10 per cent by the year 2010 and 30 per cent by 2030.

The extent to which renewables can be used can only be assessed in the context of the entire integrated energy system. This applies, in particular, to the electricity sector where the specific properties of renewables (e.g. intermittent generation) must be taken into account.

If a future-oriented picture of the total energy system is to be developed, it will be necessary to also include other technologies (e.g. highly efficient combined cycle plants, low-energy houses etc.) and their possibilities of use in addition to renewable sources of energy. Sometimes, these even compete with the renewables.

In principle, there is a wide range of possible applications for renewables on all levels of energy supply from the conversion sector up to the end-use sectors of transport and traffic, households, industry and small users (e.g. commerce and small industries). However, a large proportion of these applications is considered uneconomical from the present point of view; only

105

a small fraction is already economically efficient today (e.g. hydropower) or is on the threshold of economic efficiency (e.g. wind power). It is hardly possible to make a generally valid statement on the economic viability of a technology since it depends on many factors. It can often only be defined for individual objects as a function of individual boundary conditions. For example, the use of district heat (e.g. produced by a central heating plant) essentially depends on the heat density of the potential supply area. However, general boundary conditions are also of decisive significance for the economic efficiency of a technology, and their change (e.g. increase in energy prices) can lead to a reevaluation of economic efficiency.

The following discussion is based on a changed boundary condition brought about by the Federal Government's decision to reduce the energy-related CO_2 emissions by 25 per cent until 2005 relative to the year 1990. The role of renewables will be analysed with the aid of an energy economy optimization model developed by the Research Centre Jülich within the framework of the IKARUS[1] project initiated by the BMBF (Federal Ministry of Education, Science, Research and Technology). In this context, main emphasis is placed on electricity production.

Definition of Energy Potentials

Ideas of the extent to which renewables can be used are frequently described in terms of potentials. Relevant data cover wide ranges since they are often based on very different definitions and since assessments involve considerable uncertainties. In order to evaluate the results of the analysis illustrated by the following diagram, the definition of potential (Figure 6.1) will be briefly explained.

The *theoretical potential* (often also called physical potential) of energy sources is defined by the maximum physically exploitable amounts of energy. It is a purely fictitious information and describes the basic applicability taking physical laws (e.g. laws of thermodynamics) into account. An example is the potential energy of all rivers in a country.

The *technical potential* describes that fraction of the theoretical potential which could be theoretically used according to the current and foreseeable future state of the art. This includes, for example, availability, storage and transport losses, ecological boundary conditions or meteorological conditions.

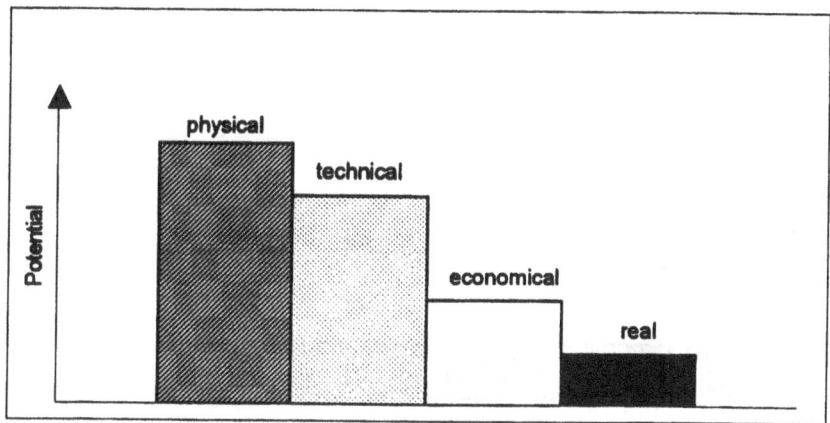

Figure 6.1 Definition of energy potentials

The *economic potential* comprises that fraction of the technical potential which is considered economical under very precisely defined boundary conditions. A differentiation is made here between individual economic potentials based on an economic approach from the aspect of an individual actor and overall economic potentials. The latter are based on a macroeconomic approach and this is also the basis of the calculation results of the IKARUS optimization model. In principle, a comparison of economic potentials must carefully take account of the given boundary conditions (e.g. interest rates, period of depreciation, external costs etc.). Moreover, it must be seen that different methodological approaches can lead to different results.

A potential assessed to be economical must not necessarily be used. Thus, for instance, a potential which is economical from a macroeconomic point of view must not automatically be economical for an individual actor. Even economic potentials are not necessarily fully exploited. For example, obstacles such as high initial investments or information deficiencies can lead to a situation where such a potential is not or only incompletely used.

The extent to which technical potentials are exploited is shown in Figure 6.2 for photovoltaics, wind and hydropower. The percentages describe the ratio of current use to technical potential. These are rough estimates since a large variety of assumptions are made in determining the potential. This may be illustrated by the example of photovoltaics. In (Kaltschmitt et al., 1994) a technical potential of 380 TWh is specified, which roughly corresponds to 70 per cent of today's total gross electricity production in Germany assuming collector surfaces of 800 million m² (roof surface) and

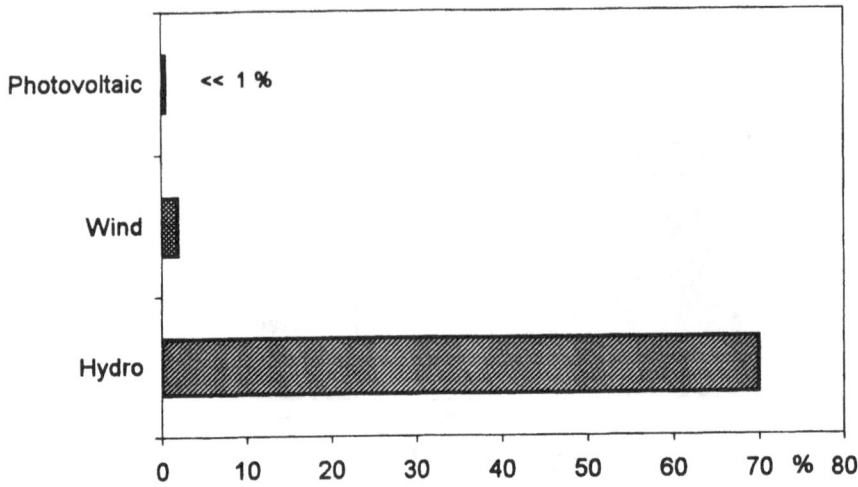

Figure 6.2 **Today's use in relation to the technical potential of renew-able energies for electricity production, in West Germany (Kaltschmitt et al., 1994)**

3,520 million m² (green surface). The assumed surface corresponds roughly to the surface area of the federal states of Saarland, Berlin and Hamburg. Taking account of restrictions on the production side, the technical potential is much less (11 TWh for 2005 and 183 TWh for 2020). Further informa-tion especially about the potential of wind energy in Germany is provided in Part II, Chapter 8.

On the whole, however, it can be stated that only a small fraction of the technical potential is used in the case of photovoltaics and wind whereas the potential of hydropower is exploited at a rate of approximately 70 per cent. Of the renewables used today, hydropower contributes most to electricity production.

The IKARUS Optimization Model

The IKARUS optimization model (Hake et al., 1993) is a technology-based model and reproduces the integrated energy system of the Federal Republic of Germany from the primary energy level (e.g. hard coal mining) up to the useful energy and energy services level (e.g. production of industrial goods). The model maps energy flows, emissions and costs of the entire energy sys-tem. The optimization criterion is minimization of the total system costs that would be necessary to modify the energy system (e.g. for a given CO_2 reduction). Among the competing technologies, the model chooses those which are most favourable taking the optimization criterion into account. By simultaneously including the supply side (conversion sector) and the end-use sector in the optimization process it is possible to weigh competing supply- and demand-side CO_2 reduction measures against each other. This approach, which corresponds to the idea of least-cost planning, is quasi automatically contained in the IKARUS model approach.

The optimum solution generated corresponds to the planning result of an "omniscient economic planner" acting on a macroeconomic level and can be interpreted as the best solution path in the sense of the stipulated goal. The results can therefore only help to identify certain benefits and disadvantages of developments. Between the results and their possible application in a recommendation it must be checked in detail, for example, whether this recommendation appears relevant in the light of existing business structures, the legal situation and acceptance by those affected.

Table 6.1 Basic data for the year 2005

		West Germany	East Germany	Total Germany
Population	in million	65.00	15.20	80.20
Living space	in billion m^2	2.59	0.48	3.07
GDP	in billion DM	4.18	0.54	4.72

Power Economy Frame

A future-oriented scenario is based on given global macroeconomic data (Table 6.1). These are, for example, population development, development of the gross domestic product or the development of housing areas.

These data are used to derive the energy-determining demands to be exogenously included in the optimization model in addition to the energy carrier import prices. Tables 6.2 and 6.3 contain the most important demands according to energy services and the prices of major imported energy carriers whose increase is assumed to be moderate.

In addition to these assumptions, further limitations must be made, which can be of an energy policy or technological nature. Examples of energy policy assumptions are the use of domestic hard coal or the future use of nuclear energy. Without any assumptions, the relatively expensive domestic hard coal in comparison to imported coal would never be selected by the model, which works on cost-minimizing criteria. However, it can already be predicted today that German hard coal will also be used in the year 2005.

Table 6.2 Prices of major imported energy carriers in DM$_{89}$/GJ

	1989	2005
Imported hard coal	3.64	3.65
Crude oil	6.03	7.18
Natural gas A	3.62	4.61
Natural gas B	4.53	5.76
For comparison:		
German hard coal	6.88	7.09

Table 6.3 Development of the most important demand variables in the old and new federal states (West Germany and East Germany) up to the year 2005

	1989 West Germany (absolute)	2005 West Germany (increase in %)	1989 East Germany (absolute)	2005 East Germany (increase in %)
Space heat (10^6 m^2)				
Single-family houses	1,327	21	157	34
Multi-family houses	871	13	262	3
Total	2,198	18	419	15
Traffic				
Billion person-km	690	22	141	50
Billion tonne-km	281	48	75	84
Industry (net production)				
Billion DM	592	35	(100)	35
Small users				
Million employees	22	9	4.6	31

The capacity utilization and construction of new power plants are optimization result, i.e. the model decides, for example, how much hydropower capacity will be added. This also takes account of the intermittent energy supply in the form of time-variation generation curves. However, additions cannot be unlimited, but are also subject to technological boundary conditions. This information is exogenously preset in the model as the lower or/and upper bounds of technological restrictions. The model can then add capacity within this given bandwidth. Restrictions of this type are contained in Table 6.4.

Table 6.4 Selection of important energy policy and technological restrictions

	West Germany 2005	East Germany 2005
Hard coal mining (PJ)	> 1,100	-
Electricity from hard coal (PJ)	> 500	-
Hard coal imports (PJ)	< 800	< 270
Lignite mining (PJ)	< 970	> 640 and < 830
Electricity from lignite (PJ)	> 750	> 550
Natural gas imports (PJ)	< 2,600	< 510
Nuclear energy (GW)	21.1	-
Coastal wind power (GW)	> 2.7 and < 3.2	> 0.17 and < 1
Solid biomass (PJ)	< 161	< 65.0
Bioethanol (PJ)	38.5	33.5
Rape oil (PJ)	< 31.0	< 20.0
Biogas (PJ)	< 83.3	< 24.9

CO_2 Reduction as a Boundary Condition

In 1990, 992 million tonnes of CO_2 emissions were released in Germany due to energy conversion. About 37 per cent was produced in the conversion sector[2] and 63 per cent in the end-use sectors[3]. At the 1995 Conference of the Parties to the Framework Convention on Climate Change in Berlin, Germany agreed to reduce the energy-related CO_2 emissions by 25 per cent up to the year 2005 relative to 1990. The reduction scenarios are based on this reduction figure.

Reference Scenarios

The reference scenarios for the old and new federal states are calculated without CO_2 reduction and are to be interpreted in the sense of a business-as-usual development which, however, already contains some of the reduction measures implemented by the Federal Government (e.g. thermal insulation ordinance). It should be noted, however, that the model only selects an energy supply for the year 2005 according to minimum total system costs. In contrast, the reduction scenarios in the model contain a specified CO_2 reduction so that the reduction goal is observed in any case. The emissions in the old and new federal states already decrease in the reference scenario by approximately 6 per cent and 43 per cent, respectively, relative to 1990 (Figure 6.3). In total, this corresponds to a reduction of approximately 17 per cent for the Federal Republic of Germany; the Federal Government's reduction goal is thus not achieved. The decrease of CO_2 emissions in the old federal states is essentially attributable to autonomous efficiency improvements, structural changes and increased use of natural gas (at the expense of coal and oil).

The reduction in the new federal states is to be explained by structural adaptation processes, for example, in industry and by a greatly reduced use of lignite.

Reduction Scenarios

Since the old and new federal states are treated separately by the model, reduction goals must be defined for East and West Germany in order to comply with the overall German reduction goal. On the assumption that no CO_2 reduction beyond the reference case takes place in the new federal states, the CO_2 emissions in the old federal states must be reduced by approximately 18 per cent (relative to 1990) (Figure 6.3). The reduction scenarios presented in the following therefore relate to the old federal states. In order to reflect a ranking of reduction measures, the CO_2 restriction is varied in a range from 6 per cent (reference case) to 25 per cent. The maximum value of 25 per cent for the old federal states and an emission reduction of 43 per cent (in the reference case) in the new federal states gives a sum of approximately 30 per cent for Germany as a whole and is thus clearly above the Federal Government's reduction figure.

The following discussion will be essentially restricted to the contributions made by renewables in the reduction scenarios and here, in particular, for the electricity sector. The contributions are to be understood as "macroeconomic potential" in the sense of a cost minimization in the energy sector. They are not necessarily an expectation in the sense of a forecast.

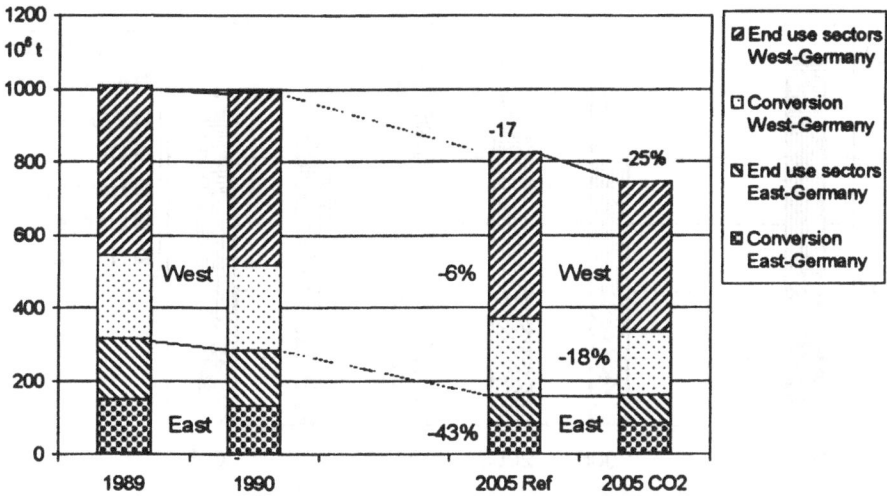

Figure 6.3 Development of CO_2 emissions in Germany (reference and CO_2 reduction scenarios)

A description of the reduction measures in other sectors is to be found in (Markewitz and Martinsen 1997a, 1997b).

Contributions by Renewables to Primary Energy Consumption

The contribution by renewables to primary energy consumption in the old federal states was approximately 2 per cent in 1995. The development between 1990 and 1995 is characterized by a constant share of hydropower, a small biomass fraction and a pronounced increase in wind power as a consequence of the Act on the Sale of Electricity to the Grid (Figures 6.4 and 6.5). See Part II, Chapter 8 for further information on the Act on the Sale of Electricity to the Grid. Part II, Chapter 9 describes biomass utilization in detail.

The reference development up to the year 2005 assumes a continued constant share of hydropower, a trebling of wind power and an increasing use of biogas. In total, the reference development leads to a 2.6 per cent share of renewables in the primary energy consumption[4] of the old federal states. As can be seen from Figures 6.4 and 6.5, the share clearly increases with increasing CO_2 restrictions and amounts to approximately 5.1 per cent for a 25 per cent CO_2 reduction. A pronounced increase is only observed

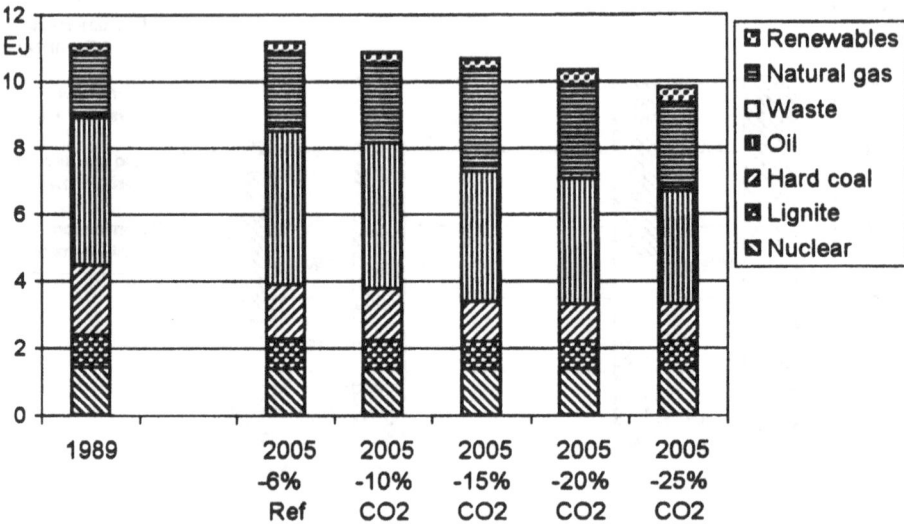

Figure 6.4 Primary energy consumption and CO_2 reduction-level, West Germany (2005)

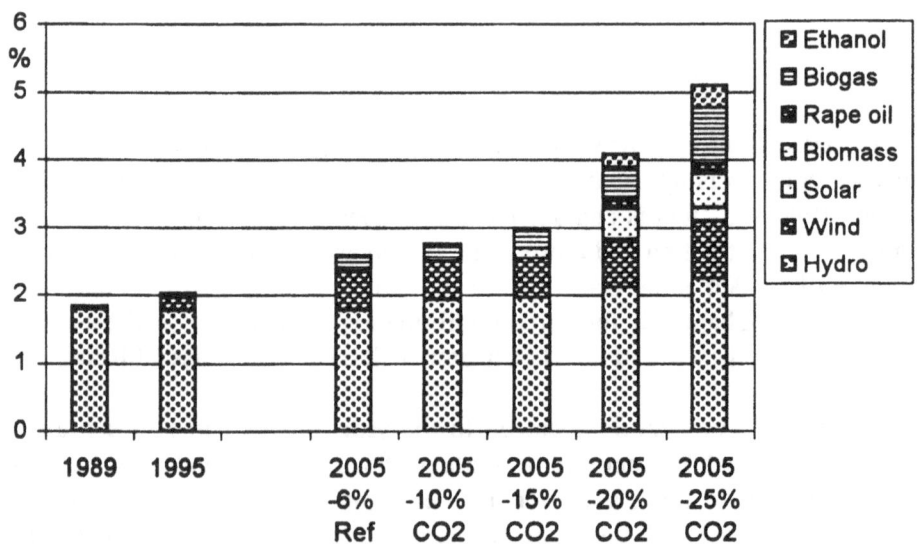

Figure 6.5 Contribution of renewables to primary energy consumption, West Germany (2005)

from a restriction of 20 per cent upwards. The moderate increase up to a restriction of 20 per cent is to be explained by the fact that the model has far more cost-efficient reduction possibilities (fuel switch, savings etc.) and prefers these according to the cost minimization approach. Figure 6.4 also shows the great influence of energy savings. In comparison with the reference development, primary energy consumption in the case of a 25 per cent restriction is lower by almost 12 per cent. This corresponds approximately to the present total final energy consumption in the small users sector.

The shares of hydro- and wind power rise with increasing CO_2 restriction and reach their maximum in the 25 per cent case (4 GW wind power as the upper bound). Solid biomass, biogas, rape oil and bioethanol are additionally used beyond a CO_2 reduction of approximately 15 per cent. Table 6.5 shows the respective applications for renewables in the 25 per cent case.

Table 6.5 Applications of renewable sources of energy for a 25 per cent CO_2 reduction in West Germany (2005)

Renewables	Applications
Hydropower	Electricity production
Wind power	Electricity production
Solar power	Thermal utilization, photovoltaics[5]
Biomass	Heating and CHP plants
Rape oil	Transport of persons and goods
Bioethanol	Passenger cars
Biogas	Heating and CHP plants

Electricity Production

Figure 6.6 illustrates public electricity production in West Germany. An increase is to be observed between 1989 and 1995; electricity is essentially produced from nuclear energy, lignite and hard coal. The values also contain the electricity produced in combined heat and power plants[6]. In comparison to 1995, almost no change in total electricity production is to be observed in 2005 for the reference development. However, the composition of energy carriers used for electricity production will change. In essence, natural gas will substitute hard coal. In this context, the assumptions made in Table 6.4 should be referred to: no construction of new nuclear plants and production of electricity from a bounded lignite volume of 750 PJ, which corresponds approximately to the present quantity.

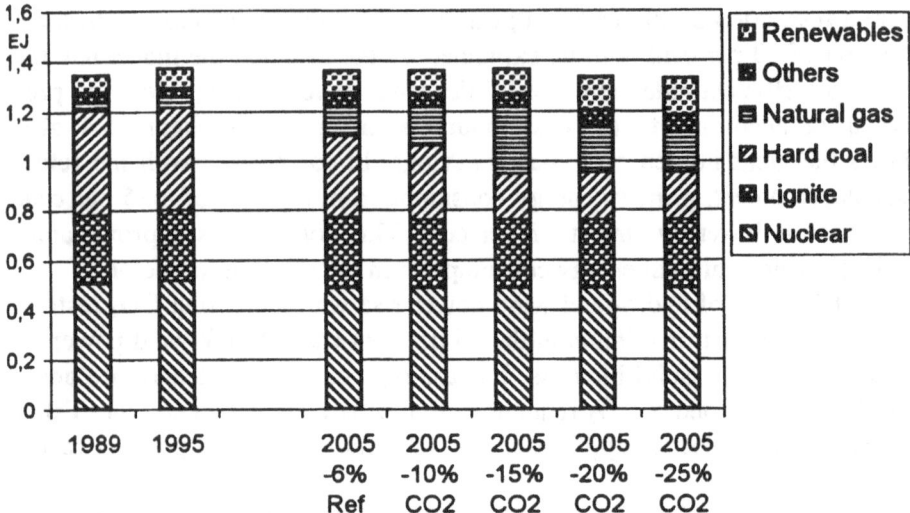

Figure 6.6 Public electricity production in West Germany

Increasing CO_2 restriction leads to a strong decline in electricity production from hard coal to a minimum input of 0.5 EJ. The share of natural gas increases correspondingly. It is also striking to note that a "moderate" CO_2 restriction leads to an increase in the share of natural gas, whereas a "stringent" CO_2 reduction rather results in an increased use of renewables in combination with saving measures.

Contributions by Renewables to Electricity Production

The use of renewables[7] for electricity production was essentially restricted in 1995 to hydro- and wind power. They maintain their dominant position both in the reference case for the year 2005 and in all reduction scenarios. The increase from 1995 up to the reference case in 2005 is exclusively brought about by an increased use of wind power, which will approximately treble in comparison to 1995, as can be seen from Figure 6.7.

With increasing CO_2 restriction, the contributions of renewables currently accounting to approximately 5.5 per cent will rise to approximately 11 per cent (for a 25 per cent CO_2 restriction). First, additional wind power plants will be built providing an increase from about 1.16 GW (1995) to 4 GW in the case of greatest CO_2 restriction. This involves typical unit sizes of 500 kW (40 m rotor diameter). Such units are described briefly in Part II,

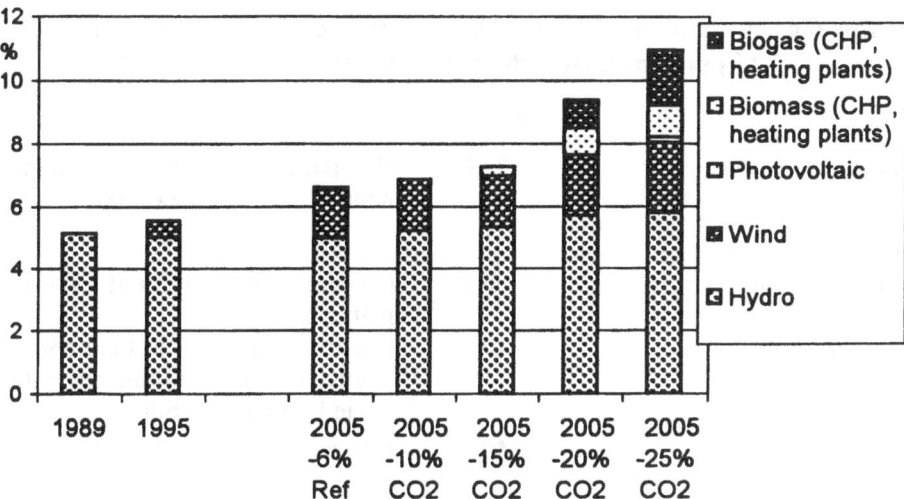

Figure 6.7 Percentage of electricity production by renewables in West Germany (2005)

Chapter 8. The share of hydropower will also increase, although the expansion potential is much smaller. First of all, the potential of larger plants (> 10 MW) will be exploited, followed by the addition and revitalization of smaller units and very small hydroelectric plants (250 kW). In total, the share of hydropower increases from 5 per cent to almost 6 per cent with rising CO_2 restriction. Only with a CO_2 restriction exceeding 15 per cent biomass and biogas will also be used in heating power plants and CHP plants and reach the defined upper bounds in the 25 per cent reduction case. The contribution of pholtovoltaics in the case of a 25 per cent restriction corresponds to a power of 22 MW and is exogenously preset in the sense of an expectation value.

The expansion of electricity production on the basis of renewables requires relatively high investments, as can be seen from Table 6.6. For the 25 per cent reduction scenario, the investments made by the model between 1989 and 2005 for the construction of new plants are listed. In the electricity and heat sector, a total of nearly DM 50 billion must be invested in this period for total new power plant construction (fossil and renewables). About 50 per cent of these investments are for electricity and heat production plants based on renewables. A precise breakdown for the renewables is also contained in Table 6.6.

Table 6.6   Investments for new plants in the period 1989 to 2005, 25 per cent CO_2 reduction in West Germany (2005)

$$10^9 \text{ DM}$$

Electricity sector:	33.0	(For power plants based on lignite, natural gas and renewables)
Heat sector:		
- District heat	6.8	(Heating and heating power plants, grids)
- Short-distance heat	10.4	(Heating and (CHP) heating power plants, natural gas turbines with waste heat boiler, grids)
Total	50.2	(100 %)
Share of renewable-based plants:		
- Hydroelectric plants	7.5	(15 %)
- Wind power plants	9.9	(20 %)
- Photovoltaics	0.2	(< 1 %)
- Biomass (CHP) heating power plants	1.9	(4 %)
- Biogas (CHP) heating power plants	4.5	(9 %)
Subtotal renewables	24.0	(48 %)

Expected Contribution for the Years 2005 and 2020 in Germany

The role attributed to renewables for electricity production in various studies, assuming that the development of the past years will continue without any major change, will be shown in the following. For this purpose, the results of the Study Commission (Enquete, 1994), of the PROGNOS Study on behalf of the Federal Ministry of Economics (PROGNOS, 1995) and the IKARUS calculations are compared. Figure 6.8 contains the expected electricity production on the basis of renewables for the years 2005 and 2020. For the scenario-based studies (IKARUS, Enquete) the values of the reference scenarios are given, which are to be interpreted as business-as-usual developments. The PROGNOS values are expectation values. The values of the IKARUS and Enquete scenarios represent reference developments (without CO_2 restriction).

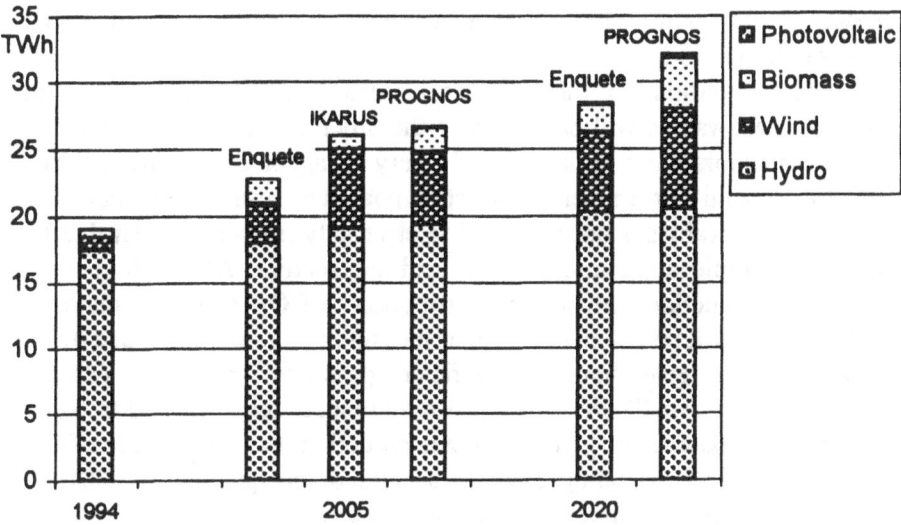

Figure 6.8 Expected electricity production from renewables for the years 2005 and 2020 in West Germany

In absolute terms, the contribution by renewables in comparison to 1994 increases by 20 to 40 per cent in the forecast and scenarios. With the exception of hydropower, whose potential is already largely exploited, the shares for wind and biomass are many times higher than the 1994 value. Relating renewable electricity production to total public net electricity production, the shares range from 4.4 per cent to 6.6 per cent for the year 2005. The percentages for 2020 are 5 per cent (Enquete) and 6.2 per cent (PROGNOS). In a comparison of relative shares, however, it must be pointed out that the electricity consumption rates calculated or predicted by the studies for 2005 and 2020 are in part very different. It can be stated, however, that the contributions made by renewables remain far behind the stipulations of the DPG memorandum (1995).

Summary, Conclusions

The shares of renewables in electricity production increase both under the changed boundary conditions of CO_2 reduction and in the reference developments or forecasts. The strongest increase is to be observed for wind and biomass, whose contributions will be many times higher than today. In all reference developments and forecasts, however, the percentage of electricity production from renewables remains far behind the stipulations of the DPG memorandum (1995).

The calculations for the old federal states show that electricity production from renewables will only achieve the order of magnitude demanded in the DPG memorandum in the case of a very stringent CO_2 reduction far beyond the Federal Government's reduction goal. The results also indicate that the use of renewables is not restricted to electricity production, but that there are also multiple applications in the end-use sectors. Although renewable electricity production furnishes a contribution to CO_2 reduction, major saving potentials will be achieved by other measures (e.g. increased use of natural gas, thermal insulation, more efficient passenger cars etc.), which are often less expensive. There is no royal road to a strategy oriented to the conservation of resources or greenhouse gas reduction, but a multitude of measures are involved extending over all sectors of energy supply. Electricity production from renewables should also be seen in this context. In order to apply a strategy in practice, the most efficient measures must be selected. Efficiency evaluation must be governed by the principles of energy supply: supply security, environmental compatibility and economic efficiency.

In the case of a stringent CO_2 restriction of 25 per cent in West Germany, corresponding to an overall German reduction[8] of about 30 per cent, approximately 50 per cent of all investments to be made in the electricity and heat sector for constructing new generation plants will be for plants based on renewables. This result is only valid for the power economy frame described above. This frame should therefore be verified before making any recommendations for action and, consequently, any investments. A modification of the energy policy frame (e.g. role of hard coal and nuclear energy) could sometimes be a more cost-efficient solution.

Notes

1   Instruments for Greenhouse Gas Reduction Strategies
2   This includes electricity and heat production, refineries, coal beneficiation, gas distribution as well as primary energy production.
3   Industry, small users, households, traffic
4   The primary energy assessment of renewables in the IKARUS optimization model is performed according to the efficiency method. See also Görgen and Ziesing, 1996.
5   The share of photovoltaics was exogenously preset in the model and corresponds to an expectancy attitude. It is not a result of optimization.

6 "Others" also contain waste incineration in heating power plants. These will not be counted among renewables in the following.

7 Excluding waste

8 43 per cent CO_2 reduction in the new federal states (reference case)

References

DPG (1995): "Energiememorandum 1995 der DPG", *Physikalische Blätter*, No. 5, pp. 388 – 391.

Enquete: Schaumann, P., Läge, E., Rüffler, W., Molt, S., Fahl, U., Diekmann, J., Ziesing, H.-J. (1994): "Integrierte Gesamtstrategien der Minderung energie-bedingter Treibhausgasemissionen (2005/2020)". Study on behalf of the Study Commission of the 12th German Bundestag "Protecting the Earth's Atmosphere".

Grawe, J. and Wagner, E. (1995): "Nutzung erneuerbarer Energien durch die Elektrizitätswirtschaft, Stand 1994", *Elektrizitätswirtschaft*, Vol. 94, No. 24, pp. 1600 – 1616.

Görgen, R. and Ziesing, H.-J. (1996): "Zur Reform der Energiebilanzen", *Energiewirtschaftliche Tagesfragen* Jg. 46, No. 1/2, pp. 34 – 36.

Hake, J.-Fr., Kuckshinrichs, W., Markewitz, P., Martinsen, D., Walbeck, M., (1993): "Modelle", in: *VDI Reports* No. 1043, pp. 23 - 48, VDI-Verlag Düsseldorf.

Kaltschmitt, M. and Wiese, A. (1994): "Technische Einsparpotentiale, substi-tuierbare End- und Primäräquivalente und Kosten erneuerbarer Energieträger in Deutschland", *Zeitschrift für Energiewirtschaft* 1/94, pp. 41 – 64.

Markewitz, P. and Martinsen, D. (1997a): "Konsequenzen für die deutsche Ener-giewirtschaft bei Einhaltung des CO2-Minderungsbeschlusses bis zum Jahr 2005", *VDI Reports* No. 1321, pp. 579 - 593, VDI-Verlag Düsseldorf.

Markewitz, P. and Martinsen, D. (1997b): "IKARUS-Minderungsstrategien für Deutschland", Workshop on 14/15 April 1997 "Modellinstrumente für CO_2-Minderungsstrategien", in: Konferenzen des Forschungszentrums Jülich 1997.

Meliß, M. (1996): "Regenerative Energiequellen", *BWK*, Vol. 48, No.4, pp. 54 - 61.

PROGNOS: Eckerle, K., Hofer, P., Masuhr, K., Oczipka, T., Schmidt, G. (1995): "Die Energiemärkte Deutschlands im zusammenwachsenden Europa - Per-spektiven bis zum Jahr 2020", Study on behalf of the Federal Ministry of Eco-nomics, Basel.

7 Photovoltaics in Germany: Between Efficiency and Cost

JENS SIMON AND HERIBERT WAGNER

Introduction

The direct, environmentally benign and economically efficient conversion of sunlight into electricity is an energy policy imperative on a long time scale. At present, solar electricity only occupies niche positions - if any - in the energy mix, but solar cell technologies could accomplish more. Cell efficiency is continuously optimized and, at the same time, approaches to lower-cost production are also pursued in research. Moreover, mass production would drastically decrease prices.

When the second American satellite, Vanguard I, orbited the earth in 1958, solar cell technology then in its infancy entered space. Vanguard I used direct solar radiation to convert light into electricity with the aid of crystalline silicon. This took place four years after the first silicon solar cell with an appreciable energy conversion efficiency of 6 per cent had been built. Until the end of the seventies, the primary application of photovoltaics, i.e. the direct conversion of light into electric energy, was in space: it supplied energy for satellites (Loferski, 1993). For this purpose, silicon cells were developed which had to be particularly reliable and above all resistant to bombardment with high-energy particles in space. Cost played a minor role in view of the sums customary in space research. Considerations to the effect of bringing solar electricity back to earth, in the true sense of the word, have already been made since the fifties. On earth, however, cost is the decisive obstacle to be overcome in competition with coal, gas, oil and nuclear energy as the classical energy carriers. For terrestrial applications, the use of solar cells is still in its infancy although the technological possibilities would allow much more.

In fact, electricity from the sun is still in the shade. Although there are some pilot projects, such as the self-sufficient solar house in Freiburg (Germany), which was conceived by the Fraunhofer Institute for Solar Energy Systems and has proved efficient since autumn 1992, solar electricity is at best noticeable in wrist-watches, pocket calculators and parking meters in everyday life. The German Federal Government's 1,000 - Roofs Programme has long been phased out and the political strategy is characterized by waiting. Waiting to be overtaken? In basic research, Germany still has a leading position, but investments into practical applications are made by others. For example, the American Enron group intends to operate integrated solar cell systems on the former nuclear test site in Nevada to achieve the output of a small coal power plant with one hundred megawatt. Venturing into powerful solar electricity production is also the maxim of the Japanese Ministry of Industry. After the first step of a 70,000-roof programme by the turn of the millennium, a total of four gigawatt is to be additionally installed in Japan up to the year 2010, which corresponds to the output of four nuclear power plants. Beginning mass production of modules from solar cells will cause a rapid decrease in prices. It is expected in Japan that a solar module will already be sold at a sixth of today's price in the year 2000 (Klein, 1995).

The costs of photovoltaic energy conversion are pure manufacturing and material costs of the solar cell energy conversion machine. The light used as fuel is freely available to an unlimited extent. Every square metre in Germany is supplied every day with roughly three kilowatt-hours of solar energy (Bonnet et al., 1990). The total energy coming from the sun adds up to a value for the entire globe which corresponds approximately to the 10,000-fold present primary energy consumption of mankind. In nature, this energy is the basis for all life in the process of photosynthesis. Light is absorbed in the chloroplasts of green cells with an efficiency of 1 to 2 per cent and water split photolytically, ultimately forming glucose from CO_2. The principles of the photovoltaic effect are at home in nature (Fritzsch, 1993). In inorganic matter, they were discovered by Edmond Becquerel in 1839. Three preconditions must be fulfilled for this effect. Light must be absorbed. This light must generate negative and positive charge carriers. And finally, the charge carriers thus produced must be spatially separated so that electric voltage and electric current result.

The Photovoltaic Effect

As far as inorganic materials are concerned, light-induced charge carriers can be generated and separated in semiconductors. For the physical principles of the photovoltaic effect and applications in solar cells see Green, 1982; Jäger et al., 1990; Meissner, 1993. At the absolute zero of temperature all electrons in a semiconductor are bound at fixed positions within the crystal structure. In order to liberate an electron from this valence state, a minimum amount of energy must be applied. This can be achieved, for example, by means of heat, so that a small fraction of the electrons can already move freely in the crystal at room temperature. However, the electron can also be carried over the energy band gap between bound and free state by a photon, the energy unit of light. In addition to the electron as a carrier of negative charge, the result is also an electron vacancy of positive charge in the previously occupied valence state, a hole. Both electron and hole are carriers of electric current as free particles. This process takes place in every piece of material of a semiconductor upon the incidence of light, provided that the photon energy is greater than the band gap. However, electric current does not directly result from temperature increase or incident light.

In order to convert light into electric current, the free electrons and holes must not impinge on each other again and recombine. The charge carriers produced must be separated by a built-in electric field in the material. Such a field can be achieved by combining at least two modifications of the starting material, a so-called p-n junction. The characteristic properties of a semiconductor can be modified by adding impurities (doping). Either type of charge carrier can become an excess carrier. If electrons are involved, n-type material is produced (n for negative) and in the case of holes p-type material (p for positive) results. Combining a p-type and an n-type material produces a diode (Figure 7.1). Charge carriers diffuse over the boundary junction and leave fixed ions in the crystal. A space charge region and thus an electric field is produced which generates a field current of charge carriers. Within a short time equilibrium is established: field and diffusion current compensate each other. Exposure to light destroys this equilibrium. In essence, the concentrations of those charge carriers change which are in the minority in the respective region (minority carriers). These are electrons in the p-region and holes in the n-region. The photocurrent is then a diffusion current of these minority carriers.

The efficiency of a solar cell is the ratio of incident light power to produce electrical output, i.e. the product of current and voltage. The maximum voltage is essentially determined by the energy gap of the semiconductor. Typically, the maximum voltage is half to two thirds of this value. However, the achievable current drops with growing energy gap, since only photons with greater energies lead to electron-hole pairs, so that only the high-frequency fraction of incident sunlight can be used. In the case of a small band gap, on the other hand, the current is higher since wide regions of the solar spectrum can be utilized, but the resultant voltage is small. More-

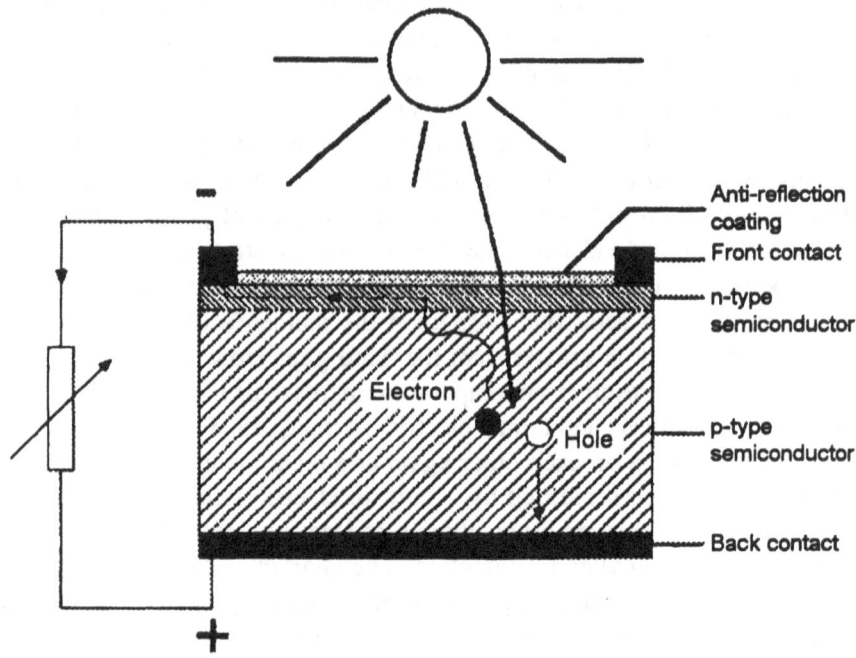

Figure 7.1 Schematic drawing of the cross-section of a solar cell (MRS, 1993). A thin n-doped film is deposited on a broad p-doped region. Absorbed sunlight produces charge carriers which migrate as diffusion current (the p-n junction acts as a "sink") to the deposited contacts. Light is converted into electric current.

over, a small band gap means that much photon energy is "given away", since most photons of the solar spectrum supply more energy than is necessary to bridge the energy gap. The excess is lost as heat. Depending on the theoretical model, slightly different statements are obtained for an optimum energy gap. In any case, however, the structure of the solar spectrum is an essential quantity (Figure 7.2). The maximum of the solar spectrum is in the yellow-green region between 1.3 and 1.5 electron-volt (eV). Optimum semi-conductor materials would therefore be indium phosphide (1.3 eV), gallium arsenide (1.4 eV) and cadmium telluride (1.5 eV). However, crystalline sili-con with its band gap of 1.1 eV is also considered to be an optimum choice according to other theoretical predictions which include certain recombina-tion paths, i.e. loss mechanisms of the charge carriers.

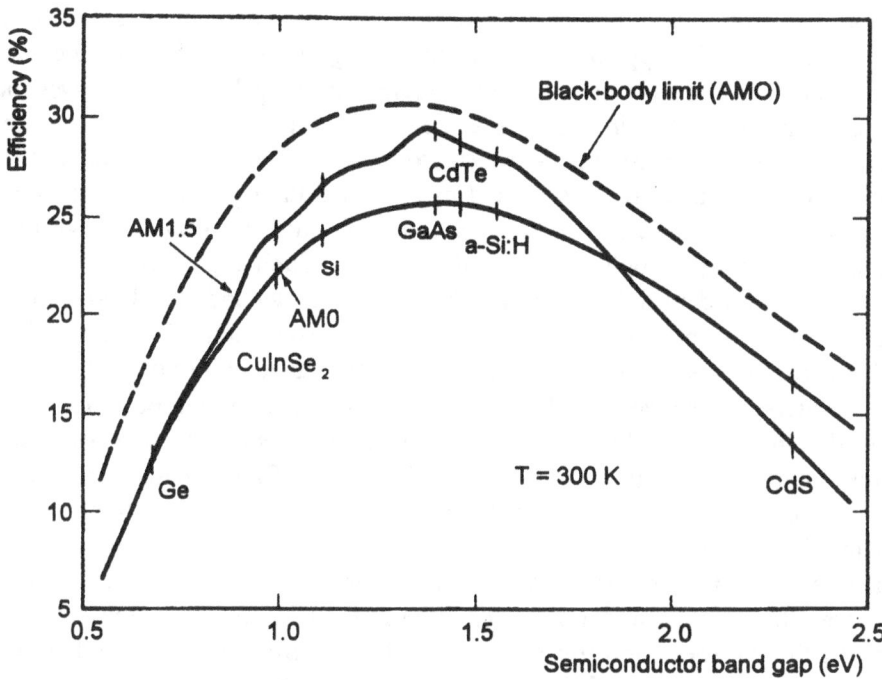

Figure 7.2 Calculation of the maximum efficiency of a model solar cell as a function of the energy gap of the semiconductor material under three different light conditions (Green, 1993). The abbreviation AM stands for "air mass": AM0 = radiation above the earth's atmosphere in space; AM1 = radiation perpendicular to the earth's surface (no curve in the figure); AM1.5 = radiation at an angle of approx. 48 degrees (standard value). The broken-line curve reflects the efficiency variation under AM0, if the sun were an ideal black emitter with a surface temperature of 6,000 Kelvin. Plotted are the energy gaps of real semiconductor materials.

The Silicon Workhorse

Silicon is the most widely used starting material for commercial solar cells. It is also the second most frequent element in the earth's crust, it is non-toxic and stable, and the processing methods are very well known from information technology and tested. Crystalline silicon is used for conventional solar cells. The atoms in silicon crystals occupy precisely defined sites and form the diamond lattice typical of the elements of group IV of the periodic system. Each atom is surrounded by four equidistant neighbours. The fewer the defects and impurities in this crystalline architecture, the better is the material suited for so-called super-efficient solar cells. The world record in efficiency for silicon solar cells is held by an Australian group of researchers who achieve an efficiency of 23.5 per cent with silicon crystals of high perfection featuring a sophisticated cell structure. Such high efficiencies can only be obtained in a few special laboratories; under industrial production conditions, currently achievable efficiencies for solar cells from crystalline silicon are far lower, the best values being in the range of 17 per cent.

Silicon is considered to be the "workhorse" of solar cell technology, especially in the crystalline form, whether single-crystal or polycrystalline. From quartz sand as the starting material silicon is first produced in several extraction and purification steps. Crystals are then grown from this starting material. Voluminous cylindrical single crystals are drawn from a silicon melt using the Czochralski method. Such a single crystal can have a weight of more than 100 kg and a diameter of more than 20 cm. From this cylinder having the thickness of a tree trunk, thin silicon wafers of a few hundred micrometres are then cut. Solar cells are produced from these wafers in the following three process steps. In the first step, the wafer is chemically treated so that its surface eventually has the texture of a waffle iron. The surface then consists of an immense number of minute pyramids so that sunlight reflection losses are minimized. The negative pattern of this structure, a kind of inverse waffle iron, is also used as a surface pattern, but the technical production process is much more sophisticated in this case (Figure 7.3). In the second step, the electronic asymmetry necessary for the photovoltaic effect, i.e. the p-n junction, must be built into the crystal. At high temperatures, the wafer is doped with an additive such as phosphorus. This additive penetrates into the surface layers of the crystal and thus produces the desired p-n junction near the surface. In the last step, finally, the cell must be contacted. Fine metal electrodes are applied onto the surface. The single cells are then connected to form the solar module. Such modules do not exhibit any inherent ageing process. The service life is primarily determined by corrosion of the metal components. Lifetimes of 20 to 30 years can be achieved with the present technologies.

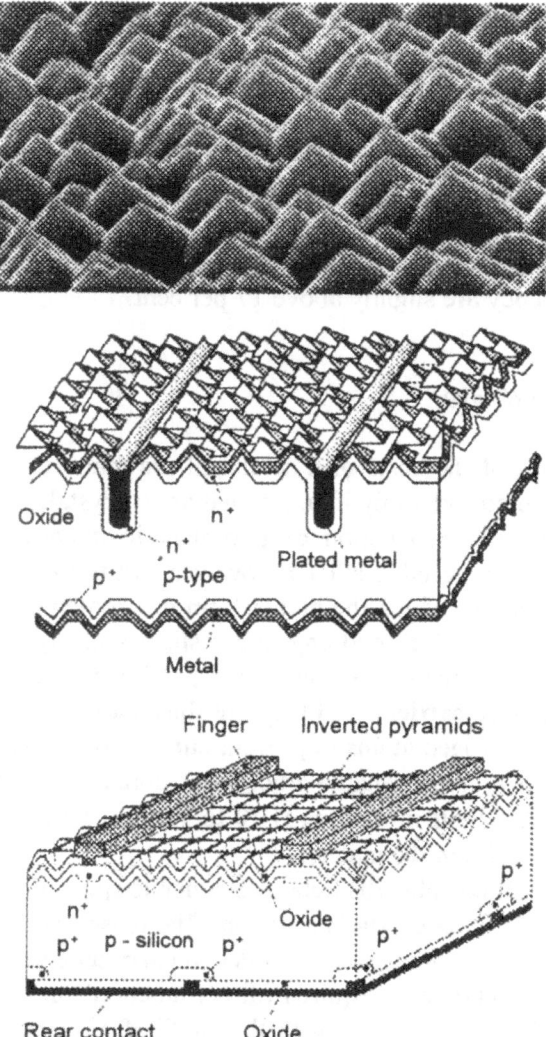

Figure 7.3 **Above: Surface of a textured silicon solar cell in the scanning electron microscope. The pyramid structures are typically 10 μm high. Centre and below: Schematic drawings of highly efficient textured silicon solar cells with pyramid and inverted pyramid structures. In the centre the electric contacts are "buried", below they are placed as "fingers" on the surface (Green, 1982).**

The advantage of solar cells from single-crystal silicon is their high efficiency, which cannot be achieved using polycrystalline material. However, the process costs for polycrystalline material are slightly lower since the crystals do not have to be produced using the expensive Czochralski technique. Instead of drawing the crystal slowly from the melt, the melt is cooled in a controlled manner in a given die. During this solidification process polycrystalline material is formed with numerous defects in the crystal structure, but the photovoltaic effect is also achieved here. Maximum laboratory values for the efficiency are slightly above 17 per cent.

Thin-Film Technologies

Roughly one third of the costs of a solar cell are material costs. The price can therefore drop considerably if an alternative to crystalline wafer technology is employed: the production of photovoltaic material in thin films. Again, a candidate material is silicon, however, not in the crystalline but in the amorphous state in which the atoms form a disordered network. In this state, the bond lengths and bond angles are slightly changed in comparison to the crystal so that some bonds break up. Open bonds act as recombination centres for the charge carriers, and they are thus saturated by the additional incorporation of hydrogen atoms to prevent current transport from being impaired. The result is hydrogenated amorphous silicon, symbolically written as a-Si:H. A typical built-in fraction is 10 to 15 per cent hydrogen in the total number of particles in the material.

Amorphous silicon absorbs light in the visible spectral region up to 100 times more strongly than crystalline silicon. The reason is the lack of lattice periodicity of the amorphous state. In order to carry an electron over the energy gap, only one photon is required (direct junction); in crystalline silicon this can mostly be achieved only with the "aid" of a quantum of the lattice vibration (indirect junction), a process which takes place more seldom. For solar cells of amorphous material, the high absorption coefficient means a reduction of the necessary material thickness and thus reduced costs. Moreover, much less energy is required to produce the cell. An a-Si:H solar cell has paid off its fabrication energy after about one to two years of operation (energy payback time), so that a so-called harvest ratio of 10 to 20 is obtained relative to the lifetime, which is a clear reduction compared to crystalline cells, which require an energy payback time of 4 to 6 years corresponding to a harvest ratio between 5 and 7.

On cheap carrier material such as glass or sheet steel foils thin, amorphous silicon layers are deposited by condensation of the material from the gas phase. A particular advantage is that films of square metre size can be produced in a single fabrication step. This base material is structured by optical writing techniques using laser so that a parallel sequence of amorphous silicon strips approximately 1 cm in width is obtained. These strips are metallically connected in series by connecting front and rear contacts between neighbouring strips. Such an integrated series connection leads to a solar module with elevated voltage (corresponding to the number of strips) and lowered current, so that conduction losses are kept low even in the case of a large total area of the solar module. This type of series connection is less expensive than the conventional non-integrated connection in solar modules from crystalline silicon cells.

Charge separation in solar cells of amorphous silicon is not possible with a p-n structure as in the case of crystalline silicon. This is due to the disturbed atomic structure of the material, which exhibits a large number of recombination centres, especially in doped material. In an undoped layer (intrinsic i-type layer), on the other hand, the free charge carriers can cover a maximum distance of several micrometres on average until they recombine. Charge carriers must therefore be produced in such an i-type layer, which is thin enough to permit electrons and holes to drift through the layer, but also thick enough to absorb a large portion of the sunlight. The field which separates the charges is obtained by a sandwich structure in which the i-type layer is placed between two thin doped layers (p-type and n-type layer). The result is a p-i-n structure (Figure 7.4).

The decisive disadvantage of a-Si:H solar cells has so far been their low efficiency, which is still further reduced by a long-time aging effect. The efficiency of a typical a-Si:H solar module decreases during operation, i.e. irradiation with light. Intensive research is being carried out to basically increase the efficiency and improve its stability. One approach is the stacked-cell concept in which two or more p-i-n structures are stacked on top of each other and the sum of the i-layer thicknesses remains constant compared to the single p-i-n cell. Due to the smaller thickness of the subcells, the charge carriers can be collected more effectively than in the single cell. The stacked cell is thus less sensitive to the defects produced in the amorphous network during solar cell operation. A tandem cell loses less than 1 (absolute) per cent of its efficiency after several thousand hours of irradiation with light, and thus degrades, for example, from 10 to 9 per cent. The so-called "stabilized efficiency" is thus perceptibly increased.

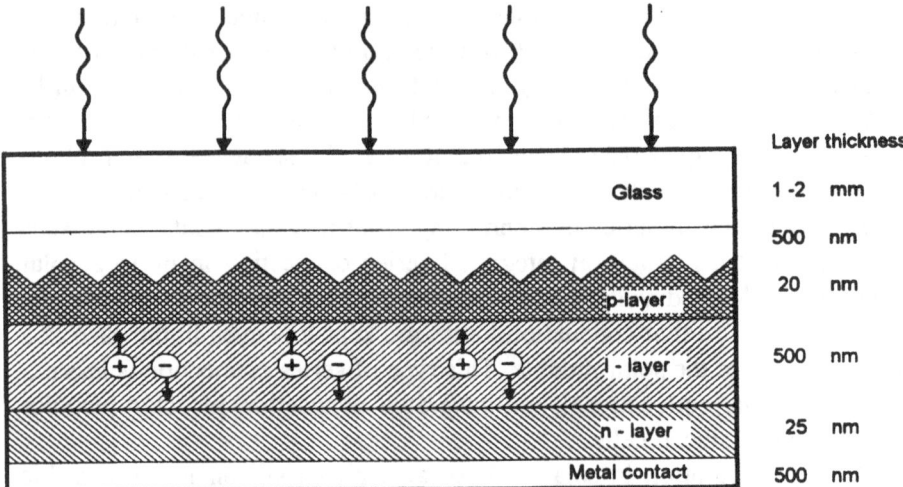

Figure 7.4 Film structure of a solar cell of amorphous silicon (a-Si:H). A typically 0.5 μm thick undoped layer (i) is sandwiched between a p- and an n-doped layer. Light penetrates into the i-type layer where it produces charge carrier pairs which drift to the contacts.

Beyond Silicon

In addition to the silicon "workhorse", photovoltaic research also investigates several other materials (MRS, 1993; Johansson et al., 1993). From a central materials perspective, two large groups can be distinguished. One group backs thin-film techniques which promise immense price advantages. The other group backs optimum efficiency, which presupposes crystalline materials with corresponding fabrication and material costs. The thin-film technology group primarily aims at increasing the efficiency, the other at lowering production costs. The aim is to jointly optimize both aspects: cost and efficiency. In the field of thin-film solar cells, above all copper-indium diselenide, $CuInSe_2$ (CIS), and cadmium telluride, CdTe, are in the focus of research and development. The efficiency record, however, is held by crystalline compound semiconductors which combine elements of the third and fifth group of the periodic system (III-V semiconductors) (Table 7.1). The frontrunner is the III-V compound gallium arsenide (GaAs). For single cells, an efficiency just under 29 per cent was achieved, for tandem cells of GaAs/GaSb of more than 35 per cent.

Table 7.1 Comparison of efficiencies for different classes of solar cell materials in per cent. The efficiencies of commercial modules are clearly below the values of prototype modules, and the latter clearly below the laboratory peak values for the single cells. Rough categories of manufacturing costs are also given.

Cell type	c-Si	Poly-Si	II-VI	III-V	a-Si
Efficiency (laboratory)	23.1	17.3	17	25	12.7
Efficiency of prototype-modules	20.8	15	11.1	-	11.0
Efficiency of commercial modules	14	12	-	-	6-7
Production costs	high	medium	low	very high	low

Different problems are encountered, however, for photovoltaic materials beyond silicon. Some of these materials contain dangerous environmental chemicals such as cadmium. The encapsulation of solar cells which, for example, in the case of silicon serves to shield the cell from environmental impacts, at the same time fulfils the opposite purpose in the case of CdTe solar cells in that it protects the environment against the chemical cell substance. Above all, however, it must be ensured for such cells after the end of their service life that toxic substances are disposed of or recycled. Moreover, material costs are relatively high. Tellurium, for example, is produced as a byproduct during copper purification. The annual production is therefore only 300 tonnes, which is by far not enough for a mass production of solar cells. A substance that can only be handled with considerable precaution is also arsenic used in GaAs cells. GaAs solar cells require crystalline material, and the achievable crystal qualities are far from being at the "silicon level". Growing facilities for GaAs, which provide high crystal perfection, are currently still under development in crystal growing research. Materials such as CdTe and GaAs, however, are of interest for special applications due to their high efficiency. CdTe, for example, has a band gap of 1.45 eV almost optimally adapted to the solar spectrum and such a high absorption coefficient that a film of one micrometre thickness absorbs 99 per cent of the visible sunlight.

Development Trends

Two strategies are being pursued in photovoltaics in order to lower the system costs and make solar cell technology economically acceptable. One strategy aims at cost reduction by large-area solar modules in thin-film technology. Such flat-plate collectors have efficiencies between 10 and 15 per cent. The second strategy avoids large-area photovoltaic material and uses lenses and other optical tools instead in order to direct sunlight to a small region of photovoltaically active material. So-called concentrator systems use materials of high efficiency (greater than 20 per cent) such as crystalline silicon and III-V materials.

Concentrator systems require direct sunlight. They cannot focus diffuse light produced by scattering in the atmosphere, on clouds and atmospheric humidity. The use of such systems makes therefore less sense in cloudy regions and is restricted to areas rich in sunshine or to space. Concentrator systems are always coupled with motors tracking the system towards the sun. In practice, one or two rotation axes are used which adapt the orientation of the solar cell to the diurnal range of the sun or additionally also to the seasonal period. A sophisticated optical system makes it possible to focus light to such an extent that a hundred times more energy falls onto the solar cell than without light-focusing optics. However, the technological input for these systems increases correspondingly. The cost for the solar cell itself is only a fraction of total costs since light is focused on a small-area solar cell. Efforts are therefore made to design above all low-cost lenses and mirrors. On account of the large number of high-technology components involved, concentrator systems are only economical in plants providing at least several kilowatts of thermal output. Flat-plate collectors, on the other hand, can effectively convert both direct and diffuse light into electricity. They can therefore practically be used worldwide. They must not be rotated into the normal direction to the sun and thus do not contain any moving parts. This leads to a relatively robust technology.

The great majority of all photovoltaic systems installed today are flat-plate collector plants. In combination with thin-film technology, this offers the most promising opportunity to substantially decrease the costs. Photovoltaics could thus become mature for terrestrial electricity production. In 1990, almost one third of all solar cells sold world wide were made of amorphous silicon thin-film material. Thin-film technology is above all attractive with respect to cost reduction for two reasons. On the one hand, thin material films absorb sunlight much more efficiently than crystalline cells.

Material savings are correspondingly immense. On the other hand, thin-film manufacturing techniques are particularly well suited for mass production. Large-area deposition with integrated connection of the cells to form modules is possible with a high degree of automation at simultaneously inherently low production costs and low energy consumption. There are good prospects for achieving the central goal of an increase in efficiency and its long-term stabilization for the single cell by the realization of stacked cells with optimized adaptation to the solar spectrum.

Dropping Costs

At present, solar electricity is not yet competitive in Germany at a cost of 2 DM per kilowatt-hour on average ($\approx$ US $ 1.25 per kWh). This cost figure relates to 20-year utilization at an interest rate of 8 per cent. Assuming 30 years of utilization and 4 per cent interest, today's cost is already at DM 1.20. These values would already drop to roughly one third at present if mass production was introduced. A further downward jump in cost would be achieved with solar cells of amorphous silicon (Figure 7.5). It is expected that thin-film technologies in conjunction with mass production could reduce the price of photovoltaic electricity below DM 0.30 per kilowatt-hour - in sunshine countries even below DM 0.20. All these figures relate to the status quo and can thus only be compared with current electricity prices from conventional energy sources.

Several considerations must be included in order to make statements on the economic efficiency of photovoltaics. For example, the cost of conventional energy supply will necessarily increase the more, the scarcer become the resources. From the aspect of national economy, however, energy is far too cheap even today. Furthermore, all external costs such as environmental damage and disposal must also be included in energy supply. Today's actual energy price would be raised by a factor of three to five even now if all social costs were included. If the present developments are extrapolated into the next century on the basis of readily foreseeable trends, the question is not whether, but when photovoltaics will reach the threshold of economic efficiency. With a high assessment of social costs photovoltaics will already undercut the price for a kilowatt-hour of electricity produced from conventional energy sources around the turn of the millennium. If social costs are not included, this will only be deferred by twenty years into the future (Figure 7.6).

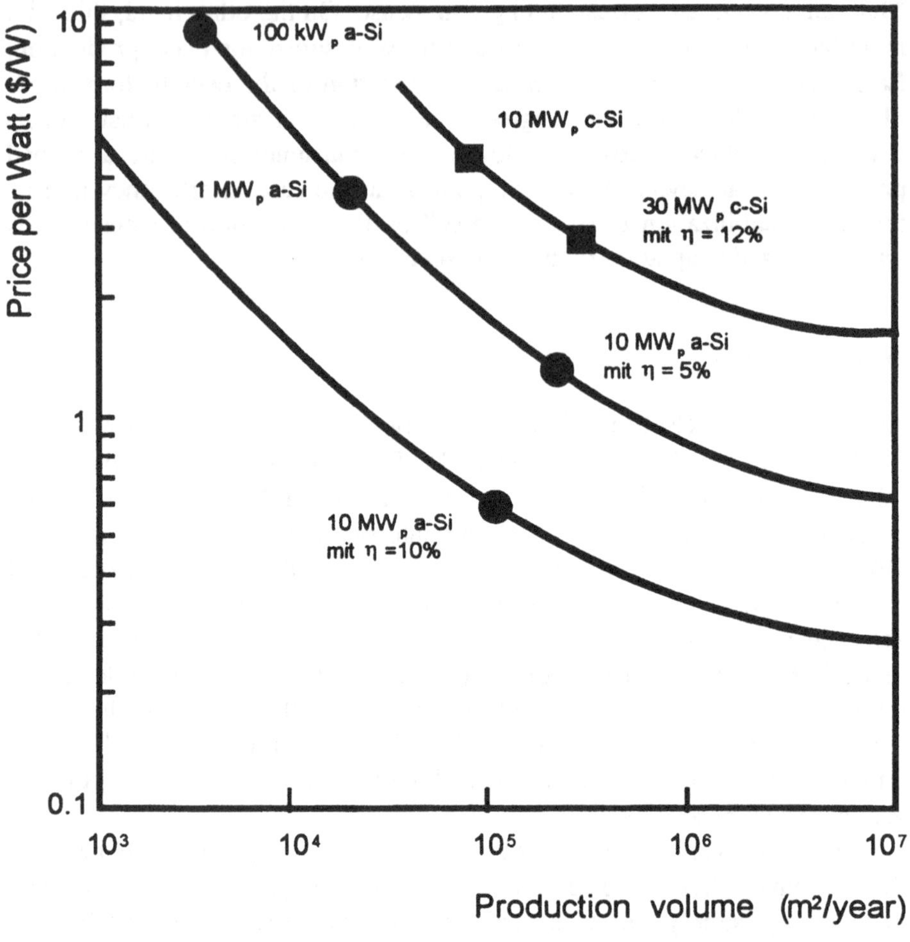

Figure 7.5 Predicted cost development for amorphous and crystalline silicon solar cells as a function of production volume for different module efficiencies η (Luft, 1992). Watt peak (W_p) is that power which a solar cell can deliver under maximum solar radiation (standard value: 1 kilowatt per square metre). As a rule of thumb, the ultimate electricity price per kilowatt-hour to be paid by the consumer is one tenth of the cost for one W_p.

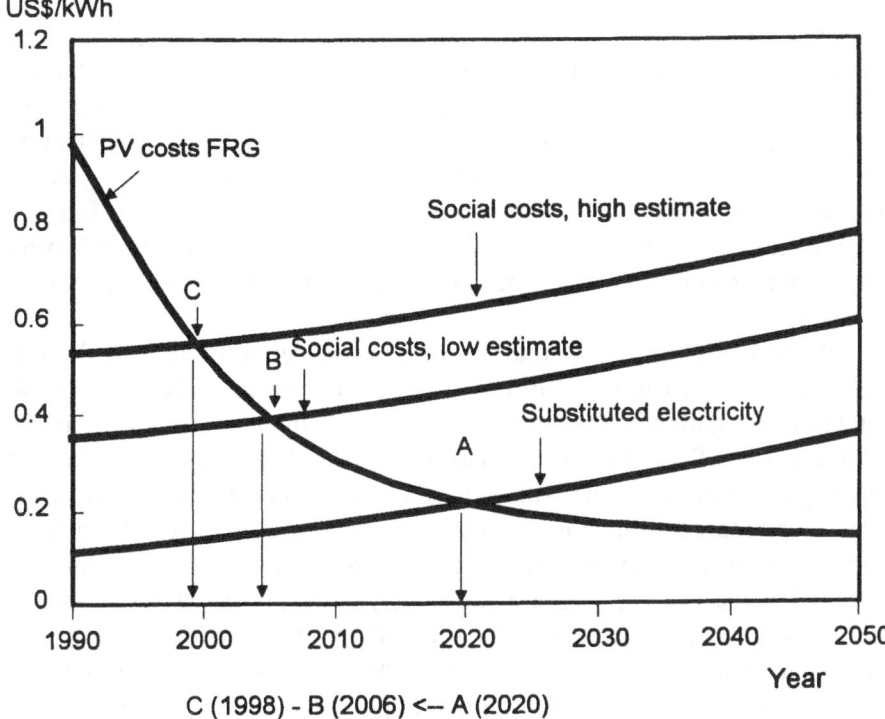

Figure 7.6 **Assessment of the price development for solar electricity in comparison to the costs for electricity from conventional energy carriers in the Federal Republic of Germany (FRG). A high weighting of the social costs (environmental damage, damage to health, waste disposal etc.) would make solar electricity already "competitive" around the turn of the millennium (Hohmeyer, 1994).**

Outlook: Energy Scenarios

The future energy mix will display a completely different "mixture" of energy sources compared to the currently practised energy supply. Moreover, not only the way in which energy is produced must fundamentally change, but also the way in which it is handled. It will be indispensable to save and efficiently use energy irrespective of how it is produced. A simple numerical example: The present per-capita consumption of energy in the industrialized countries is 57 megawatt-hours per year corresponding to 7 tonnes of coal equivalent per year. If this were taken as a target value for every individual and assuming that the world population would double to 10 billion within the next few decades, as expected, the demand for energy would rise to the six-fold of current world energy consumption. This represents a quantity which cannot be provided by any energy supply system in the world. Efficient energy conversion and use is therefore a prerequisite in any energy scenario and, at the same time, a decisive step to be made in the immediate future in order to realize the CO_2 emission reduction propagated at the United Nations summit meetings on environmental protection in Rio de Janeiro (1992) and Berlin (1995).

Photovoltaics is not a suitable means for effectively solving the CO_2 problem on a short-term basis because electric current only accounts for roughly one eighth of total primary energy consumption. However, photovoltaics is one of the envisaged pillars in the overall concept of a future energy supply. Such concepts will be based to an increasing extent on renewable energy sources which, in the final analysis, are all solar-operated (apart from direct solar radiation: wind, biomass, hydropower, ocean thermal energy and wave energy, geothermal energy). The power of renewables is enormous. Scenarios drawn up, for example, for the environmental protection summit meetings (Johansson et al., 1993) show that about 30 per cent could be covered by wind and solar power plants and another 30 per cent by hydropower and biomass even if the world wide demand for electric current were to triple up to the year 2050. Energy storage only comes into play from a stage at which there is a high renewable fraction of delivered energy. Storable solar-produced hydrogen will be integrated into a network of directly used fluctuating energy (sun, wind), continuously arising energy (hydropower) and remaining tolerable fossil and nuclear energy plants (Nitsch, 1993). Hydrogen requirements will grow about linearly with increasing renewable energy.

An argument often put forward against photovoltaics is the area requirement for solar cells in order to produce large quantities of electricity as direct energy or hydrogen as an energy storage medium. Many numerical examples could be given here. In most cases, however, too many parameters are included to present them here. Therefore, just a minor example: Even in a country poor in sunshine like the Federal Republic of Germany the sun radiates 100 times the energy currently consumed as primary energy in Germany. Referred to electricity consumption, this figure is even 800 times as high. In order to produce this energy for electricity by photovoltaic modules with an assumed efficiency of 15 per cent, 0.8 per cent of the German land area would be needed. (In comparison: the overbuilt area fraction in Germany is 11 per cent.) If calculations are performed using global values, it becomes apparent, in particular, that the area requirement is not the decisive obstacle to the introduction of photovoltaics. There is no (future) alternative to the sun.

References

Bonnet, D., Fuhs, W., Hoffmann, W. (1990): "Stromerzeugung durch Solarzellen. Physik – Technologie – Märkte", in: Hessisches Ministerium für Wirtschaft und Technik (Ed.), Technologie-Monitor Solarenergie und Wasserstofftechnik III, Batelle Congress.

Fritzsch, P. (1993): "Photovoltaik und Photosynthese", in: Meissner (1993).

Green, M. A. (1982): "Solar Cells. Operating Principles, Technology, and System Application", Englewood Cliffs, USA.

Green, M. A. (1993): "Crystalline- and Polycrystalline Silicon Solar Cells", in: Johansson et al. (1993).

Hohmeyer, O. (1994): "The Future of Photovoltaics and the Probable Costs of Climate Change in the Context of a Sustainable World", in: Hill, R., Palz, W., Helm, P. (Ed.), Twelfth European Photovoltaic Solar Energy Conference, Vol. II, Proceedings of the International Conference, Amsterdam, The Netherlands, 11.-15. April.

Jäger, F., Räuber, A. (Ed.) (1990): "Photovoltaik - Strom aus der Sonne. Technologie, Wirtschaftlichkeit und Marktentwicklung", Karlsruhe.

Johansson, Th. B. et al. (Ed.) (1993): "Renewable Energy. Sources for Fuels and Electricity", Washington, D.C.

Klein, S. (1995): "Solarstrom im Schatten der Atomruinen", Süddeutsche Zeitung, May 24/25th.

Loferski, J. J. (1993): "The First Forty Years: a Brief History of the Modern Photovoltaic Age", *Progress in Photovoltaics Research and Applications*, Vol. 1, pp. 67-78.

Luft, W. (1992): Panel discussion: 11th E.C. Photovoltaic Solar Energy Conference, Montreux.

Materials Research Society (MRS) (1993): *Bulletin Materials for Photovoltaics*, Vol. XVIII, No. 10.

Meissner, D. (1993): "Solarzellen: Physikalische Grundlagen und Anwendungen in der Photovoltaik", Sommerschule Physik und Chemie der photovoltaischen Solarenergieumwandlung, Braunschweig.

Nitsch, J. (1993): "Szenarien einer zukünftigen Energieversorgung - Fallbeispiel Deutschland", in: Meissner, 1993.

8 Potentials and Constraints of Wind Energy Utilization for Climate Protection in Germany

MANFRED KLEEMANN

Introduction

In the seventies various activities were started in Germany in order to develop modern wind power plants. The aim was to respond to the so-called oil price crisis. By the end of the eighties the technology had been steadily improved but market penetration still remained very low. This started to change during the early nineties. Due to an intensive political promotion programme wind energy utilization increased. During the last 6 years this technology has made the greatest progress compared to other technologies based on renewable energies. Although the installed capacity has grown at high annual rates, the absolute amount of electricity generated is still low and the contribution to national CO_2 savings is still minor. The future role of wind is a matter of controversy in Germany and expectations differ tremendously.

The purpose of this section of the book is to discuss the potentials and constraints on wind energy utilization with respect to carbon dioxide mitigation. The first chapter presents an estimation of the technical potential in TWh. The next three chapters describe the development of respectively the installed capacity, the expansion of the wind power industry and the state of the art. Environmental impacts and cost of electricity generation are presented in the following two chapters. Conclusions for CO_2 reduction are drawn in the last chapter.

Wind Energy Potential

Using the technical term wind energy potential one has to clearly distinguish different levels such as:

1. Theoretical potential
    This type is also called meteorological and site potential. It refers to the physical properties of the wind at a certain site.
2. Technical potential
    The technical potential is determined by the available theoretical potential, the topography, the sites available for wind power production and the efficiency of the wind turbine. Due to this restrictions the technical potential is considerably lower than the theoretical potential.
3. Economic potential
    Not all the technical potential which can be identified is economically competitive. Therefore the economic potential is far below the technical. Some energy economists say that it is difficult to define an economic potential because at present the electricity generation costs of wind power plants are higher than the avoided variable costs of conventional power plants.
4. Utilized potential
    Due to various restrictions the expected level of utilization can be below the economic potential. Such restrictions are for instance: inadequate information, lack of money, lack of acceptance and other uncertainties.

The following Table 8.1 presents the technical potential of wind energy in Germany. The identified suitable land area is based on an annual mean wind speed of more than 4.5 m/s at 10 m height and amounts to 4,140 km², which is equal to 1.2 per cent of the total land area of Germany. With the exception of the summit areas of some mountain ranges in Central and Southern Germany all high-potential areas are preferably situated in the flat coastal regions of Northern Germany.

Since the gross electricity generation of all power plants reached 563 TWh in 1994, the technical potential of wind energy could contribute in the range of 2.5 to 14.2 per cent in Germany.

Table 8.1 Technical potential of wind energy and its utilization

		Onshore
Mean wind speed at 10 m height	m/s	> 4.5
Area potential of Germany	km²	4,140
Capacity potential	GW	7 - 60
Energy potential (electricity)	TWh	14 - 80
Electricity generated from wind (1996)	TWh	3.8

Sources: Diekmann, 1995 and own estimates

Recent studies identified an additional wind energy potential of the same order of magnitude for the offshore areas of the Baltic Sea. Although offshore wind energy converters have a higher electricity output, the additional construction costs mean that at present they are not cost effective compared to onshore machines.

Development of Installed Capacity

The German Government has promoted many wind energy utilization projects since the seventies. But until 1989 the total installed wind turbine capacity increased very slowly and reached only 20 MW.

The 250 MW Wind Programme

A new phase of wind energy development was initiated in 1989 with *The 250 MW Wind Programme*. The purpose of this programme was to carry out comprehensive test and demonstration activities on an industrial scale. With accompanying scientific measurements and evaluations various useful statistical data were collected for further improvement of the state of the art. The usual subsidy for a participant in *The 250 MW Wind Programme* amounts either to DM 0.08 per kWh generated and used by themselves or DM 0.06 per kWh if fed into the public grid. For comparison: the generation cost without any subsidy is in the range of DM 0.14 to 0.26 per kWh. The additional grant was limited to a maximum of 25 per cent of the total investment (IEA, 1995). The programme was closed to new applicants at the end of 1995. However, support for the existing programme will continue for about 10 years.

Act on the Sale of Electricity to the Public Grid

In January 1991 the new *Act on the Sale of Electricity to the Public Grid* came into force. The act regulates the supply of electricity generated from renewable energies to the public grid. The respective utilities are obliged to buy the current from private producers at a fixed price. This price level has to be at least 90 per cent of the average price which the utilities received in the previous year from their final consumers. For 1996 the rate amounted to DM 0.172 per kWh.

Table 8.2 Development of installed wind turbine capacity and of electricity generated

Year	Annual	Cumulative	Electricity production
	GW/a	GW	TWh
1987	0.001	0.018	0.04
1988	0.001	0.019	0.04
1989[1]	0.001	0.020	0.04
1990	0.040	0.060	0.13
1991[2]	0.051	0.111	0.25
1992	0.072	0.183	0.42
1993	0.151	0.334	0.77
1994	0.309	0.643	1.48
1995	0.494	1.137	2.62
1996[3]	0.513	1.650	3.80

[1] Initiation of The 250 MW Wind Programme
[2] Implementation of the Act on the Sale of Electricity to the Public Grid
[3] Estimate

Sources: Rehfeld, 1996 and own estimates

These two political measures caused a rapid expansion of wind power utilization in Germany. Since 1989 the cumulative rated capacity has nearly doubled every year. At the end of 1996 an installed level of about 1.65 GW was reached (see Table 8.2). The electricity generated by wind energy converters contributed about 0.7 per cent to the total electricity production of Germany in 1996.

About two years ago utilities started to file objections. Electricity companies located in windy areas of Northern Germany stressed, among other issues, that the additional costs for the enforced purchase of wind energy are too high and are unevenly distributed across the country. Moreover, most of the utilities are of the opinion that the subsidy is too high and mistargeted.

Wind Power Industries in Germany

In 1996 about 20 companies manufactured wind turbines in Germany with unit sizes ranging from some kW to 1.5 MW (Wind Turbine Market, 1995). About 90 per cent of the capacity installed is supplied by the seven largest producers. The total turnover of all manufacturing and service companies is expected to reach DM 1.2 billion in 1996. Nearly 5,000 jobs have been created in the wind business.

The growing restrictions on the domestic market are giving rise to increasing export activities. In 1991 exports amounted to 1 percent of the capacity installed in Germany. Although the figure reached 7 per cent in 1995 the export share is still low.

Due to the significant technical progress achieved, the unit size of wind turbines installed in Germany has increased distinctly. From 1989 to 1995 the average unit capacity increased from 145 kW to 475 kW. This trend will continue in the future. Table 8.3 presents the prototypes with a rated capacity (rated power) of more than 1 MW. The first successful development of these units already started during the late eighties and has now reached commercialization.

Table 8.3 German prototypes with a rated capacity of more than 1 MW (1995)

Capacity MW	Type	Site	Year
1.2	AWEC	Cabo Villano (Spain)	1989
1.2	WKA60	Helgoland	1990
1.2	WKA60II	Kaiser Wilhelm Koog	1991
3.0	AEOLUSII	Wilhelmshaven	1993
1.5	E66	Aurich	1995
1.5	TWI500	Emden	1996
1.2	A1200	Brunsbüttel	1996
1.5	TWI1500	(Planned)	1996/97

Source: IEA, 1995

Status of Wind Turbine Development

Important improvements to the state of the art in wind turbine technology have been achieved during the past decades. The main developments have been:

- a steady increase of rated unit capacity of commercial turbines from about 20 kW in the seventies to 1,500 kW today,
- a significantly higher reliability and hence a better availability which reaches 95 per cent or even more,

- the reduction of investment cost due to cheaper technologies, larger units and higher production rates,
- increased performance and higher efficiencies,
- a more variable speed control to allow the rotor to operate at optimum efficiencies in a wide range of wind velocities.

At present the wind turbines have preferably three blades manufactured from glass-reinforced plastic. Table 8.4 presents a summary of characteristic data of commercially available machines from 100 to 1,500 kW.

Table 8.4 Size and weight of commercial wind turbines

Rated capacity kW	Rotor diameter m	Hub height m	Total weight[1] t	Rated wind speed m/s
100	21 - 23	25 - 45	12 – 30	12 – 13
250	29 - 30	30 - 65	30 – 60	13 – 17
600	42 - 47	40 - 70	60 – 120	12 – 16
1,500	65 - 70	70 - 100	200 – 1,000[2]	13 – 15

1) Without foundation
2) Steel-concrete tower

Environmental Impacts

The environmental impacts of wind energy utilization such as effects on bird life, noise emissions, and visual impacts can place constraints on the long-term market development in Germany.

Impacts on Birds

From studies in the Netherlands it is expected that a total installed wind turbine capacity of 1 GW would cause about 21,000 bird deaths per annum (Kasteren, 1995). This could on average amount to 1 to 2 victims per turbine per year. Other studies present lower mortality rates. Since the German coastal area has similar characteristics, this number can also be applied there. The present capacity could then cause more than 20,000 bird deaths per year. Although the number of birds killed by traffic is considerably higher, more and more ornithologists are concerned about the impacts of the increasing number of wind turbines on bird life. This is also due to the reduction of breeding grounds and of resting places for migrants caused by rotating blades and noise disturbances.

Noise Emissions

Wind turbines are often sited in areas of low background noise level, where even relatively low sound levels are detectable. Noise is defined as sound that is unwanted by the hearer because it is unpleasant, bothersome, interferes with important activities, causes stress, or is believed to be physically harmful (Erp, 1996). The allowable sound level in Germany is prescribed by regulations. It depends on the time of the day and on the type of settlement as shown in Table 8.5.

The noise output of modern wind turbines can reach more than 100 dBA near the rotor. To meet the legal requirements considerable distances between the site of the plant and the next settlement have to be maintained. This results in a loss of potential areas for wind energy utilization.

Visual Impacts

The high tower, the rotating blades and the white or light grey colour of the wind energy converters cause visual impacts. Especially the moving blades attract the human eye. These impacts are difficult to quantify and they cause much controversy. Local residents in part fear a decrease in the number of tourists and establish pressure groups against wind energy utilization. On the other hand, studies indicate that not all tourists see significant disadvantages caused by the large machines. However, the regulations for protected areas are so strict that great care has to be taken in the planning process to ensure that the regulations are met. This leads to a further reduction of potential areas for wind turbines.

Table 8.5 Recommended noise levels in Germany (dBA)

	Day	Night
Commercial areas	< 65	< 50
Mixed areas	< 60	< 45
Generally residential areas	< 55	< 40
Purely residential areas	< 50	< 35

Electricity Generation Cost

The electricity generation cost for a given 500 kW wind turbine is determined by the wind potential of the site and the fiscal regime under which the costs are calculated. The wind power input to a turbine varies in proportion to the cube of the wind speed. The cost of electricity generation is therefore highly sensitive to the mean wind speed of a location. Table 8.6 therefore shows a range of the annual average wind speed from 5.5 to 7.5 m/s and the respective capacity factors. The levelized generation cost presented in Table 8.7 is based on the data in Table 8.6, which reflects the situation in Germany in 1996.

Table 8.6   Cost data for a 500 kW turbine

Cost of a 500 kW unit	DM 980,000
Incidental expenses	27 %
Operating and maintenance costs	2 %
Interest rate	5 %
Repayment period	12 years

A comparison of the levelized generation cost in Table 8.7 with the subsidies according to the *Act on the Sale of Electricity to the Public Grid* of 0.173 DM/kWh (1996) shows that the breakeven point is reached at an average wind speed of 6.5 m/s at 40 m height; this means about 5.2 m/s at 10 m height at the same location. Sites with higher wind potential have to be chosen by an investor in order to earn money with wind energy if he does not receive any other subsidies.

Table 8.7   Levelized electricity generation cost based on 500 kW units (without subsidies)

Mean speed at 40 m height	Capacity factor[1]	Cost
m/s	h/yr	DM/kWh
5.5	1350	0.26
6.0	1690	0.21
6.5	2080	0.17
7.0	2500	0.14
7.5	2840	0.13

[1] Expressed in full load hours per year

Avoided Fuel Cost

From the point of view of an utility, which has to buy the investors electricity, or from the point of view of society as a whole the economic situation looks different. The fuel cost avoided in conventional power plants when wind energy is utilized is three to four times lower than the cost of wind power generation even at locations with good wind potential. This means, the additional cost of wind energy utilization can not be compensated by the fuel cost savings in conventional power plants.

Therefore the wind turbine market will remain an artificial one which depends to a great extent on considerable subsidies. The high generation cost are due to the still high investment cost and to the very low capacity factors (see Table 8.7). The latter is caused by the variation of wind speed (calm periods). Due to many windless periods and the low resulting capacity factor wind plants can never replace conventional plants, they can only save fuel and the associated fuel costs.

Conclusions for CO_2 Reduction

Electricity generation based on wind energy is generally considered to be environmentally more benign, because the major pollution effects of the fossil fuels are avoided. Table 8.8 shows for instance the CO_2 savings of wind energy utilization in comparison to hard coal power plants in Germany. The capacity of 1 MW wind turbines can save about 2,000 tonnes of CO_2 per annum. Such savings can be achieved in coastal or mountainous areas which have a good wind potential.

The German Government aims for a 25 per cent reduction of CO_2 emissions in 2005 compared to 1990 (see Part I, Chapter 2). This percentage corresponds to about 246 million tonnes of carbon dioxide per year. Because of economic and ecological restrictions, declining public acceptance and site scarcity it is expected that the installed wind power capacity will double

Table 8.8 CO_2 saving of wind power plants in comparison to hard coal power plants

		tonnes/year
500 kW	wind turbine	974
1,650 MW	capacity installed in 1996	3.2×10^6
3,500 MW	expected capacity in 2005	6.8×10^6

from 1996 to 2005.

If this becomes true, then wind would contribute about 7 million tonnes to the CO_2 reduction goal. In Part II, Chapter 6 an upper limit of 4 GW has been assumed. However, the contribution of wind energy will remain minor compared to other reduction measures in the sectors of household, traffic and industry such as energy conservation and application of more efficient conventional technologies (see Part I, Chapter 2).

References

Diekmann, J. (1995): "Kosten und Potentiale der Nutzung von Windenergie in der Bundesrepublik Deutschland" (Costs and Potential of Wind Energy Utilization in Germany), IKARUS-Projektbericht 3-07, Forschungszentrum Jülich (Research Centre Jülich).

Erp, F. van, August (1996): "Siting Process for Wind Energy Projects in Germany", Arbeiten zu Risikokommunikation, Heft 60, Research Centre Jülich.

IEA Wind Energy (1995): "Annual Report, International Energy Agency", Paris.

Kasteren, J. van (1995): Bird Society Satisfied, *Wind Power Monthly*, Vol. 11, No. 9.

Kleemann, M. (1996): "Stürmische Perspektiven – Nutzungsmöglichkeiten und Grenzen der Windenergie", *Physik in unserer Zeit*, VCH Verlagsgesellschaft, Weinheim, Vol. 27, No. 2.

Rehfeld, K. (1996): "Wind Energy Use in Germany", *DEWI Magazin*, No. 8, Wilhelmshaven.

Wind Turbine Market (1995): "The International Overview 1995", Publisher: WINKRA-RECOM Verlags GmbH, Hanover.

9 Utilization of Biomass in the German Energy Sector

MARTIN KALTSCHMITT

Introduction

The energy and environment discussion in Germany is currently governed by the negative consequences of the greenhouse effect and its mitigation. Among the large number of conceivable options, renewable energies are often regarded as major "sources of hope". If, however, the level of current utilization is taken as an indicator of the relative proximity to the market there only remain biomass, hydro and wind power from among the multitude of renewable energy options. Next to hydropower biomass is by far the most used option in Germany today.

Biomass can be used to meet the demand of final and useful energy with the aid of a variety of different technologies and processes. The options differ substantially according to the type of biomass used (e.g. liquid manure, sewage sludge, forest residual wood, rape seed, wheat) and according to the desired form of useful or final energy (e.g. heat, electricity, ethanol, motor fuel, pyrolysis oil). For this reason, the current state of the art regarding the various possibilities for using biomass will first be analysed in the following chapters. Subsequently, the technical biomass potential will be assessed and its current utilization described in order to better evaluate the already applied and still available opportunities provided by this form of renewable energy within the German energy system. This will be followed by an analysis of the supply costs for final and useful energy. Based on this, the possible reduction of CO_2 equivalents due to current and still conceivable biomass utilization - determined over the entire life cycle - and the associated reduction costs will be calculated and discussed. The CO_2 equivalents are understood to be the sum of all radiative forcing anthropogenic greenhouse gas emissions weighted with the respective greenhouse potential. Since chlorofluorocarbons (CFC) and non-methane hydrocarbons (NMHC) do not practically occur in the life cycle of bioenergy carriers, these trace gases are not considered; the study exclusively comprises CO_2 from fossil energy carriers, CH_4 with a greenhouse potential of 21 kg CO_2/kg CH_4, and N_2O with a greenhouse potential of 310 kg CO_2/kg N_2O

151

(IPCC, 1995). The CO_2 released during the conversion of biomass into energy is not included in the calculation of CO_2 equivalents since it has been previously extracted from the atmosphere by the plants and does not additionally enhance the greenhouse effect (Kaltschmitt and Reinhardt, 1997).

State of the Art

The state of the art of the methods suitable for a utilization of residues of organic origin and of energy crops, respectively, is very different.

Residues

Combustion is the "classical" process for the utilization of solid fuels of organic origin. This technology is available and already reliably used on a large technical scale within a very wide capacity range. The legal requirements for protecting the environment can also be fulfilled in most cases with modern plants even under rapidly changing load conditions and at partial load. The plants currently available are primarily designed for heat supply. Although it is basically possible to produce electricity, this is technically more sophisticated due to the for some biofuels low ash melting point and the danger of high-temperature chlorine corrosion of some bio-energy carriers. For electricity production, in particular, co-firing in existing coal power plants is a comparatively promising option (Sontow et al., 1997).

Biomass gasification seems to be one of the most promising options especially for electricity production, on the one hand, due to the high electricity generation efficiencies and, on the other hand, due to comparatively greater environmental acceptability (i.e. lower emissions) in comparison to electricity generation by biomass combustion. For this reason, considerable research efforts have been made in recent years to make this technology available on the market. However, this has been hardly successful to date; only a few gasification plants are at present commercially operated exclusively for heat supply in Sweden and Finland. Plants for electricity production - and this is where the actual advantage of gasification takes full effect - currently only exist as pilot projects within the framework of research and development activities. Problems are especially encountered with gas cleaning; the gas turbine or gas engine installed behind requires a largely tar- and dust-free fuel gas. The necessary purity can currently only be achieved with high technical expenditure involving additional costs and un-solved technical problems, which make large-scale implementation difficult under the present economic conditions in the energy sector (Kaltschmitt and Bridgewater, 1997). Gasification therefore only represents an option - although important - for the future and has no practical significance for biomass conversion at present.

Pyrolysis with the aim of an efficient liquefaction of solid organic sub-stances has been the object of intensive research for many years. A large-scale application of the relevant techniques, however, has not been accom-plished to date, especially against the background of the high costs in-volved and the still unsolved technical problems; biomass pyrolysis is not expected to be reliably available on a large technical scale within the next few years (Kaltschmitt and Bridgewater, 1997). This technique has also no importance for a utilization of solid organic residues so far.

Liquefaction after gasification and subsequent methanol synthesis is not available either on a small or a large technical scale from the present point of view, although it has already been commercially applied in the past. In view of the high costs and the technical problems involved in gasification, methanol production cannot be assumed to appreciably contribute towards covering German energy demand within the next few years.

Alcoholic fermentation for the production of beverage alcohol has been state of the art for many years. Beverage alcohol is currently produced from sugar- or starch-containing feedstock. For the cellulose-containing residues a saccharification is first necessary; this technique has been occasionally applied on a large technical scale in the past, but cannot be regarded as commercially available without any problems from the present point of view due to the associated technical requirements (e.g. application of ac-ids). Moreover, the costs are so high that these techniques are currently not applied at all. A production of alcohol from solid residues must therefore be ruled out for the German energy supply in the foreseeable future.

Energy Crops

The concepts for biomass supply from energy crop growing are largely still at the stage of research and development. This applies to cultivation and harvesting techniques as well as to storage and, in part, to the respective energy utilization technologies.

Biomass produced in plantations can, in principle, also be converted into secondary or useful energy with conversion technologies other than combustion. As far as the current state of the art is concerned, the statements made in connection with residues are essentially valid for these options, too.

Whole-crop cereal (straw and grain) harvesting, for example, is not very effective due to the high grain losses involved. No satisfactory solution has been developed so far; this applies to both bale and pellet lines. Storage also still poses a number of unsolved problems. For example, stored whole-crop cereals are particularly susceptible to being eaten by mice and rats due to the high fraction of grains in comparison to straw. There is also the danger of germination in the case of a high water content.

Combustion is the technique currently best suited for this kind of biomass. However, there may arise difficulties resulting from the high nitrogen content of the grain or chlorine content of the straw, respectively, the different combustion properties of grain and straw and the relatively low ash melting point.

Grasses The situation is similar for concepts aiming at the utilization of annual and perennial grasses. In contrast to whole-crop cereals, whose cultivation has been state of the art for decades, both the selection of suitable grass varieties for German conditions and their cultivation are still at the stage of research and development. Harvest techniques are not mature either, although the machines available from cereal production can also be used in part for the harvest of grasses. Storage, on the other hand, is largely unproblematic assuming a dry harvest and compaction. In contrast, there are still quite a number of combustion- and process-engineering difficulties caused by the structure and constituents of this biofuel.

Wood plantations This largely also applies to the supply chains on the basis of short rotation plantations. Planting does not pose any major problems, although quite a number of different tree species are still being examined for cultivability. Harvesting, on the other hand, is still characterized by a considerable development potential despite already existing prototype harvesters. This also applies to storage, where mould formation and self-warming can occur in particular in the presence of wet chips due to dry recovery being hardly possible. In contrast, the combustion of wood can be regarded as having reached a sufficient state of the art; the legal requirements for emission protection can be (largely) met without any problems. Difficulties can only arise if the fuel is very inhomogeneous and characterized by considerable water content and water content variations, respectively.

Potential and Utilization

Potential of Residues

Energetically usable solid organic residues arise in agricultural and forest plant production. In addition, industrial residual wood, demolition wood and other ligneous biomass can be used for energy production.

Ligneous biomass Forest management provides, in addition to stem and industrial timber, biomass which, at present, is not utilized. Unused wood pieces (thinning material, logs and thicker branches with a diameter of ≥ 8 cm with bark) is particularly suited for energy production (Wegener et al., 1994; Becher et al., 1995). The corresponding potential is determined from the average annual wood growth rates (approximately 63 million m^3/yr) less felling (approximately 38 million m^3/yr) and annual firewood utilization of approximately 9 million m^3/yr (approximately 85 PJ/yr). This gives a wood potential of roughly 16 million m^3/yr or 142 PJ/yr. The additionally arising biomass in the forest (non-compact wood, twigs, bark and foliage) cannot be meaningfully utilized. The recovery of stump and root wood, for example, constitutes an intervention in the forest soil and is therefore not considered. Moreover, part of the biomass volume should be left in the forest to contribute to the humus and nutrient cycle and can therefore not be used as an energy carrier.

In addition, ligneous biomass arises as wood residues in industrial woodworking, discarding from the utilization process (e.g. packing material), management of public parks and gardens and in roadside planting. In the producing industry, roughly 6.7 million t/yr (dry matter) of industrial wood residues arose in 1992 in the sawmilling industry and in timber processing alone, of which, however, about 4.5 million t/yr are already utilized in the paper and chipboard industry (Becher et al., 1995). For the remaining 2.2 million t/yr, an energy potential of roughly 40 PJ/yr is calculated. In addition, between 8 and 10 million m^3/yr of demolition wood (without waste paper) arises, which corresponds to an energy potential of about 81 PJ/yr (Hrubesch, 1996). Ligneous biomass from wind shielding hedges, woody plants at rivers and lakes, along roads, railway lines and waterways and small wood from fruit-tree pruning amounts to a total of about 1 million m^3/yr; this corresponds to roughly 7 PJ/yr (Hrubesch, 1996). In other sectors of the timber trade and industry there is a certain additional potential which, however, cannot be precisely quantified at present.

In total, the energy potential from wood residues amounting to approximately 270 PJ/yr corresponds to a share in the German final energy consumption (9,630 PJ in 1996) of approximately 2.8 per cent.

In comparison, roughly 85 PJ/yr of firewood was sold and presumably also used as an energy carrier (Hrubesch, 1996). Together with roughly 55 PJ/yr forestry residues used as firewood, 40 PJ/yr industrial residual wood used almost completely, roughly 12 PJ/yr other waste wood and just under 1 PJ/yr other wood used, the current wood exploitation of roughly 193 PJ/yr corresponds to a fossil energy share of just under 2.0 per cent in final energy consumption.

Culmiferous biomass The main agricultural byproduct for energy generation is straw arising in cereal production. It is already utilized in many ways - as a rule, however, not for energy conversion but for ploughing into the topsoil, litter in livestock breeding or sales to market gardens. Only the remainder then still left can be used as an energy source.

The total volume of technically recoverable straw can be estimated from the arable land used for the respective cereal species, the regionally different grain yield and the average grain-straw ratio. For Germany this gives a technically recoverable straw volume of roughly 39.1 million t/yr. If only one fifth is regarded as usable due to the restrictions described, an energy potential of about 104 PJ/yr is obtained (Kaltschmitt, 1997). This corresponds to roughly 1.1 per cent relative to the final energy consumption in Germany. This potential is hardly used. At present only about 3 PJ/yr are converted.

In Germany, culmiferous biomass is additionally produced on areas which are tended. However, this biomass volume is difficult to estimate, depends considerably on changing legal and administrative conditions and since it is composted in most cases, it is not further discussed here - nor is the additionally arising culmiferous biomass from other different sources (e.g. grass cut from road verges, public parks and front gardens).

Total potential Germany has a total energy potential from ligneous and stramineous organic residues of 374 PJ/yr (roughly 3.9 per cent relative to the final energy consumption in Germany in 1996). In addition, roughly 85 PJ/yr (approximately 0.9 per cent of the final energy consumption) of firewood is currently sold.

Potential of Energy Crops

For plant-based energy carrier production, whole-crop cereals (grain and straw), grasses with high biomass yield or fast-growing tree species can be grown (Kaltschmitt, 1994). The respective technical potential is primarily determined from the arable land available and also from agronomic aspects.

Due to the current overproduction of food, areas for cultivating renewable substrates are even available in densely populated Germany. In the medium term, a maximum area of 4 million hectares could be available for energy crop cultivation. With currently achievable yields this gives a maximum energy potential of about 690 PJ/yr for whole-crop cereal cultivation, roughly 840 PJ/yr for elephant grass production (miscanthus) and approximately 800 PJ/yr for fast-growing tree species like willow and poplar. This corresponds to a maximum of just under 9 per cent of the final energy consumption. Due to the high energy generating costs especially for cultivated biomass, this potential is not used at present.

Comparison Between Potential and Use

A comparison between biomass potential and use in existing plants shows that nearly all of the industrial wood residues and part of the forest demolition wood is already utilized, whereas other ligneous biomass is hardly used as energy carrier. Accordingly, of the solid biomass fractions considered here, the demolition wood potential has been unused in part to date, the potential from straw and from other ligneous biomass is largely unused and the potential from energy crops is not yet used at all (Table 9.1).

Costs of Feedstocks, Plants and Energy Supply

Fuel Costs of Wood Residues and Waste Wood

The energy carrier costs for forest residues arising in timber harvesting are calculated from the expenditure incurred for collecting and chopping; the average total costs are in the range of 10 to 11 DM/GJ. In the case of utilizing forest residues from thinning operations, the costs for chips vary between 5 and 8 DM/GJ depending on the process variant, tree spe cies, age and terrain (free forest road).

Firewood also constitutes a regular commodity; current prices range between 50 and 70 DM per stacked m^3 for coniferous wood or 60 and

Table 9.1 Potentials and current use of biomass in Germany

	Technical potential	Used in			Unused technical potential
		very small plants	*small plants*	*large plants*	
	PJ/yr	PJ/yr	PJ/yr	PJ/yr	PJ/yr
Firewood	-	39.0	46.0	-	-
Forest wood residues	142	25.0	30.0	-	87
Industrial wood residues	40	-	18.3	21.7	-
Demolition wood (without waste paper)	81	1.0	2.6	8.4	69
Other wood	7	0.5	0.5	-	6
Straw	104	0.3	2.5	0.2	101
Energy crops (max.)	840	-	-	-	840
Total (without firewood)	1,214	26.8	53.9	30.3	1,103

90 DM per stacked m^3 for hardwood. This corresponds to prices between 7 and 10 DM/GJ for coniferous and 9 to 13 DM/GJ for hardwood.

In addition to the forest residues discussed here, industrial residues (such as bark, sawing byproducts, shavings) arise in sawmills and can be processed into fuel at low cost. However, a large proportion of these industrial residues are utilized as a raw material. The remainder is mostly used for heat and electricity supply in the plants of the respective industrial companies. The fuel costs for industrial residual timber are thus above all based on the market prices for material use and range between roughly 1 DM/GJ for bark and about 2 DM/GJ for sawing byproducts, with variations depending on the respective economic conditions (without delivery charges). Under certain conditions, fractions of such industrial wood residues may be available free of cost. The situation is similar for uncontaminated demolition wood, where the market prices of wood range between 1 and 1.5 DM/GJ.

Other ligneous biomass comprises a variety of different fractions for which no costs can be specified due to the great inhomogeneity. It could be assumed in this case that the supply costs correspond to the disposal proceeds.

Wood can be stored unchopped in the forest or in storage places, chopped it can be stored in open-air bulk storage places and in halls. Storage in the forest or in similar places does not cause any additional costs, whereas other storage procedures partially involve considerable extra costs.

The transport of wood chips can be carried out by tractor-drawn vehicles or other commercial transport equipment. Costs of 0.6 DM/GJ are calculated for a transport distance of approximately 5 km and 1.5 DM/GJ for about 30 km.

In total, fuel costs between 6 and 13 DM/GJ arise for forest wood residues delivered free to the combustion plant and between 8 and 15 DM/GJ for firewood. Costs between 2 and 4 DM/GJ delivered free to the combustion plant are assumed for industrial wood residues, between 0 (contaminated demolition wood) and 3 DM/GJ for uncontaminated demolition wood and 0 DM/GJ (excluding disposal) for other ligneous biomass.

Fuel Costs of Straw

If the straw arising in cereal production is regarded as a residue, it is only necessary to include the costs of straw collection. They are composed of the costs incurred for pressing and transporting the straw to the farmyard or storage place including vehicle loading and unloading as well as the costs for storing and removal from the store and they amount to about 3 DM/GJ. On the other hand, straw is to be treated as a byproduct if its incorporation into the soil contributes to the nutrient and humus supply. In this case, the value of the nutrients contained in the straw (1 to 4 DM/GJ) and the possible contribution to the humus supply (2 to 5 DM/GJ) must be included in addition to the costs for collecting and making the straw available. The energy carrier costs are then between 5 and 7 DM/GJ on average. Straw is also a regular merchandise in some regions of Germany; at present, the market price ranges between 80 and 130 DM/t (i.e. 5 to 9 DM/GJ).

Additional costs arise for storage and transportation. For example, straw should not be stored uncovered in the open air, since the fuel quality is impaired by penetrating moisture. The corresponding storage costs are in the range of 0.7 DM/GJ.

Tractor-drawn vehicles or normal trucks can be used for transportation. The most economic form of transport up to 30 km is the use of tractors with corresponding trailers; costs of 0.6 DM/GJ arise, for example, for a distance of 5 km. For longer distances, trucks are used, for example, at costs of about 1.9 DM/GJ for 30 km. In summary, this gives a fuel cost between 4 and 12 DM/GJ delivered free.

Fuel Costs of Energy Crops

Biomass can also be produced by cultivating special plants. A differentiation is made here between the cultivation of energy cereals, perennial grasses and fast-growing tree species. The resultant energy carrier costs are composed of the production expenditure for the respective plant and the expenditure for making the biomass available.

Cereals are among the crops chiefly cultivated in Germany, so that the production expenditure for different yield and climate conditions is known. Based on average conditions, energy carrier costs of between 13 and 15 DM/GJ arise for whole-crop cereals without transport charges from areas under cultivation.

The production costs are far less well known for fast-growing grasses such as miscanthus. Energy carrier costs of between 8 and 21 DM/GJ arise, for example, on the basis of yields currently achieved in Germany and average expenditure for the plants within the life expectancy of such crops, as far as this can be calculated at present. Lower fuel costs may also be possible in the case of very high yields and a dry biomass harvest.

Poplars can be grown in agricultural plantations and harvested as chips in perennial cycles. Energy carrier costs of between 10 and 16 DM/GJ are calculated for the yields possible in Germany. However, this does not include the cost of extracting the rootstocks after timber production.

Additional costs arise for storage and transportation to the combustion plant. Assuming storage similar to that for residues and transportation by tractor-drawn vehicles or trucks, additional costs of 1 to 2 DM/GJ will arise.

Plant Costs

Current specific expenditure for biomass-fuelled combustion plants shows a pronounced dependence on power output, in part decreasing considerably with increasing thermal capacity. Accordingly, average prices of between 600 and 780 DM/kW must be assumed at present (bandwidth between 250 and just under 1,500 DM/kW) for small plants in the 12 to 25 kW range (e.g. single-family houses). The average specific expenditure ranges between 450 and 650 DM/kW with a bandwidth from 200 to approximately 1,100 DM/kW for installed capacities between 20 and 40 kW (e.g. two-family houses). If plants with an even higher capacity are examined, e.g. for industrial enterprises, the average prices in the 150 kW range are just under 300 DM/kW, but vary between 150 and 450 DM/kW. The specific investments for large industrial plants with thermal outputs of up to 10 MW range between 100 and 800 DM/kW and sometimes even higher. For underfeed stokers, for example, they are approximately 250 to 300 DM/kW and for grate firing systems with thermal capacities of up to roughly 30 MW they vary between 300 and 600 DM/kW; the average is about 500 DM/kW. In comparison, fluidized-bed and gasifier firing systems are even more expensive.

Heat Generating Costs

The costs arising annually can be determined from the fuel costs, the other operating costs and the plant investments (period of depreciation corresponds to the technical lifetime, interest rate 4 per cent). Total annual costs are used to calculate the heat generating costs under the assumed boundary conditions for possible heat supply in the course of a year. Since very different plant technologies in very different power ranges with different biofuels can be used for different applications, the heat generating costs are subject to large variations. For example, the heat generating costs are between 20 and 43 DM/GJ for a small wood-fired plant (lump wood boiler) with roughly 40 kW thermal output. In comparison, heat generating costs of between 25 and 41 DM/GJ are calculated for a chip combustion plant of similar capacity using forest residual wood as fuel. If a heat supply from large plants with capacities of slightly less than 3 MW thermal output is assumed, heat generating costs of between 44 and 48 DM/GJ are calculated for the end consumer (including a short-distance or district heating network); this results from the comparatively high fuel costs, on the one hand, and the high plant investments and costs for the short-distance or district heating network, on the other hand. Heat supply from straw in large-scale plants is thus much more expensive than that from forest residual wood, where the heat generating costs for the end consumer are only between 35 and 45 DM/GJ. If low-cost biofuel is available, as may be the case for industrial residual wood, for example, the heat generating costs decrease significantly and are only between 31 and 35 DM/GJ under the conditions assumed here. If energy crops are used, the heat generating costs are higher due to higher energy carrier costs; they can increase up to 41 to 49 DM/GJ for chips from short-rotation plantations (Lux, 1997).

Reduction Possibilities and Reduction Costs of CO_2 Equivalents

Based on the energy carrier potentials described and the present utilization the emissions of CO_2 equivalents will first be determined which would occur if fossil energy carriers were used instead of solid biomass; this corresponds to the reduction already realized for CO_2 equivalents in Germany at present ("realized reduction"). Subsequently, the additionally available reduction potentials in the conventional energy system will be calculated from the unused technical potentials ("additional reduction"), considering the CO_2 equivalents instead of the actual CO_2 emissions. CO_2 equivalents are understood to be the weighted sum of radiative forcing trace gas releases according to the aspect of the "anthropogenic greenhouse effect". Since CFCs and NMHCs practically do not occur in the life cycle of bioenergy carriers, this only includes carbon dioxide (CO_2) from the conversion of fossil energy carriers, methane (CH_4) with a greenhouse potential of 21 (i.e. methane is 21 times more climate-forcing than CO_2 for a residence time of 100 years in the atmosphere) and nitrous oxide (N_2O) with a greenhouse potential of 310 (IPCC, 1996); other anthropogenic greenhouse gas releases are not considered. The CO_2 extracted from the atmosphere during plant growth is not considered either since it is not additionally climate-forcing. In addition, the respective reduction costs are calculated for the reduction potentials still available.

In order to estimate the reductions of CO_2 equivalents already realized and still possible, it is assumed that the major fossil energy carriers currently used were replaced when using the biomass under consideration in the German energy system. The reference scale for quantifying the reduction possibilities is the final or useful energy, since the utilization rate of conversion plants can be different for different fuels (e.g. the utilization rate of wood-fired combustion plants is below that of plants operated with light fuel oil). In this way, the useful energy is determined from the biomass and then the fossil energy input needed to provide this useful energy is calculated. This is always done under the most realistic conditions (e.g. use of forest waste wood for heat supply replacing light fuel oil) (Kaltschmitt, 1997).

Realized Reduction

Solid biomass fuels are currently mainly used for supplying heat. In order to determine the reduction of CO_2 equivalents already undertaken, the calculations are based on the following boundary conditions:

1. The firewood and straw used in very small plants exclusively replace hard coal briquettes in single coal furnaces. Efficiencies of 65 per cent are assumed for biofuel- and fossil-fired furnaces.
2. Firewood, industrial residual wood and straw used in small plants replace half of the oil- and half of the gas-fired central heating systems. Efficiencies of 75 per cent are assumed for systems fired with solid biofuels and 86 per cent for conventional oil and gas burners.
3. The currently existing large plants essentially provide process heat and to a limited extent also district heat. They are thus competing with corresponding oil- or gas-fired heating plants, half of which are assumed to be replaced. The efficiency is about 85 per cent for modern wood- and straw-fired large-scale plants. Oil blast burners of this power class have efficiencies of 89 per cent and gas blast burners 92 per cent.

This gives substitutable fossil final energy equivalents of slightly more than 179 PJ/yr calculated from roughly 196 PJ/yr of biomass utilized at present. Due to the generally better utilization rates of fossil-fired plants, the fossil substitution potential is thus between 8 and 9 per cent below the energy input of biomass. On this basis, the additional savings of CO_2 equivalents due to the whole life cycle can be determined. In this connection, biomass is not burdened with combustion-related CO_2 emissions. Accordingly, roughly 15.4 million t/yr of CO_2 equivalents of fossil origin are not released in Germany due to the biomass utilization already realized. This corresponds to about 1.4 to 1.5 per cent compared with the roughly 1,060 million t of anthropogenic releases of CO_2 equivalents in Germany in 1995.

Additional Reduction

The reduction potential of CO_2 equivalents involved in the currently still unused technical potentials of solid biofuels, i.e. the potential from forest residual wood, demolition wood, other ligneous biomass, straw and energy crops, depends considerably on the respective use of the biomass in the energy system and thus also on the substituted fossil energy carrier. In order to analyse the entire bandwidth given in Germany, the reduction possibilities for three different, but typical variants accounting for the currently discussed spectrum of use will be determined in the following:

1. Utilization of the biomass potential still available in new small plants (up to 1 MW) to be constructed for heat supply, i.e. use in central heating plants and heating systems in households, commercial and in-

dustrial enterprises (case A "small plants"). Corresponding oil- and gas-fired small state-of-the-art plants are taken as fossil reference systems.

2. Use of the total biomass potential still usable in new large-scale plants to be constructed for supplying heat (heating plants above 1 MW) (case B "large plants") replacing corresponding oil- and gas-fired heating plants.

3. Utilization of the entire unused potential as additional fuel in existing conventional coal power plants for electricity production (case C "co-firing") balanced against existing power plants exclusively fired by hard coal and lignite. The utilization rate of an exclusively coal-fired system does not essentially change in the case of a fuel mix mainly composed of 90 per cent coal and 10 per cent biomass (Sontow, 1997).

For these three cases it is possible to determine the final energy substitution potential of fossil energy carriers corresponding to the unused biomass potential with a methodology comparable to the procedure previously applied. For the remaining technical potential from forest residual wood, demolition wood, other ligneous biomass, straw and energy crops, substitution potentials between 224 (without energy crops) and a maximum of 940 PJ/yr (energy crops on 4 million ha) are obtained for case A "small plants", between 240 and a maximum of 1,041 PJ/yr in case B "large plants" and between 263 and a maximum of 1,103 PJ/yr for case C "co-firing". On this basis, the corresponding possible reductions in CO_2 equivalents can be calculated from the respective emissions including all upstream chains as shown in Table 9.2.

Due to the still unused potential of solid biofuels in Germany, it would therefore be possible to achieve reductions of CO_2 equivalents of between 13 and a maximum of 125 million t/yr depending on the assumed fossil substitution process. The lower values of the bandwidths shown in Table 9.2 are obtained without cultivation of energy crops and the upper bound reflects an assumed energy crop acreage of 4 million ha. The lowest savings of CO_2 equivalents are to be observed if gas-fired small plants are replaced (case A "small plants" / natural gas). In contrast, the replacement of lignite in existing power plants is associated with the highest possible reductions of CO_2 equivalents (case C "co-firing" / lignite), since lignite combustion is characterized by very high specific CO_2 emissions. The CO_2 equivalents are essentially dominated by CO_2 emissions from fossil energy carriers; the other radiative forcing trace gas releases (i.e. CH_4, N_2O) hardly influence the result. The greater reduction potential in heating plants (case B "large plants") in comparison to small-scale heat supply (case A "small plants") is essentially due to the higher efficiencies of large plants com-

Table 9.2 Reduction potentials of CO_2 equivalents from technical biomass potentials in Germany

	Case A "small plants"		Case B "large plants"		Case C "co-firing"	
	Fuel oil	*Nat. gas*	*Fuel oil*	*Nat. gas*	*Hard coal*	*Lignite*
	In million t CO_2 equivalents per year					
Forest residues	6.1	4.4	6.7	4.7	9.3	10.5
Demolition wood	4.8	3.5	5.3	3.7	7.4	8.3
Other wood	0.4	0.3	0.5	0.3	0.6	0.7
Straw	6.8	4.9	7.6	5.2	10.8	12.2
Energy crops	≤ 48.5	≤ 32.3	≤ 54.9	≤ 35.4	≤ 81.9	≤ 93.3
Total 1[1]	18.1	13.1	20.1	13.9	28.1	31.7
Total 2[2]	≤ 66.6	≤ 45.4	≤ 75.0	≤ 49.3	≤ 110.0	≤ 125.0

[1] without energy crops
[2] with energy crops

pared to small plants.

In total, between 13 and 32 million t/yr of CO_2 equivalents can thus be saved by utilizing the existing unused organic residues alone (without energy crops). Of this saving potential, which can be realized on a relatively short-term basis, about one third results from forest residual wood, slightly more than one third from straw, slightly less than one third from demolition wood and about 2 per cent from other ligneous biomass. This corresponds to 1.2 to 3 per cent relative to the total anthropogenic emissions of CO_2 equivalents of roughly 1,060 million t in Germany in 1995. In the medium term, roughly 32 to 93 million t/yr of CO_2 equivalents could be avoided by the additional cultivation of energy crops on areas of up to 4 million ha. This is between 3 and just under 9 per cent relative to the currently released emissions of CO_2 equivalents. In total, the current emissions of CO_2 equivalents in Germany could thus be reduced by up to roughly 12 per cent by utilizing the previously unused potential of solid biofuels.

CO_2 *Reduction Costs*

Based on the specific useful-energy-related supply costs discussed, the corresponding reduction costs can be estimated. These are monetary expenditures to be theoretically raised when using solid biofuels as a substitute for fossil energy carriers to provide the same useful energy per tonne of avoided CO_2 equivalent. The extra costs associated with heat and electricity supply from biomass in comparison to the substitutable useful energy supply from fossil energy carriers are compared for this purpose to the corresponding savings of CO_2 equivalents. The bandwidths of the reduction costs thus obtained result from the very different and thus greatly varying supply expenditure for bioenergy carriers, which is site-dependent, and from the high expenditure for combustion techniques compared to fossil technologies. By definition, the reduction costs can only be specified for the still unused biomass potential; the reduction costs for already utilized biomass are zero or sometimes even negative.

Assuming that the still usable biomass potential is utilized in small plants (case A "small plants") and would replace light fuel oil or natural gas, reduction costs of up to 216 DM/t of CO_2 equivalent are obtained for forest residues, 104 to 293 DM/t for straw and between 79 and 386 DM/t for energy crops (Table 9.3). In contrast, only low (up to 18 DM/GJ) or no reduction costs result for demolition wood and other ligneous biomass. These figures also show that the fraction of "other ligneous biomass" and the uncontaminated demolition wood can be used most economically. Since these biomass fractions can already be largely used economically today, the reduction costs are correspondingly low. In comparison, forest residual wood utilization is on average slightly more expensive and straw utilization is much more expensive, so that the reduction costs are also correspondingly high. Only energy crop utilization is still more expensive and characterized by still higher reduction costs (Table 9.3).

Biomass options with lower heat and electricity generating costs than fossil reference systems are associated with cost savings. By definition, they do not involve any costs for the reduction of CO_2 equivalents.

Assuming, on the other hand, a utilization of these potentials in heating plants (case B "large plants"), specific reduction costs for CO_2 equivalents are obtained which are on a higher level compared to case A "small plants". In the case of a replacement of light fuel oil, for example, they range from 172 to 270 DM/t for forest residues, from 154 to 268 DM/t for straw and from 244 to 456 DM/t for energy crops. If natural gas is replaced, they are on average higher by roughly one third. Natural gas is characterized by lower specific CO_2 emissions in comparison to light fuel oil, while the heat generating costs are comparable. In this case, too, the CO_2 emissions from fossil energy carriers largely determine the result of the balances of CO_2 equivalents. These higher reduction costs in comparison to small plants are essentially due to the fact that a heat supply from biomass in

Table 9.3 **Reduction costs of CO_2 equivalents from unused technical biomass potentials (without industrial residues)**

	Case A "small plants"		Case B "large plants"		Case C "co-firing"	
	Fuel oil	*Nat. gas*	*Fuel oil*	*Nat. gas*	*Hard coal*	*Lignite*
			DM/t of CO_2 equivalents			
Forest residues	0 - 162	0 - 216	172 - 270	233 - 374	24 – 89	24 -82
Demolition wood	0 - 18	0 - 18	103 - 157	135 - 211	0	0
Other wood	0	0	103 - 123	135 - 163	0	0
Straw	104 - 21	137 - 293	154 - 268	209 - 375	6 – 81	6 - 74
Energy crops	79 - 264	109 - 386	244 - 456	362 - 691	57 – 201	53 - 179

large plants compared to that from fossil energy carriers is relatively more expensive than for small plants. The main reasons are as follows:
1. The investments for biomass firing systems are much higher due to more sophisticated combustion technology to meet the more stringent environmental protection standards.
2. There are hardly any reductions in fuel expenditure for bioenergy carriers in contrast to fossil energy carriers for purchasing larger quantities of fuel (i.e. the cost degression for fossil energy carriers is markedly greater than for biofuels).
3. The operating costs are clearly higher in comparison to fossil-fired plants.
4. The costs for ash disposal have to be considered.
5. Own funding for the plants, which is hardly affordable in contrast to small plants.

However, the still unused biomass potential can also be co-fired in existing coal power plants and can thus contribute to covering the given electricity demand. For a replacement of imported hard coal, reduction costs between 24 and 89 DM/t are obtained for forest residues, from 6 to

81 DM/t for straw and from 57 to 201 DM/t for energy crops. Conversely, no additional costs arise for demolition wood and other ligneous biomass. In the case of replacing lignite, on the other hand, the reduction costs are slightly lower (Table 9.3); this is due to the slightly lower efficiency of a lignite power plant in comparison to a hard-coal-fired steam power plant.

In total, analyses have shown that the use of uncontaminated waste wood and other ligneous biomass (including wood from wind shielding hedges, wood on the banks of rivers and lakes, along roads, railway lines and waterways, and from fruit-tree pruning) leads to the lowest reduction costs for CO_2 equivalents in all cases examined. However, the possibilities of using these biomass fractions for a reduction of the energy-related radiative forcing trace gas releases are very restricted due to the small technical potential, on the one hand, and the limited possibilities of making this biomass volume available, on the other hand. Reasons are, first, the very widely dispersed occurrence of other wood and, second, the possible pollutant load in the case of demolition wood burning and the resulting licensing problems. In contrast, the use of forest residues and straw is markedly and that of energy crops significantly more expensive. However, these biomass segments can be exploited in a simpler and less problematic manner.

Among the possibilities examined of incorporating biomass in the German energy system, co-firing in conventional coal power plants involves the lowest reduction costs. Biomass utilization in small plants for heat supply is more expensive, but still comparatively economic. In contrast, the use of organic substances in large plants for the production of process as well as district heat is characterized by the highest reduction costs on average; this also represents the possibility of a biomass utilization in the German energy system involving the highest additional costs in comparison to substitutable fossil energy carriers.

Summary and Conclusions

The aim of this section is to describe the technology, the technical potential of solid biomass and its current use, the costs for the provision of energy carriers and useful energy as well as the corresponding reduction potential and reduction costs for CO_2 equivalents in Germany. The results discussed can be summarized as follows.

1. Biogenic solid fuels can be converted into the desired useful energy by a variety of different technologies and procedures, but up to the present, combustion has been the only technology of significance. Plants

are available in all power ranges needed and permit reliable and largely low-emission operation.

2. In Germany, a technical potential of approximately 142 PJ/yr is available from forest residues, about 40 PJ/yr from industrial residual wood and roughly 81 PJ/yr from demolition wood, approximately 7 PJ/yr from other ligneous biomass, roughly 104 PJ/yr from straw and up to 840 PJ/yr from energy crops depending on the cultivated area of max. 4 million ha. Together with the current firewood consumption of roughly 85 PJ/yr this maximum potential of just about 1,300 PJ/yr corresponds to a maximum share of 13.5 per cent of the final energy consumption in Germany in 1996.

3. Part of this potential is currently already being utilized. In particular, industrial residual wood is used almost completely, forest residues at a rate of two fifths, demolition wood at a rate of nearly one seventh and straw as well as other ligneous biomass at a very small rate for meeting the energy demand. In total, roughly 196 PJ/yr of biomass including firewood is probably used at present in Germany.

4. Without this biomass which is already used in the energy system and if fossil energy carriers were used instead, the releases of CO_2 equivalents in Germany would be approximately 1.5 per cent higher (CO_2 equivalents are here understood to be the weighted sum of CO_2, CH_4 and N_2O from the aspect of the "anthropogenic greenhouse effect"), including the overall life cycle in the case of biomass and fossil energy carriers.

5. If the additionally available biomass potential including energy crops producible on a maximum of 4 million ha were utilized, the releases of CO_2 equivalents could be reduced by 45 million t/yr using this biomass in small plants as a substitute for natural gas or by 125 million t/yr using it in lignite-fired large power plants. This corresponds to a maximum of 12 per cent relative to the total emissions of CO_2 equivalents amounting to roughly 1,060 million tonnes in Germany in 1995.

6. The costs incurred for realizing this reduction potential vary within a large bandwidth. The use of uncontaminated demolition wood and other ligneous biomass (e.g. wood from wind shielding hedges, small amounts of wood on the banks of rivers and lakes, along waterways, from fruit-tree pruning) generally leads to the lowest reduction costs for CO_2 equivalents. In contrast, the use of forest residues and straw is markedly and that of energy crops significantly more expensive. Among the possibilities of incorporating biomass into the German energy system, co-firing in conventional coal power plants involves the lowest reduction costs for CO_2 equivalents. Biomass utilization for

supplying heat is slightly more expensive in small plants and significantly more expensive in large plants.

Solid biofuels could thus furnish a considerable contribution towards meeting the energy demand in Germany, exceeding by far the current level and additionally involving a marked and cost-effective reduction of the anthropogenic greenhouse effect.

References

Becher, S., Frühwald, A., Kaltschmitt, M. (1995): "CO_2-Substitutionspotential und CO_2-Minderungskosten einer energetischen Nutzung fester Biomassen in Deutschland", *BWK* 47; 1/2, pp. 33 – 38.

Hrubesch, P. (1996): "Holzverbrauch in den Haushalten Deutschlands", Study of the German Institute for Economic Research, Berlin.

IPCC, Intergovernmental Panel of Climate Change (Ed.) 1996: "Climate Change 1995 - The Science of Climate Change", Cambridge University Press, Cambridge.

Kaltschmitt, M., Reinhardt, G. A. (Ed.) (1997): "Nachwachsende Energieträger – Grundlagen, Verfahren, ökologische Bilanzierung", Vieweg, Braunschweig/ Wiesbaden.

Kaltschmitt, M., Bridgewater, A. V. (Ed.) (1997): "Biomass Gasification and Pyrolysis"; CPL-Press, Newbury.

Kaltschmitt, M. (1997): "Systemtechnische und energiewirtschaftliche Analyse der Nutzung erneuerbarer Energien in Deutschland", Habilitationsschrift, Forschungsbericht des Instituts für Energiewirtschaft und Rationelle Energieanwendung, Vol. 38, University of Stuttgart.

Kaltschmitt, M. (1994): "The Benefits and Costs of Energy from Biomass in Germany", *Biomass & Bioenergy* 6, No. 5, pp. 329 – 337.

Kaltschmitt, M., Reinhardt, G. A., Stelzer, T. (1997): "LCA of Biofuels under Different Environmental Aspects", *Biomass & Bioenergy* 12, No. 2, pp. 121 – 134.

Kaltschmitt, M.; Wiese, A. (Ed.) (1997): "Erneuerbare Energien - Systemtechnik, Wirtschaftlichkeit, Umweltaspekte", Springer, Berlin, Heidelberg.

Lux, R., Kaltschmitt, M. (1997): "Regenerative Energien zur Niedertemperaturwärmebereitstellung - Eine vergleichende energiewirtschaftliche Analyse", *Erdöl, Erdgas, Kohle* 114, No. 1, pp. 31-37.

Sontow, J., Siegle, V., Spliethoff, H., Kaltschmitt, M. (1997): "Biomassezufeuerung in Kohlekraftwerken", *Energiewirtschaftliche Tagesfragen* 47 (1997), No. 6, pp. 338 – 344.

Wegener, G., Frühwald, A. (1994): "Das CO_2-Minderungspotential durch Holznutzung", *Energiewirtschaftliche Tagesfragen* 44, No. 7, pp. 421 – 425.

10 CO_2 Reduction Potentials Through Renewable Energy Sources and Rational Energy Use in India

NARENDRA BANSAL

This chapter discusses the following aspects of CO_2 reduction potentials through the use of renewable energy sources and rational energy use in India:

1. The Indian commercial and non-commercial energy consumption.
2. The greenhouse gas emission levels.
3. The renewable energy technologies and their potential for specific CO_2 emission reductions.
4. The rational energy utilization and the potential of specific CO_2 emission reductions.

The paragraphs 1 and 2 can be considered as a supplement to Chapter 3 in Part I. The figures presented in this paper are indicative. Detailed studies need to be done to improve the data and to assess the overall reduction potentials of all greenhouse gas emissions resulting from various energy uses.

India's Commercial and Non-commercial Energy Consumption

The pattern of total energy consumption in India is shown in Figure 10.1. The non-conventional energy sources like firewood, agricultural waste and dung still contribute about 47 per cent of the total energy requirements.

There has been a steady growth in energy demand of over 6 per cent per year in the eighties corresponding to a GDP growth rate of 5.6 per cent. There has been a gradual shift to commercial sources of energy from 35 per cent of the total energy supply in 1970 to 53 per cent in 1994.

171

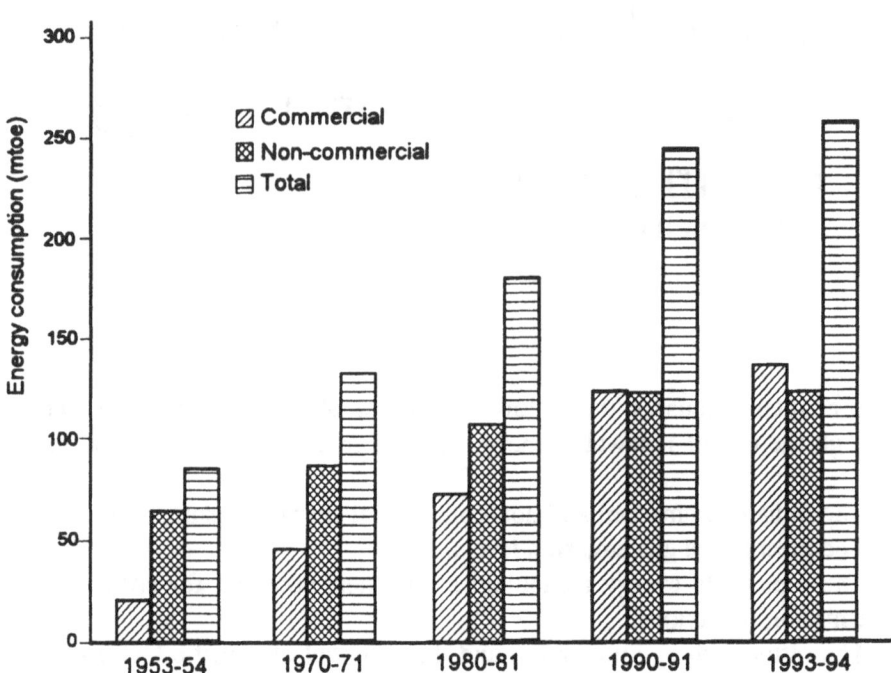

Figure 10.1 Pattern of energy consumption in India

The main primary energy sources are coal, oil, natural gas, hydro- and nuclear power, the consumption patterns of which are given in Figure 10.2, with sectoral energy consumption in Figure 10.3.

While emissions of CO_2 occur whenever fossil fuels are burnt, their rate of emission varies. The variation is primarily dependent upon the quantum of carbon and hydrogen in fuels. Coal has been and is likely to continue to be the largest primary source of commercial energy in India. At present, coal accounts for 60 per cent of fossil fuel use in calorific terms, followed by liquid petroleum (30 per cent) and the rest being accounted for by natural gas. Steel, power, cement and railways are the major industrial consumers of coal and account for over 70 per cent of domestic consumption. The present patterns of petroleum product distribution and consumption indicate that more than 80 per cent of petroleum consumption contributes to CO_2 emissions.

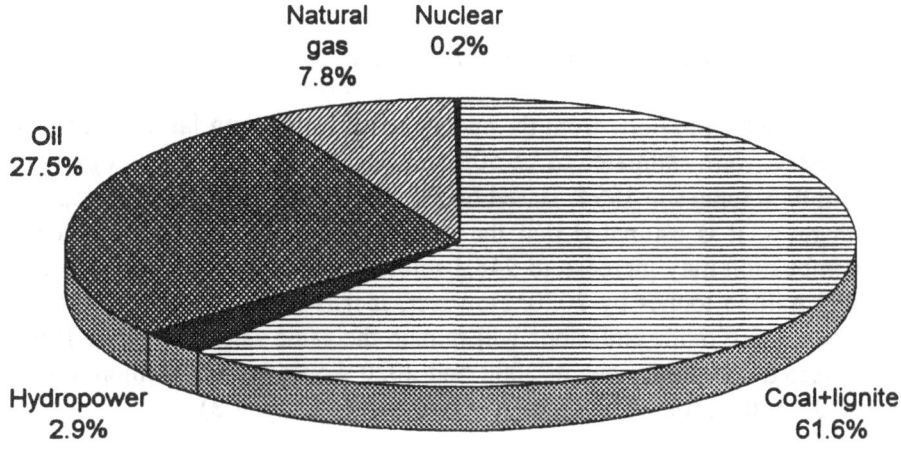

Figure 10.2 Pattern of commercial energy consumption (1995-96)

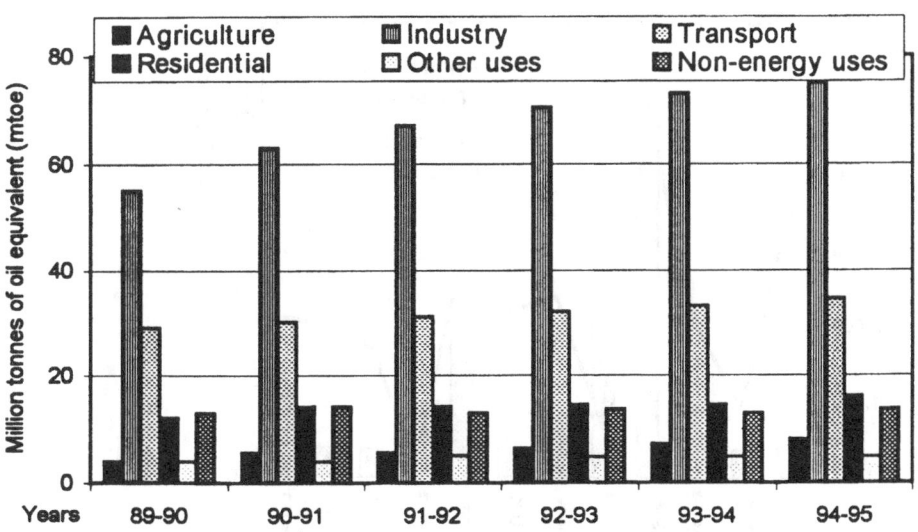

Figure 10.3 Sectoral consumption of commercial energy

Greenhouse Gas Emissions in India

CO_2 Emissions from the Energy Sector in India

Carbon dioxide emissions from the energy sector, excluding land use change and forestry, were estimated to be 508.6 million tonnes in 1990 and grew to 628.2 million tonnes in 1994. Based on the projected fossil fuel consumption growth rates, it is estimated that the carbon dioxide emissions from fossil fuel combustion may increase to 948.1 million tonnes by the year 2000 and to 2,862 million tonnes by 2020. However, if it is assumed that the growth rate of carbon dioxide emissions will remain the same as it was up to 1994, the projected CO_2 emissions in 2000 and 2020 would be 842 million tonnes and 2,233 million tonnes, respectively (see Part I, Chapter 3).

Indian Carbon Dioxide Emissions in Relation to Other Countries

India is the world's fifth largest carbon dioxide emitter but its per capita emission is very low. Figure 10.4 compares the carbon dioxide emissions of the world's dirty dozen.

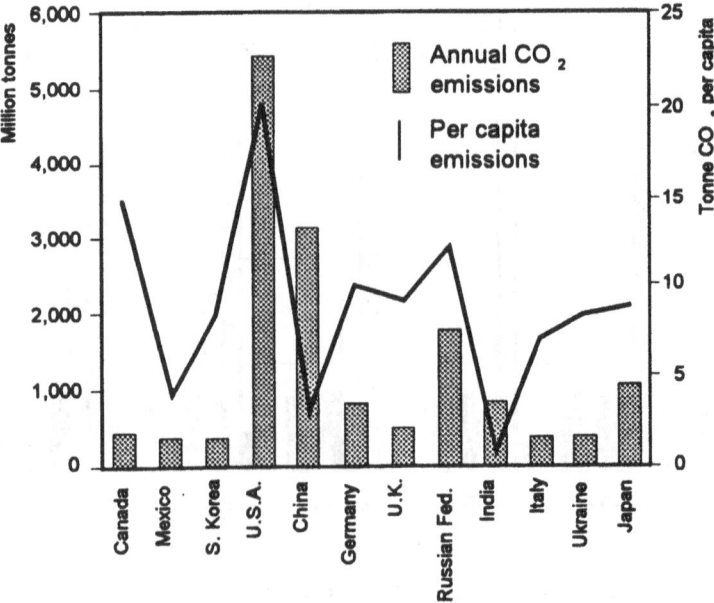

Figure 10.4 The world's top twelve CO_2 emitters

Nitrous Oxide Emissions

Nitrous oxide has 310 times the global warming potential of carbon dioxide. The major source of N_2O emissions in the country is traditional biomass burning contributing approximately 3.4 million tonnes of carbon dioxide equivalent emissions in 1990.

Methane Emissions

Methane has twenty-one times the global warming potential of carbon dioxide. Methane emissions from the Indian energy sector are confined to fugitive emissions from fossil fuel mining and handling.

The Central Mining Research Institute (CMRI) has calculated the methane emission coefficients and according to their estimates, 1.09 cubic metres of methane are emitted per tonne of coal mined by opencast methods and degree I underground mining. The methane emission coefficients for degree II and degree III underground mining are 11.07 and 23.53 m³ per tonne of coal mined, respectively. Methane emissions from coal mining and handling in 1990-91 are estimated to be 0.396 million tonnes or 8.3 million tonnes of carbon dioxide equivalent in 1990. In 1994, methane emissions from coal mining and handling increased to 0.53 million tonnes or 11 million tonnes of carbon dioxide equivalent. The IPCC emission coefficients for underground mining are more than double the CMRI coefficients and as per IPCC estimates, coal mining and handling will contribute 20.5 million tonnes of carbon dioxide equivalent. This is still not significant when compared to the net carbon dioxide emissions from the energy sector.

Fugitive emissions of methane from oil exploration, production, transport, refining and storage are 9.5 kilotonnes per year or nearly 0.2 million tonnes of carbon dioxide equivalent.

Methane emissions from natural gas production, transmission and distribution, venting and flaring are 0.63 million tonnes or 13.2 million tonnes of carbon dioxide equivalent.

Renewable Energy Technologies – Potentials, Costs and Emission Savings

The use of renewable energy sources as a replacement for fossil energy sources can contribute significantly to the reduction of CO_2. Though the current non-conventional energy sources account for merely 0.2 per cent of total power generation, their estimated potential is large as seen in Table 10.1.

A comprehensive programme to implement renewable energy technologies has been undertaken by the Ministry of Non-conventional Energy Sources (MNES). Data for achievements up to the end of March 1995 are presented in Table 10.2. Special information on the state of art of the photovoltaic technology and on promotion programmes is provided in Part II, Chapters 11 and 12. The increasing role of wind energy is discussed in Part II, Chapter 13 and the important role of biomass for energy supply is presented in detail in Part II, Chapter 14.

Technologies for power generation from wind, canal-based small hydropower projects and biomass cogeneration compare favourably with conventional power projects (Table 10.3).

Capital costs of new conventional power projects are estimated at Rs. 40 million ($\approx$ 1 million US $) per MW and the generation cost is estimated at Rs. 2.25 per kWh.

Allocations for renewable energy sources are, however, meagre, being only 0.3 per cent of the total plan expenditure for the 8th Plan. For this reason some important future technologies are not taken seriously in the Indian programme. In the long term solar produced hydrogen is a very promising option for CO_2 reduction. This, however, needs serious R&D effort with higher allocation.

Table 10.1 Renewable energy potential in India

Energy source	Estimated potential in MW
Hydropower	84,000
Small hydro	10,000
Ocean thermal power	50,000
Wave power	20,000
Tidal power	10,000
Wind energy	20,000
Solar energy	5×10^{15} kWh/year
Bio-energy	17,000
Cogenerating	8,000
Draught animal power	30,000
Energy from waste	1,000

Source: Internal documents of MNES, Government of India.

Table 10.2   Achievements in renewable energy sources

Programme	Unit	Achievement
Wind energy		
Wind farms	MW	733
Wind pumps	Nos.	3,158
Small hydro		
Mini micro	MW	129
Bio-energy		
Biomass-based cogeneration	MW	29
Biomass combustion power	MW	14
Biomass gasifiers/Stirling engines	MW	30
Family-sized biogas plants	Nos.	2.3×10^6
Community biogas plants	Nos.	1,623
Improved cookstoves	Nos.	22.6×10^6
Solar thermal		
Solar thermal systems		
- Collector area	m²	364,354
Solar cookers	Nos.	406,642
Solar PV		
Power units	KW_p	909
Community lights	Nos.	270
TV and community facilities	Nos.	640
Domestic lighting uses	Nos.	37,359
Lanterns	Nos.	81,059
Street lights	Nos.	32,870
Water pumps	Nos.	1,820

Source: MNES, Government of India.

Table 10.3   Comparative costs

	Capital cost 10^7 Rs./MW	Generation cost Rs./kWh$_{el}$
Wind power	3.5	2.3
Small hydro	3.5-6.0	1.5-3.5
Cogeneration	2.0-2.5	2.0-2.5
Solar photovoltaic (grid connected)	30	15.2
Solar thermal (grid/hybrid mode)	12	5.0-7.5
Sea wave	9.0	5.8

Based on a study by Kolb et al. (1989), the specific CO_2 emissions for power generation for various technologies are given in Table 10.4.

The last two columns in Table 10.4 show the specific savings in CO_2 emissions by the renewable energy technologies as compared to the reference technologies. Since the electricity-generating technologies have no emissions, the CO_2 emissions of the reference technology can be fully booked as savings. The CO_2 emissions of an electrically driven heat pump are relatively high because it was assumed that the driving electricity is produced by the existing power station mix of the Federal Republic of Germany (0.65 kg CO_2 /kWh$_{el}$). The electricity production emissions are assigned to the heat pump. For the coefficient of performance (ratio of total heat output to electricity input) an average number of 2.5 was assumed.

Table 10.4 Specific CO_2 emission savings

Renewable energy technology	CO_2 Emissions Kg/kWh[*]	Conventional reference technology	CO_2 Emissions kg/kWh[*]	Savings	
				kg/kWh[*]	kg/kWh[**]
Wind energy converter	0.0	Coal power plant	0.92	0.92	0.33
Photovoltaic cell	0.0	Coal power plant	0.92	0.92	0.33
Hydropower plant	0.0	Coal power plant	0.92	0.92	0.33
Electric heat pump	0.26	Oil-fired boiler	0.34	0.08	0.06
Gas heat pump	0.12	Gas-fired boiler	0.24	0.12	0.10
Solar heater	0.0	Oil-fired boiler	0.34	0.34	0.27
Biogas-fired heater	0.51[***]	Oil-fired boiler	0.34	0.34	0.27
Wood-fired heater	0.48[***]	Oil-fired boiler	0.34	0.34	0.27
Geothermal system	0.0	Oil-fired boiler	0.34	0.34	0.27

[*] CO_2 emissions related to energy output
[**] CO_2 emissions related to fossil primary energy equivalent
[***] CO_2 assimilated by growing biomass (assumption)

More favourable is the gas-driven heat pump. The figures are based on the assumption that the ratio of heat output to gas input is 1.6 and that the heat pump works as a total energy system (utilization of exhaust gas heat).

Solar water heating does not cause any CO_2 emissions, so that the emissions of the reference technology fully appear as savings.

The combustion of biogas and firewood involves significantly higher CO_2 emissions than a comparable oil-fired system. Energy uses of biomass can only contribute towards reducing the CO_2 problem if the CO_2 released is assimilated again by growing biomass. This is assumed to be the case for the specific savings of Table 10.4.

The real CO_2 reduction potential by renewable energy sources can be assessed only after the possible substitution based on a comprehensive energy and environmental policy. In any case, an estimate of the cost of CO_2 savings by implementing renewable energy sources is given in Table 10.5. The cost figures are derived from Kolb et al., 1989. They reflect only partly the present situation in India as shown by a comparison with Table 10.3. The range is due to the selected fiscal parameters, the unit size and the annual operating hours. The cost figures can only serve as a rough indicator. In the last column the additional cost per kg CO_2 saved is shown. A comparison of these numbers shows that hydropower plants have the least reduction costs. Further expansion of the hydropower capacity is desirable. At present photovoltaic cells are unfavorable due to the very high electricity generation costs. For the heat-generating systems geothermal heat and fuel wood have the lowest costs, but the expansion of their future application is also re-

Table 10.5 Estimated cost of CO_2 savings in power-generating systems

Technology	Range of energy generation costs	Additional costs compared to the reference technology[*]	Range of costs of CO_2 savings
	Rs./kWh	Rs./kWh	Rs./kg
Hydropower	2 - 5	(-2.8) - 0.2	(-3) - 0.2
Wind energy (25-55 kW)	5 - 7	0.2 - 2.2	0.2 - 2.4
Photovoltaic			
kW unit size	20 - 50	15 - 45	17 - 50
MW unit size	10-15	5.2 - 10	5.7 - 11
Wood stove	4-6	0.2 - 0.22	0.6 - 6
Solar water heater	8-20	4.2 - 16.2	12.4 - 48

[*] For reference technologies see Table 10.4

stricted because of the limited resources. Due to the uncertainty of the cost figures they should not be multiplied by the potential future CO_2 savings given in column four of Table 10.4 in order to obtain overall additional costs of CO_2-saving measures.

Some technologies have the potential for cost reductions by further technical improvement and by industrial mass production. This is valid in particular for photovoltaic cells and wind energy converters. Beyond that it can be expected that the market price for oil will rise further making renewable energies more attractive.

General Aspects of Rational Energy Use

Transportation Sector

The transportation sector is one of the major (after power) sectors contributing to environmental pollution and emission of CO_2. It is possible to achieve considerable efficiency improvements with gasoline and diesel engines. It is desirable to enforce statutory limits to the fuel consumption as has been done in the USA (Figure 10.5).

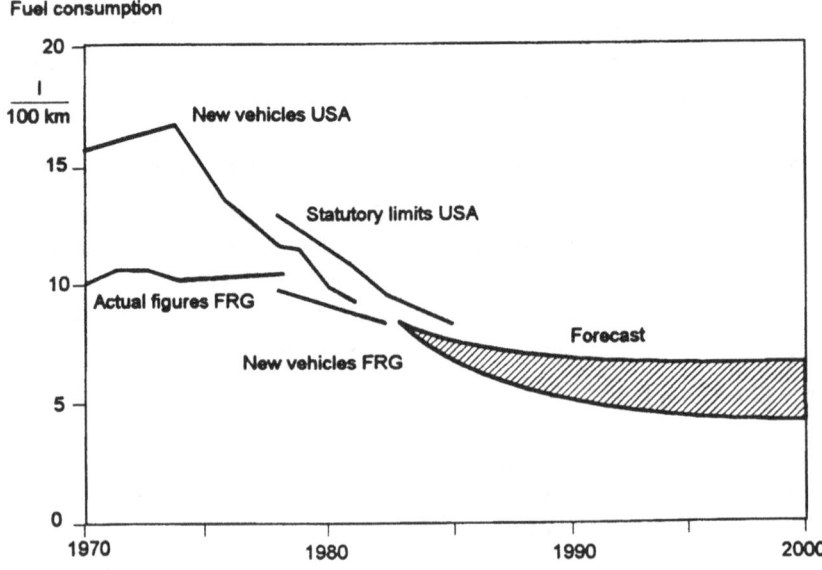

Figure 10.5   Development of fuel consumption of new cars in the USA and the Federal Republic of Germany (FRG)

The goal of reducing fuel consumption will continue by reducing vehicle weight, the drag and rolling resistance, by optimizing the transmission and drive, by increased use of fuel injection and by smaller cooling systems. An interesting market development is to be observed for diesel engines. Modern diesel engines consume up to 25 per cent less fuel than gasoline engines, i.e. the CO_2 emissions also decrease by this order of magnitude. Use of methanol, bioalcohol and vegetable oil in motor engines is a possibility. Other measures include improvement of roads, better traffic management and more efficient mass transport systems.

Industrial Sector

The industrial sector consumes nearly 50 per cent of the total energy supply with its breakdown into energy carriers as given by Table 10.6. Thus 50 per cent of the CO_2 emissions results from the industry sector. Some calculations done by Kolb et al. (1989) give figures for different industrial sectors (Table 10.7). Since no precise figures do exist for Indian industry, the figures in Table 10.7 can serve as a first indicator.

In the medium and long term, an effective strategy for reduction in energy use by industry and consequent greenhouse gas emissions is shifting to more energy-efficient process technologies. For very high energy intensive industries such as iron and steel, cement, fertilizers, and chemicals, cogeneration of electricity and process steam by industries is an important area for development.

Long-term technological solutions for building materials such as cement and bricks, some of the most energy-intensive products, will depend on development of new building materials that are less energy-intensive, non-biodegradable polymers produced from agricultural products or biotechnological processes.

In the short term, the use of efficient motors, compact fluorescent lamps or other energy-efficient lighting systems, improved refrigerators, and space conditioning systems are all candidates worth pursuing.

Table 10.6 Industrial energy consumption in India 1990

	Million tonnes	Billion kWh	Million tonnes CO_2
Coal	43.3	254.6	83.0
Oil and gas	12.1	145.2	43.6
Electricity	-	25.7	16.2

Table 10.7 CO_2 emission factors for selected efficient industries

Branch of industry	Fuels kg CO_2/ kWh	Electricity[1] kg CO_2/ kWh
Iron and steel	0.37	0.50
Chemistry	0.26	0.56
Non-metallic mineral	0.29	0.65
Cement	(0.33)	(0.65)
Brick	(0.21)	(0.65)
Lime	(0.26)	(0.65)
Paper and pulp	0.27	0.47
Non-ferrous metals	0.25	0.65
Industry in total	0.26	0.63

[1] Taking into consideration the primary energy input in industrial self-supply of electricity

Fossil Power Plants

One of the largest sources of carbon dioxide emissions in the country is the electric power sector which is heavily dependent on coal as a fuel - coal that contains up to 50 per cent ash or inert matter - which exacerbates the problem of low conversion efficiency and present technology based on pulverized coal combustion. Only 60 per cent of the Indian coal-fired power plants operate at an efficiency of over 30 per cent, averaging around 33 per cent, with a few of the best power plants operating at an efficiency of 34.5 per cent. 25 per cent of the coal-based power plants operate at an efficiency of between 20 and 30 per cent and the rest at below 20 per cent. The coal-fired power plants need to adopt efficiency improvements as regular operation and maintenance practices along with the modernization and rehabilitation of old power plants to enable them to operate at optimum possible efficiency given the life of the plant and the wear and tear of its components. Many power plants are in need of urgent renovation and modernization to extend their lives and maximize power production from the present installed capacity.

The power sector in India consumes about 160 million tonnes of coal and about 6 million tonnes of petroleum products per year, releasing 310 million tonnes of CO_2 into the atmosphere. This contributes to nearly 40 per cent of the total CO_2 emissions. A major improvement in the efficiency of power generation will not only increase the utilization capacity but also reduce CO_2 emissions. Conventional power plants typically have the following efficiencies:

Coal	0.38
Lignite	0.37
Oil	0.39
Natural gas	0.40

There are many methods to improve these efficiencies as shown in Figure 10.6. The possible efficiencies and CO_2 reductions are given in Table 10.8.

Residential and Commercial Sector

Though accurate estimates are not available about energy consumptions in the residential and commercial sectors, it is however estimated that 25 per cent of the commercial energy is used in India for space heating and cooling and lighting. Depending on the energy consumed per m² of floor area, some of the figures are given in Table 10.9.

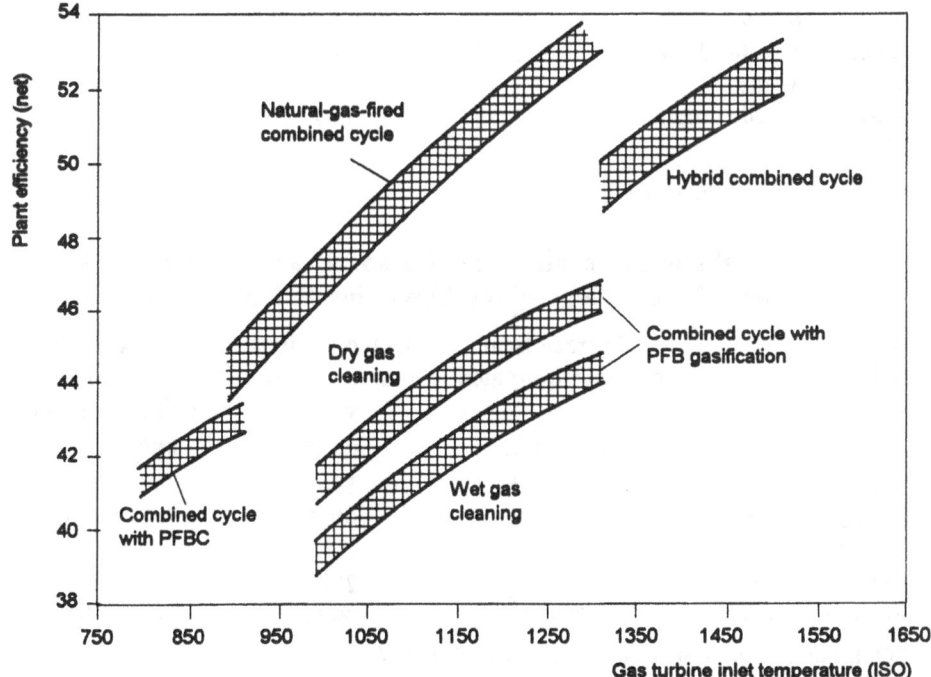

Figure 10.6 Efficiency comparison of advanced power plant concepts

Table 10.8 Efficiencies and CO_2 emissions of fossil power plants

Technology	Net efficiency (at full load)	CO_2 emissions (kg/kWh_{el})	Specific CO_2 reduction related to conventional systems (%)
Hard-coal-fired power plants			
Conventional hard-coal-fired power plant with desulphurization and DeNO$_x$	0.38	0.87	
Combined cycle with PFBC	0.415	0.80	8
Integrated gasification combined cycle (IGCC)	0.42	0.79	9
IGCC with hot gas cleaning	0.45	0.73	16
Hybrid combined cycle	0.48	0.69	21
IGCC with natural gas turbine[*]	0.415	0.73	16
In comparison: natural gas combined cycle	0.51	0.37	57
Natural-gas- and oil-fired power plants			
Conventional oil-fired power plant	0.39	0.70	-
Oil-fired combined cycle	0.49	0.55	21
Conventional natural-gas-fired power plant	0.40	0.48	-
Natural-gas-fired combined cycle	0.51	0.37	23

[*] 82 % hard coal, 18 % natural gas

Table 10.9 Final energy requirements for space heating and CO_2 emissions for buildings with different insulating standards

Building standard	Average final energy requirement kWh/m²a	CO_2 emissions[1] (current heating stock) kg/m²a	CO_2 savings (related to building stock) kg/m²a (%)
Houses in stock[2]	220-270	59-73	-
Heat Insulation Ordinances 1982[2]	150-180	40-49	19-24 (32-34)
Swedish standard	100-120	27-32	32-41 (54-56)
Low-energy[3] houses	30-70	8-19	51-54 (74-86)

[1] CO_2 factor: heating systems in stock 0.27 kg CO_2/kWh
[2] In Germany
[3] Intensified heat insulation, ventilation system with heat recovery

References

EIS (1996): Economic Intelligent Service, Centre for Monitoring Indian Economy, Private Ltd., Bombay.

GOI (1996): "Economic Survey 1995-96", Government of India Publications, New Delhi.

Kolb, G., Eickoff, G., Kleemann, M., Crzykalla, N., Pohlmann, M., Wagner, H.-J. (1989): "CO_2 -Reduction Potential Through Rational Energy Utilization", Jul-Spez-502, KFA-STE Internal Report, Research Centre Jülich, Germany.

Wagner, H.-J. and Walbeck, M. (1988): "CO_2-Emissions due to Energy Supply", *Energiewirtschaftliche Tagesfragen*, Heft 2, (in German).

Walbeck, M. and Wagner, H.-J. (1987): "Anhalts-Zahlen für die CO_2 Emissionen durch die Energieversorgung", KFA-STE, IB-1/87, Internal Report (in German).

11 Status of Photovoltaic Science and Technology in India

VIRESH DUTTA AND PRABHAT KUMAR KONER

Introduction

The sun has always been treated reverentially in India and was recognized as the source of life in ancient literature. The utilization of solar energy for solar thermal applications is well known and widespread. Sir J.C. Bose had contemplated a wider usage for solar energy, since it is available in abundance ($5x10^{15}$ kWh/yr) throughout the country. This suggestion was ahead of its time, though the photovoltaic (PV) effect had been discovered in 1839 by Becquerel in an electrochemical cell and in 1877 by Adams and Day in selenium (Green, 1990; Dutta, 1994). The oil crisis of 1973 provided the fillip for renewable sources of energy in general and solar (photothermal and photovoltaic) energy in particular. The initial efforts of research and development in the universities and national institutes/laboratories had been mainly for developing photovoltaic devices for space applications. This now encompasses terrestrial applications, keeping stride with international efforts in this area (Garg and Dutta, 1995). The governmental effort promoted the applications of PV systems in the form of demonstration projects and this has slowly found acceptance in the market place. As more and more systems are being developed and implemented all over the country, PV has assumed the role of one of the leading renewable sources of energy.

Solar Photovoltaic Energy System

A solar photovoltaic (SPV) system comprises a PV array for converting the solar energy into the required voltage (series connection of modules) and current (parallel connection of modules in the panel) to run the DC/AC appliances by means of appropriate storage and interfacing devices (Balance of System or BOS) (Bureau of Indian Standard, 1989; Bhattacharya, 1991). Storage is generally in the form of electrochemical batteries (Pb-acid e.g.) which provides the electrical energy storage for operating the load during the night or no sunshine days. Special batteries are available which allow deep discharge (75 per cent from top) without any damage to the batteries. The batteries can be sealed for mobile applications or vented for stationary application. These require maintenance by way of topping, contact cleaning etc. and have limited life (1,000 cycles of charging/discharging at C/10). A variety of charge controllers are available in the country to maintain proper charging and discharging of batteries for enhanced operation lifetime. Since most PV systems are installed in remote areas, the requirement for maintenance-free or low-maintenance batteries is obvious. Several battery manufacturers have introduced such batteries specially for PV applications (Chaurey and Deambi, 1992). High-efficiency, high-frequency inverters have been developed for operating PV lighting systems. Use of CFL (5, 7, 9 or 11 W) lamps allows more effective utilization of expensive PV electricity in the form of higher light output. Availability of high efficiency inverters for utility applications has been poor, since most inverters for conventional AC appliances have an efficiency of about 75 per cent, unlike the international figures for PV inverters (about 90 per cent or above). Grid-interactive PV inverters have been designed for experimental purposes and more effort is needed in this direction.

Single-Crystal Si Solar Cells Manufacturing

Figure 11.1 shows a block diagram of the different steps involved in solar cell module manufacturing. It is heartening to note that all the processes are available in the country and have been developed under an active collaboration between academic institutions and PV industries. The METKEM-IISc (Vasudevan, 1997) process utilizes hydrogen reduction of $SiCl_4$ for the production of Si, which is then used for crystal growing by means of the standard Czochralski technique. The Si ingots are cut into wafers by diamond-impregnated internal diameter (ID) cutters or by a multiple wire saw.

There are several solar cell manufacturers (Central Electronics, Bharat Heavy Electricals Limited (BHEL), Udhaya Semiconductors, Renewable Energy System etc.), who utilize indigenously available or imported solar-grade Si for cell fabrication. Some other companies (WEBEL-SL, Pentafour etc.) have imported cell fabrication technology. As shown in Figure 11.1, cell fabrication has several steps (Parthasarathi, Madhaven and Kaul, 1994), all of which are critical for obtaining high efficiency and yield over a large number of wafers used for device fabrication. The starting point is the

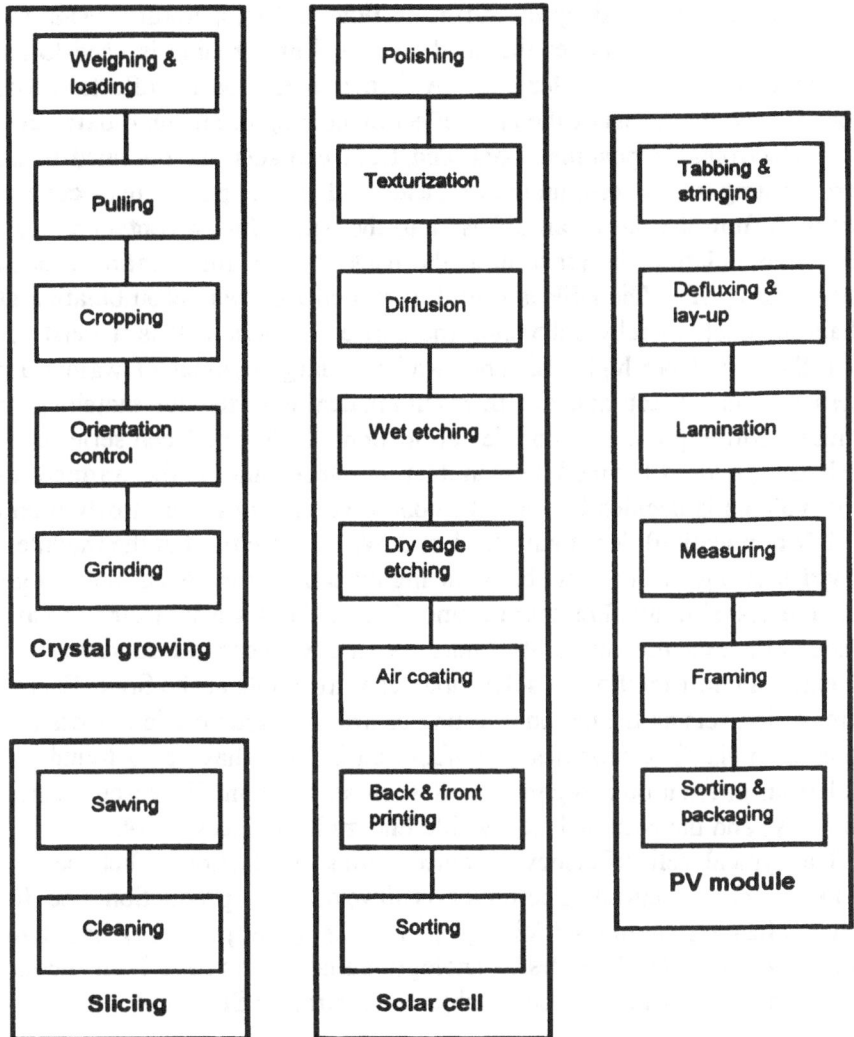

Figure 11.1 Block diagram showing Si crystal, solar cell and module processing

cleaning and polishing of wafers to remove any contaminants like grease and saw marks from wafer cutting. A surface texturization by chemical etching creates pyramidal structures on the surface which results in light trapping, thereby reducing reflection from the surface. Diffusion of phosphorus through the textured surface converts the top of the wafer into n^+, with the diffusion depth controlled by the diffusion time and temperature inside the furnace. Wet etching removes the dead layer and dry etching is used to remove shunt paths at the wafer edge. A further reduction in reflection loss can be effected by means of the anti-reflection coating of silicon dioxide created by electroless deposition. Back and front contacts are obtained using screen printing of silver-aluminium paste and silver paste, respectively. Aluminium from the paste can diffuse into the wafer during contact annealing, thus annihilating the junction at the back contact and creating a back surface field (BSF). The BSF is useful in reducing carrier recombination at the back contact, thereby enhancing the carrier collection. It is a must for solar cells made from high-resistance wafer. A large number of wafers are processed in one batch and are then automatically sorted for matching at maximum power point for module fabrication. A 33- or 36-cell series-connected string is used for module manufacture. Depending on the wattage required (voltage is decided by the cells connected in series and mostly refers to a 12 V application), less than 1/2, 1 or 2 W_p cells are used in the modules. The series string is enclosed between highly transparent glass and tedlar sheets and sealed in an aluminium frame. The modules are subjected to various standard tests for suitability under harsh environmental conditions. A more elaborate test facility for solar modules is available at the Solar Energy Centre, which acts as the national testing centre for photovoltaic devices and systems in India. The modules manufactured in India have also found approval from international organizations such as the Joint Research Centre, Ispra (Italy) and the National Renewable Energy Laboratory, USA.

The typical cell efficiency obtained during production is between 12 and 14 per cent. Central Electronics is developing a production line for commercialization of high-efficiency solar cells (>18 per cent) based on University of New South Wales technology. Initial efforts have been encouraging and high efficiency has been achieved on circular Si wafers.

Thin-Film Solar Cells Manufacturing

These are major contenders for replacing single-crystal Si devices for large-scale PV application at a relatively low cost. This optimism stems from the advantages offered by thin-film technology (Chopra and Das, 1990) - less material required, use of different types of substrates, low process temperatures, possibility of integrated manufacturing process etc. The efficiency of these cells for small areas has already reached >10 per cent in labs (Bloss,

Pfisterer, Schubert and Walter, 1995). The research effort is now aimed at adapting all the process steps for production of these cells over a large area. The major materials for this category of cells are:

1. copper indium diselenide (CIS),
2. cadmium telluride (CdTe) ,
3. thin-film Si and
4. amorphous Si .

CIS is a promising photovoltaic material in view of its near ideal band-gap and it can be deposited by a variety of techniques like co-evaporation, selenization of Cu/In layers. Internationally, the active area cell efficiency for $CuInGaSe_2$ (CIGS) solar cells has reached 17.7 per cent for an area of 0.41 cm^2, which is a record for all thin film solar cells (Gay, 1996). Ga alloying has been a key development in achieving such efficiencies. The effective band-gap increases thus raising the open-circuit voltage with a slight reduction in short circuit current. The window layer of CdS is normally deposited by the solution growth technique. Attempts have been made to replace this layer by other n-type films eliminating Cd from the cell structure. In fact, by varying the doping levels in CIGS, CdS and conducting oxides, it is perceived that more efficient cell structures can be created.

The IACS Calcutta group has adopted the co-evaporation technique, in which three separate sources of Cu, In and Se evaporation are used for the deposition of CIS under controlled conditions (Bhattacharya, Dutta, Chaudhuri and Pal, 1996). A composite CIS film, having the initial film with excess Cu followed by a film with excess (In+Se), is used as the absorber layer. The CIS cell efficiency with this design yields a cell with 11.4 per cent efficiency. Alloying with Ga, improvements in CdS window layer and contact materials are required for further enhancement in efficiency to achieve a value of 15 per cent and above. The University of Tirupathi group is working on the selenization process for CIS solar cells.

CdTe with its band-gap of 1.5 eV has been thought of as the best semiconductor for PV applications. This has been proven by the fact that efficiency in the range of 12–17 per cent has been reported by several groups preparing CdTe by a variety of techniques (closed space sublimation (CSS), electroplating, spray pyrolysis etc.). The NPL Delhi group is developing the electroplating technology and the IIT Delhi group is developing the spray technology for CdTe solar cells. Efficiency values of 8 per cent have been achieved for CSS CdTe with in-situ $CdCl_2$ treatment. In situ $CdCl_2$ treatment (Paulson and Dutta, 1996) has been found to improve the microstructural and electronic properties of the CdTe films, which then improves the efficiency. Improvement in other cell layers is expected to enhance efficiency beyond 10 per cent. A thin CdS window layer is a must in order to have an increased blue response of the cells. Use of dual SnO_2 improves Voc for cells using thin CdS. One of the major problems facing these cells is the rear contact to CdTe. CdTe cannot be easily doped due to self-compensation effects (and hence the layer is highly resistive) and has a high work function. No metal can, therefore, make proper ohmic contact with CdTe. Graphite paste doped with copper has been shown to be one of the best contact materials. The other way to make contact is to etch the CdTe surface before contact metal (Au) deposition. The etching makes the surface Te rich (and hence p+). However, both graphite contact and etching/contact deposition are not well understood and are still the subject of research. Electroless Ni-P has been reported to make good contact with CdTe (Ghosh, 1996).

There are two companies, Ecosolar in Pune and Polyplex in Delhi, who are trying to produce CdTe solar cell modules prepared by physical vapour deposition and screen printing, respectively. Obtaining large area CdTe film for modules is a critical problem which is being solved by these companies. Toxicity-related issues are of great importance for CdTe cells, because of the use of Cd in cell structure. Extreme care is taken in laboratories and industry to establish ways of limiting researchers exposure to Cd.

Use of compound semiconductors in CdTe and CIS solar cells can lead to degradation over the required period of operation (10 yrs. or more). Unlike Si solar cells, the Si thin-film cell on an inexpensive ceramic substrate combines the advantages of Si with those of thin film technology. With an efficiency of about 15 per cent for 1 cm^2 area these cells have proven that such cells can be manufactured at a lower cost than any other commercial cell. The Jadavpur University group is establishing a liquid-phase epitaxy Si facility to make these solar cells. The cell design requires diffusion lengths of about 100 μm by grain boundary passivation, use of light trapping etc.

Amorphous Si solar cells utilize the better optical absorption characteristics of amorphous Si and the possibility of doping/alloying hydrogenated amorphous Si. The plasma CVD technique used for deposition has been successfully developed for large-area deposition, making a-Si:H a major macroelectronic material with applications in other areas also. The device structure utilizes a p-i-n structure with light absorption in the i-layer and then the internal field causes drift conduction for photogenerated carrier separation. Such single junction solar cells have yielded efficiencies >10 per cent for small areas. For as-deposited devices, however, photodegradation due to the Staebler-Wronski (SW) effect results in a rapid decrease in cell efficiency initially which then stabilizes. An (engineering) approach to counteract the SW effect is to have thin absorber layers, so that the high electric field present removes the photogenerated carriers before the dangling bond states are created. However, in order to effectively absorb the solar spectrum, such thin absorber layers have to be made into a tandem structure. The reported efficiency of a triple junction solar cell is 13.7 per cent for small areas and 10.2 per cent for modules (Bloss, Pfisterer, Schubert and Walter, 1995).

The Energy Research Unit, IACS Calcutta has developed double junction solar cell technology (Barua, Roy and Chandhuri, 1996). The cell shows an efficiency of 10 per cent with a stabilized efficiency of 8 per cent. Using a-SiGe:H for the bottom cell and a-SiC:H or a-SiO:H for the top cell, a triple junction cell can be created.

A pilot plant facility has been established for a-Si modules by BHEL and MNES at Gwalpahari near Delhi (Bhattacharya, Reddy, Singh, Saxena, Prasad, Kumar, Nangia, Bhatnagar and Barua, 1997). Single junction technology is used to fabricate the module using glass-in-panel-out technology. Figure 11.2 shows a block diagram of the process steps involved in this tech-

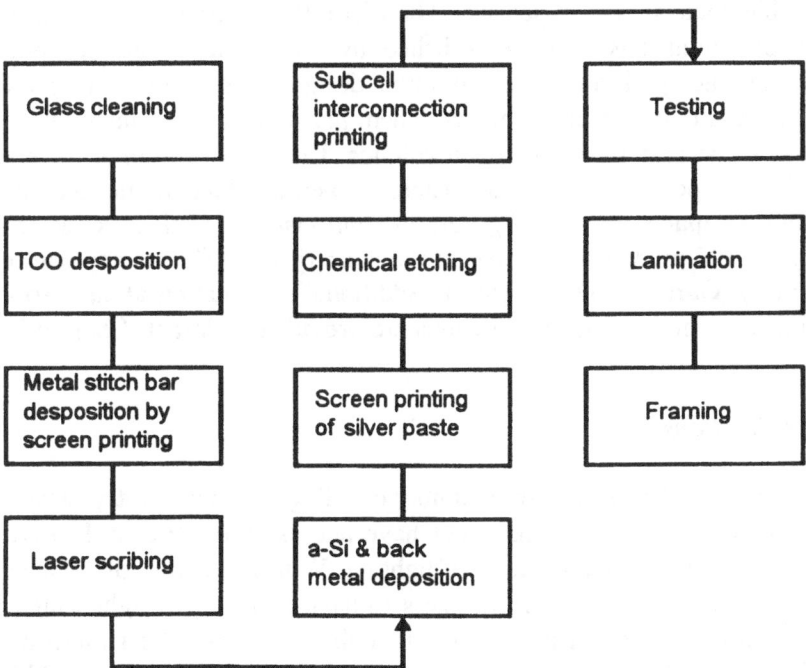

Figure 11.2 Block diagram of a-Si:H thin film solar cell manufacturing

nology. The glass substrate (30x30 cm) is cleaned in a cleaning station using a detergent solution and manual scrubbing. A clean and dry substrate is inserted into a conveyrized atmospheric pressure chemical vapour deposition system for the deposition of SiO_2 and SnO_2:F. The top grid pattern is screen printed on the TCO coated substrate and then laser scribed to create isolated strips of cells. Sequential depositions of P, I and N a-Si:H layers are done in separate PECVD chambers. A top silver contact is deposited to complete the cell structure. 75 subcells are thus created which are interconnected (isolating the poorer cells) to make the module. A typical module output is 4.5 W after deposition and there is about 25–30 per cent light degradation due to the SW effect.

Several different types of PV cells and modules are available on the Indian market.

Photovoltaic Applications

In spite of the advantages like low pollution, little/no maintenance and operation cost, modularity, reliability and long life-time, PV is not commercially viable because it is expensive. Therefore, the suitability of PV in different applications has to be established by considering socio-economic, techno-economic, pollution cost, optimum design, load profile of specific application and environmental factors. Then, the stand-alone remote DC application can be best suited for photovoltaics. Unlike other sources of electricity, the cost per unit of electrical energy generated does not depend drastically on the capacity of the PV generating unit installed. This is reflected in the range of PV products available in the country for different applications (Table 11.1) (Garg and Dutta, 1995). Additional information about various possibilities of photovoltaic applications are provided in Part II, Chapter 12.

Rural Applications

Solar lanterns   There is a large number of villages in the country, where a large population resides and does not have access to electricity. Kerosene lanterns have been the main source of lighting. With the advent of solar lanterns, it is now possible for the villagers to have a source of light which is cheaper, non-polluting and has a high availability factor. The lantern consists of a CFL-5 light source operated by means of a 12 V, 25 – 40 kHz high-efficiency (>80 per cent) inverter. A sealed lead-acid battery stores the

Table 11.1 Photovoltaic systems for different applications

Rural applications	Remote applications	Urban applications
Lighting system: street, solar lantern, domestic and community	Telecommunication and telemetry	Grid-connected peak saving applications
Communication application: telephone sets and exchange	Satellite applications, Antarctica and Mount Everest expedition	PV in buildings
Water pumping: irrigation and drinking water	Cathodic protection: oil, gas, water pipelines etc.	Captive/emergency power generation
Health application: water purification and medical refrigeration	Lighthouses, warning lights at airports and railway level crossings	Petrol and diesel dispensing station
Recreational application: power for radio, TV etc.	Hydrometeorological stations, offshore platform	-
Village power plant	Remote defence applications, solar fencing	-

solar electricity from a 10 W module during sunshine hours. The battery's state of charge is maintained using a low-loss charge controller. PV lighting for higher light output using CFL-7, 9, 11 lamps for domestic, community and street lighting is also manufactured. Obviously an enhanced PV generation and battery storage is required in such systems.

Solar water pumps PV water pumps utilize DC or AC pumps (centrifugal, submersible etc.) to lift water from wells, streams etc. at different depths. The water pumps can then be used for irrigation and drinking water. They are particularly suitable for irrigation since the water output from the pumps and water consumption are highly correlated.

As the cost of PV modules has decreased over the years and higher-efficiency photovoltaic pumps have become available, the cost of PV water pumps has decreased steadily and these pumps are found to be cost-competitive with conventional diesel pumps. A study conducted by the Administrative Staff College of India (ASCI), taking into account technical evaluation and user response, on the performance of photovoltaic pumps showed a high user satisfaction with the overall performance of the system.

Solar refrigerators The availability of health care in villages has been poor. One of the reasons is that the medicines, vaccines etc. are not easily available. The lack of electricity means that these cannot be stocked. Vaccine refrigerators operated on PV are therefore a viable alternative and have been recommended for global immunization by WHO. The reliable performance of PV-operated refrigerators is helping to extend the benefits of modern medicines and vaccines to the villagers. PV-operated radio and TV have also been made available to provide infotainment all over the country. Apart from the economic benefits, the sociological impact in terms of imparting education and information about health, agriculture etc. is enormous.

Large grid connected units Two 100 kW grid-interactive power plants are installed at the villages of Kalyanpur in the Aligarh district and Saraisadi in the Mau district in Uttar Pradesh as a demonstration project for grid-connected rural application. From each of these, 25 kW of power is fed to the grid, while the remaining 75 kW of power is used to energize domestic lights (600), street lights (60), campus lights and irrigation pumping sets in each village. The total cost of Kalyanpur and Saraisadi is Rs. 42.5 million and Rs. 45.0 million respectively. The PV modules cost is around 55 per cent, the battery cost 7–15 per cent, the PCU is around 10 per cent and the cost of electrical and mechanical parts, appliance including transmission and distribution lines, etc. is around 20 per cent, and the cost of all civil works (residences, battery room, land development etc.) is around 10 per cent of the total cost.

Figure 11.3 shows the number of PV systems for lighting and water pumping installed in different years since 1992-93. It can be noted that the number of solar lanterns and domestic lights are increasing, showing the preference of villagers for individual lighting as against street lighting. The data for 1996-97 take into account the number of PV systems up to Dec.'96 and not Mar.'97, as in other years. In fact, the number is expected to increase.

Remote Applications

The telecommunication network has been expanding to cover all the parts of the country by means of satellite and land-based equipment. This requires locating equipment like telephone exchanges, repeater stations, satellite ground stations etc. in remote and inaccessible places. The Department of Telecommunications (DOT) has recognized the inherent advantages of PV

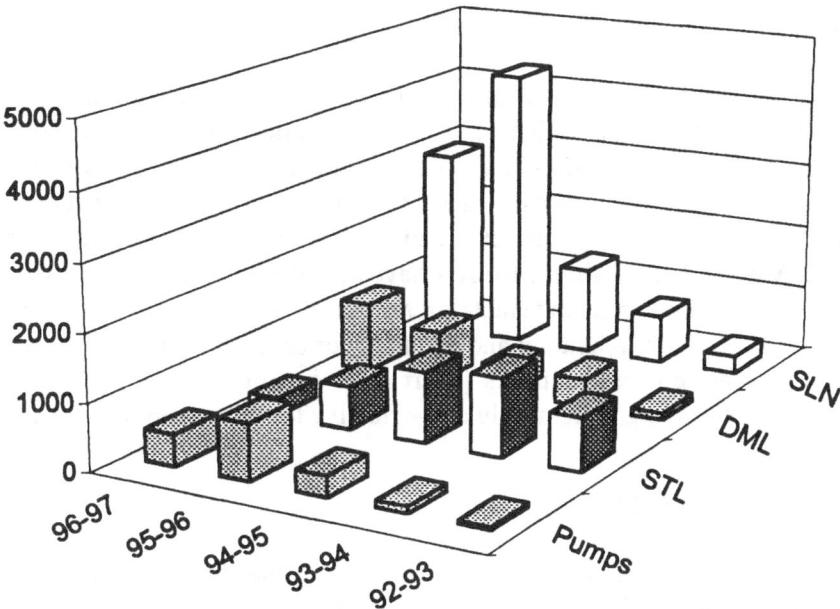

(SLN - solar lanterns; DML - domestic lighting; STL - street lighting)

Figure 11.3 Number of PV systems for rural applications installed in different years

power generation to operate this equipment reliably without much maintenance. In fact, DOT is a major consumer of PV modules in the country. The
systems mostly require low power (a few hundred to 4-5 kW), which can be
easily generated by properly designed PV systems, even for places where the
insolation is low. PV generation will in future play the role of "conventional"
power generators for such systems.

Cathodic protection There are underground pipelines carrying various
types of fluids across the country over large distances. These pipelines are
subject to electro-chemical corrosion and need to be protected by supplying
charge through an anode (cathodic protection). A voltage has to be applied
to cause corrosion of the sacrificial anode instead of the pipeline. Indeed, this
method requires a reliable electric generator for the remote areas through
which the pipelines pass. A 140 W_p PV generator along with a 150 AH battery storage can protect a 10 km pipeline. An electronic control unit to control the anode current, which depends on the soil potential, a charge control-

ler and lightening protection unit are also required (Mishra, Joshi, Roy and Gupta, 1996).

Railway signalling   PV-based railway signalling eliminates the dangers of unmanned rail crossings which have been the cause of several accidents throughout the country. Since PV modules are not affected by poisonous gases and many other chemicals, these modules have found applications in the offshore platforms for telemetry and other applications. Indian expeditions to Antarctica and Mount Everest have also demonstrated the effectiveness of PV modules in such remote areas. As the cost of transportation of diesel, grid extension, operation and maintenance cost etc. has to be added to the conventional power generators (apart from the normal cost factors), PV generators are proving increasingly cost-effective for remote applications.

Various Aspects of Urban Applications

The demand for electricity has been growing in urban areas, leading to severe power shortage throughout the year. This has led to a proliferation of inverters/diesel generators (DG) sets to combat load shedding and has resulted in dependence on utility electricity for battery charging and utilization of diesel for electricity generation. Overloading of transformers and conductors, harmonic injection has further deteriorated the quality of power.

PV output is in general highly correlated with the local distribution system peak loads. Thus, PV can reduce the thermal overloads of transformers and conductors. Since the current and power flowing through these can be limited to their rated capacity, this obviates the need for reconductoring the line, upgrading the transformer bank or addition of new circuitry. Further, such a PV system can reduce electrical loss, provide kVAr support, and increase reliability. PV studies in the USA have also proven that PV can be an economic alternative, taking into account all the benefits accrued, to serve the utility supply and demand side needs (Wenger, Hoff, Shugar and Farmer, 1994).

A first order cost analysis of photovoltaics power generation and DG power generation for urban emergency load has been made to evaluate its suitability in urban areas (Koner and Dutta, 1998). The unit cost of emergency load energy is calculated by using different parameters like the interest rate of commercial loans at the present value of the Indian market, the Indian Renewable Energy Development Agency (IREDA) loan facility to promote PV, the depreciation cost, operation and maintenance cost of PV and DG sets, and the fuel cost of DG sets. The unit cost of PV energy is found to be cheaper or comparable to the unit cost of existing DG-generated energy for emergency application for up to 500 hours of load shedding. The PV emergency generation system can also serve towards peak saving at the site.

The pollution cost of DG, increasing trend of salary/wages hike in the operation of DG, escalation of fuel price and decreasing trend in PV system cost are also favourable to PV economics. The modular characteristics of the PV system lead to the use of decentralized generation units to save wiring loss and cost and to provide for the stepwise expansion of power generation according to growing demand. PV-operated petrol pumps for dispensing petrol and diesel have been operating in several locations. A programme is under way to boost this application on a national basis.

Technological Growth of PV in India

During the period 1985 to 1990, domestic photovoltaic module production was in the range of 0.8 MW to 1 MW per year. In the last six years, the annual production of PV modules has increased significantly and in the year 1996 production was 800 per cent compared to 1990 production (Bhargava, 1995). The turnover of the PV industry, over Rs. 250 crores (1 crore = 10 million), during 1995-96 is almost double that of 1993-94 (Rs. 130 crores). The production of PV modules was 8 MW during 1995/96. The production of PV cells and PV modules in different years is given in Figure 11.4. It can be seen that there is a gap between the production of PV cells and PV modules. The production of PV modules during 1995-96 is just the double of the production of PV cells, the excess demand for PV cells is met by imported cells. METKEM produces 30 tonnes of polysilicon ingot equivalent to the 24 tonnes of monocrystalline ingots which produced 2 million wafers during 1996, against the demand of about 4 million wafers (Vasudevan, 1997).

The Ministry for Non-conventional Energy Sources has the distinction of being the only such ministry around the world. The ministry is promoting different sources of non-conventional energy including the PV activity through the state nodal agencies. According to the annual reports (Ministry of Non-conventional Energy Sources), the cumulative capacity of PV installed in India up to March '97 is 27 MW. 42 per cent is rural telecommunication, 8.8 per cent street lighting, 8.7 per cent PV pump, 7.8 per cent rural home lighting, 5.5 per cent PV power plant, 4.5 per cent solar lantern and 22.7 per cent is for other applications of PV (Figure 11.5).

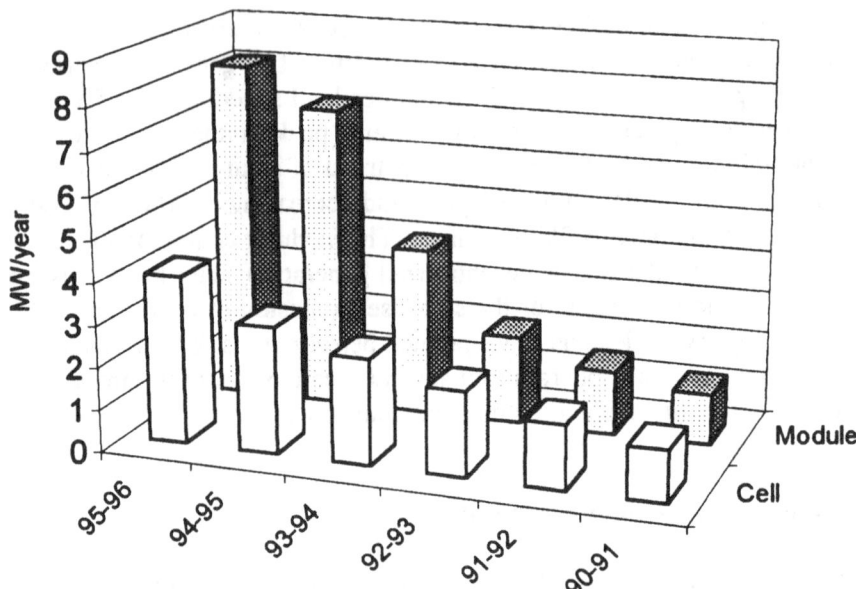

Figure 11.4 Production of PV cells and modules in different years

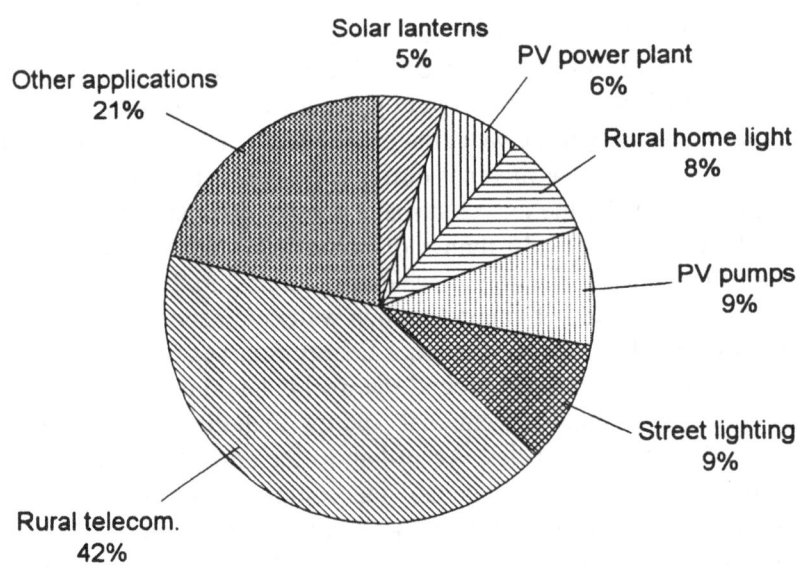

Figure 11.5 Distribution of total installations for different applications based on PV systems

In November 1995, the Ministry launched a scheme to augment and supplement grid power by installing photovoltaic power projects in the range of 25 - 100 kW for two niche applications:
1. rooftop systems on public buildings to demonstrate peak load shaving applications in major urban centres,
2. distributed grid T&D support systems in remote rural areas at tail-end grid sections.

Financial Assistance for PV

There is a reduced rate of customs duty and exemption of excise duty for the imported materials, equipment and systems related to PV technologies, and sales tax exemption on PV products to promote the growth of PV industries in India. The customs duty on raw materials like silicon ingots and silicon wafers, consumables for manufacturing silicon wafers, solar cells, modules etc. is only 15 per cent. Capital equipment for PV and related silicon industries can be imported by paying customs duty of only 25 per cent. The customs duty is 35 per cent to import complete solar cells, PV modules and PV systems.

A direct subsidy is available to the users of solar lanterns and PV pumps by MNES as follows:
1. Rs. 1,500 per lantern and
2. Rs. 125 per W_p for PV arrays up to 1.5 lakhs (1 lakh = 100,000) per system.

The maximum subsidy of 2 crores at the rate of 66 per cent of project cost for urban roof top peak load shaving application is also available at present.

The PV technology involves high initial investment and there is little encouragement from commercial banks or conventional financial institutions. The Indian Renewable Energy Development Agency (IREDA) has been established to cater to this need. A soft loan is provided to PV users/manufacturers at an interest rate of 2.5-5 per cent to cover 80–85 per cent of the project cost, with a moratorium of 1-2 years and a repayment period of 8-10 years (Indian Renewable Energy Development, 1997). IREDA is also responsible for implementing the projects under World Bank assisted schemes (e.g. Photovoltaic Market Transformation Initiative). 39 projects with an aggregate PV capacity of 531 kW_p have been sanctioned.

Testing, Standardization and Reliability

A National Photovoltaic Test Facility (NPTF) has been established at the Solar Energy Centre, Gwalpahari, Haryana with the equipment necessary for the testing and evaluation of solar cells, modules (according to the JRC-Ispra specification 503), balance of system components, and complete systems to ensure high product quality. The following tests are available: I-V characteristics and efficiency in STC and outdoor conditions, hot spot endurance, visual inspection of cracks, deformation of cells etc., and degradation tests.

Other facilities available are testing of solar lanterns and small lighting systems, efficiency of inverters, PV array and system evaluation under field conditions and calibration of pyranometers. The centre has also established facilities for the testing and evaluation of PV water pumping systems for submersible and surface pumps under outdoor conditions. Solar lanterns, PV modules, array and water pump evaluation facilities are also available at the Photovoltaic Laboratory, IIT, Delhi. Additional test facilities at the Electronic Research & Test Laboratory, Calcutta, the Electronic Testing and Development Centre, Bangalore, and the Central Power Research Institute, Thiruvanathapuram are also operational.

The establishment of national standards of PV systems has been taken up with the Bureau of Indian Standard (BIS). Three Indian Standards have been published based on the Bureau's participation in the work of IEC/TC-82. These standards are identical to the corresponding IEC proposal. Indian standards for items like module qualification testing, balance of system components, batteries, inverters etc. are under consideration.

Conclusion

Photovoltaics has assumed a major role as an alternative source for meeting diverse requirements ranging from a few watts to hundreds of kWs. This has been brought about by the progress made in all the aspects of photovoltaics: materials, devices, systems, balance of systems. Stand-alone applications to grid-connected applications have been developed for rural and urban areas, taking advantage of the unique features of PV technology, namely, modularity, ease of system design and implementation, freedom from pollution, virtually no operation/maintenance cost, long system component life (except batteries), reliable operation etc. The growing importance of PV can be gauged by enhancement in the targets set by the Ministry of Non-conventional Energy Sources (see Part II, Chapter 12).

References

Barua, A. K., Roy, Swati and Chandhuri, P. (1996): "Fabrication of High Efficiency Double Junction Amorphous Silicon Solar Cells", Proceedings of the NSEC '96, Calcutta, pp. 155 - 158.

Bhargava, B. (1995): "Solar Photovoltaics: Market Poised to Expand", IREDA NEWS, pp. 11 - 21.

Bhattacharya, D., Dutta, J., Chaudhuri, S. and Pal, A. K. (1996): "CuInSe$_2$/CdS Solar Cells with Efficiency 11.4 per cent Produced by Bilayer Technique", Proceedings of the NSEC '96, Calcutta, pp. 172 - 175.

Bhattacharya, S., Reddy, S.R., Singh, S.P., Saxena, A. K., Prasad, B., Kumar, K., Nangia, O.P., Bhatnagar, R.B.L. and Barua, A. K., (1997): "Glass-in Panel-out Amorphous Silicon Solar Cell Pilot Plant-Commissioning Experience", 14th EC PVSE Conference, Barcelona, Spain.

Bhattacharya, T.K. (1991): "Design and Development of Photovoltaic Systems", Vol. I-III.

Bloss, W. H., Pfisterer, F., Schubert, M. and Walter, T. (1995): "Thin Film Solar Cells", *Progress in Photovoltaics*, Vol. 3, pp. 3-24.

Bureau of Indian Standard (1989): "Solar Photovoltaic Energy Systems-Terminology", No. IS-12834.

Chaurey, A. and Deambi, S. (1992): "Comparison of Commercially Available PV Batteries in India", Proceedings of the 6th PVSEC, New Delhi, pp. 587 – 592.

Chopra, K. L. and Das, S. R. (1990): "Thin Film Solar Cells", Plenum Press, London.

Dutta, V. (1994): "Physics of Photovoltaic Devices, Photovoltaic System Design and Implementation", FITT HRD Programme at R.E.S. Hyderabad, pp. 1–33.

Garg, H. P. and Dutta, V. (1995): "Status of Solar Photovoltaic Technology in India - An Industrial Outlook", Applied Energy, Vol. 52, pp. 395-419.

Gay, R. R. (1996): Technical Digest, 9th PVSEC, Miyazaki, p. 149.

Ghosh, B. (1996): "Deposition of Ni-P Composite on CdTe/CdS Thin Film by Modules", Proceedings of the NSEC '96, Calcutta, pp. 188 - 191.

Green, M. (1990): "Photovolatics: Coming of Age", Proceedings of the 20th IEEE Photovoltaics Specialist Conference, Kissimmee (U.S.A.), pp. 1-8.

Indian Renewable Energy Development Agency Limited (1997): Guidelines for LOAN assistance.

Koner, P. K. and Dutta, V. (1998): "An Economic Feasibility Analysis of Photovoltaics Power During Urban Load Shedding Time", Solar Energy Materials and Solar Cells (in press).

Ministry of Non-conventional Energy Sources, Government of India, Annual Reports 1993-94, 1994-95, 1995-96, 1996-97.

Mishra, P. R., Joshi, J. C., Roy B. and Gupta, P. (1996): "SPV Based Mini Cathodic Protection System", Proceedings of the NSEC '96, Calcutta, pp. 224 – 227.

Parthasarathi, A., Madhavan, D. and Kaul, V. K. (1994): "Solar Photovoltaic Energy Products: From Semiconductor Physics to Advanced Energy Technology", International Conference on Physics and Industrial Development: Bridging Gap, Jan.17-19, New Delhi.

Paulson, P. D. and Dutta, V. (1996): "An in situ Method for $CdCl_2$ Treatment on CdTe Thin Film", Technical Digest, 9th PVSEC, Miyazaki, Japan, p. 423.

Ramamurthy, V. (1997): "Application of Photovoltaics - A Social and Techno-Economic Perspective", Proceedings of the National Conference on Alternate and Renewable Technologies, Jan. 10-11, Hyderabad.

Sharma, M. P. (1994): "Utility Grid-Connected Solar Photovoltaic Power Plants for Meeting Energy Needs for Rural Area in Developing Countries - A case of India", *Solar Energy Materials and Solar Cells*, Vol. 35, pp. 469 – 476.

Vasudevan, A. P. (Feb. 1997): "METKEM Silicon Activities", Symposium on Current Status on Solar Energy Materials and System, Crystal Growth Centre, Anna Univ., Chennai.

Wenger, H. J., Hoff, T., Shugar D. S. and Farmer, B. (1994): "PVUSA 500 kW Grid-Support Photovoltaic Project: Interim Results on Value", Proceedings of the 12th EC PVSE Conference, Amsterdam.

12 The Photovoltaic Promotion Programme in India

BHARAT BHARGAVA

Introduction

Energy has become an integral part of the overall development of a society. Energy is required for agriculture, drinking water supply, lighting, health care, telecommunications, industrial activities and for all aspects of everyday life. Provision of lighting and cooking energy for rural and remote areas is still a major issue in many developing countries including India.

There is a vast scope and potential for the use of photovoltaic (PV) technology in India. There are still over 90,000 villages in the country which remain to be electrified. About 50,000 villages have a population of up to 500 inhabitants and they are likely to have a low electricity demand in the next 5-10 years, making the cost of rural electrification very high. 10,000 villages are estimated to be located in difficult areas such as forests, hills, deserts and islands. Even in electrified villages, only about a third of the households have electricity connections. This leaves about 60-70 million households which are dependent on kerosene for meeting a basic need such as lighting. Given the unreliable nature of electric power supply in most rural areas, there are about 100 million kerosene lanterns of various types in use. Likewise, there are millions of diesel pump sets employed for irrigation and other purposes. A sizeable quantity of oil is needed to run these devices which can be avoided if PV systems are used on a large scale.

Photovoltaic technology and its applications have come to be regarded as an important thrust area in India's quest for development and utilization of non-conventional energy sources. It is widely recognized that photovoltaics will have an important role to play as an environmentally benign technology, capable of meeting electrical power requirements specially in rural and remote areas yet to be electrified. The technology has already proved to be reliable and cost-effective in various fields such as telecommunications, TV transmission, remote area power source etc. Further advances in technology development and the expected cost-reduction in large-scale manufacturing will expand photovoltaic applications substantially.

The Indian Photovoltaic Programme

The Ministry of Non-conventional Energy Sources (MNES) is responsible for the overall planning and programme formulation as well as the supervision of the implementation of various programme activities. The Indian programme on photovoltaics seeks to develop and nurture basic scientific and technological capabilities for undertaking state-of-the-art research and development and to promote the dissemination of technology through demonstration, industrial production and commercialization.

The programme for development of photovoltaic technology and its applications in India was initiated as far back as 1976. After more than a decade of industry-based technology development, the crystalline silicon solar cell technology has reached a mature stage. Substantial indigenous capability has been developed covering silicon material, solar cells, PV modules and systems. A variety of PV systems have been developed and deployed in the field for the purposes of demonstration and for field testing and evaluation. The programme is currently focusing on further improvements in material technology, crystalline silicon cell and module efficiencies, development of thin-film technology, development of new systems and improvements in balance of systems (BOS) designs.

In June 1993, MNES prepared a new strategy and action plan for accelerating the development and utilization of renewable energy technologies. As part of this plan, the PV programme was also significantly expanded to achieve a deployment level of 25 MW during the 8th five-year plan through a combination of policy initiatives and support for market development. Among the elements of the new action plan are:

1. Deployment of solar lanterns as a substitute for kerosene lanterns.
2. Electrification of villages/hamlets through PV systems.
3. A special programme on water pumping systems for agriculture and related uses.
4. Intensified R&D on technologies which can lead to a reduction in costs.
5. Commercialization of PV systems for various applications by giving a market orientation to the programme and promoting manufacturing and related activities.

To implement the new strategy and action plan, the MNES adopted a two-pronged strategy: a socially oriented programme in which the use of PV systems is promoted through subsidies and other measures, especially in rural areas; and a market-oriented programme in which soft loans and other incentives are provided for manufacturers and users. Other supporting measures include removing barriers to foreign investment and foreign technology, encouraging private investment and manufacture, reducing custom duties on imported materials and components and improving quality through provision of test facilities.

As a result of these measures, India has achieved a leading status among the countries of the world in the development and use of PV technology. The Indian market and programme are the largest among developing countries. India has emerged as the second largest manufacturer in the world of PV modules based on crystalline silicon. Industrial production which was around 1 MW per year before the start of the 8th plan touched a level of 8 MW during 1995-96. There are over 70 companies now engaged in the production of solar cells, modules and systems. PV systems are being used widely in telecommunications, railways and for other specialized purposes. Export of PV products to other countries has also begun.

Currently there are 7 manufacturers of crystalline silicon solar cells and a total of 12 manufacturers of PV modules. The present Indian production is based on single-crystal silicon solar cells. The total domestic installed capacity of solar cell manufacture is about 12 MW per year. Similarly the present annual installed capacity for the manufacture of PV modules is about 18 MW. Most of these units have semi-automatic production lines. Details of some important programmes/applications are given in the succeeding sections.

Solar Lighting

Lighting is one of the basic needs in households. It is also required in community centres, clinics and dispensaries, adult education centres, in streets and in a variety of other isolated locations. In most cases kerosene lanterns of various types including Petromax are widely used in the majority of these locations. Besides requiring imports of vast quantities of oil, such lanterns often provide inadequate lighting, cause pollution and can entail fire hazards.

A number of solar lighting systems have been developed in the country to cater to these requirements both in rural and urban locations. Among the systems available are street lights, fixed domestic lights, portable solar lanterns and larger community systems. All these products have been developed indigenously and manufactured on a commercial scale in the country.

A street lighting system consists of 70 watts of PV modules mounted on a pole, a battery at the base and an 11-watt compact fluorescent lamp with an inverter and charge controller. The lamp comes on automatically at dusk and switches off at dawn. The components and batteries used in these systems have been optimized over the years. Over thirty thousand of these systems have been installed in the country through State Electricity Boards and Renewable Energy Agencies.

Solar lanterns were developed and introduced about four years ago on a trial basis. A solar lantern consists of a small module (typically generating 10 watts of power) and a lantern unit which uses a battery, electronics and a compact fluorescent lamp (usually of 7 watts). The system requires no installation and is easy to operate. The battery is charged during the daytime by the power from the PV module and provides energy for the lamp for 3-4 hours at night. As a portable lighting unit, the lantern can be used anywhere indoors and outdoors.

After evaluating the performance of lanterns and their popularity, the MNES has expanded the programme considerably during the last two years. The solar lantern programme is being implemented through the State Nodal Agencies. The MNES has also opened additional channels for the distribution of solar lanterns such as showrooms. Training and after-sales arrangements are also being provided for in the programme.

Another lighting system supported under the MNES programme is a fixed-type domestic lighting unit. In this case, a full single PV module is installed on a rooftop or on a small pole; a battery unit is placed inside the house, two lamps of the compact fluorescent type are provided along with independent switches. MNES meets 50 per cent of the cost of such systems which is about 10,000 to 12,000 rupees (Rs.) per system. Such systems are popular in Uttar Pradesh, Rajasthan and some other states.

Solar Water Pumping

Water pumping was one of the earliest applications of photovoltaic technology developed in India. The demand for electrical energy and diesel fuel for running irrigation pump sets has been increasing year after year leading to shortages and supply constraints. A photovoltaic pumping system, used on a large scale, can cut down the need for extending the distribution grids in rural areas and the resultant losses in transmission. The pumps can also bring the benefits of irrigation and drinking water supply to backward areas which are not served by the existing grid and where it is difficult to supply diesel.

Small pumping systems of 300-360 watts were developed and tested during the eighties. Seeing the need for larger quantities of water, the MNES sponsored the development of larger capacity pumping systems fitted with efficient DC motors. Separately, the Ministry also supported the trial of deep well submersible pumps powered by PV. Such pumps were used mainly for drinking water supply.

Based on the experience gained the MNES evolved a special programme for the supply and installation of PV water pumping systems. The programme aimed at achieving a high volume of installation, leading to increased scale of manufacture, improvement in technology and reduction in cost. A scheme for the installation of water pumps was approved during 1993-94. The scheme provides for a subsidy and a soft loan for the remaining cost of the pumping system. Loans were available to manufacturers for establishing or expanding the production facilities. The entire scheme is operated through IREDA (Indian Renewable Energy Development Agency).

An element of market orientation and competition is built into the programme by leaving it to the manufacturers to find potential buyers and provide after-sales services. The scheme is open to all types of users, individuals as well as institutions. The pumping systems could be used for any purpose required by the users. Systems of up to 2,250 watts array capacity are allowed under the scheme. A subsidy of Rs. 125 per watt of the PV array subject to a maximum of Rs. 150,000 is provided to the users. A soft loan of up to Rs. 100,000 is also available to the users at an interest rate of 5 per cent per annum with a repayment period of 10 years. A total of 1,778 pumping systems have been installed so far.

PV Power Plants

One way of meeting all the electrical energy requirements of a village is to establish a power plant using PV modules of the required total capacity. Such plants employ a large battery bank and an appropriate power conditioning system. A line is drawn from the plant to provide power to all houses and other installations. Power is usually provided for a certain fixed duration every day.

The reliability and availability of PV power plants has been found to be on the whole better than stand-alone systems mainly because of the presence of a local person trained in the operation and routine maintenance of the systems. The typical sizes of power plants range from 2 kW to 10 kW.

In order to generate experience with grid connected systems, the MNES has supported a few demonstration plants. Among them are two plants in Uttar Pradesh, each with a capacity of 100 kW, of which about 25 kW is fed into the grid. The Ministry has also evolved a programme to encourage State Electricity Boards to introduce grid-connected systems for peak load shaving or voltage support system.

Other Applications

Over the years, MNES has supported the development and demonstration of a variety of applications in different sectors. As a result of these efforts PV power systems are now being used for railway signalling, off-shore oil platforms, microwave repeaters, TV transmission and reception and for providing power to border outposts of the BSF (border security taxes) and border police IRBP. Many of these applications have become fully commercial, i.e. PV systems are being used by the organizations concerned at full cost and in preference to conventional options. The largest example of this kind is in the telecommunication sector, where thousands of rural radio telephone systems are being operated with solar power by the Department of Telecommunications. There is further scope for expanding the use of PV technology by the defence services, railways, post department etc.

The MNES is continuing to support the introduction of newer applications. Among the systems proposed for support are refrigerators used for storing vaccines and medicines, solar water purifiers and educational kits.

Prospects for Further Growth

Over the years more than 350,000 photovoltaic systems aggregating to over 22 MW have been installed for a variety of applications in different parts of India. This has contributed in a significant way to the process of commercialization of photovoltaics in India. At present 50 per cent of the off-take is for commercially viable applications. About 9 MW of PV systems have been deployed for telecommunication applications. More than 6 MW of PV systems have been deployed for lighting applications such as street lighting, domestic lighting, community lighting, village power plants and solar lanterns. About 2 MW has been used for deployment of water pumping systems. It is estimated that about 5 MW of PV systems have been deployed for other sectors like use in railways, off-shore well head oil platforms, very low power transmitters for television, battery charging by defence and paramilitary forces, medical refrigeration etc.

Barriers in Rapid Growth of PV Applications

While significant growth has been registered in the past few years, still there are many issues which need to be addressed to achieve further growth of PV applications and aim for a sustainable market. Some of these issues are:
1. Initial high cost,
2. Reliability of the products due to site specificity,
3. Marketing and after-sales service network and
4. Financing mechanism.

Cost of PV Systems

There has been a downward trend in the cost of Indian-made PV modules, partly on account of reduction in customs duties and partly due to the large volume of production. Prices of PV modules have come down from about Rs. 225 per watt in 1990-93 to Rs. 165-175 during 1995-96.

At present the initial cost of PV systems is high. Typically a 70 W module-based street light unit costs about Rs. 22,000. Each individually owned 35 W domestic lighting system costs about Rs. 11,000 and a 10 W module-based solar lantern costs about Rs. 3,500-4,000. The PV modules account for a significant share of the overall costs of a PV system.

Despite the fact that the initial cost of photovoltaic systems is high, it turns out that for certain decentralized applications involving relatively low capacity utilization and loads, the photovoltaic systems are cost-effective for a number of applications on a life-cycle cost basis.

Studies have shown that PV systems of up to 2 kW capacity are competitive in those locations which are generally 3-5 km away from the grid-line. On life-cycle cost analysis, a number of small PV systems for lighting, water pumping, telecommunications, etc. have been found to be viable, when compared to the extension of the grid. Devices such as solar lanterns are commercially viable if the real cost of kerosene is taken into account. Small solar power systems which can provide lighting for a few hours are also cost-effective compared to petrol generators.

Typical costs of the electrification of a new village by the grid are estimated to be about Rs. 300,000/kW and this shoots up to Rs. 900,000 in the case of hilly, remote and far-flung areas. The cost of the electrification of a rural household, where a rural grid is available, is estimated to be around Rs. 1,200 per service connection.

Photovoltaics would appear to be a more technically and economically viable answer for pre-electrification to provide lights to such hilly, rural, remote and far-flung areas. The cost of electrification of a village by PV is estimated to be about Rs. 350,000-400,000 per kW including the cost of the local transmission distribution network etc. Therefore, for a small village of around 80 households in a remote area photovoltaic systems appear to be economically competitive in comparison to the extension of the grid for meeting lighting needs.

PV System Reliability

PV systems need to have reliable technology to ensure high system availability. Though considerable improvements have taken place, there is still a need to ensure quality and training of the local staff in basic repairs and maintenance.

The establishment of national standards for PV systems has been taken up with the Bureau of Indian Standards (BIS). Six Indian Standards have been published based on the Bureau's participation in the work of IEC/TC-82 (Indian electric company).

MNES and other major user organizations have formulated performance specifications for the PV systems. A photovoltaic test facility has been set up by MNES at the Solar Energy Centre (SEC), Gwal Pahari, to qualify PV modules to the recent BIS/JRC-Ispra specification, and to test the BOS (balance of systems) and complete PV systems to ensure product quality. The test facility is equipped to undertake routine testing and development testing activities, and to provide service to the PV industry by way of establishing standards and certification and to ensure quality of the products made in the country. At present SEC is able to test some of the PV systems like solar lanterns, small lighting systems, and to conduct performance tests on DC pumps and efficiency tests on inverters. Calibration of pyranometers is also possible.

Marketing and After-Sales Service Network

The overall requirement of the PV products in the country can be divided into two broad market segments, namely the institutional market and the consumer market. At present most of the PV systems in the country have been deployed through the institutional market route. In this case the PV manufacturers sell their products to various government organizations and other institutional users, who distribute these systems to the actual beneficiaries. The State Nodal Agencies for renewable energy systems, which are implementing the MNES schemes, are one of the major institutional buyers of the PV systems. The other major buyer is the Department of Telecommunications. This arrangement of bulk purchase by the user organizations requires limited marketing efforts by the manufacturers. In most of the cases the network of the user organizations has been used for system failure reporting and after-sales services also.

One of the limitations of the present industrial scene is lack of adequate marketing and after-sales service network. It is realized that the cost of setting up a nationwide network will be very high. Some efforts have been initiated in this direction. In the last few years some of the manufacturers have taken the initiative to set up limited dealer/distributor and servicing networks. Many of the PV manufacturers still do not have any visible marketing and after-sales service arrangements. Due to this limitation the vast potential of the consumer market/applications has remained virtually untapped. It is estimated that products like solar lanterns and solar modules for transistorized radio sets alone may have a multi-megawatt market.

Financing Mechanism

In view of the initial high cost of the PV systems, the financing problem needs specific attention. There is a large potential for the commercialization of several PV products if suitable financing arrangements are made available to individuals and commercial users and appropriate marketing efforts are made by PV manufacturers. In order to promote the development of markets for PV products, MNES has introduced soft loan schemes through the Indian Renewable Energy Development Agency (IREDA). Under this scheme soft loan assistance is available to individuals as well as commercial organizations for the purchase of solar photovoltaic systems. The loans can also be accessed by financial intermediaries, PV manufacturers, product distributors, cooperative societies, non-governmental organizations etc. These organizations are expected to market PV products and be responsible for the timely return of the loan to IREDA. It is expected that manufacturers, their dealers and financial intermediaries will take the lead and set up a countrywide sales and servicing network to offer a variety of photovoltaic systems for different uses. The World Bank has also provided US $ 55 million to

IREDA for a "PV Market Development Project". The World Bank project envisages the creation of a revolving credit facility at IREDA for loan support to the users for purchasing of variety of PV systems.

Government Policy

There is a growing recognition that PV technology perhaps offers the best prospects for a breakthrough. Therefore, the policy is clearly directed towards a greater thrust on all aspects of PV technology and applications. The recent policy measures and duty rationalization provides excellent opportunities for increased investment in this sector, technology upgrading, introduction of new technologies, market development and export promotion.

At present there are no barriers to setting up a manufacturing unit by any private sector or foreign manufacturer. Guidelines issued by the Reserve Bank of India and the Ministry of Industry are applicable for this sector also. MNES is encouraging technology upgrading for the manufacture of various PV products. Manufacturers can set up new units in domestic areas of export processing zones. The Government has given a major impetus to PV applications in the most extensive manner possible. The policy direction and programme thrust aims at increasing the commercial role for photovoltaics more than ever before.

Fiscal and Financial Incentives

To encourage the domestic manufacture of PV products and applications, over the years custom duties on PV-related items have been progressively reduced. There is no excise duty on local manufacture of silicon wafers, solar cells, modules and various PV systems. In most of the states, many PV products are exempt from sales tax. The other incentives to this sector include 100 per cent depreciation during the first year and soft loan to the users and PV manufacturers.

Conclusions

It has been realized that there is a niche for photovoltaic systems in the near term in unelectrified areas away from the grid. Applications like solar lanterns are useful in even those areas which have intermittent electricity supply. A vast number of applications pursued so far has contributed in a significant way to the process of commercialization of photovoltaics in India. The present demand for PV products in the country is about 8 MW per year. Some of the important application areas which are expected to grow further include lighting, water pumping and telecommunications. Other emerging applications include battery charging, railway signalling, water purification, medical refrigeration and various consumer applications.

In the next 3-5 years the demand for the PV systems is likely to go up to about 12-15 MW per year for stand-alone decentralized applications. With expected cost reduction, increase in volume production and improvements in system design, photovoltaics will become more and more commercially attractive for decentralized power applications. In that case the demand for PV systems may go up to a level of about 25-30 MW per year. If centralized grid connected systems are commercially feasible, this may increase considerably. This will result in further expansion of activities. It is expected that the Indian PV industry will gear up to meet this challenge.

13 Wind Power Development in India

AJIT GUPTA

Introduction

Wind energy has been exploited for thousands of years. In India, too, there are references about windmills dating back to 1879. The first systematic efforts to harness wind energy in the country were undertaken during the fifties and early sixties by the Council of Scientific and Industrial Research (CSIR) at the National Aeronautical Laboratory (NAL), mainly in the field of water-pumping windmills. However, due to limited interest and relevance in the energy scene at that time, this work was closed down in 1966. The oil crisis of 1973 revived interest in wind energy utilization, and in the National Science and Technology Plan specific recommendations were made on the harnessing of renewable sources of energy, including wind energy. Up to the mid-eighties, work in this area continued to be concentrated on water-pumping windmills. In the Seventh Plan, commencing in 1985, wind energy development received a new thrust with programmes for wind resource assessment and wind power generation.

International Status and Trends

Although it has been exploited for thousands of years, the re-emergence of wind energy for electric power generation in the grid-connected mode is of relatively recent origin. Since the mid-seventies, when work began in earnest on harnessing the wind, the development of wind energy technology has made significant progress. Modern wind turbines are far removed from their historic predecessors. They are highly sophisticated machines built on aerodynamic principles developed from the aerospace industry, incorporating advanced materials and electronics, and are designed to deliver energy across a range of wind speeds. The technical feasibility of using wind as a major source of energy has been established, and wind energy today ranks as one of the most promising of the renewable energy technologies for generating

217

electricity. During the next few years, wind installations are likely to rise by as much as 20 per cent annually. Today wind power is a truly global phenomenon and is beginning to figure in national energy plans as an important source of energy, income and employment.

The world's total wind turbine capacity has passed the 6,000 MW mark with over 33,000 wind turbines in operation world-wide, producing about 10 billion kWh annually. The United States, in particular the State of California, set the pace in the early eighties. A total wind power capacity of 1,600 MW, comprising about 17,000 machines, has been installed in the United States producing over three billion units annually. The National Energy Strategy envisages 4,000-8,000 MW of wind turbine capacity being on-line by the turn of the century.

Several European nations, especially Germany, Denmark, the Netherlands, The United Kingdom and Spain, now have committed wind energy programmes. Against a present installed wind power capacity of about 3,500 MW, the strategy for Europe envisages a capacity of 4,000 MW by the year 2000. The total installed capacity in Germany has risen to 1,550 MW. The country now leads Europe in the production of electricity from wind, and is well on its way to achieving the target of 2,000 MW by the year 2000. A total of over 4,000 wind turbines has been installed in Denmark, giving an installed capacity of 850 MW. The Danish Government's target for the year 2005 envisages a wind power capacity of 1,500 MW. 300 MW of wind power capacity have been installed in the Netherlands, and the target is 1,000 MW by the year 2000. In the United Kingdom the installed capacity stands at 270 MW. In Spain, a capacity of about 250 MW has been installed.

Wind is one of the most cost-effective of the renewable energy technologies and the resource is widely distributed around the world. The capital costs have been halved and now average about $ 1,000/kW. They are expected to decline to $ 750-850/kW within the next few years. Operation and maintenance (O&M) costs have dropped fourfold over the past decade to 1-1.5 c/kWh, and are likely to drop to less than 1 c/kWh by the year 2000. Availability factors have increased from 60 per cent to over 95 per cent, and generation can be predicted with certainty on a long-term basis. Capacity factors now vary from 20-30 per cent and are expected to increase to 30-45 per cent by the year 2000. With the output from a modern turbine in a good wind area now averaging 800-1,000 kWh/yr m² of rotor swept area, the specific energy yield has nearly doubled. The output is generally about 2 million kWh/MW. The construction lead time is less than six months, and wind turbines are highly modular. The new variable speed wind turbines are expected to improve energy capture by 10 per cent or more, reduce stresses, and lengthen turbine life. This concept, as well as the evolving wind turbine technologies employing flexible, lightweight blades, improved ailerons, teetering attachments, direct drive transmission, increased height and aerodynamic tower design, and advanced electronic controls will help to break the 5 c/kWh barrier down from the present cost of 7-9 c/kWh, and dropping to below 3 c/kWh by the year 2000. In terms of land area, with installations of 8 MW/km², the output is typically 160,000 kWh/ha yr.

The experience of other countries has provided useful information on policy initiatives, technology development, institutional linkages, legislation, pricing etc., which are necessary for successful programme development, particularly in developing countries. India has taken up a fairly ambitious programme, faced as we are with a growing shortage of power and energy. The interest stems not only from the fact that wind power is proving to be cost-effective, but also because it is modular, has short gestation, and is environmentally benign.

Wind Resource and Potential in India

The most prominent feature of the wind climatology in India is the monsoon circulations. Winds in India are influenced by the strong south-west summer monsoon, which starts in May or June, when cool, humid air moves towards the land and the weaker north-east winter monsoon, which starts in October, when cool, dry air moves towards the ocean. During the period March to August, the winds are uniformly strong over the whole Indian Peninsula, except the eastern peninsular coast. Wind speeds during the period November to March are relatively weak, though higher winds are available during a part of this period on the Tamil Nadu coastline.

A Wind Energy Data Handbook was published in 1983, based on an analysis of information and data on wind available from the vast network of meteorological observatories. This served as a preliminary data source for the early initiatives in India during the Seventh Plan (1985-90). In 1985, an extensive Wind Resource Assessment Programme was taken up comprising wind monitoring, wind mapping and complex terrain projects. The programme now covers 25 States, and is today the world's largest wind resource assessment effort covering over 600 stations. Today, 92 masts of 20-25 m height with sophisticated continuous recording instruments and 58 masts of 5 m height with cup counter anemometers are operational. A number of complex terrain studies has also been undertaken. Four volumes of the Handbook on Wind Energy Resource Survey for India have been published so far, which cover wind data from 118 wind monitoring stations.

Potential windy locations have been identified in the flat coastal terrains in southern Tamil Nadu, Kerala, Gujarat, Lakshadweep and Maharashtra. Favourable sites have also been identified in some inland locations of Karnataka, Andhra Pradesh, Madhya Pradesh, and Rajasthan. 98 locations having a potential of about 5,000 MW have so far been identified in these States with annual mean wind speeds greater than 18 km/h, which could be considered for wind power projects. The wind system in Tamil Nadu is influenced by high winds accelerated by the three passes, namely Aralvaimozhi, Shencottah and Palghat, resulting in annual mean wind speeds between 5.6 to 6.9 m/s.

Wind survey efforts have so far mainly concentrated on relatively simple, flat or coastal terrains. The zone of influence of a windy station identified in such terrains extends over several square kilometres, where wind farm projects can be planned with a higher degree of confidence. However, it is expected that similar or even better wind conditions exist in the yet to be explored areas particularly in the mountainous and hilly areas of north and north-eastern India. In fact, some of the best locations identified so far in the country such as Muppandal in Tamil Nadu, Jogimatti in Karnataka and Rammakkelmedu in Kerala have been found in complex terrains. Different methods for wind resource assessment, such as Geographic Information System (GIS), Wind Atlas etc. are proposed to be employed for complex terrains in view of the extreme variations over relatively small areas on account of local factors.

According to a first order estimate, the resource potential in India is about 20,000 MW. According to another estimate, the potential, on the basis of land availability only (particularly along the coastal regions), could be of the order of 50,000 MW. The potential in the Southern States and Gujarat alone is estimated to be about 10,000 MW. Wind data is required for a precise estimate of the total potential, and this will, therefore, have to await the results of the country-wide resource surveys.

Wind Farm Siting Considerations

The main evaluation criteria for the assessment of sites for wind farm projects are:

1. Wind resource: The annual mean wind speed should be at least 5 m/s, preferably above 5.6 m/s, for economic harnessing of wind power. It is not enough to obtain general wind data. Site-specific information on wind speed, direction, frequency, shear, gusts and turbulence is necessary. The energy content should be more than 1,500 kWh/m²/yr. Complex terrains require micro-level wind resource studies.

2. Land use: Assuming 200-250 kW wind turbines (rotor diameter D=25 m), distance between rows 7 D, and between turbines 5 D (with rows perpendicular to the prevailing wind direction), the total area required is about 10 ha/MW installed. However, only 5-10 per cent of this area is directly required for foundations and roads on the site. Array efficiency should normally be above 95 per cent, but this will depend on the specific configuration and orientation. Wake and shadow effects should be evaluated carefully. For wind farm projects, it is not necessary to acquire the entire land. In most remote far-flung potential areas, sufficient waste or barren land, which is of little value, is available, and the installation of wind turbines does not affect the local population or economic activity. In other areas, conjunctive use for grazing, agriculture, salt pans, etc. is possible, and only the small portion occupied by the wind turbines gets disturbed.

3. Accessibility: Easy accessibility should be available for movement and erection of the heavy wind turbines and electrical equipment, and for civil construction work. Only limited road construction should be required. Contours, topography, terrain and soil characteristics should also be considered. In remote locations, where large cranes may not be available, a manual mode of erection should be possible.

4. Grid system: Power quality of the grid should be free from frequent interruptions, and voltage and frequency variations should be within prescribed limits in order to be able to operate grid-connected wind turbines. Integration of wind turbines into the power systems does not pose serious technical problems as long as the wind capacity does not greatly exceed the minimum demand. In India, demand almost always outstrips supply, and the additional energy from the wind turbines is immediately absorbed. A spread-out wind capacity, less than 20 per cent of the grid capacity, is normally recommended. In general, the grid system should fulfill the following criteria:

   • Frequency should be within the 47-52 Hz interval.
   • Voltage variations of 15 per cent at the common coupling point, when the wind farm is connected or disconnected.

- Voltage increase at each wind turbine should be below 13 per cent of the rated voltage.
- Asymmetry should be within 15 per cent.
- The short circuit level at the common coupling point should not be below 5 to 10 times the maximum power output of the wind farm.
- Wind turbines should be provided with start current limiting devices: I (start) < 1.3 I (rated).
- Wind turbines should be provided with a capacitor band for full compensation of the idle running reactive power consumption.

The evaluation of the grid should take into consideration the availability of the grid as well as the quality of the existing transmission and distribution lines. The quality of the lines is the main factor for possible breakdowns of the system. Also, configuration of the existing grid and the power consumption at sub-stations near the wind farm and consumer should be taken into account. Evacuation of power should preferably be through 33 kV lines or above, as these are more stable, and the sub-station should be less than 30 km from the project.

Status and Experiences in India

In India, the total wind power capacity has reached 900 MW, and about 2 billion units of electricity have been fed to the grid from wind farm projects so far. The programme for the demonstration of wind farms was initiated in 1985, and experience has been favourable - the technology has generally performed up to expectations, and the wind resource assessment programme continues to reveal even more promising sites. An aggregate capacity of about 50 MW has been established at 23 locations in 8 States. In the demonstration projects undertaken so far, the unit size of machines has gone up from 55-100 kW in the first few projects to 400-600 kW in recent projects. Different types and designs of wind turbines have been demonstrated and new potential areas have been opened up. The wind machine availability in these projects has been of the order of 90-95 per cent and annual capacity factors of up to 30 per cent have been reached. Annual generation of 2-2.5 million units per MW has been achieved.

A few problems arose in the early demonstration projects as at that time the selection of sites had to be undertaken on the basis of inadequate wind data, lack of compatibility of the machines with Indian environmental conditions and poor grid quality, stability and outages. Grid faults occurred on account of conductor snapping, insulator failure, lightning, transformer panel, cable faults, low voltage, load shedding etc. Machine faults were mainly attributable to blades, generator, controller and sensors. Inadequate temperature control in the equipment, corrosion and earthing also caused problems. These have largely been overcome as a result of the feedback obtained from the early projects and a better understanding of the various requirements. With better siting, adaptability of wind turbine equipment to Indian conditions, detailed and thorough project planning and implementation and improved O&M services, availability and performance have now improved considerably.

The demonstration projects have helped to create awareness about the new technology, to provide useful operating experience for industry and utilities, to establish technical and economic viability; and to clarify technical and economic issues for investment decisions involving large-scale wind farm development and commercialization in the country. Basic capability has been developed in industry, technical institutions, electricity boards, nodal agencies and consulting organizations towards planning, siting, layout and configuration design as well as execution of foundations and other civil and electrical site works, and also grid interface. Indigenous expertise and capability for handling, transportation, storage as well as local erection (with and without large cranes), commissioning, start-up, testing, maintenance and repair have also grown, and foreign expertise is not now necessary for undertaking this work any more.

DANIDA (Danish International Development Assistance) support for three wind farm projects aggregating to 20 MW in Gujarat and Tamil Nadu during 1989-91 also helped the move from demonstration to commercial projects. Among the factors which contributed to the success of these pioneering projects were: commitment and active involvement of Central, State Governments and utilities; clear definition of objectives; adequate project size; focus on a single technology and application; use of local infrastructure and expertise for construction and erection; progressive local production; sufficient resources for planning and appraisal; and technical assistance for planning, implementation, training and service.

A notable feature of the Indian programme is the interest among private investors/developers in setting up commercial wind power projects. A capacity of 850 MW of commercial projects has been established so far, mainly in Tamil Nadu, Gujarat and Andhra Pradesh. About 167 MW of additional capacity was achieved during 1996-97 up to March 1997. It is expected that at least another 200 MW will be added during the year by March

1998. The largest installation of wind turbines in the country has so far taken place in the Muppandal-Perungady area near Kannyakumari in Tamil Nadu, with an aggregate capacity of about 350 MW. This represents one of the largest concentrations of wind farm capacity at a single location.

R&D support is being provided for indigenous design, development and field testing of wind turbines and of rotor blades. The indigenous 55 kW machines and the first two prototypes of an indigenous 200 kW machine have performed satisfactorily. A Wind Power Systems Development and Test Centre is planned in Tamil Nadu, with initial financial and technical assistance from DANIDA. The Centre will be responsible for technology development suited to local conditions and will undertake testing, certification and standardization. It is likely to become functional during 1997-98.

A large number of companies have tied up with foreign collaborations for joint venture/licensed production of wind electric generators in India, of which six companies account for the major market share at present. The progress of phased indigenization has been good and nearly complete indigenization has been achieved. A joint venture has been established at Bangalore for blade production. Two other manufacturers have initiated blade production. Machines of 400-600 kW unit size have been installed for the first time in India during the past year. Introduction of higher capacity machines will enable more cost-effective harnessing of wind energy. The annual turnover of the wind industry has reached Rs. $1,500 \times 10^7$ (US $ 450 million).

New Thrust Given During the Eighth Plan

During the Eighth Plan (1992-97), the Ministry of Non-conventional Energy Sources (MNES) consolidated and strengthened technology development and commercialization by providing a market orientation and creating a favourable policy environment. The goals were re-defined and aim at generating 2,000 MW of power from renewables during the Plan. Attractive opportunities were created and procedural formalities were simplified to foster private investments. A key element of the new strategy of commercialization is to utilize the Government's limited budgetary resources to demonstrate the technical and economic viability of "emerging" technologies and applications with a view to leverage institutional finance and private investments, and attracting external assistance. The development of entrepreneurship and greater competition is expected to reduce costs and improve the quality of equipment, and to lead to the establishment of a large number of market outlets, a service network, and repair and maintenance infrastructure.

Renewable energy is expected to create maximum impact in the production of electricity. Projections indicate that by the end of the decade it would be cost-effective to generate and supply renewable electricity, aggregating to several thousand megawatts, as its efficiencies and costs are decreasing while the costs of conventional electricity are increasing. Besides grid supply augmentation renewable electric technologies offer possibilities of distributed generation at or near the points of use, which can reduce peak loads and save on costly upgradation and maintenance of transmission and distribution networks to serve growing demand. The Eighth Five Year Plan accordingly gave special emphasis to generation of grid power from renewables including wind power. Large wind farm projects are under finalization in the States of Andhra Pradesh, Tamil Nadu, Gujarat, Karnataka, Maharashtra, Madhya Pradesh and Kerala. The 100 MW goal of the Plan has not only been achieved, but exceeded many times.

Costs and Environmental Benefits

Wind power has the potential to become the cheapest method of generating power by the turn of the century. The present capital cost of wind power projects ranges between Rs. $3.50 - 4.00 \times 10^7$/MW, including local civil, electrical works and erection. The cost of generation varies from Rs. 1.75-2.25/kWh, depending upon the site. Though these costs compare quite favourably with those for new thermal power projects located away from coal mining areas, cost data from the small wind farm projects is not strictly comparable with large scale coal thermal projects. During the peak or power shutdown period, wind could replace diesel power which has very high operating costs. The costs of wind power generation will decline further through higher efficiencies obtained from advances in technology, larger-scale and more efficient manufacturing, discovery of windier sites, as well as with increase in size of wind turbines and wind power projects. Wind power will turn out to be even more competitive in comparison with conventional power if the classical cost calculations for conventional power also reflect all the external social and environmental costs. Studies have shown that these costs are roughly equal to the commercial costs of conventional electricity, indicating that the total cost to society is actually double the commercial cost.

India's energy production, because of heavy dependence on coal for thermal power generation and on wood and crop residues for household energy needs, is associated with environmental problems, including land degradation, water and air pollution, and the depletion of biomass and soil capacity. There is a growing awareness of the hazards of local and regional (particulates, SO_2, NO_x) and global CO_2 emissions from fossil-fuel-based power generation and the potential destruction of India's forest resources (CO_2 sinks). Wind turbines are the most "environment-friendly" method of producing electricity. They have no adverse effects on the global environment, unlike conventional coal- or oil-fired power plants or large hydropower projects. The emissions that can be saved per year from a typical 200 kW wind turbine, having an average yearly output of 400,000 kWh and involving the replacement of 120-200 tonnes of coal, have been estimated as follows:

sulphur dioxide (SO_2): 2-3.2 tonnes;
nitrogen oxide (NO_x): 1.2-2.4 tonnes;
carbon dioxide (CO_2): 300-500 tonnes; and,
particulates: 160-280 kg.

The specific CO_2 savings amount to about 2 tonnes per year per kW. A similar figure has been derived in Germany (see Part II, Chapter 8).

Promotional Incentives and IREDA Financing

A package of incentives is available which includes tax concessions such as accelerated depreciation, tax holiday, soft loans, customs and excise duty reliefs, improved foreign investment procedures, etc. Major initiatives in the recent past have also been taken to create remunerative and assured markets for power generation based on non-conventional energy. Guidelines have been sent to all the States on general policies and facilities for wheeling/banking/purchase of power from such projects. It has been proposed that the States may consider purchasing such power at least at the rate of Rs. 2.25/kWh. Supplementary guidelines have also been circulated, which provide for annual escalation at the rate of 5 per cent and suggestions for security of payments for the power sold. It is hoped that this will lead to attractive and assured returns on investments by developers and investors. Twelve States have already come forward and announced attractive policies for private sector power projects based on non-conventional energy sources, including wind power. In order to encourage the small investor, a concept of "Wind Energy Estates" in the joint sector with private sector, State and MNES (Ministry of Non-conventional Energy Sources)/IREDA (Indian Renewable Energy Development Agency) participation has been mooted. This is expected to reduce the gestation period, provide infrastructural facilities and reduce costs for small investors. The first such company has become functional in Madhya Pradesh and has set up a capacity of 9 MW in its wind energy estate near Indore.

The income tax, import and excise duty regimes are constantly being reviewed to allow the induction, development and deployment of the latest technologies, and to provide for healthy competition. The Government has issued comprehensive guidelines to bring about healthy and orderly growth of the wind power sector and to discourage the induction of poor technology and other misuse. The incentives should be utilized to optimize generation from identified windy sites using tested, proven equipment.

The Indian Renewable Energy Development Agency Ltd. (IREDA) was established in 1987 with the main objective of operating a revolving fund for the development, promotion and commercialization of renewable energy technologies by providing soft-term finance. It serves as a model for other developing countries and has received considerable international assistance. It has operated a World Bank and Global Environment Facility (GEF) line of credit amounting to US $ 78 million, co-financed by DANIDA, to promote commercial wind power generation. An ADB (Asian Development Bank) line of credit for commercial wind power development has also become available to IREDA. A KfW (Reconstruction Loan Corporation, Germany) line of credit is being negotiated.

Future Directions and Outlook

Additional power requirements in the developing countries to meet their growing developmental needs, and increased consciousness of the natural environment are expected to lead to increased installation of wind turbines, as no other new electricity-producing technology has attained the same level of maturity. There are no major technical barriers to large-scale penetration of wind power, except for the technical adaptations required to suit the existing power distribution networks. The main constraints are non-technical pertaining to land utilization, pricing, institutional, legal aspects, etc.

The programme in the Ninth Plan will seek to promote further commercialization and to create healthy market conditions. The role of the Government is to act as the "mission" leader and facilitator, to focus on policy and planning, and to support resource assessment, research and development, testing and standardization, demonstration, training and information dissemination. The State government agencies and the State Electricity Boards are working in unison to promote wind power development in the potential States. In order to take a long-term view, and to realize the full potential of renewables, the Government is formulating a comprehensive renewable energy policy, which will encompass the Government, industry, financial institutions, research institutions, non-government organizations, investors, developers, and users. The policy will help to create awareness, foster development and demonstration, accelerate commercialization, and create an effective support infrastructure and delivery mechanism for installation, operation, maintenance and repair. The Government also plans to introduce special legislation to promote renewables, as the present legislation governing the electricity sector is considered inadequate for the effective and rapid development of the renewable energy sector.

The World Watch Institute has predicated a fundamental change in the world's energy production and use, with wind power well-positioned to contribute to the emerging energy system based on new, renewable, decentralized energy technologies. Modern renewables could meet up to half of the world's energy demand by 2060, having a wind power share of 10 to 20 per cent. A report by Arthur D. Little, commissioned by the American Wind Energy Association, predicts 2,000-3,500 MW new wind capacity by the year 2000 outside the United States. Among the ten countries surveyed, India will see by far the highest wind capacity additions by the year 2000.

India has now gained sufficient experience, both technological and operational, and is now on the threshold of "takeoff" in wind power. It offers a viable option in the energy supply mix, particularly in the context of the present constraints on conventional sources. It also offers an attractive investment option to the private sector in the context of the recently announced policies and drive towards private sector power generation. Setting of broad goals will accelerate commercialization, and help in the development of a stable industry and its sustained growth. The resource, technology and commercialization prospects will have to be evaluated to determine the level of deployment, so that additional capacity are by and large techno-economically viable. A target for additional capacity of 2,000 MW by the year 2002 has been set. If a goal of another 7,000 MW is set for the year 2012, the total wind capacity of 10,000 MW then would amount to about a 4 per cent share in the total anticipated installed capacity of the country. Given the vast potential of wind energy in India and a successfully demonstrated technology, the time has come for a major policy and planning thrust for harnessing this vast natural resource. Actions are being initiated towards realization of the goals.

14 Biomass-Based Power Generation Prospects in India

SUDHIR MOHAN AND JAYANT RAMAKRISHNA MESHRAM

Biomass-Based Power Generation Prospects in India

The attractiveness of biomass as a fuel for power generation derives from its many similarities to fossil fuels. Some of the important similarities are:
1. its ability to generate "firm" power;
2. its amenability to storage and use as per power demands;
3. its broadly similar combustion characteristics, which may even enable co-firing;
4. absence of a need for elaborate pre-firing preparation.

This similarity with fossil fuels means that equipment designed for fossil fuels can be easily adapted for firing biomass materials; no major new investments would be required for setting up industries to fabricate new conversion equipment; manpower trained for work with fossil-fuel-fired power plants could be deployed for biomass fired power plants; and, as a result, replacement of fossil fuels by biomass could be brought about without major transitional economic costs and adjustments. Therefore, unlike many other renewable energy technologies (e.g. solar power generation), which are considered "back-stop" technologies, biomass-based power generation is termed a replacement technology.

Also on its own, biomass is being recognized as a valuable energy source. Especially in India, its importance cannot be underestimated when it is realized that it helps to meet over 75 per cent of the energy needs of rural areas, which cover roughly 70 per cent of our population. Further appreciation of its role in recent times could be derived from:
- its wide and equitable availability in the country,
- its less polluting nature as compared to fossil fuels,
- the fact that if biomass use in rural areas was to be "replaced" by oil, India would need to import an additional 15 million tonnes of crude oil every year.

Additionally, it is now being recognized that if used for power generation, Indian surplus biomass power resources alone could:

231

- save over 70 million tonnes of coal energy per year – the importance of this would be extremely significant in future when almost 80 per cent of coal mined in India will be used for power generation and availability of coal itself could constrain the creation of new power capacity,
- save over 162 million tonnes of net carbon-dioxide emissions into the atmosphere, helping the country to fulfil its global obligations (for detailed estimation, see Table 14.1),
- generate 20-30 crore (1 crore = ten million) mandays of additional employment every year in rural areas through local collection, storage, handling and transportation of biomass to power plant sites.

The above comments have attempted to bring out the background to the surging interest in biomass-based power generation in India. The following pages give an overview of the status of biomass power technology in the country through answers to the following questions:

- What is the potential?
- What are the Government programmes, policies and incentives?
- What has been achieved so far?
- What technological capabilities exist?
- What could the future hold?

Table 14.1 Estimation of net reduction in greenhouse gas emissions by biomass power in comparison to coal power

Assumptions

Load	1	MW
Distance of coal project from load	200	km
Transmission losses	3	%
Specific coal consumption	0.65	kg /kWh
Specific biomass consumption	1.1	kg /kWh
Carbon content in coal	55	%
Carbon content in biomass	40	%
Calorific value of coal	4,000	kcal/kg
Calorific value of biomass	3,500	kcal/kg
Present method of disposal of biomass*	Open burning	
Annual hours of generation	6,000	

Estimation

Net capacity	1	MW
Carbon dioxide emitted by coal project	8,100	t/yr
Net carbon dioxide emitted by biomass project	0	t/yr
Total reduction in carbon dioxide emission	8,100	t/yr
Potential from 20,000 MW of biomass power	162×10^6	t/yr

* if not used for power generation

Potential of Biomass Power in India

Types of Biomass

The term "biomass" in the Indian context primarily means material derived from the field residues of crops; waste by-products of crop processing; woody produce of forests; and also, the woody produce of plantations grown especially for this purpose. In accordance with the general practice followed in the country, municipal and industrial wastes, cattle and human wastes, etc. are taken as a separate category, not part of biomass.

Biomass Production

For agriculture-related biomass, the most exhaustive survey to assess the quantity of biomass produced in the country was carried out by the National Productivity Council in 1985-86. The survey recorded the ratios for the production of various types of crop residues and the useful product, and on the basis of these ratios, went on to estimate the statewise and cropwise biomass production. The survey concluded that 322 million tonnes of various field residues were produced in 1985-86. In addition, the quantity of waste by-products of crop processing was placed at 50 million tonnes, which evidently did not include bagasse.

Assuming that the ratios of wastes to useful products would still be valid, one can work out the quantities of these materials produced in recent times. These estimates are given in Table 14.2.

Surplus Biomass

The total quantity of agricultural-related biomass is estimated to be of the order of 480 million tonnes every year. The most substantial portion out of this quantity is produced during rice cultivation. In fact, 140 million tonnes of paddy straw estimated to be produced every year can itself sustain a power capacity of over 15,000 MW. However, as is obvious, not all of this quantity can be made available for power production without affecting other uses. The present uses of the materials are also given in Table 14.2. As can be seen, almost all the materials find some other use in the rural Indian economy. Therefore, more important than estimating the total quantities produced every year, it is necessary to estimate the quantities which can be spared for power production without affecting present uses.

Table 14.2 Estimates of biomass production in India (1995-96)

Crop	Production 10^6 tonnes	Residue or by-product	Ratio t/ha	Waste 10^6 tonnes	Typical uses
Rice	80	Straw	3.5	140	Roof thatching, cattle feed, packing, burnt in fields
		Husk	0.5	40	Mainly small industry and brick kilns
Wheat	63	Straw	1.3	82	Almost exclusively as cattle feed
Maize	9	Cobs	0.3	3.0	Cattle feed, domestic fuel
		Stalks	1.0	9.0	Almost exclusively as cattle feed
Coarse, cereals	25	Straws	1.0	25.0	Sometimes as cattle feed Also as domestic fuel
Sugarcane	250	Green tops	0.05	12.5	As cattle feed
		Trash	0.05	12.5	Left in the field and sometimes burnt in situ
		Bagasse	0.3	48 organized	Mainly as captive fuel, 5 per cent goes for paper
				27 unorganized	Used exclusively as fuel for jaggery making
Cotton	2.2	Stalks	8	18	Used as domestic fuel or burnt in field
		Ginning waste	0.1	0.2	Used as fuel by brick kilns/small industry
Groundnut	8	Shell	0.33	2.6	Fuel by small industries, specially by oil extractors
Rapeseed, mustard	6	Stalks	1	6	Partly as domestic fuel
Other oil-seeds	8	Stalks	1	8	Partly as domestic fuel
Jute and mesta	1.6	Sticks	2	3.2	Partly as domestic fuel, partly as industrial fuel
Pulses	13	Strains	1.0	13.0	Partly as domestic fuel
Coconut (10^8 nuts)	140	Shell	0.135 kg/nut	1.8	Domestic and small industrial fuel
		Pith	0.246 kg/nut	3.4	Fuel, or burnt off
		Fibre	0.164 kg/ nut	2.3	As coir, packing, etc.
Jowar	10	Stalk	2	20	As cattle feed
Bajra	5	Stalk	1	5	Domestic fuel
Total	-	-	-	482	-

Notes to the table on the next page

1. The ratios were mainly taken from the report of the NPC survey of biomass availability in India (1986). The values of production for 1995-96 are from various published data (e. g. most recently Hindustan Times, 14.4.1997).
2. The values were rounded to nearest whole number, where such rounding would not significantly affect the numbers.
3. Although waste ratios for various coarse cereals, pulses and oilseeds vary from product to product, yet, for the sake of rounding off, an approximate average value has been taken to represent the whole sector.
4. The ratios in most cases would indicate values within ± 10-20 per cent rather than definite values as these would vary with yield, soil, type of seed, irrigated/non-irrigated, etc. In some cases though (e. g. bagasse and husk), these are more definitive.
5. Many other minor materials e. g. de-oiled cakes from solvent extraction, minor husks from pulses and oilseeds, etc. have been neglected.

No comprehensive attempt has however been made, apart from the aforementioned NPC study, to estimate the surplus biomass materials which could be made available for power production. A recent effort in this direction has been the taluka-level biomass studies sponsored by MNES, initially in around 100 talukas, spread over the entire country. The studies utilized household surveys of a sample of the population to arrive at the pattern of biomass consumption for various applications. However, since the responses to household interviews were largely guesstimates, exact quanta of surplus left after meeting the domestic applications could not be arrived at and only orders of magnitude figures were derived. These show that generally in the Northern Indian States of Punjab and Haryana surpluses are much higher, especially as paddy straw is not generally used as a cattle feed and a larger percentage of domestic fuel requirements are met by petroleum fuels, biogas and dried animal dung. The surveys show that while in Punjab a typical taluka could support a 20-40 MW power project, in the Southern States of Andhra and Tamil Nadu not more than 5 MW could be supported.

Indirect estimation of the biomass which can be made available may also be attempted. Since it has been proposed that around 250 million tonnes of biomass (excluding bagasse) is used as fuel in households and small industry, and since it is also known that while in households use efficiency is not more than 10 per cent and in industry it is less than 50 per cent, it could be envisaged that by promoting energy efficient technologies, significant surplus quantities of biomass could be released. The success of such technologies would, however, depend upon the price paid by the power project for the biomass or the financial benefits which will accrue to farmers on changeover. Obviously, such improvements can only be carried out up to the present socio-technological limits of around 25 per cent for domestic cooking and around 70 per cent for small industrial applications.

Thus, it could be said that provided the financial benefits are attractive to present users, at least 100 to 125 million tonnes of biomass can be made available for alternative uses by savings from the present uses, without replacement by alternative fuels. This will depend upon payment of suitable prices for the biomass by power producers and, as can be appreciated, is *bound* to take place because of market forces as power demand increases. This quantity, added to around 10 per cent present normal surpluses out of total production, brings the quantity which could be available for power generation, out of total present biomass production, to 140 to 160 million tonnes per year.

In addition, biomass is also produced from forests. However, since only the sustainable/renewable quantities are considered, only that quantity of biomass which could be produced on a recurring basis from India's forest area of around 0.35 million km^2 should be taken. Thus, yields from forests should be taken as only naturally falling branches, twigs, and deadwood. If the quantity of these was to be considered as around 1 t/ha, it can be seen that forestry biomass would not be very significant compared to total biomass produced from other sources. Most of these woody forestry biomass materials are also used for burning in domestic stoves and hence the same logic as that applied for agricultural biomass would apply in respect of quantities that become surplus as a result of efficiency improvements. Approximately half of the total sustainable production of around 35 million tonnes per year can thus be made available for power production.

Therefore, altogether 160-170 million tonnes of biomass could be made available through efficiency improvements and collection of present surpluses. The 160-170 million tonnes of biomass should, on a conservative basis, be sufficient for sustaining 16,000 to 18,000 MW of power generation capacity. In addition, surplus power which can be produced by optimization of cogeneration in sugar mills (using bagasse as a fuel) has been estimated by a MNES Task Force at 3,500 MW. Thus, the total potential for generation of power from biomass in India could be stated to be around 20,000 MW.

Government Programmes, Policies and Incentives

Biomass has been recognized as an important renewable energy resource by the Government right from the inception of renewable energy programmes. Programmes have been initiated for both efficiency improvements for the use of biomass in traditional applications, as well as for promotion of higher value addition to surplus biomass through the power generation route. Technologies of improved briquetting for cooking stoves are being promoted in the former category while biomass combustion, cogeneration and gasification are promoted in the latter category. Only brief details of biomass power programmes are given in following.

Gasification Programme

This was one of the first biomass power programmes to be initiated by the Ministry. The programme intends to promote the development, demonstration and commercialization of biomass gasifier-based systems for water pumping and mechanical power applications, thermal applications (production of producer gas) and generation of electrical energy for captive industrial application or rural electrification.

A network of research institutions has been built up over the years for developmental work on various facets of biomass gasification, such as development of application packages; testing and evaluation; characterization of biomass materials etc., apart from developmental work on basic gasification and power generation systems. The present generation of biomass gasifier-dual fuel engine power packs can use a variety of woody biomass materials for power generation of up to 400 kW (electric) with around 80 per cent diesel displacement. The gasifiers are of the down-draught type and require sizing and moisture control of feedstock. More versatile gasifiers, using powdery biomass, are also reported to have been successfully tested. Rice husks, coconut shells, etc. are some other materials reported to have been successfully tested in gasifiers.

The demonstration programme provides financial support of up to around 30 per cent of the cost of gasifiers for thermal applications and up to around 60 per cent of mechanical/electrical applications. Around 1,600 gasification systems, aggregating to around 26 MW equivalent capacity, have so far been installed in the country.

Grid-connected, gasifier-based power generation systems have recently been taken up for promotion and the first of such projects - a 500 kW system, based on wood grown on state plantations - is being installed with substantial financial support from the central Government in the Kutch region of Gujarat. The hardware is being supplied by an Indian company.

Biomass Combustion

It has been proposed that beyond a certain capacity perhaps Rankine cycle based power projects may prove to be more economical. This will specially be true until the time biomass integrated gasifier cum gas turbine combined cycle systems, which can increase the efficiencies of biomass conversion to over 60 per cent, are finally established. The Ministry therefore initiated a pilot programme on biomass-combustion based power generation in 1994-95. Two projects were provided with capital subsidies under the Programme to demonstrate the technology. At present, the Government is promoting this technology through financial incentives in the form of a subsidy for reduction in rate of the interest. The scheme is being implemented through financial institutions.

Bagasse Cogeneration

India is one of the largest sugar cane producers in the world. More than 150 million tonnes of cane is crushed in the organized sector to produce sugar. Around 45 million tonnes of bagasse is produced during this process, most of which is burnt in sugar mill boilers to produce steam and power for captive use. Approximately 10 per cent of the bagasse which remains surplus is partly sold off for paper production and partly disposed of to small industry.

A task force set up by the Government in 1993 estimated that 3,500 MW of additional power could be produced by the sugar industry if they were motivated to adopt high pressure/high temperature steam generation along with steam-saving measures in the sugar process. Thus, the process of "optimum cogeneration" will lead to augmentation of grid power as well as economic benefits to the sugar mill.

The national programme on bagasse-based cogeneration being implemented by the Ministry intends to promote optimum cogeneration through demonstration of state-of-the-art technologies, providing financial incentives to other projects, and providing support for information dissemination, R&D and training activities.

The limited number of "demonstration" projects will be provided with capital subsidies to partly compensate for the risks which pioneering mills would take by adopting untried technologies. Minimum surplus power generation of 5 MW by using at least 60 bar/450°C steam pressure/temperature conditions have been stipulated. The scheme is designed in such a manner as to provide encouragement to cooperative/public sector sugar mills which constitute over 75 per cent of the mills in the country.

General Incentives

Apart from the programmes for promotion of these technologies, announced by the Ministry of Non-Conventional Energy Sources of the Central Government, many other incentives are also available for their users. These include fiscal incentives such as a 5-year tax holiday (as announced for all power projects), accelerated depreciation, concessional excise/customs duties and sales tax exemption in many States.

A major development which has occurred in recent years relates to the announcement of general policies for purchase/wheeling/banking of power generated from various non-conventional energy sources. Eight States have announced general policies to purchase this power at rates varying from Rs. 2.0/kWh to Rs. 2.25/kWh, escalated at 5 per cent per year for 10 years. This facility assures a ready market for the generated power and makes the projects bankable.

In addition to the mandatory purchase of power by the State Electricity Board (SEB), some states also allow facilities for wheeling of generated power through the state grid to the generator's own unit located in another part of the state or, as in some states, even to third-party consumers for sale at mutually negotiated rates. The biggest concern, where third-party sale of power is not permitted, is surety of payments for the energy sold to the SEB. Unfortunately, no worthwhile solution to this has so far emerged.

Indian Technological Capabilities

The power equipment manufacturing sector in India is quite well developed with a large number of public sector/private sector companies manufacturing boilers, turbines, handling equipment, electrical switchgear, etc. Due to similarities between conventional power equipment and that required for biomass, as pointed out at the beginning of this paper, no difficulty is expected in the manufacture of equipment for biomass power projects. The capabilities in each of the areas are given below.

Boiler Manufacturing

Biomass-fired boilers for power projects can be of the suspension firing type with travelling grate/dumping grate or the fluidized-bed type. A number of large manufacturers (some with turnovers exceeding Rs. 4,500 million, apart from BHEL, which has a total turnover of over 50,000 million) have established capabilities for manufacturing spreader-stoker-fired, travelling grate/dumping grate boilers; atmospheric pressure fluidized-bed boilers and circulating fluidized-bed boilers (BHEL = Baharat Heavy Electrical Limited). The capacity which can be manufactured in the industrial boiler range is generally up to 150 tonnes per hour/100 bar, while larger boilers could be made by power boiler manufacturers. Though for power generation applications apart from bagasse, only a few boilers have been made as yet. For industrial steam generation applications, many large boilers have been supplied. Biomass successfully fired in these boilers includes rice husk, straw, cotton stalk, coconut shells, soya husk, de-oiled cakes, moist coffee process waste, jute wastes, groundnut shells, etc. Boilers have also been made with multi-fuel capabilities for firing coal/biomass, or a combination of biomass materials.

Bagasse-fired boilers have been made in the country for sugar mills for many decades past, and at least 1,000 of such boilers would be working today. Almost all manufacturers have capabilities to cater to high pressure/high temperature steam needs if required by the sugar industry. Due to the recent upsurge of interest in cogeneration for surplus power, leading manufacturers are upgrading their capabilities for high-efficiency boilers.

Steam Turbine Manufacturing

The market for small (less than 15 MW) steam turbines has primarily been represented by demand from the sugar industry. Since the sugar industry had been catering to only captive power requirements, the maximum generation in any mill was around 6 MW, and hence this became the upper end of Indian industrial turbine manufacturing capability. In exceptional cases, for large mills where captive demand was greater, multiples of smaller rating would be deployed. Efficiency of turbines was never a consideration, as long as the electricity and the steam demands of the process matched. Opening up of the market for power sales has brought in its wake premiums on efficiency and, as a response to market requirements, the main manufacturers have started the process of technical upgrading. Initially, high-efficiency turbines are being offered either with mainly imported components, or in fully imported versions. Phased local manufacturing has simultaneously been initiated. Three of the world's leading engineering companies are in this business in India, apart from BHEL.

Almost all combinations - condensing, single extraction/double extraction condensing, back pressure etc. - are now being offered in the country with full after-sales service guarantees. The efficiencies of turbines now being offered are comparable to the best in the world.

Biomass Gasifier Manufacturing

India is among the leaders in the biomass gasification area. Though development efforts started in the early eighties, today there are at least three manufacturers who offer systems of up to 500 kW_{el} single unit capacity. Technology for these systems has been developed fully indigenously either with the support of central government research institutions or by the private sector manufacturers themselves.

The gasifiers are at present almost exclusively of the down-draught atmospheric pressure design and are primarily designed for firing woody biomass. Some preparation, especially sizing, is necessary before firing the biomass into the reactors. The systems are generally of the batch-feed type. The cooling/cleaning systems have also evolved considerably and at present gas qualities suitable for operation of dual fuel engines are being guaranteed. On the engine side, obviously, fully indigenous capabilities exist.

Progress in Biomass Power in India

Indian efforts for a promotion of biomass power started with a 10 MW project using rice straw in the agriculturally rich State of Punjab. The project was initiated in 1988 and installation was completed in 1992. The project uses a custom-built overfeed fluidized bed boiler designed and fabricated by BHEL. The firing of straw is in the form of bales, which are pushed into the furnace with continuous pushes. The bales are supposed to be broken on entering the hot furnace, but because the ropes used to tie the bales were not breaking fast enough, many trials were necessary before the right rope was arrived at. The firing system was apparently an adoption from the "cigar firing" arrangement used with travelling grate boilers in Denmark. Apparently also, bale feeding was preferred to loose/pneumatic feeding in view of the large chopped quantities involved (around 15 tonnes per hour).

After initial trials, it was found that there was a severe slag deposition problem on the superheater and first boiler bank as well as in the bed. Modifications were then carried out to increase overfire air, reduce bed temperatures and add limestone to reduce alkali content in the ash. The modified version was recommissioned in early 1994 and the problems appeared to have been resolved. The plant, however, could not be operated any further due to the severely reduced availability of straw in the vicinity of the project because of a change in cropping patterns. This underscores the need to have multifuel boilers for biomass projects.

The second simultaneous project in the private sector was commissioned around 1992 in Haryana. The project was designed primarily as a 4 MW captive power plant for a medium density particle board company. The company considered it a synergizing of their operator, since they would anyway have procured substantial quantities of agricultural wastes for their main activity. The main fuel is cotton stalk which is chopped to around 1" (one inch) before firing into a spreader stoker, travelling grate boiler. The boiler is capable of using a variety of alternate biomass materials. The project has been running successfully.

In recent times, two biomass power projects, one based on rice husk, and the other on Prosopis juliflora, have been taken up in the private sector with a capital subsidy from the Government under a pilot programme to demonstrate the viability of such projects. Both the projects are under installation. Details of these are given in Table 14.3. In addition a 12 MW project, proposing to use cane trash and bagasse, and a few other smaller projects mainly for captive consumption, using fuels such as rice husk, de-oiled cakes, etc., have been commissioned.

Around 25 MW of electricity equivalent capacity through 1,500 biomass gasifiers, ranging from 5 kW to 500 kW, has also been installed, mainly through partial financial support from the Indian Government. The systems are meant for water pumping, captive electricity, captive gas generation, etc.

Though possibilities for surplus power generation through cogeneration in sugar industry have been long known, their exploitation could start in a significant manner only after 1994, following the announcement of the national programme on bagasse based cogeneration by the Central Government. The programme offered a mix of promotional and financial incentives to cogenerating sugar mills which, more than anything else, assured the sugar industry, the State Governments and the SEBs (State Electricity Boards) of Government backing for the technology and hence a ratification of its viability. In the initial rush, surprisingly, more enthusiasm was shown by cooperative sugar mills than by mills in the private sector.

This is perhaps explained by the innate desire of cooperative mill managements to increase the value addition, so that they could increase payouts to farmer members. It is a different matter that these mills have so far been constrained by their own fund-raising capabilities.

Table 14.3 Demonstration biomass power projects

Unit 1

Capacity	6 MW
Total cost	Rs. 18 crores (1 crore = 10^6)
MNES subsidy	Rs. 4.2 crores
Balance	IDBI, IREDA and promoters
Main fuels	Prosopis juliflora
Location	Village Vedadri, District Krishna, Andhra Pradesh
Type of boiler	Spreader stoker, travelling grate
Storage provisions	2 months
Fuel preparation	Chopping to less than 3-inch size
Yearly requirement of fuel	45,000 tonnes
Back-up fuels	Coal
Alternate biomass	Bagasse, pump mill rejects

Unit 2

Capacity	5 MW
Total cost	Rs. 22 crores
MNES subsidy	Rs. 3.5 crores
Balance	IDBI, IREDA, promoters and public issue
Main fuel	Rice husk
Location	Jharouda village, Raipur district, Madhya Pradesh
Type of boiler	Atmospheric fluidized bed, 62 bar/485°C
Storage provisions	3-4 months
Fuel preparation	Fired as it is
Back-up fuel	Coal
Alternate biomass	Nil

A capacity of 55 MW surplus power generation has so far been commissioned in 15 sugar mills. Projects range from 1.5 MW if incidental power to 8 MW from a mill with 2,500 tonnes of cane per day. More than 80 MW of projects in another 15 mills are under construction. The encouraging point is that so many of these mills have chosen steam pressures of more than 60 bar and have made serious attempts to optimize cogeneration. Details of typical optimum cogeneration projects being considered by many sugar mills are given in Table 14.4. Most of these projects sell electricity to the state grids for which general policies have been announced by eight major sugar-producing states.

Table 14.4 Details of a typical "optimum" bagasse cogeneration project

Mill capacity (on 24 hrs. basis)	2500 tonnes per day
Capacity/hour	104 tonnes
Bagasse produced at 30 % on cane	31.25 tonnes
Bagasse available after losses and non-fuel consumption	30 tonnes
Moisture in bagasse	50 %
Calorific value	2.250 kcal/kg
Steam consumption at 2.5 ata at 3% on cane	3.12 tonnes per hour
Deaerator steam consumption at 2.5 ata	1 tonne per day
Power consumption including hydraulic drives	3.0 MW
Boiler efficiency	69 %
Steam pressure	66 bar
Steam temperature	485°C
Total steam generation	67 tonnes per hour
1st extraction	3.2 tonnes per hour
2nd extraction	45 tonnes per hour
Condensing steam	18.8 tonnes per hour
Total power generation	13.0 MW
Total internal consumption including auxiliary of power plant	4.3 MW
Net power export	8.7 MW

Future Possibilities and Conclusions

Biomass is a very important renewable energy source of the country. More than 20,000 MW of power could be supported on the surplus biomass which could be made available, without displacing present uses, if a suitable price was paid to biomass producers/users. The technology for such projects is available, the market for power is assured and government policies are becoming conducive. There would thus be no reason to suspect the inherent replacement potential of biomass power in the country and it may not be overly optimistic to expect a biomass power capacity of more than 10,000 MW in the next two decades. However, a need exists to consolidate and build upon the modest beginnings. During the Ninth Five Year Plan, which commenced in April 1997, it is envisaged that R&D efforts on advanced gasifications systems will be intensified to improve efficiencies of biomass use so that more power can be extracted from the same quantities.

The views expressed in the paper are those of the authors and not necessarily those of the Government of India.

PART III

Reduction Options in the Residential Sector

15 Instruments to Realize Energy Saving Potentials in the German Residential Sector

WOLFGANG FEIST AND WITTA EBEL

High Energy Saving Potentials in Existing Buildings in Germany

Carbon dioxide emissions into the earth's atmosphere must be drastically reduced in order to mitigate global climate change (Bundestag, 1995). The most important aim is to avoid unnecessary energy consumption by efficient energy use. Efficient energy use is the safest, most environmentally friendly and least expensive way to "energy acquisition". It is economically attractive, rapidly feasible and can be integrated into our economic process without any structural changes. Efficient energy use therefore plays a key role in solving the climate problem. It is a precondition for meeting residual needs with renewable energy in the more distant future. Efficient energy use creates the scope for action for future generations to decide on supply technologies without unavoidable constraints.

At present, about one third of the final energy in Germany is used for space heating. A technical energy saving potential of about 70 per cent is exploitable with commercially available technologies for thermal insulation in existing buildings (Ebel et al., 1996) (Figure 15.1). The technical potential even increases to over 85 per cent with the passive-building technologies currently under development.

The most important measures for saving heating energy are the subsequent insulation of structural components of the external envelope of buildings, the installation of high-grade thermal insulation glazing, improved automatic control technology and more efficient heat generation (e.g. by gross calorific-value technology, cogeneration or heat pumps).

The energy demand for the production of the required insulating materials is insignificant. In order to ensure adequate air quality, controlled ventilation with the aid of exhaust fans is recommended for kitchens, bathrooms and toilets. Additional energy savings can be achieved by retransferring the heat from exhaust air to fresh air using heat exchangers. These meas-

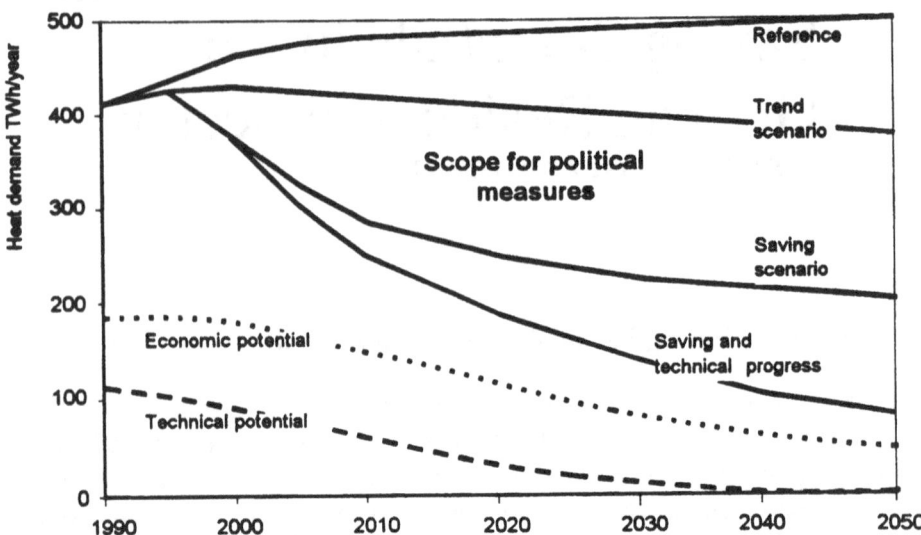

Figure 15.1 Scenarios for the development of heating demand of private households in Germany

ures serve not only for energy conservation, but also prevent damage to buildings and lead to increased housing quality.

Numerous insulating materials and insulating systems are available on the market for thermal insulation in old buildings, which lead to high energy savings in the case of physically proper workmanship.

Thermal insulation measures must be carried out within the framework of modernization or repair work which is necessary anyhow (coupling principle). The underlying principle is to "go the whole hog", since insufficient insulating thickness leads to long-term loss of the saving potential. Insulating material thickness of 20 cm should be provided in roofs, 12 cm for outer wall external insulation and 6 cm for internal insulation. These values are economically reasonable in view of today's energy prices and are a meaningful precaution against future rising energy prices.

A catalogue of measures for optimum thermal insulation in old buildings has been developed with the aid of model calculations, cost accounting and determining optimum insulating material thickness (Ebel et al., 1996). On the basis of the upper price scenario given by the Study Commission "Preventive Measures to Protect the Earth's Atmosphere" in 1991, achievable economic energy savings amount to more than 50 per cent over time (Figure 15.1). Completed demonstration projects confirm that the assumed thermal insulation standards are achievable in existing buildings (Görg, Kienzle et al., 1996).

However, the specified energy saving potentials are only exploitable with reasonable economic expenditure if structural energy saving measures are coupled to normal renewal cycles for the respective components. This coupling only takes place by itself in individual cases or involving an inadequate scope of measures. Savings of 10 - 20 per cent can therefore only be expected under the present legal and economic boundary conditions ("trend" curve, Figure 15.1). If, on the other hand, the coupling principle is consistently pursued and thermal insulation measures are optimally executed, the economic potential can be exploited almost completely up to the year 2050 ("saving" scenario). The difference between "saving" and "trend" curve is the scope for action that can be used by a joint effort of all those involved (politics, economy and owners).

Using the Potentials Identified

As shown in (Ebel et al., 1996), more than 50 per cent of the heating energy needed today in the residential building stock could be economically saved using thermal insulation techniques already available on the market. However, this potential can only be realized with economically reasonable expenditure if structural energy saving measures are coupled to renovations of the respective components within the normal renewal cycle. It is therefore not easy to achieve the goal of a 25 - 30 per cent reduction of carbon dioxide emissions within 15 years envisaged by the federal government and the Study Commission "Protecting the Earth's Atmosphere" of the German Bundestag. The long investment cycles of plants and buildings using or converting energy make it necessary to steer investment decisions at an early stage and create the required political boundary conditions in good time.

In order to be able to assess the impact of energy policy actions a priori, however, instruments are required enabling the dependence of energy consumption on controllable parameters to be assessed. Current technology-based prediction models are unsuitable due to the long investment cycles and the dependence of individual options for action on the "history" of buildings and structural components.

For this reason, a specific scenario model has been developed which is based on a cohort method. The entire residential building stock is divided into representative types of houses. Types of buildings and their components are divided into age classes (cohorts). Each of these cohorts is observed over time. At the time of repair, the "energy-related age" of the component concerned is zeroed in the model. The repair times are given by the component-specific renewal periods and are described by distributions. The more time has elapsed since the last renovation, the greater is the probability for renewal in the year under consideration.

Energy saving measures can be carried out for the respective component at each time of renewal. The specific energy consumption of the building will then decrease accordingly. The extent to which the measures are actually carried out is determined by different assumptions for the respective scenarios.

Living floor space activated from the building stock is considered separately, since this additional floor space does not lead to correspondingly increased energy consumption (see Figure 15.2). Annexes or extensions of buildings have much lower specific energy consumptions than the already existing stock.

Energy saving potentials beyond the already described measures available on the market have not been included in the model calculations, although more intensive energetic renovations become possible in the long term due to technological progress and will also be economically efficient due to rising energy prices.

On this basis, total useful and final energy consumption depends on the following parameters:

1. specific energy demand (relative to the floor space in m^2): whereas this service is assumed to be constant for centrally heated flats, increased heating requirements must be expected when changing over from decentralized to central heating since, in most cases, all rooms are then heated, including side rooms;
2. heating facility measures: unless they lead to changes in behaviour (see above), they only relate to final energy consumption and emissions;
3. scenario assumptions with respect to building renovation and the insulation standard of new buildings.

The assumptions on the overall development of housing stock are based on the forecast by the German Study Commission "Protecting the Earth's Atmosphere".

The renewal cycles are in some cases given by the very long service life time of components such as roofs and facing plaster. It is between 30 years for softwood windows and 100 years for tiles. A precondition, however, is very good workmanship which is not given especially for large proportions

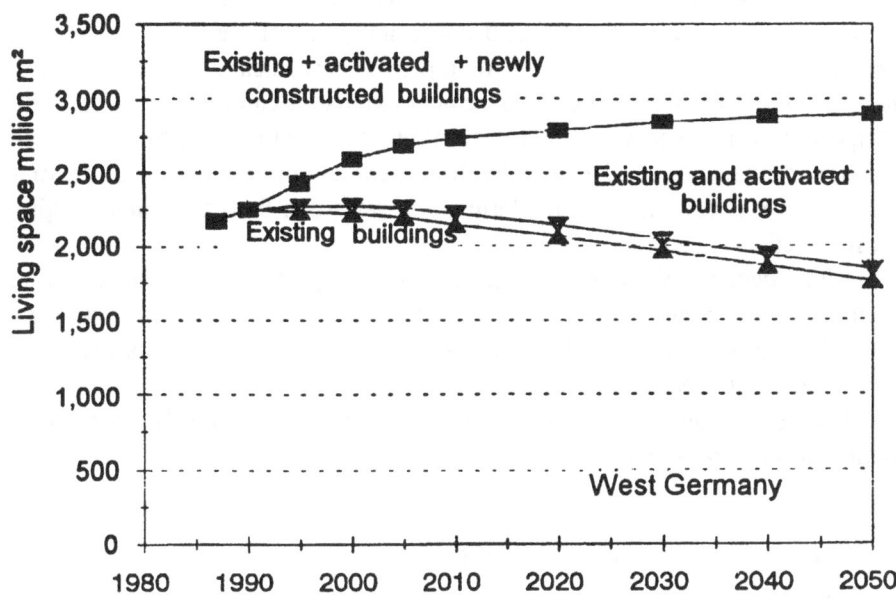

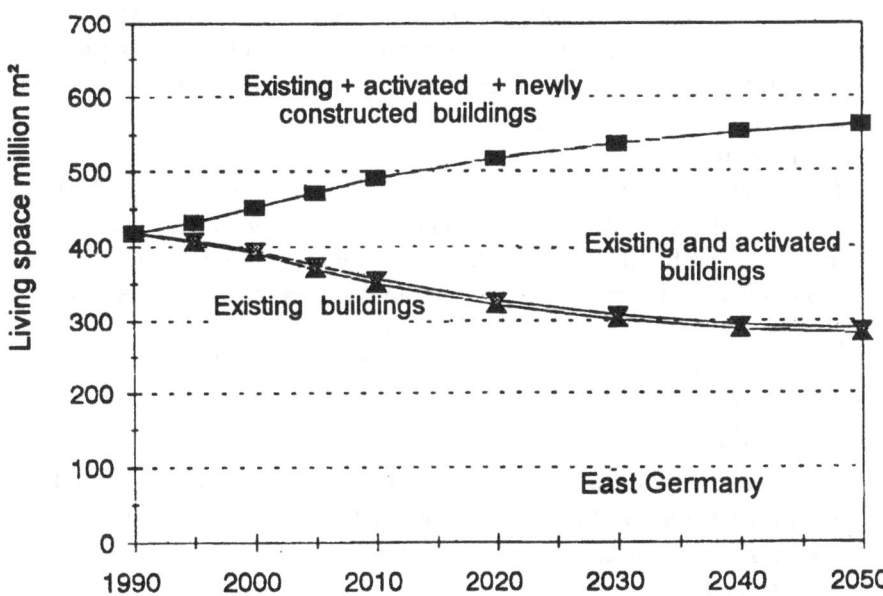

Figure 15.2 Forecast concerning the future development of living floor space in West and East Germany

of more recent building stock (built after the second world war). However, renovations of relevance from a heat insulation point of view are in part also carried out for aesthetic reasons to improve convenience or comply with changed user demands. A roof or basement extension can also be linked with energy saving measures. Furthermore, there are saving possibilities which are largely independent of other measures, such as core insulation of the masonry. Future renovation and modernization rates can therefore only roughly be estimated.

More decisive than precise renovation rates, however, is the question whether saving measures are carried out to a sufficient extent at a given time. The replacement periods assumed for the model calculations are taken from (Ebel et al., 1996).

Figure 15.2 shows the expected development of the overall floor space, divided into existing, activated and new buildings.

Base Scenarios for Existing Buildings

The following scenarios are shown in Figure 15.1:
1. Zero reference scenario
    No further energy saving measures are carried out. Although such a reference scenario itself does not represent a realistic development, it provides suitable reference for the quantification of saving potentials due to structural measures.
2. Trend scenario
    Measures are carried out with suboptimal insulating layer thickness (trend catalogue of measures from (Ebel et al., 1996)) executed with the following probabilities at replacement times, provided that they are economically reasonable in the individual case and at the given time:
    -   roof: 50 per cent
    -   window: 100 per cent (insulation glazing)
    -   wall: 20 per cent
    -   floor/basement: 10 per cent

    The energy prices are based on the reference price development without additional taxes or charges, as stipulated for the studies by the Study Commission "Protecting the Earth's Atmosphere".
3. Saving scenario
    Since 1995, 100 per cent of the measures of the saving catalogue have been carried out at the respective replacement times, provided that they

are economically reasonable in the individual case and at the given time of replacement. The scenario is based on the price development stipulated for this case by the Study Commission "Preventive Measures to Protect the Earth's Atmosphere", which leads to significantly higher energy prices. The upper bound assumed for the mean future energy price is 13 Pf/kWh. Consideration is given to the conservation of monuments and to restrictions of architectural design.

4. Economic potential

   All measures of the saving scenario are carried out up to a cost of 13 Pf for the kilowatt-hour saved, but the most favourable time of replacement is not taken into account. The *economic potential* thus does not reflect a realistic development, but constitutes the lower bound for development in the saving scenario.

5. Technical potential

   All measures of the saving catalogue from (Ebel et al., 1996) are executed without paying regard to restrictions for reasons of economic efficiency, conservation of monuments, architecture or limited implementation speeds.

In the *reference scenario* the specific heating demands in the building stock change slightly because the ratios of the building types are shifted due to demolitions. The demolition of older buildings rather leads to a reduction in the specific heating demands of the remaining buildings, whereas the increased demolition of compact large multi-family houses above all in the new federal states (East Germany) has the opposite effect. Moreover, additional floor space is activated in the stock. However, the additional floor space created by extensions has a lower specific energy demand even with relatively poor thermal insulation.

The *trend scenario* extrapolates the previous development in executing structural energy saving measures and thus reflects a probable consumption development in the case of modest political efforts.

The *saving scenario* represents a development which is characterized by major political efforts at energy conservation, but simultaneously considers the aspects of individual economic profitability. The lower bound for the development in the "saving" scenario is reflected by the *economic potential*. This will only be reached in 50 - 60 years due to the in part very long implementation periods.

The energy saving measures in the *saving scenario* involve total additional investment costs of DM 208 billion distributed over 50 years. This sum which initially appears high only represents the additional costs compared to normal repairs. Figure 15.3 shows the development of these additional costs and, in comparison, the pure modernization costs for those measures which can be reasonably coupled to the energy saving measures under consideration. The additional costs only account for 11 per cent of the total cost in the period mentioned. They are marginal in comparison to the - still much higher - total cost of repair and modernization.

In the *trend scenario* the additional costs for energy savings amount to DM 1 billion per year. In the *saving scenario* they initially reach a peak with DM 12 billion per year - that is about 28 per cent of the total costs for measures capable of being coupled - but then perceptibly decrease with increasing implementation of the "saving" development (Figure 15.3).

The difference between trend and saving development indicates the scope for energy policy actions. Whereas only 11 per cent heating energy can be saved in the *trend scenario* compared to the reference development without structural energy saving measures, savings amount to 39 per cent in the *saving scenario* (cumulative saving rates in 2050).

Instruments for Exploiting the Saving Potentials

The aim of environmental policy must be to exploit as far as possible the technical energy saving potential in buildings up to the year 2050. Only then this sector can make its contribution to the required reduction of CO_2 emissions by 80 per cent.

Characteristic Figures of Energy Consumption and Energy Identification Cards of Buildings (IDs)

An important step towards achieving sufficient heat insulation standards is the definition of reference scales. They permit, on the one hand, a classification of the energy consumption of an existing object and, on the other hand, they make the market of energy saving technologies more transparent.

Energy data for heating load, heating energy and primary energy demands in buildings have already been defined on several occasions. However, binding terms and uniform, easily verifiable modes of calculation still remain to be determined. These energy data can then be generally made available in energy IDs for old and new buildings. The introduction and spread of characteristic figures of energy consumption of a building would trigger a number of positive effects:

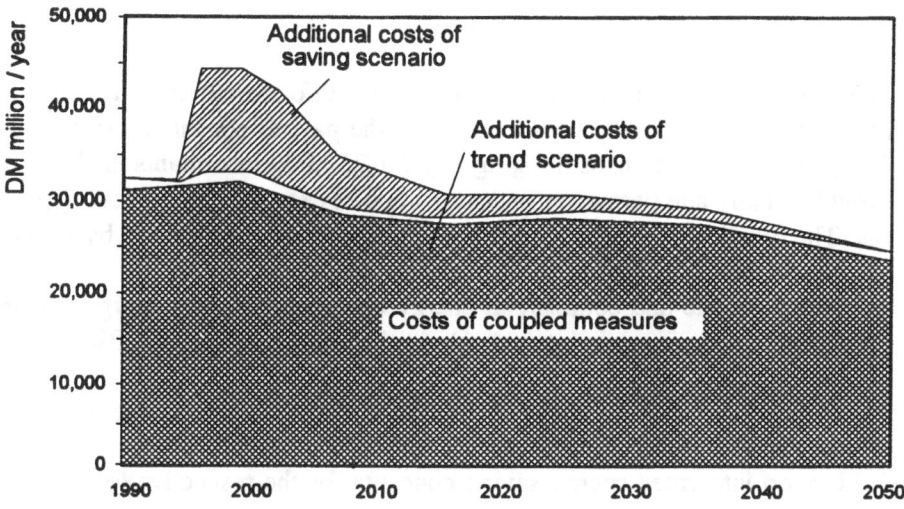

Figure 15.3 Investment costs in the building stock

1. Clear orientation aids will be given for the actual target value, i.e. energy consumption.
2. Various ways are possible to comply with the data. This will provide leeway for modernization and planning new buildings and promote innovative solutions.
3. By the issue of energy IDs the data will become a quality feature for buildings, which has an influence on the rents and sales proceeds achievable on the market.
4. Compliance with the desirable standard can be verified by owners and users of buildings with the aid of consumption measurements, which in turn promotes the careful execution of thermal insulation measures.

The calculation procedure for the annual heating demand stipulated in the 1995 Thermal Insulation Ordinance does not provide realistic values. The "Guideline for an Energy-Conscious Planning of Buildings", on the other hand, provides a realistic and easily verifiable method for calculating energy data (Ebel, Feist, 1994). In contrast to the heating demand IDs of the 1995 Thermal Insulation Ordinance, energy IDs should also include the heating system to enable an overall optimization of the energy supply. Energy IDs should initially be issued on a voluntary basis and only become mandatory within the framework of support programmes.

Establishing a Consultancy Infrastructure

Independent energy consultancy can reduce information deficiencies and prejudices against energy conservation on the part of consumers (see Table 15.1). An established consulting agency for 250,000 inhabitants each would provide locally and permanently strong impulses for the energy saving process. The creation of a suitable infrastructure should be supported by a funding programme. The energy consulting agencies should

1. inform private and commercial energy consumers free of charge and independent of economic interests about the possibilities of an efficient, environmentally and socially compatible energy use,
2. provide them with an object-related basis for decisions on energy-saving investments,
3. develop integrated energy saving concepts for the respective local conditions and
4. increase the general level of knowledge concerning the significance of energy conservation by continuous public relations work.

Table 15.1 Selection of consultancy instruments

- *Discussion of specific problems* with the aid of rough analyses, product descriptions and execution guidelines.
- *Permanent exhibition* at the consulting agency to support the discussions.
- *Computer programmes* to generate heat balances for buildings and simulate energy saving measures.
- *Evaluation of applications for funding* heat engineering renovations of buildings (see below) and implementation of a performance control.
- Development of *integrated energy concepts* for residential building cooperations.
- Creation of a *regional building typology* in which house owners recognize their buildings.
- *Elaboration of typical packages of measures*; implementation of demonstration objects in cooperation with local craft enterprises.
- Generation of *local information material* such as trade directories.
- *Public relations* by participation in regional fairs, travelling exhibitions, press releases.
- *Cooperation with local or municipal authorities* for urban development and renewal measures as well as development of energy concepts.

- *Cooperation with executing craft and business enterprises* in presenting the product range; creation of market transparency.
- *Provision of further consultancy services* by architects and engineering consultants for planning work.
- Participation in *further training* for craft enterprises.
- Implementation of *performance controls* for energy saving measures.
- Implementation of *dynamic cost efficiency calculations* and description of the ecological and social implications of energy use.

The topics to be covered include thermal insulation in the building stock, low-energy houses, modern heating technology, electricity savings in households and industry, cogeneration, use of renewables and water saving. The independence of consultancy ensures its credibility, exemption from charges guarantees a widespread impact. The financial expenditure for 320 consulting agencies amounts to roughly DM 190 million per year for running costs and a nonrecurring sum of DM 80 million for setup. This could be shared among the federal government, federal states, municipalities and other institutions. In view of this modest expenditure, energy consultancy can be promoted immediately and need not be linked to the introduction of an energy tax.

Tightening the Thermal Insulation Ordinance and Improving Construction Legislation

The Thermal Insulation Ordinance of 1995 must be improved as soon as possible by finalizing the low-energy house as a standard for new buildings. At the same time, existing weaknesses in the present demonstration procedure must be eliminated by close reference to the European EN 832 standard.

As long as there are no effective standard federal measures, land use and development plans constitute a possibility for local governments - even though restricted - to become active themselves. In the case of municipal building land and land replotting in the course of urban development measures, in which the local government appears as the interim owner, the sale or resale can be tied to thermal insulation requirements or energy data. Similar possibilities of influence exist for settlement projects of residential building cooperatives owned by local governments.

Energy Tax

The "emission uptake capacity of the biosphere" is an asset which has so far been used almost free of charge. Energy taxes may serve to allocate the external costs of energy use to the polluter. They are then incorporated in his economic calculation.

Ideally, a corresponding tax would have to be assessed on the basis of the respective emissions from economic activities. However, this would require a very high technical and bureaucratic effort. Since more than 90 per cent of the relevant emissions come from energy conversion, it is self-suggesting to directly use these for taxation. The non-renewable primary energy used constitutes a good measure for energy taxation. On the one hand, all conversion steps are thus covered and incentives given for efficient energy use at all levels. On the other hand, primary energy generation and imports are statistically recorded in detail even today and can therefore be taxed with minor additional effort. In addition to a basic amount, surcharges for specific substances contained in energy carriers, for example carbon or uranium, would be conceivable. An energy tax must be introduced step by step and must be calculable on a long-term basis in order to leave enough time for adaptation processes. In discussions it is claimed again and again that such a tax must not lead to an increase in the so-called government expenditure rate and that therefore relief in other sectors would be appropriate. The possibilities include:
1. bonus payments per capita of the population,
2. reduction of other indirect taxes such as the value-added tax as well as
3. easing of the incidental wage cost burden by government subsidies to the pension insurance fund.

However, a precise analysis shows that economic reasons alone are not responsible for the reluctance concerning energy saving investments. The energy tax revenue should therefore also be used for financing other instruments such as energy consultancy and support programmes.

Support Programmes

Financial support for thermal insulation measures in the building stock is indispensable despite the high economic potential shown in (Ebel et al., 1996), even if the economic boundary conditions are improved by an energy tax:

1. Capital recovery for energy saving investments generally takes place over long periods, whereas house owners rather expect short-term return.
2. In rental housing construction, obstacles must be compensated by the law of tenancy. Savings in heating costs remain with the tenant, but the owner must make the investment. A rent increase after allocation of modernization expenses can also be achieved by the rising local reference rent even without energy saving investment.
3. Financial support is an ideal incentive with a widespread impact for all groups of owners.

Since 1996, the federal government has promoted savings in heating energy in the stock of buildings to the amount of DM 200 million annually for an initial period of five years. Several federal states like Hessen, Bremen and Baden-Württemberg have already operating support programmes since years, but the funds available without federal support have so far been moderate. It will be necessary to harmonize the different programmes and orient them towards optimum thermal insulation measures. A catalogue of these measures under heat engineering aspects is shown in Table 15.2. The funds of the federal programme should be increased to DM 4 billion per year from energy tax revenues. Funding must be based on three principles:

1. Funding should cover the difference between the modernization costs of a structural component with and without improvement of the thermal insulation.
2. Funding should include measures with an optimal scope going beyond the standards stipulated in the Thermal Insulation Ordinance.
3. The funding conditions should be such as to prevent inflationary effects. The funding rate should therefore not be based on the respective total cost, but on fixed grants towards costs.

The modalities of funding should be oriented to the necessary implementation speed. For owner-occupants, the non-repayable grant is meaningful since modernization measures are generally not loan-financed in this case. For residential building associations and private landlords, loans or reduced interest rates should be made available. The federal state of Hessen, for example, promotes this segment via loans at a 3.5 per cent annual interest rate and redemption. The granting of funds in the form of tax write-off facilities, on the other hand, has the disadvantage that it favours persons with high income, causes take-along effects in the case of measures planned anyway, and facilitates coupling to consultancy for the selection of meaningful measures.

Table 15.2 Catalogue of measures for a public support programme on the rehabilitation of buildings under heat engineering aspects (Ebel et al., 1996)

Measure	Requirement	Funding
External insulation of the outer wall as a curtain wall or composite thermal insulation system	12 cm	40 - 60 DM/m^2
Internal insulation of the outer wall	6 cm	20 - 25 DM/m^2
Core insulation of the outer wall	4 cm	10 - 15 DM/m^2
Steep roof insulation	16 - 20 cm	30 - 40 DM/m^2
Loft insulation	16 - 20 cm	20 - 30 DM/m^2
Flat roof insulation (staggered according to current k-value)	12 - 20 cm	20 - 30 DM/m^2
Basement ceiling insulation	6 cm	10 - 15 DM/m^2
Installation of thermal insulation glazing	$U^* = 1.3\text{-}1.5$ W/(m^{2}K)	40 - 60 DM/m^2
Special expenditure for buildings subject to the conservation of monuments	-	up to 50 % of the additional cost
Heat recovery boiler	-	DM 1,500 per building
Other thermal insulation measures at itemized expenses with substantiation	-	up to 50 % of the cost
Conversion to district heating (only for cogeneration)	-	DM 2,500 per building

*U = Heat transmission coefficient

Model Projects and Research Funding

Regional building typologies It is important to establish building typologies on a regional level which, from the very outset, do not only differentiate buildings according to construction age classes as well as single- and multi-family houses, but also according to large urban, medium-sized and small urban/rural development. For each building type, a standard package of suitable thermal insulation measures should be proposed. This typology does not have to be complete. However, it should enable experts to supplement and correct it so that it becomes an effective instrument of energy consultancy.

Thermal rehabilitation concepts   Thermal rehabilitation in the building stock requires instruments helping architects, civil engineers and energy consultants to design measures specifically tailored to concrete objects:

1. manuals for building modernization under heat engineering aspects: an excellent example is the manual on the rehabilitation of buildings under heat engineering aspects issued by the Swiss Federal Office for Economic Issues, which could also render very good services for Germany;
2. flow charts for establishing building concepts under energy saving aspects as well as
3. computer programmes for the energy balancing of buildings.

Model projects accompanied by research   The coupling principle considerably reduces the cost of thermal insulation measures. However, the target values of the heat consumption data are only reached on an object-by-object basis after a relatively long time, i.e. after running through all renewal cycles. This is entirely tolerable for the majority of existing buildings, since the total period for complete realization of the 80 per cent CO_2 reduction extends until the year 2050.

In order to obtain a tangible idea of the target values, however, it is necessary to perform model rehabilitation concepts for selected typical objects, where the envisaged target condition is achieved directly and not only in the course of the renewal cycles. Abandoning the rehabilitation cycles means, however, incomparably higher additional expenditure which does not pay back due to energy conservation and must therefore be booked under the research or demonstration aspect.

Model rehabilitation implies at the same time pilot and demonstration projects from which owners of comparable houses, building trade as well as planners, engineers and energy consultants may obtain clues for execution details and the effectiveness of measures.

Adapted design details for typical rehabilitation cases   The structural designs for the energy-efficient rehabilitation of buildings are, in principle, available on the German market. In a number of cases, however, adapted detail solutions are required for certain building types and rehabilitation measures:

1. low-cost prefabricated components for the physically proper fitting of
   - windows to external insulation,
   - window sills on composite thermal insulation systems,
   - shutter boxes and their subsequent insulation,

- walls to roofs and perimeter insulations,
- internal insulations to window reveals and inner walls;

2. system solutions for structured outer walls;
3. special solutions for half-timbered houses;
4. low-cost subsequent installation of ventilation systems.

New components for further energy savings From a physical, technical and practical point of view, there are in principle no limits to a steadily progressing reduction in heating energy consumption even in existing buildings. Further research could help to develop additional energy saving measures and thus bring the technical potential ever closer to the theoretical potential. There is a need for research in the following areas:

1. Development of prefabricated components (composite units) for both internal and external vacuum superinsulations.
2. Development of new edge bonding techniques for windows to avoid the thermal bridge effect of the usual aluminium spacer.
3. Development of highly insulating window frames.
4. Development of insulated attachment sections that can reduce the heat bridges in existing glazings (e.g. with metal frames).
5. Development of glazing techniques with low-cost panes for k-values below 0.7 $W/(m^2K)$ (e.g. triple heat absorbing glass with sandwiched inner pane and only one edge bonding spacer).
6. Development of automatic control systems for demand-guided air-quality-controlled ventilation.

It is entirely conceivable that such techniques can be developed until the end of the nineties at costs between 8 and 25 Pf/kWh for the final energy saved.

Need for a Matched Bundle of Instruments

The instruments of energy policy presented in this chapter form a matched bundle which can only take full effect in the case of a *joint use of all measures* (Table 15.3). The instruments reinforce each other by synergy effects and only thus offer the opportunity of reaching the ambitious goal of an energy conservation in the building stock ultimately exceeding 50 per cent.

The above mentioned 50 per cent reduction goal can neither be achieved without expanding the instruments nor in the absence of individual measures. This interdependence may be explained by the example of omit-

Table 15.3 Options for political action

German Government

- Stepwise introduction of an energy tax.
- Amendment of the Thermal Insulation Ordinance (introduction of the low-energy-house standard).
- Amendment of the Energy Saving Act and of construction legislation.
- Introduction of validated and comparable energy consumption figures.
- Implementation of large pilot projects.
- Financing an energy consultancy infrastructure.
- Federal support programme for low-energy houses.
- Federal support programme for the rehabilitation of old buildings.
- Research funding.

Federal States of Germany

- Establishing and financing an energy consultancy infrastructure.
- Implementation of medium-scale demonstration and pilot projects.
- Modification of the training regulations for architects and civil engineers.
- Support programmes for low-energy houses.
- Support programmes for the rehabilitation of old buildings.
- Organization of further training measures for architects, engineers and craftsmen.

Local Government

- Creation of energy consultancy centres.
- Development of rehabilitation concepts for the old building stock.
- Incorporation of improved thermal insulation standards in development plans.
- Implementation of small demonstration and pilot projects.
- Moderator role between local authority, municipal utilities, craft shops, banks, house owners.

ting one component in each case:

1. If it is not possible to establish a generally accepted standard for the energy quality of buildings (*energy consumption figures*), the success of the other instruments is not measurable. An opportunity of activating free-market driving forces for the saving process will then remain unused. There is a lack of orientation for energy consultancy and a lack of application criteria for support programmes.

2. If there is no quantitative and qualitative *establishment of energy consultancy*, the information costs remain high for the owner in addition to the actual cost of thermal insulation measures. Since, according to experience, the necessary specialized knowledge is not widely spread, it's very likely that suboptimal or even contraproductive measures are taken.

3. Without *increasing the energy price* a high portion of the conservation potential being on the threshold of economic efficiency today remains unexploitable. Information, advice and even financial support will not induce owners to take any measures that appear unprofitable against the background of low energy prices.

4. Without the *support programme* proposed, a high quota of lost opportunities must be expected since rehabilitation measures must generally be carried out together with repairs required anyway. At precisely this time the necessary additional investments relating to environmental protection must be made. In this connection, a selective incentive programme may be helpful especially for owners who are not themselves also users. In order to achieve the envisaged goal, three essential criteria must be fulfilled:
   - the political boundary conditions must be created at an early stage,
   - clearly more than 70 per cent of all owners must be won for coupling heat engineering rehabilitation to renewal measures and
   - rehabilitation measures must be applied which are markedly above the currently usual level (high insulating material thicknesses).

   The last two points are only feasible in conjunction with a support programme.

5. Without *further scientific research* the expenditure for implementing the structural measures proposed would be insurmountably high in practice.

Complementing Strategies

In the case of a reduction of carbon dioxide emissions, modernization apparently competes with a more efficient energy supply. Simple considerations show, however, that this is not true. Starting points in energy supply are the average efficiency of the heating system and the fuel used. The present average efficiencies of roughly 70 per cent can be increased up to 90 per cent. Natural gas combustion involves CO_2 emissions that are lower by one quarter compared to oil. The sole conversion to natural gas provides the smallest environmental advantages. Energy consumption will then decrease by just about 10 per cent and CO_2 emissions by just about 20 per cent. The values are only slightly better if only the heating systems are improved, whereas a combination of the two measures can reduce energy consumption by 30 per cent and CO_2 emissions by 38 per cent. In contrast, thermal insulation measures alone already have a conservation potential of 70 per cent in both categories. This can be improved up to 80 per cent by a combination with other strategies.

The use of renewables cannot replace thermal insulation either. This may be seen from publications according to which solar heat will in future be available at costs of 25 to 40 Pf/kWh. In comparison, the average cost of the energy saved is below 13 Pf/kWh for all thermal insulation measures under consideration. The use of solar energy is therefore especially justified after exhaustive energetic modernization.

Acknowledgements

This chapter is based on two studies prepared at the Institute for Housing and Environment (IWU):

- Institute for Housing and Environment, 1994: Empirical study of the possibilities and costs for saving energy and increasing energy efficiency in existing and new buildings (old and new federal states). Final report for the German Federal Environmental Foundation in cooperation with the Study Commission "Protecting the Earth's Atmosphere" of the German Bundestag, Darmstadt.
- Institute for Housing and Environment, 1990: Energy saving potentials in the building stock. Study series on energy policy issued by the Hessen Ministry for the Environment, Energy and Federal Affairs, Wiesbaden.

Contributions to these two studies were made by:

Dipl.-Ing. Rolf Born	Dipl.-Ing. Michael Jäkel
Dr. Witta Ebel	Dr.-Ing. Jobst Klien
Dipl.-Ing. Werner Eicke-Hennig	Dipl.-Ing. Wolfgang Kröning
Dr. Wolfgang Feist	Dipl.-Phys. Tobias Loga
Dipl.-Ing. Wilfried Gabler	Dr. Helmut Schmidt
Dipl.-Ing. Olaf Hildebrandt	Dipl.-Ing. Benedikt Siepe
Dipl.-Ing. Hans-Peter Hilpert	Dr. Storch,
Dipl.-Ing. Eberhard Hinz	Dr. Uwe Wullkopf

The authors would like to thank these persons as well as Dr. Helmuth-Michael Groscurth who participated in (Ebel et al., 1996).

References

Ebel, W., Eicke-Hennig, W., Feist, W., Groscurth, H. M. (1996): "Der zukünftige Heizwärmebedarf der Haushalte", Institut Wohnen und Umwelt GmbH, Darmstadt.

Ebel, W., Feist, W. (1997): "Leitfaden "Energiebewußte Gebäudeplanung"", 5th edition,. Study series on energy policy, issued by the Hessen Ministry for the Environment, Energy and Federal Affairs, Darmstadt/Wiesbaden, 1994; revision: Loga, T., Ebel, W., Feist, W. 1997, Institute for Housing and Environment.

Görg, Kienzle et al. (1996): "Dokumentation der Modellprojekte (Thermie-Altbau-Programm)", Stadtwerke Hannover AG.

Study Commission "Protecting the Earth's Atmosphere" of the 12th German Bundestag (1995): *Mehr Zukunft für die Erde*, Economica Verlag, Bonn.

16 A Modelling Approach to Energy Saving and CO_2 Mitigation in the Residential Sector of Germany

RAINER HECKLER

Introduction

Since it is one of the major consumers in the German energy sector, careful evaluation of the household sector and its impact on CO_2 mitigation is essential. The IKARUS project's space heating model calculates the annual heating energy demand of a building or a set of buildings using the European EN 832 standard as the mathematical basis (IKARUS = Instruments for Greenhouse Gas Reduction Strategies). The model further calculates the corresponding emissions for various types of buildings in the Federal Republic of Germany. Buildings are classified according to their physical size, age, building use and the heating technology applied. The model calculates the heating energy demand of a building in the steady state where the capacity is considered only as a lumped parameter. For parametric analysis it also facilitates the integration of various calculation methods like the periodic solution method. The modelling approach, used to evaluate the energy demand of existing and new residential buildings and their impact on CO_2 emissions and to forecast the trends of subsequent measures required to reduce these emissions, is discussed in this paper.

Introduction to the IKARUS Project

Various models are available to the user predicting the energetic performance of detailed architectural and engineering proposals. These models arrive at a given output depending on the user input. Most of these models are designed to calculate the energy demand of a single building or a group of buildings, but the impact of each of them on the overall energy demand of a region/country remains in question. Although it is relatively easy to say that a building is energy-efficient, it is essential to know what the level of efficiency is and at what cost it has been achieved. Given the fact that for the next fifty years electricity is going to be the most extensively used form of energy, the impact of its production on CO_2 emissions will be enormous. The effect of this is shown by world-wide discussions concerning the "Climate Change" issue. The energy models are important in this regard.

The IKARUS (Instruments for Greenhouse Gas Reduction Strategies) model has been developed with the aim of deriving an instrument consisting of a set of models that evaluate the present status of greenhouse gas emissions (CO_2, NO_2, SO_2, CO, C_mH_n) in Germany and study the impact of various strategies to reduce them. The model basically consists of five sub-projects: primary energy, conversion, households and small consumers, industry and transport. A further sub-project "cross-sectional technologies" is a link between the final energy sub-projects. A central model reproducing the energy flow of various sectors in the Federal Republic of Germany and optimization as an objective has been developed using the Linear Programming (LP) method. The optimization criterion is basically the cost of the overall system with given CO_2 reduction requirements. The data base consists of the technology and the general data basis. The technology data base contains data on technology, energy, economy and ecology of current technologies and systems for the reference years 1989, 2005 and 2020, separately for the federal states of the former East and West Germany. The general data base contains structural and inventory data for the base year 1989, and scenario data for the reference years 2005 and 2020. The technology model offers the possibility of comparing technology chains (e.g. hard coal production – coal-fired power plant, electric storage heating versus crude oil import, refinery oil-fired central heating) and individual technologies (e.g. heat pump versus thermal insulation). Thus for a given strategy, its effect is envisaged within the technology mix on the basis of certain criteria, e.g. minimal cost of energy production leading to reduced greenhouse gas emissions.

The IKARUS project includes the following models:
- optimization model for the whole energy sector (described above),
- traffic sector simulation model,
- residential space heating model, as described in the following sections.

Introduction to the Space Heating Model

There is a high potential for energy saving and emission reduction in Germany concerning energy consumption for the space heating of private households. Nearly 77 per cent of the final energy consumption of 36 million private households is for space heating purposes and 12 per cent for water heating (1994). Amongst the energy-related CO_2 emissions of the energy sector, the household and small consumers sector alone contributes 20 per cent of the total emissions after the industry sector. 20 per cent of the primary energy sector is related to district heating and electricity production. If this is also taken into account in the residential sector, then the energy-related CO_2 emissions of the household sector increase to 40 per cent (Figure 16.1).

The inevitable use of heating systems makes it an important sector. Every technology has its impact on the environment. The impacts can range from hazardous effects to less harmful ones. With the given scenario of climate change and ozone depletion, it is imperative that the problem be tackled sector-wise. Keeping the above in mind, the space heating model has been developed for analysing the scenario in the residential sector. The aim of the space heating model is to derive a simulation tool that analyses the impact of new technologies and various other measures on the reduction of energy consumption and thus CO_2 emissions. Since the model is dynamic in nature, the user has the freedom to decide change of values in discrete time steps and specify measures over time (for example the use of efficient heating technologies or renovation of building components etc.). In this part various types of buildings are adequately linked with approximately 10 renovation measures and 20 heating systems to form a large number of building variants for storage in a result file of the data base. An inventory file serves to store the number, living floor space and occupancy of each variant so that the data for the Federal Republic of Germany can be extrapolated by multiplying the inventory data by the specific result data of a variant. Inventory data can also be generated for future scenarios. In addition to the single types, the data base also contains a building mix of typical buildings.

The aim of the model is to calculate the final energy demand, the energy consumption of energy carriers, emissions and the total investment costs of adopting the measures required to reduce the energy consumption and the related emissions.

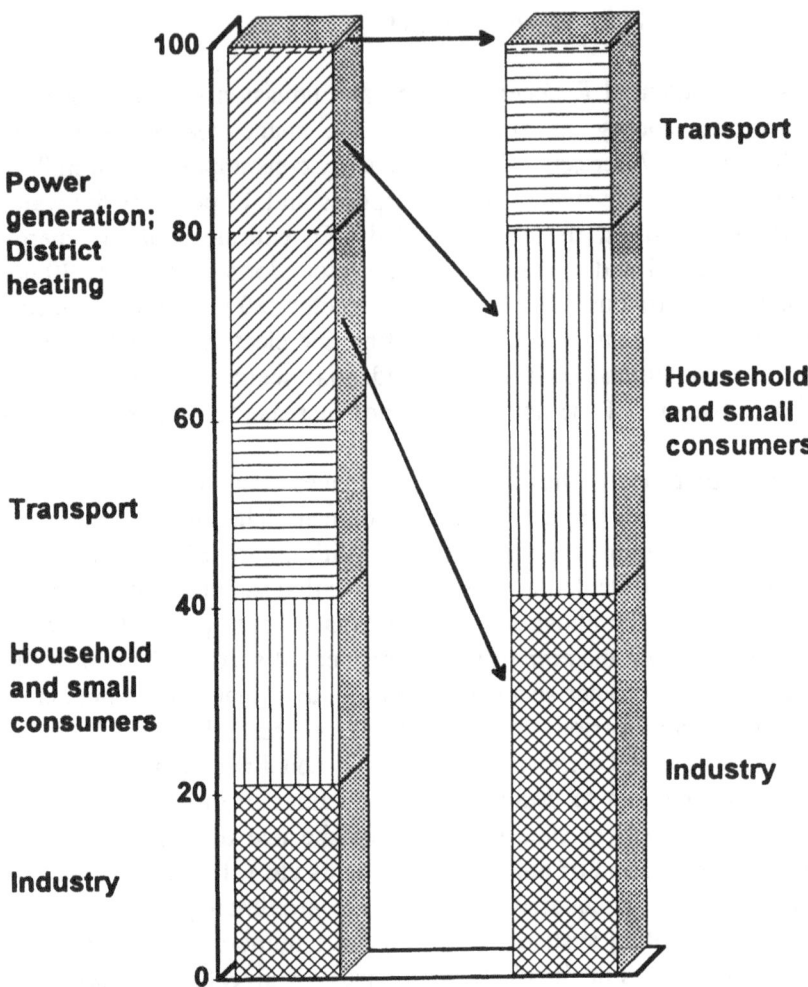

Source: Energieversorgung Schwaben AG.

Figure 16.1 Energy-related CO_2 emissions in 1990 (1,008 x 10^6 tonnes)

Analysis of Energy Demand in Buildings

If we firstly concentrate on buildings, then it is known that the energy gain is caused by solar radiation through the walls, windows and the roof and by internal sources of heat other than the heating system, i.e. equipment and occupancy (see Figure 16.2). To contain the heat within the building is thus very important. Furthermore, a definite temperature difference between the outside and inside needs to be maintained through reduced transmission losses. Infiltration losses and user behaviour are also important aspects that ascertain how much heat can be contained in the building. For Germany, heating of the indoor spaces is a predominant requirement. With the best possible design of a building, the maximum reduction in the number of heating degree days is about 60 per cent and hence space heating has to be supplemented by a mechanical system. Thus an efficient heating system is also of equal importance.

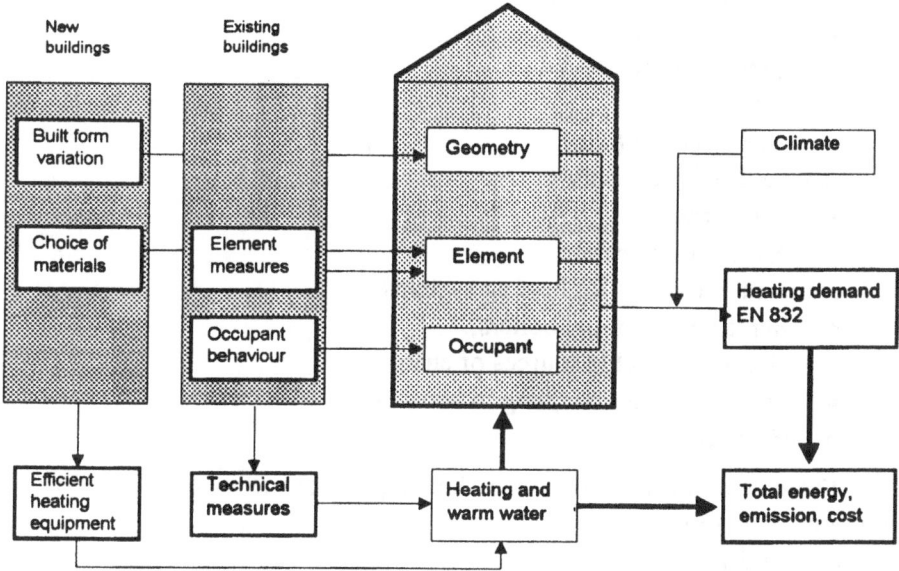

Figure 16.2 Factors influencing space heating

The impact for energy consumption in a building can be outlined as follows:

1. Building envelope - smaller surface area to volume ratio, so that losses through the building envelope are reduced. Hence the area to volume ratio is important.
2. Building elements - building materials with lower heat transmission coefficients reduce the heat losses through the building envelope.
3. Heating and warm water - efficient heating equipment with control systems for its efficient use.
4. Heat recovery - waste heat recovery for recycling and re-use.

Modelling Approach

The model is designed keeping the following aspects in mind:
1. New building aspects
2. Construction measures
3. Reduction in heat losses
   - Additional insulation,
   - Winter garden.
4. Minimizing the physical (construction deficiency) errors
   - Administrative (governmental) regulations,
   - Heat insulation,
   - Energy codes,
   - Subsidies,
   - Energy consultancy.
5. Behaviour of occupants
   - Temperature,
   - Air exchange rate.
6. Technical measures for heating systems
   - Replacement of old boilers,
   - Use of renewable sources of energy,
   - Power and heat coupling in households,
   - Heat recovery.

The calculations for the space heating model are in principle divided into three main modules:
1. Time-independent.
2. Time-dependent, steady-state: EN 832.
3. Economics.

The modules from M0 to M2 contain subroutines that calculate the heat transmission coefficients of the building element, heat exchange area, the geometry form and the corresponding input data. On the basis of the EN 832 norms modules M3 to M7 calculate the monthly heating load, night-time gains, warm water demand, final heating energy demand of the system and the total emissions. The modules M8 to M11 calculate the costs of the timely measures, and trends of energy consumption and emissions in the future. The structure of the model is shown in Figure 16.3.

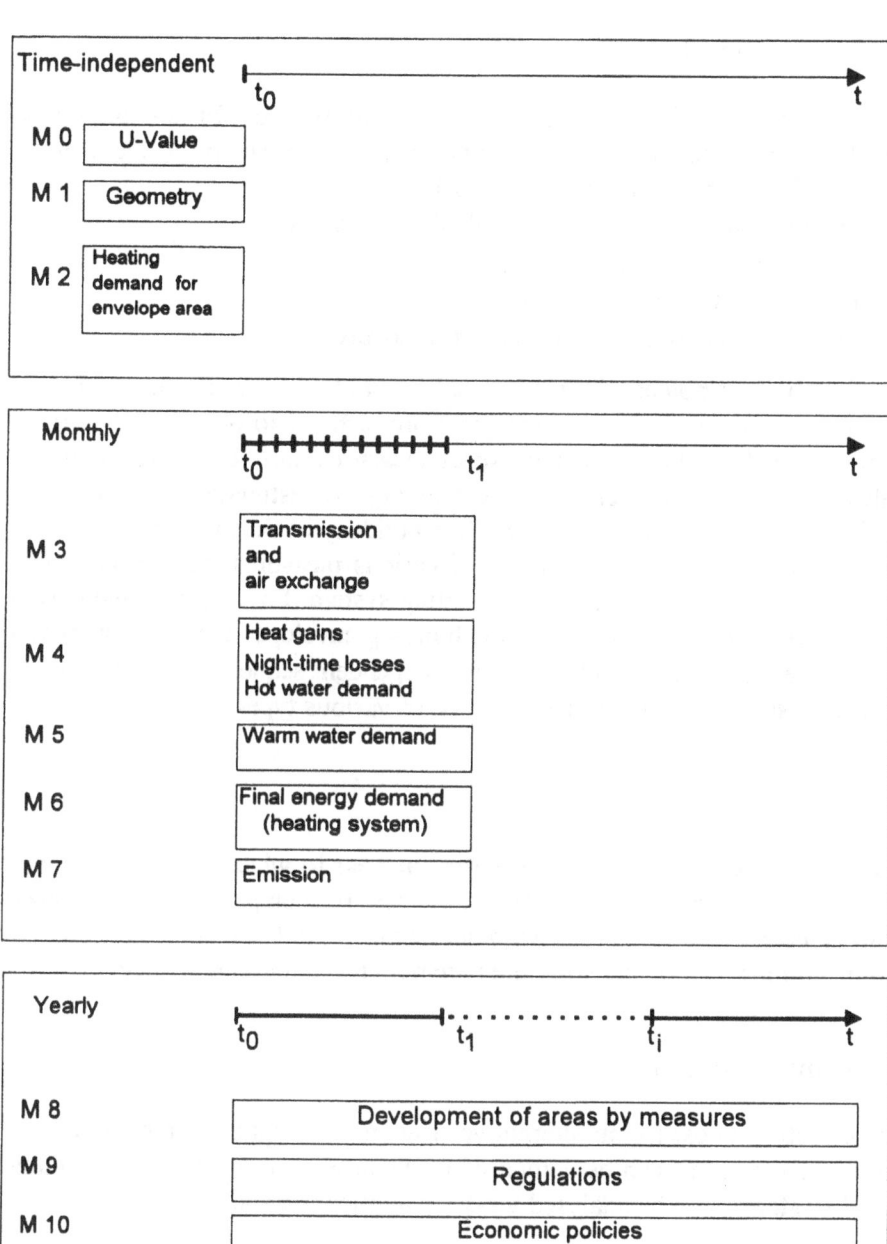

Figure 16.3 The modules of the physical model

Strategic Approach

By optimization of the planning process and construction for new buildings, two-thirds of the heating demand can be saved in comparison to the average demand of the current total building stock:

- by the choice of building materials for insulation,
- by passive use of solar energy,
- by efficient heating equipment,
- by controlled air exchange and heat recovery.

The highest potential is represented by old buildings. But here the necessary measures for energy saving are more difficult to plan and to realize. In any case, from the economic aspect measures can be realized together with necessary reconstruction of the building. To estimate this potential a detailed knowledge of the structure of the building stock is required.

The model allows the analysis of various measures for old buildings, the design of new buildings and the heating system. For a given time period the measures can be simulated on the building envelope, heating system and warm water applications. The total time-dependent sequence of all measures is called a strategy. The strategies can be of various types:

Base Strategy

This is a reference strategy for a particular year to which energy consumption, emissions and costs of other strategies are compared. The reference strategy is characterized by a minimum of measures ("business as usual" or "doing nothing"). Existing structures are not changed in this strategy.

Alternative Strategies

The investment cost for an alternative strategy, its impact on the energy demand and emissions can be compared to the base strategy. Likewise a number of strategies can be analysed vis-à-vis application and feasibility.

Strategic Calculations

This can be done for the analysis of a single old/new building as well as for a larger number of old/new buildings. The user interface for the model is shown in Figure 16.4. The interface in the form of a flow diagram enables the user to proceed accordingly:

- *For a single building* Specified by age and type the heating energy demand for a single building can be calculated with a single measure or a combination of measures, the main aim being to reduce the overall energy consumption index of the building type.
- *For a larger number of buildings* The specific heating energy demand is kept constant, and various steps are then studied:
  1. The energy demand of a set of buildings (depending on the frequency of each type of building) can be calculated as per the actual data. The corresponding emissions are calculated accordingly.
  2. Depending on the target emission reduction figure to be reached, measures for the buildings can be analysed at 3 levels, i.e. improved building elements (renovation measures) and use of efficient heating systems (heating technologies). The third level can be the use of both renovation of the building envelope and the heating system.
  3. The cost implications can be ascertained for every strategy or measure chosen.
- *For new buildings* Depending on the permissible area for new houses, the heating energy demand can be calculated on the basis of certain strategies to be adopted for reduced CO_2 emissions (e.g. low heat transmission coefficients of walls, use of super glazing for windows, use of gas burners).

The model extends its use over various aspects:
1. It enables the user to choose a given calculation method, e.g. steady-state, periodic solution etc.
2. It uses the chosen calculation method to calculate the overall energy demand of a single zone, multi-zone, single building, set of buildings etc. It further allows the use of various strategies for reducing the energy demand and therefore the emissions.
3. It enables parametric studies of individual components e.g. roof forms, building shapes, building elements, heating/cooling system etc.

Emission Reduction Strategies and Area Development

Organization of strategic variants:
1. The target year for analyses is a fixed year, the specific energy demand for this target year being fixed for each building. The analysis gives a

variant which differs from the original by a specific amount, which is constant over time. Thus it is a sequence of stationary demands.

2. There is a high demand for living space/person (area/person). Hence another task of the model is the development of areas over time. This calculation is dynamic in nature. Depending on the existing building scenario (buildings that are habitable, buildings that need to be demolished), the population and the area required for new buildings, the final energy demand and the final emissions can be calculated. For example:

Population × Living area/person [m^2] = Total building area required

$$A_i(t+1) = \quad A_i(t) \quad - \quad A_i(t) \quad + \quad A_i(t)$$
$$\text{(existing)} \qquad \text{(demolished)} \qquad \text{(new)}$$

3. For a given heating system, the final energy demand and the related emissions are calculated depending upon the efficiency of the system, its surface properties, regulation control and costs. The heating system details are calculated from the characteristic curve, which is independent for each system. The input from the curve is the load factor, from which the final energy demand is calculated.

Forecasting

Here the development of the future energy demand and the resulting emissions of the residential sector can be estimated in view of the development of new buildings (vis-à-vis available land and population growth), new technologies and new materials as well as their cost.

Economic Analysis

The present value method is used for calculating the costs of various measures. The investment costs based on the cost of the measures are calculated annually and are then normalized over the entire lifetime of the measure to obtain the present value. The strategy costs for reduction of emissions are also discounted to the present value.

The Computer Model: (Main Interface)

The computer model is structured around the following main elements as shown below:

1. Building stock (individual buildings, building elements and geometry).
2. Measures for the building envelope (building elements), heating technology (heating equipment).
3. Strategies - combination of building envelope and heating equipment measures.
4. Total energy and emissions.

Structure of the Model

The physical model contains a routine for the calculation of different parameters used in heating demand calculation. More routines can be added to this part. The core contains the control programme and dialog programme (Figure 16.4). The control programme controls the data and time for simulation and applies the mathematical algorithms, e.g. iteration etc., for solving the equations. It sends and receives data from the graphical user interface. The dialog programme is written to check the routines and obtain the results without a graphical interface. It is a faster and easier way to check the results. The graphical user interface (GUI) is used for showing the results in graphic or tabular form.

The basic principle in the model's structure is that the individual elements are modelled from the uppermost and most comprehensive level, down to a more detailed description of the elements, constituents and functions. The model is thus built up hierarchically or in a structure where the next level gives the detail of the current level.

Data Structure

The input data are separated into five independent categories:
1. Building elements,
2. Building geometry,
3. Heating technology,
4. Climatic zones,
5. User-specific data.

The input information is as described below:
1. Building description,
   - volume of the building,
   - area and orientation of walls, roof, floor and windows.

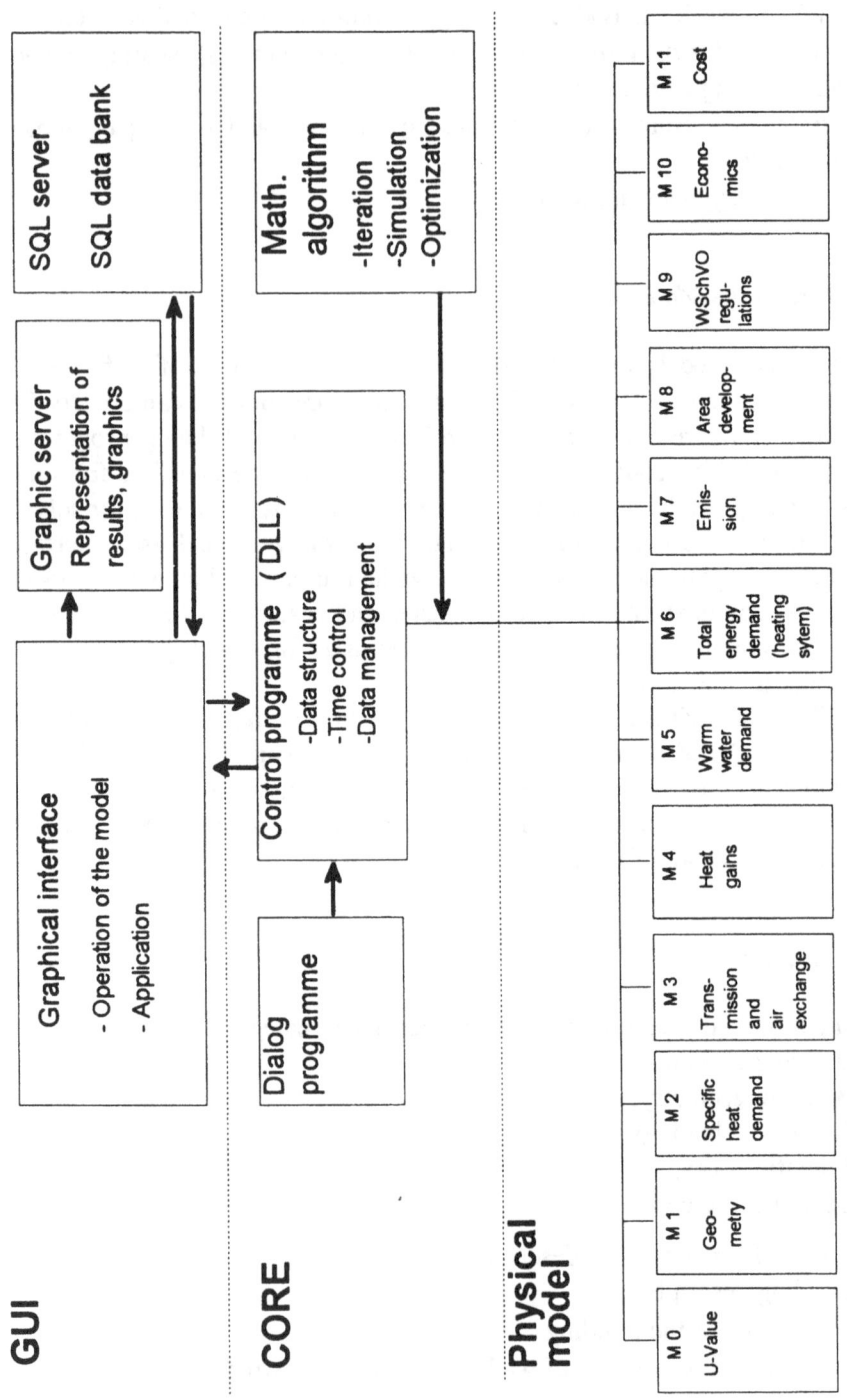

Figure 16.4   The hierarchical structure of the software

2. Design data
    - level of insulation for walls, floor and ceiling,
    - infiltration rate,
    - equipment efficiencies,
    - material type and thermophysical properties.
3. Weather data
    - monthly average ambient temperature,
    - monthly average global solar radiation for different orientations.
4. Economic data
    - cost of auxiliary fuel,
    - fuel escalation rate,
    - cost of conservation.

The outputs from the model are:
1. Auxiliary energy consumption and costs
2. Annual/monthly heating and cooling loads for the building
3. Economic performance of energy conservation measures and reduction of greenhouse gases

The stocks of buildings are mapped as types of buildings. The buildings are classified according to size, age, heating technology and building use. For Germany, the data base consists of 32 building types classified on the basis of the regions:
- Old Germany (West),
- New Germany (East).

User Interfaces

For the usage of the model there are a lot of forms building the graphical user interface. A short description is given for the most important forms.

Form "Stock" In this form, the building stock made up of representative buildings of different regions can be selected and analysed. With this form the development of new building stocks, i.e. present and future, is also possible. Since it is directly linked to the strategy form, future forecasting in terms of area development for buildings can also be analysed.

Form "Building geometry" This form, essentially created for the analysis of new buildings, calculates the input data for energy demand calculations.

For a given region, a building can be analysed to arrive at an optimum form. The form consists of 25 possible combinations of building shapes. A building can also be analysed for the optimum glazing area on a surface and choice of building materials for the walls, floor, roof and windows. The data can be saved and the user can create a data base independently.

Form "Element" This form simulates the variation of building elements and the subsequent layer combination. There is a possibility of defining new measures (e.g. adding insulation, increasing thickness of wall etc.) and analysing the impact of the element measures on the specific heat demand of a building. Moreover, since the form is directly linked to the material data base, it is possible to view the latter and choose from it accordingly.

Form "Measures" This form contains single measures and ensembles of measures. The measures can be analysed for different time periods, for different types of buildings (single or stock of buildings), as a result of which variants are produced. The best combination of measures with respect to reduced energy consumption and emissions and cost can be obtained.

Form "Heating demand" The form calculates the specific energy demand based on norm EN 832. It also gives the heat balances vis-à-vis losses and gain: transmission through walls, windows, cellar, roof and heat bridges, infiltration, air exchange etc. This enables the user to ascertain which part of the building component requires careful evaluation and the measure or strategies can be accordingly adopted. For rigorous analysis it is also possible to choose a calculation method, e.g. periodic solution method, WschVO'95 (German Thermal Insulation Ordinance), steady-state method, EN 832 standard etc. The analysis can be carried out on a monthly or yearly basis.

Form "Heating technology" With this form information on various types of heating systems is possible. The other information available is: efficiency of the system, temperature of the system, various distributions possible etc. and the specific cost and emissions of each of the technologies introduced.

Form "Final energy" Information on the specific energy demand of a building type and ensemble of buildings can be obtained. In addition, the primary energy consumption vis-à-vis electricity, district heating, coal etc. and the related emissions and cost can also be obtained by this form.

Form "Strategies" This form enables a user to carry out the analysis of various strategies. The strategies could include government incentives, forced regulations, choice of materials, various technologies etc.

Form "Parametric variation" With this form the other sensitive parameters like air exchange rate, average indoor temperature, user behaviour, internal heat gains, system controls etc. can be analysed for their effect on the specific energy demand.

Conclusions

The space heating model calculates the energy demand and the corresponding emissions for space heating. The stocks of buildings are mapped as type of buildings and the buildings are classified according to building size, age of building, heating technology and building use. The model calculates the implication of strategies, single measures, combination of measures for energy saving and emission reduction with cost and efficiency. It has a user-friendly interface which allows the users, who have no experience in mathematical modelling and the physical parameters required for the simulation, to work with the model. The main features of this model are:

1. It can simulate an individual building or a set of buildings.
2. The data base contains 32 different types representing all the buildings in Germany. It is flexible and thus can be modified and extended. A data base of different building types for different countries can also be integrated into the data base.
3. The data base is external to the model and thus the model allows different methods of energy demand calculations to be integrated, e.g. steady-state, periodic solution method etc.
4. The effect of different energy conservation measures on the energy demand can be easily analysed. The measures are defined as single measure or as a combination of measures, e.g. an additional layer of insulation is added to a wall/walls (single measure) or insulation is added to a wall/walls, roof etc. (combination of measures). With these measures it is possible to simultaneously analyse the effect of measures in parts and the corresponding effect on the energy demand. For instance, combinations like 20 per cent of the buildings of one type in one region are equipped with one set of measures and the rest with another set of meas-

ures and can be studied simultaneously. This is a very important aspect for the renovation of old buildings.

There are a number of software tools currently available on a commercial, shareware or freeware basis for the energetic performance of buildings with a varying degree of user support. Along with the parametric study of the energy demand and energy reduction/optimization strategies, it is essential to evaluate the impact of the set of measures on the overall CO_2 emission reduction status. Addressing such issues including both functionality and practicality, is thus an important issue for future development.

References

Comité Européen de Standardisation, CEN (1991), CEN TC89/ WG 4, Residential Building Energy Requirements for Heating Calculation Method.

DIN Deutsches Institut für Normung (1993): DIN EN 832 "Wärmetechnisches Verhalten von Gebäuden", Berlin.

Ebel, W., Eicke, W., Feist, W., Gabler, W. (1991): "Dokumentation der Referenzgebäude Institut Wohnen und Umwelt", IWU Darmstadt, Bericht BMFT TP 5.02.1.

Gruson, C., Kerschberger, A. (1992): "Kostenermittlung für wärmetechnische Maßnahmen an der Gebäudehülle", IKARUS-Bericht No. 5-10, Jülich.

Heckler, R., Kolb, G. (1997a): "Mögliche Entwicklungen des Energieverbrauchs im Sektor Raumwärme", IKARUS Workshop on 14/15 April 1997 in Bonn, "Modellinstrumente für CO2-Minderungsstrategien", Proceedings (Eds. Hake, J.-Fr., Markewitz, P.), Forschungszentrum Jülich, Vol. 4200003, pp. 37-61, Jülich.

Heckler, R., Kolb, G. (1997b): "Strategien zur Emissionsminderung im Raumwärmesektor", Beitrag zum 3. Ferienkurs "Energieforschung", Jülich.

Kolmetz, S., Ostermeier, U., Rouvel, L. (1994): "Endenergiebedarf der Privaten Haushalte für Raumheizung und Warmwasserbereitung in der Bundesrepublik Deutschland", Bericht TP 5.28.3 im Rahmen des IKARUS- Projekts, Jülich.

Kolmetz, S., Rouvel, L. (1993): "Energieeinsparpotential im Gebäudebestand durch Maßnahmen an der Gebäudehülle", Bericht TP 5.22.1, IKARUS-Projekt, Jülich.

VDI-Richlinien (1983): "Berechnung der Kosten von Wärmeversorgungsanlagen. Betriebstechnische und wirtschaftliche Grundlagen", VDI 2067, Sheet 1.

Werner, H. (1991): "Berechnung des Jahresheizwärmebedarfs von Gebäuden", IBP-Bericht EB-29/1991, Stuttgart.

17 Energy Requirements and Alternate Energy Uses in the Residential Sector of India

NARENDRA BANSAL AND HARI PRAKASH GARG

Abstract

The domestic sector is the largest consumer of energy in India accounting for 40 to 50 per cent of total energy consumption. The bulk of this energy consists of traditional fuels such as firewood, animal dung, and agriculture residue. In urban as well as in rural households, consumption of LPG, kerosene and electricity is increasing. Since the burning of traditional fuels is superimposed by the increasing trend of commercial energy use, the domestic sector also contributes significantly to greenhouse gas emissions into the atmosphere.

In the absence of real estimates about energy consumption in the residential sector it is also difficult to estimate the emissions. This section therefore discusses only the alternatives to traditional and conventional fuels for various uses in the household sector.

Introduction

Data about energy consumption in the household sector in India is available in terms of the number of households using a particular type of fuel, and not the actual or estimated quantities of fuels used. The available data indicate a distinct shift from firewood use to LPG for cooking, which remains the dominant energy use for domestic purposes. In some areas though, particularly in the North East, firewood still remains the dominant fuel for cooking and space heating purposes. Field surveys broadly indicate a rise in the per capita energy consumption as well as a shift away from non-commercial fuels with increased incomes in urban areas. There are significant urban-rural differences in the energy profile of households, with regard to both supply and consumption.

285

While traditional fuels in the household sector are normally used for cooking, water heating and space heating, commercial energy forms may be used as well for lighting, cooking and running domestic appliances. In 1991/92, commercial energy consumption was estimated to be 13 mtoe, which was 10 per cent of the total consumption. Among the commercial fuels, petroleum products in the form of kerosene and LPG are most important, accounting for nearly two-thirds of the consumption of commercial fuels, the share of coal being one quarter and that of electricity one tenth. As stated earlier, information on the pattern of household energy consumption is available only from sample surveys. Table 17.1 shows the percentage of fuel used by urban and rural households of different income categories.

Table 17.1 Fuel used by urban and rural households of different income categories (the figures show the share of each fuel in terms of useful energy (%))

Fuel	Up to 3,000	3,000-6,000	6,000-12,000	12,000-18,000	18,000 and above	Average
	Annual household income (rupees)					
Rural						
Soft coke	1.3	1.6	4.7	4.9	7.3	2.1
Kerosene	2.7	2.6	2.3	1.8	1.8	2.6
Electricity	0.2	0.4	0.6	0.9	1.0	0.4
Firewood	60.8	59.0	56.8	53.5	49.3	59.2
Vegetable wastes	16.1	14.6	15.6	18.2	16.6	15.6
Dung cake	18.9	21.8	20.0	20.7	24.0	20.1
Commercial	4.2	4.6	7.6	7.6	10.1	5.1
Non-commercial	95.8	95.4	92.4	92.4	89.9	94.9
Urban						
Soft coke	14.9	23.6	31.1	20.0	19.8	23.2
Kerosene	19.4	23.8	19.6	17.7	14.8	21.1
Electricity	0.8	1.7	2.6	3.5	4.9	1.9
LPG	-	5.2	15.9	34.0	41.3	9.8
Firewood	54.9	37.3	22.8	16.7	13.9	35.5
Vegetable wastes	2.6	1.4	1.4	2.7	1.5	1.7
Dung cake	5.2	4.5	3.9	4.1	2.3	4.5
Charcoal	2.2	2.5	2.7	1.3	1.5	2.3
Commercial	37.3	56.8	71.9	76.5	82.7	58.3
Non-commercial	62.7	43.2	28.1	23.5	17.3	41.5

Source: NCAER, 1981: Domestic Fuel Survey with Special Reference to Kerosene (1978/79), New Delhi: National Council for Applied Economic Research.

The shares of different fuels for various end uses in the urban and rural households are given in Tables 17.2 and 17.3 respectively and the projected demand for different fuels in the domestic sector is given in Table 17.4.

It is evident from Tables 17.2 and 17.3 that cooking, water heating and lighting are the major uses of energy consumption in the residential sector,

Table 17.2 Share of each fuel for different end uses in urban households (%)

Fuel	Cooking	Water heating	Lighting	Space heating	Space cooling	Others
LPG	47.1	11.6	-	-	-	-
Kerosene	12.6	23.2	7.9	-	-	-
Soft coke	5.0	3.3				
Firewood	31.6	33.9				
Dung cake	3.2	4.5				
Electricity	0.5	23.5	92.1	100.0	100.0	100.0
Total	100.0	100.0	100.0	100.0	100.0	100.0

Table 17.3 Share of each end use in consumption of different fuels in rural households (%)

Fuel	Cooking	Water heating	Lighting	Space heating	Space cooling	Others	Total
LPG	96.3	3.7	n. a.	n. a.	n. a.	n. a.	100
Kerosene	71.2	20.6	8.2	n. a.	n. a.	n. a.	100
Soft coke	90.9	9.2	n. a.	n. a.	n. a.	n. a.	100
Firewood	85.6	14.4	n. a.	n. a.	n. a.	n. a.	100
Dung cake	82.1	17.9	n. a.	n. a.	n. a.	n. a.	100
Electricity	1.0	7.6	34.7	3.8	25.3	27.6	100

Table 17.4 Annual demand for different fuels (all India) (mt)

Fuel	Total consumption				Domestic requirement	
	1987/88	1988/89	1989/90	1994/95	1999/2000*	2004/05*
LPG	1.4	2.8	2.3	12.6	17.3	23.7
Kerosene	7.2	7.7	8.2	n. a.	n. a.	n. a.
Soft coke	1.7	1.8	n. a.	9.0	14.0	20.0
Firewood	n. a.	n. a.	n. a.	n. a.	n. a.	258.5
Dung cake	n. a.	n. a.	n. a.	n. a.	n. a.	150.5
Electricity (TWh)	188.0	187.0	208.1	40.9	82.6	145.6

* Projections by the Planning Commission

for which either fossil fuels are used or wood and dung, all contributing to greenhouse gas emissions because even biomass is not completely replenished. For space heating, the biomass used is actually always credited to cooking and therefore there is no reliable data on energy consumption for space heating. Only when electricity is used for heating or cooking can some estimates be made.

It is the purpose of this section to discuss alternate technologies using solar energy for partial replacement of commercial as well as traditional fuels and simultaneously discuss the methods of reduced energy consumption for heating and/or cooling of buildings.

Energy Consumption for Space Heating and Cooling

India possesses a large variety of climates ranging from extremely hot desert regions to high altitude locations with severe cold conditions. On the basis of monthly mean data recorded at 233 stations, located in all parts of India, it was found convenient to divide the country into six climate zones (Figure 17.1). The representative locations chosen for studying the effect of efficient windows are Leh (cold and sunny), Shillong (cold and cloudy), Delhi (composite), Jodhpur (hot and dry), Madras (warm and humid) and Bangalore (moderate). The number of degree days for each of these representative locations (with set point temperature of 20 °C) are given in Table 17.5.

Table 17.5 **Degree days for representative locations of different climatic zones in India (set point temperature =20°C) (window area = 30 per cent of the floor area).**

Location	Leh	Shillong	Delhi	Jodhpur	Madras	Bangalore
January	880	326	178	93	140*	0
February	714	232	90	0	163*	87*
March	620	124	81*	161*	245*	174*
April	432	33	258*	310*	312*	219*
May	313	13	419*	447*	394*	214*
June	183	0	430*	429*	382*	129*
July	81	0	347*	316*	332*	100*
August	96	0	307*	285*	313*	100*
September	207	0	279*	282*	290*	100*
October	415	84	183*	236*	251*	100*
November	582	201	0	78*	174*	51*
December	766	298	133	41	143*	0

* Degree days for cooling

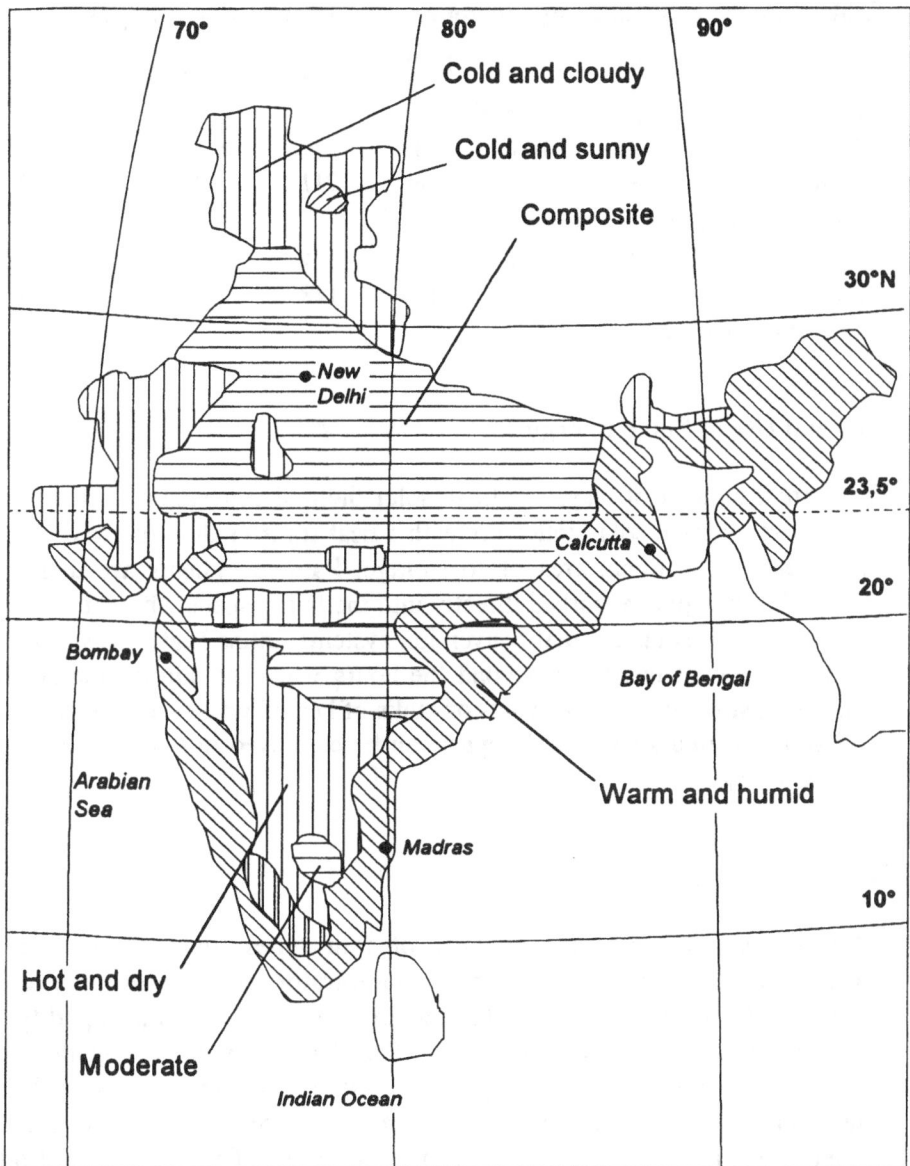

Figure 17.1 Climatic zones of India

Based on the number of degree days, specific energy requirements for heating and cooling of buildings per unit floor area in selected representative locations are given in Table 17.6.

Table 17.6 Specific heating/cooling energy demand (kWh/m²yr)

Location	Leh	Shillong	Delhi	Jodhpur	Madras	Bangalore
Single glazing ($U_{Building}$ = 2.89 W/m²K) [*]						
Heating	418	103	31	11	-	-
Cooling	-	-	180	211	250	99
Double glazing ($U_{Building}$ = 2.15 W/m²K) [*]						
Heating	307	76	23	8	-	-
Cooling	-	-	133	148	182	75

[*] U = heat transmission coefficient

Thermal Use of Solar Energy

There are a number of ways to utilize solar thermal conversion. Active systems utilize external solar collectors with a heat transfer fluid to convey collected heat to the living area or to storage. Passive systems are those in which solar energy is absorbed directly into the living space where it is to be used. Almost all solar thermal conversion systems utilize heat storage to extend the period of operation beyond the hours when the sun is shining. In most cases, storage simply consists of tanks of heated water. However, other more sophisticated storage techniques can be employed in many cases with some advantages.

Solar Collectors

Solar energy collectors are generally of four types: flat-plate collector, evacuated tube collector, non-imaging concentrator, and concentrating collector. The flat-plate collector is further divided into two types: liquid-type flat-plate collector and air-heating-type flat-plate collector. Flat-plate collectors have been used successfully for the last 50 years for various applications such as for heating water, heating space, air conditioning, water pumping, distillation of water, power generation etc. There are several advantages of a flat-plate collector such as: they are relatively simple, can utilize both the diffuse and direct components of solar radiation, no tracking arrangement is required, low in cost and can easily be manufactured. The only limitation with the flat-plate collector is that the temperature attained is less than 100 °C. The basic components of a typical liquid heating flat plate collector are shown in Figure 17.2. There are a great variety of flat-plate collectors and they are discussed by Garg (1982).

The collector can be all metallic or plastic, single-glazed or double-glazed, selectively coated or simply painted black, depending on the temperature of operation and outside climatic conditions. Some of the parameters which need attention while designing a liquid flat-plate collector are: number and transmittance of glazing; absorptance and efficiency of the absorbing plate; construction materials; size, number and location of the manifold and tubes; heat transfer efficiency from the absorber plate to the fluid in the tube; insulation properties; tilt, orientation and place; etc. The efficiency equation for such a collector (liquid type) is of the form

$$\eta = F_R (\tau \alpha)_e - U_L (\Delta t)/I_T$$

where η is the efficiency of the collector, Δt is the temperature difference (°C) between the collector inlet (t_{in}) and the ambient air temperature (t_a), and I_T is the solar radiation incident on the collector plate (W/m²). F_R is the heat removal efficiency factor depending on the collector geometry and flow conditions and $(\tau \alpha)_e$ is the effective transmittance - absorptance product of the glazing absorber plate system. U_L is the heat transfer coefficient. The final selection will depend on its conversion efficiency, operating temperature, and cost. Generally the efficiency of a liquid flat-plate collector in the temperature range of 50-80 °C is in the range of 60-40 per cent and the costs vary from Rs. 3,000-6,000 per m² of collector area.

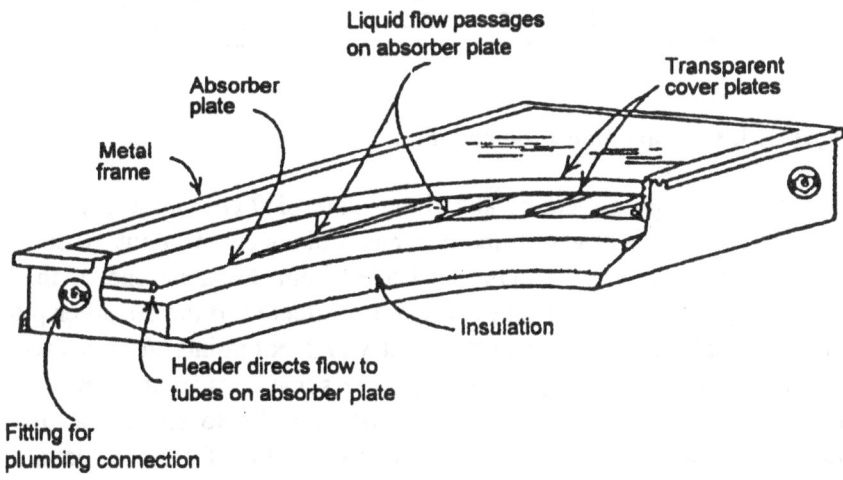

Figure 17.2 Typical liquid flat-plate collector

In a conventional flat-plate collector the radiative, conductive and convective heat losses are significant and these can be considerably reduced in an evacuated tube collector. As the name suggests, these collectors are tubular in design where the cylindrical or flat absorber is coated with a selective coating and the space between the absorber and the cover tube is evacuated (10^{-4} torr). This vacuum should be maintained for the operating life of the collector, typically 20 years, leading to the choice of glass over other materials as the main construction material. There are several designs of evacuated tube collectors (Garg, Vol. 3, 1987). A typical evacuated tube collector is shown in Figure 17.3.

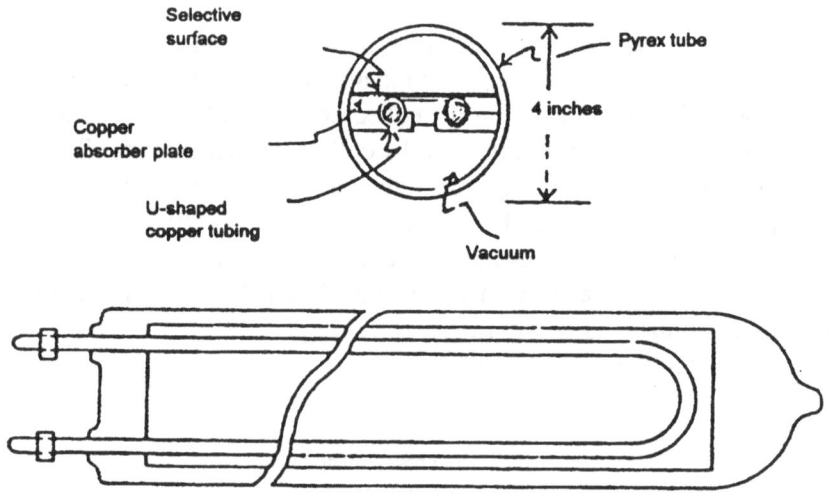

Figure 17.3 Evacuated tube collector

In this design a metallic absorbing plate of 9 cm width is fixed in the centre of a cylindrical glass tube that has a diameter of about 10 cm and is sealed at one end. Fluid enters and leaves from the same end of the glass tube through copper metal tubes which are soldered to the absorber plate. A glass-to-metal seal is formed at these entry and exit points. A high vacuum is pumped down in the air space. Getters are sometimes used to maintain the vacuum. Stand-off clips are incorporated in order to locate the absorber plate in the glass tube. A number of such tubes generally spaced equal to the outer tube diameter are arranged in a frame with either a white plane diffuse reflector on the rear side or a cusp reflector behind the tubes to enhance the solar radiation. These evacuated tube collectors are able to supply fluid in the temperature range of 100-150 °C. They are produced commercially in many countries.

Solar Water Heating

Solar energy has been used to heat water for many years, and the design requirements of solar water heating equipment have been studied for more than 90 years. Technical advances in solar water heating have been very rapid in the last 30 years, and the obvious benefits to the households can no longer be overlooked where the climate is ideally suited for the application of solar energy for water heating. Solar water heaters employing flat-plate collectors can be divided into the following four types according to their main application, temperature of operation and capacity.

1. Swimming pool water heater where a cheap plastic collector can be used without any cover and insulation. A high flow rate is maintained to limit the temperature rise to less than 2 °C.
2. Built-in-storage type solar water heater where all the three functions/components, i.e. collection, storage and control, are combined into a single unit. Hot water up to 60 °C from such water heaters has to be used up during the day, otherwise the heat would be lost during the night.
3. Domestic solar water heaters where the maximum temperature required is no more than 70 °C. Here the collector and the storage functions are separate. The control function is still accomplished through the use of natural principles and this technology is frequently employed for domestic systems in the form of the well known "thermosiphon systems".
4. Large-size solar water heaters designed for community and industrial use. Since requirements for hot water are great, a large number of collector banks is employed with a storage tank plus a control system which is to be built-in as required by the application.

In a natural-circulation-type solar water heater, there is a separate collector and storage tank and the storage tank is placed at a certain height (30 to 60 cm) relative to the top of the collector to prevent reverse circulation during off-sunshine hours. In this system, as is shown schematically in Figure 17.4, cold water from the mains is fed in through the bottom of the insulated storage tank and hot water is drained and supplied to the utility points from the top of the storage tank. Water is automatically circulated between the storage tank and the collectors.

Two alternatives are suggested to protect the system from damage due to freezing. In one simple system the collector is drained manually in the evening through a gate valve provided in the bottom of the collector by closing the collector isolation valve provided in the flow line connecting the tank bottom to the collector bottom.

In the second system, which is the preferred one, a heat exchanger is provided in the solar hot water storage tank and an antifreeze mixture is used in the collector storage loop to permanently freeze-proof the system. This natural circulation type of solar water system can be used with or without an auxiliary heating system. In case auxiliary heating is required it is provided in the storage tank itself due to convenience. This type of solar water heater is popular in many countries and is used for the supply of hot water at up to 70 °C for domestic purposes.

In India only natural circulation type solar water heaters are used to some extent in houses. Their costs vary from Rs. 15,000-20,000 per 100 litres of water.

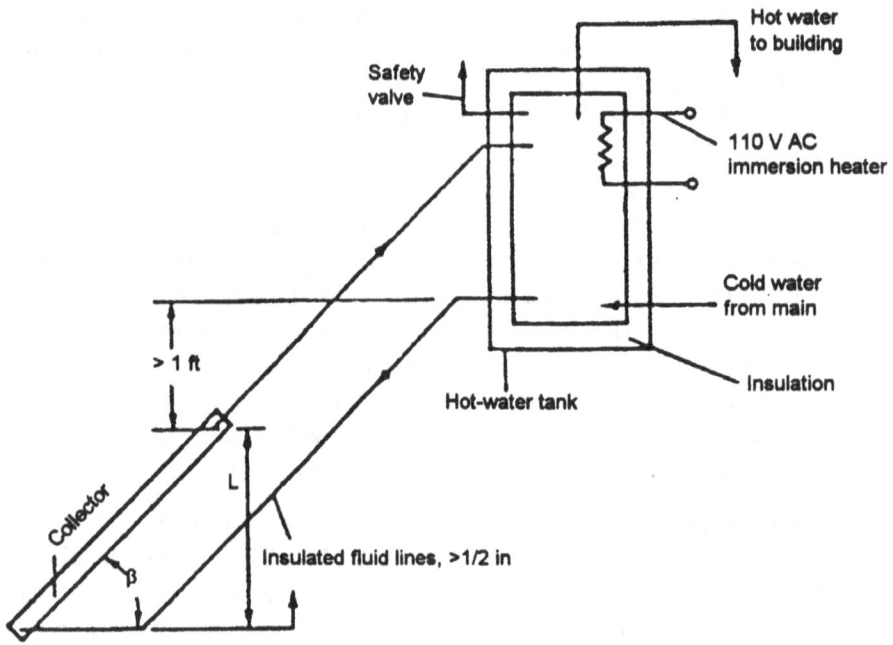

Figure 17.4 Natural circulation solar water heater

Solar Cooking of Food

The solar cookers developed so far are broadly divided into three types (Garg, Vol. 3, 1987):
1. direct or focusing type
2. indirect or box type
3. separate collector and cooking chamber type.

The most popular direct type solar cooker is the one developed at the solar laboratory of the University of Wisconsin, Wisconsin, USA. The plastic reflector uses a drape-formed, high impact polystyrene sheet of 120 cm diameter with a focal length of 45 cm and 0.15 cm thickness at the rim with a ring of 1.25 cm diameter thin-walled aluminum sheet. A reflective lining of aluminized Mylar polyester film is applied to the shell with an adhesive, so that the clear film forms a protective covering over the speculum surface. The azimuth adjustment and vertical stability in this cooker are provided by two spun discs at the base, which fit one within the other and are turned with respect to one another. The cookers, which have an effective area of about 1.1 m², deliver about 40 to 55 per cent of incident beam radiation to a cooking vessel 18 cm in diameter, e. g. a maximum delivery rate of 400-500 watts at an incident beam total energy of 1.0 kW on the unshaped reflector.

A box-type solar cooker popularized in India uses an insulated double rectangular box and a single reflector. The cooker is shown schematically in Figure 17.5.

The dimensions of the inner box, which is generally made of metal sheet and blackened afterwards, are 45x45x10 cm. The outer box is also made of metal, sometimes of fibreglass, and the spacing between the outer and inner boxes of about 4-5 cm is filled with fibreglass insulation. Two clear window glass sheets are used on the top of the inner box and are fixed in frames and hinged to the box to serve as the box door.

The reflector is a mirror of 45x45 cm fixed on a plane metal sheet and hinged to one side of the box. The angle of the reflector can be changed with the help of the rod and tube arrangement. Castor wheels are provided in the bottom of the cooker for easy adjustment towards the sun. The maximum temperature in this cooker under Delhi conditions remains at about 125 °C and therefore this cooker can cook the food at a very slow rate and it takes two or three hours to cook about 1 kg of rice or vegetables. The box-type solar cooker is simple and low cost. In India more than 0.3 million such cookers have been sold.

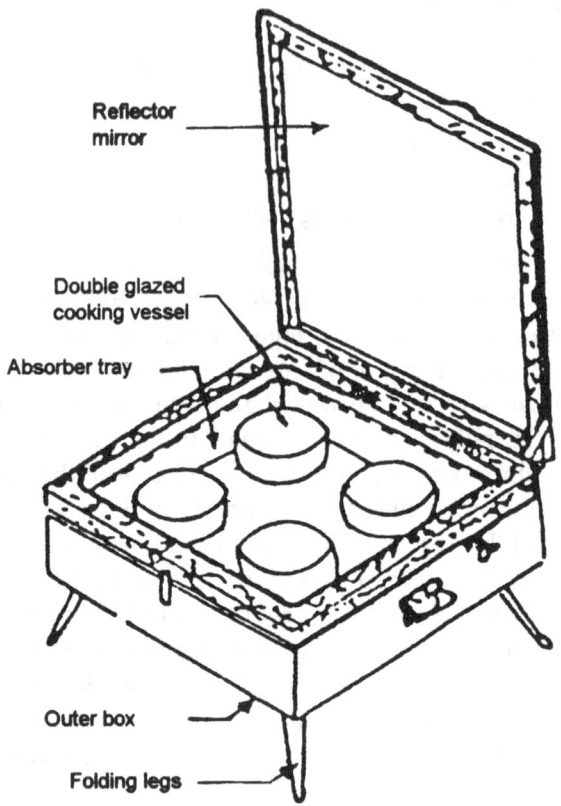

Figure 17.5 Box-type solar cooker

Solar Still

Potable or drinking water is a fundamental need of all people. In many places around the world drinking water is not available. Solar energy if available can be used for providing drinking water. By using equipment known as a "solar still" the saline or impure water can be desalinated using solar energy. As a result of the great interest in solar distillation several types of solar stills have been devolved (Malik et al., 1992). Out of several stills like single affect basing stills, multiple affect stills, single or multiple wick stills, inclined tray or step stills, and solar concentration stills, only basing stills using single effect distillation have been used for the supply of large quantities of water for isolated communities or for small supplies of water such as for battery charging, analytical purposes, etc. The conventional basin-type solar still, as shown in Figure 17.6, consists of an insulated (sometimes uninsulated) shallow basin lined or painted with a waterproof black material holding a shallow depth (5-20 cm) of saline or brackish water to be distilled and covered with a sloped (single or double sloped) glass/plastic sheet supported by an appropriate frame and sealed tightly to reduce vapour leakage. The condensate channel runs along the lower edge of the glass/plastic pane which collects the distillate and carry it outside the still. A pipe is used to fill the basin with saline water and another pipe is used to control the level of the saline water and to flush the brine. The still can be fed with saline water either continuously or intermittently but the supply is generally kept at twice as much as the amount of fresh water produced by the still. The ratio of saline water supply and amount of water to be flushed depends on the salinity of the basin water and is found to be proportional to the amount of fresh water produced. The still is erected in an exposed area with its long axis facing the east-west direction.

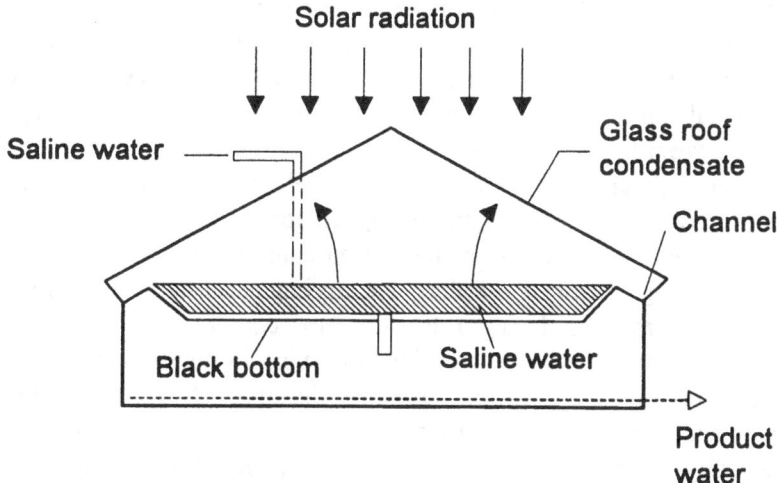

Figure 17.6 Schematic of shallow basin-type solar still

In operation, solar radiation after transmission through the transparent pane (cover) is absorbed in the water and basin. Therefore, the water temperature is raised compared to the cover. The water now loses heat by evaporation, convection and radiation to the cover and by conduction through the base and edges of the still. The evaporated water from the basin increases the moisture content in the still and is finally condensed on the inner side of the glass sheet and then slips down into the condensate channels and through them out of the still for use. The main aspects in this still are that only durable materials should be used in its construction, the basin should be waterproof, and the whole enclosure should be airtight.

There are several small variations in the geometric configuration of single basin stills but in general the efficiency of solar stills remains between 20-30 per cent only, since the latent heat given off by the water to the glass is completely lost to the outside. The performance (distillate output) of the solar still depends on many parameters including solar radiation, ambient temperature, wind velocity, water depth in the still, insulation at the bottom, inclination of the glass slope, temperature of the brine etc. A few thousands of such solar stills made of fibreglass body and glass cover are used in India.

Solar Drying

Drying is a traditional method for preserving food. The traditional age-old practice of drying food crops in developing countries is spreading food products in thin layers in the open sun, which may be termed open sun drying or natural sun drying. This natural sun drying has several advantages but also suffers from many drawbacks.

In conventional controlled drying, the fuel used is electricity, oil, natural gas or coal. Solar energy can be applied for drying crops economically and therefore in the past attempts have been made in this direction. Actually controlled drying means controlling the drying parameters like drying air temperature, humidity, drying rate, moisture content, and air flow rate. Therefore, a solar dryer is to be designed keeping in mind all the above drying parameters and the appropriateness of the dryer. Since there are many options in the design of the solar dryer, there is a large variety of solar dryers. Basically all the dryers, depending on operational modes and practicability, can be classified into two types: the direct type or natural convection type dryers and indirect type dryers or forced circulation type dryers. Direct type dryers can be used for drying small quantities for domestic use.

Natural convection type dryers appear to be more attractive for use in developing countries since they do not use any fans or blowers to be operated by electrical energy. Moreover, they are low-cost and easy to operate.

However, the problems with these dryers are: slow drying, not much control of temperature and humidity, only small quantities can be dried, and some products change colour and flavour due to direct exposure to the sun.

In their simple form, they consist of some kind of enclosure and a transparent cover. A simple cabinet dryer (Garg, Vol. 2, 1987) is shown schematically in Figure 17.7. Here the food product is heated due to direct absorption of heat and also due to high temperature in the enclosure. Therefore moisture from the product evaporates and escapes by the natural circulation of air. There are several designs of direct type dryers and these are developed keeping in mind the availability of local materials required for fabrication and for drying a particular product. Several dryers have been fabricated, tested and analysed in India.

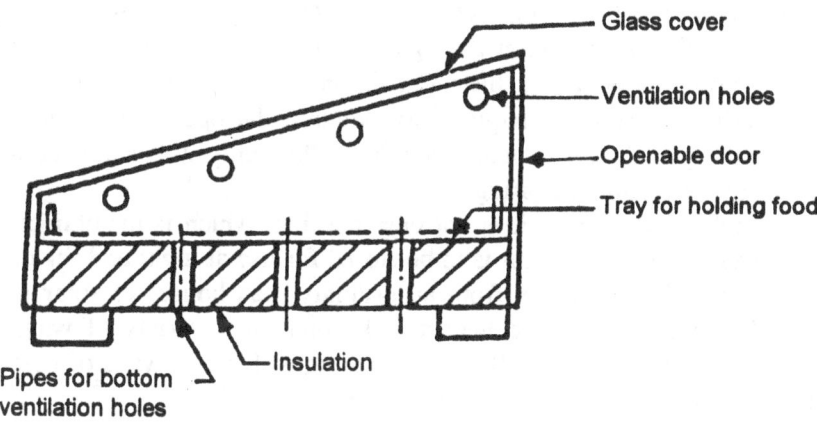

Figure 17.7 Solar cabinet dryer

Solar Greenhouse

Solar greenhouses are enclosures where crops, vegetables, or flowers are provided with a proper environment under adverse climatic conditions for plant growth and production (Bansal et al., 1994). Certainly all greenhouses receive the sunlight required for photosynthesis and also supplementary heat from the sun during cold months. In tropical countries the solar radiation and the ambient temperatures are quite high and therefore summer greenhouses can be designed in such a way that the inside temperature remains low and the plants receive sufficient sunlight for photosynthesis. Greenhouses are also nowadays used for growing vegetables and flowers throughout the year even out of season since the light and temperature in the greenhouses can be controlled. Some greenhouses are also designed to conserve water resources. Naturally, each plant type requires a slightly different type of environment for optimum production, but basically the desirable needs are moderate temperature, light, carbon dioxide, oxygen, mineral nutrients, air movement and water. The greenhouses are generally made to provide low energy-related needs, i.e. moderate temperature and light. Temperature is a dominant environmental factor in plant growth and optimum temperatures must be maintained to obtain optimum conditions during all stages of plant growth. Light is absolutely essential for plant growth and development and the light intensity, light spectral distribution and its duration affects plant growth. Therefore one of the most essential requirements of the greenhouse is the light transmission of solar radiation through the greenhouse's covers (glazings). Since in cold climates during the night the inside temperature can drop severely, auxiliary heating is required to maintain the optimum temperature. Therefore the greenhouse structure should be thermally well insulated to reduce the cost of auxiliary heating.

In a solar greenhouse, it is not only the light which is maintained at a desired level, but the solar heat is to be stored for use at night and for cloudy days, and therefore it differs from an ordinary glasshouse. In solar greenhouses, the solar energy is collected and stored in a variety of ways and therefore solar greenhouses differ in their designs. Several ways of heat loss from a greenhouse are shown in Figure 17.8.

Moreover, the solar collection storage system depends on many factors like climate, greenhouse size, plant type, orientation, economics, and whether a new greenhouse is to be planned or an existing one modified. Further, there can be a design difference if the collection storage and distribution system is by passive means or by active means. Former greenhouse designs, where the energy is stored directly (in heavy brick walls or rock walls and/or water pools or water containers exposed to solar radiation) and heat is distributed inside the greenhouse by natural means are known as passive greenhouses. Greenhouses where solar energy is collected and stored and distributed and where some auxiliary energy is employed either for circulation or for distribution or for both are known as the active type. Generally a combination of both active and passive features is employed in a solar greenhouse with the objective of minimizing the use of auxiliary energy either for heating the greenhouse or for a collector-storage-distribution system. Another class of

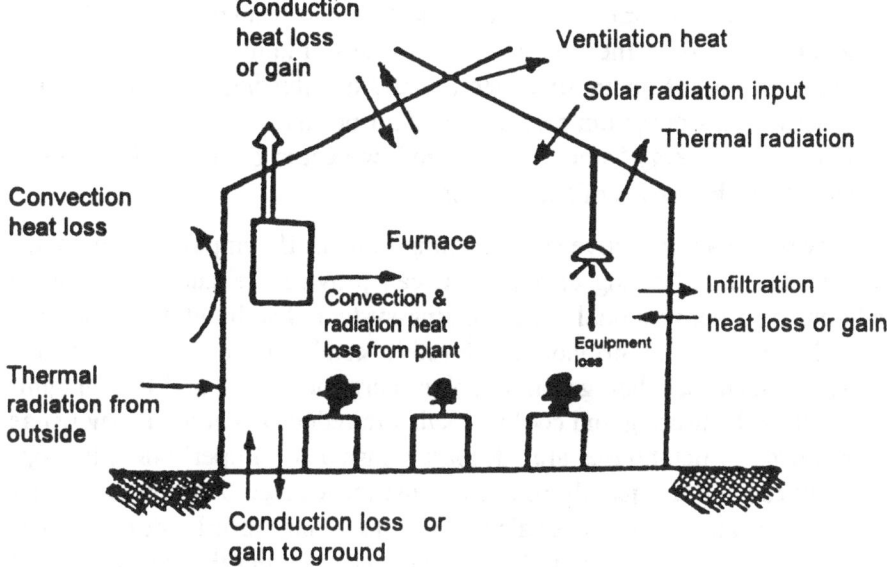

Figure 17.8 Energy flow in a greenhouse

greenhouse is known as the attached greenhouse where a greenhouse is built into a house (house-attached) and where a free exchange of air between the residence and greenhouse takes place maintaining the house temperature at a comfortable level and reducing heat losses from the greenhouse. At isolated locations a small greenhouse can help in growing vegetables and flowers.

Active Heating of Buildings

Basically building heating systems are divided into two categories: passive heating and active heating. Passive systems do not need any mechanical system and are designed in such a way that the glazed area, walls and roofs are used for collecting, storing, and distributing the heat indoors by natural processes of conduction, radiation, and convection. In active heating systems, separate solar collectors are used to heat a fluid, storage devices are used to store heat for use at night and on intermittent days, auxiliary heating systems to supply heat when required and distribution systems along with control to supply heat to the required spaces.

Active heating of buildings can be performed in any of the following three ways:

1. Solar heating of water in liquid collectors and transferring the heat to living spaces from the storage unit by means of liquid or air.
2. Solar heating of air in air collectors and transferring the heat to living spaces from storage units by means of air or liquid.
3. Using solar energy "stored" in the environment in the form of heat (ambient heat) by means of heat pumps.

Any of the above active space heating systems if compared with an appropriate auxiliary heating arrangement can provide the same comfortable conditions as a conventional space heating system. The buildings which are especially designed to provide comfortable conditions using solar active heating are such that they get more solar energy in winter and less in summer and thus the heating and cooling loads are reduced. These are known as "solar houses". Such houses are adequately insulated, properly oriented, optimally glazed and adequately sealed against air leakage. Appropriate materials and combinations of materials are used to admit, absorb, store, release, and distribute solar energy to reduce the heating load and thereby the size of the heating systems. In different countries the climate varies, as do the building codes, economic prosperity, the building materials available and therefore the structure and thermal characteristics of buildings. Therefore, there cannot be a common "solar house" design for all locations. Indeed the greatest need of the day is to develop a cost-effective active solar heating system. Therefore the problem is twofold, improved thermal performance at lower system costs.

There is a large variety of solar active space heating systems ranging from small heaters with only a few m² of collector area to large and sophisticated systems used for heating community and industrial buildings where the collector may be several thousands of m². Yet there is a large similarity in the basic layout of these systems. A typical active solar space heating system is shown in Figure 17.9.

All these active systems may be small or big and they consist mainly of the following five subsystems (Garg, Vol. 1, 1987):

1. The solar energy collectors, generally the flat-plate liquid or air collector, converting the solar radiation into heat.
2. A suitable heat storage device, generally water or pebble bed, a mix of these two or sometimes latent heat storage materials in order to synchronize heat supply and heat demand.
3. An auxiliary heat supply arrangement required in case of poor sunshine.

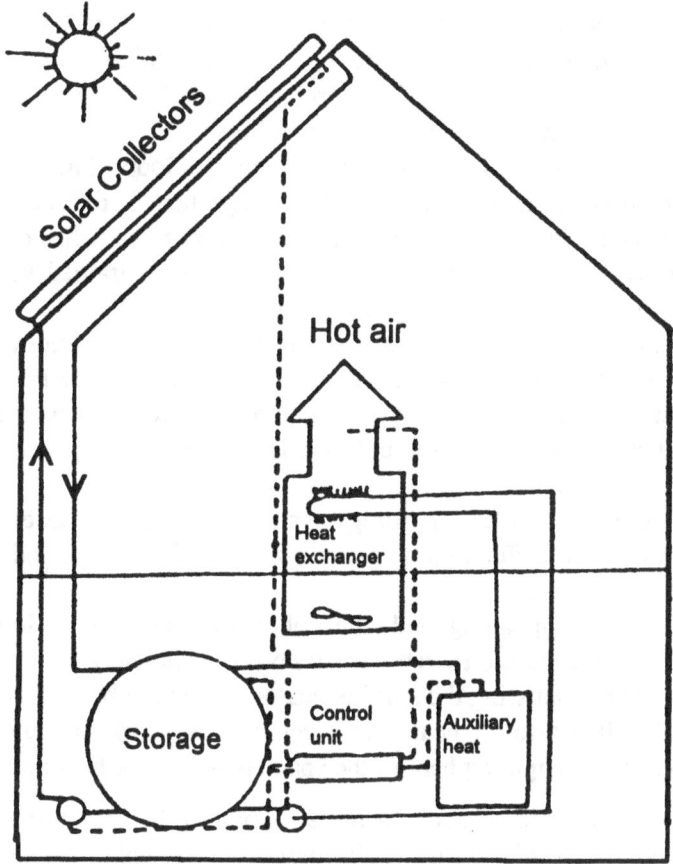

Figure 17.9 Elements of an active solar heating system

4. Control system and fluid flow devices, controlling the various operations.
5. Pumping and duct work or the distribution systems supplying the heat at an appropriate place.

It has been seen earlier that in most of the solar heating systems, the temperature requirement of the fluid is in the range of 50 to 80 °C, which makes the system much simpler in terms of fluid selection. The obvious choice is water or air in terms of solar liquid or air heating collectors. In terms of storage device the most obvious choice is a water or rock bed storage system.

Apart from the above main components of an active solar heating system, there are many other additional components that are generally required and which depend on the climatic and operating conditions, material used, purpose and size of installation and the preference of the individual designer. Some of these additional components are as follows:

1. A heat exchanger in the collector and storage loop. This is required when the fluid in the collector and the storage tank is different, such as water in the storage tank and antifreeze solution in the collector loop.
2. Drain-down type of collectors where the water is drained in the evenings to protect it from damage due to freezing.
3. A heat exchanger in the delivery and storage loop, also required when the fluids in the storage tank and the delivery pipe are different.
4. The distribution system can also be quite complex and may not only supply heat for space heating but also for hot water supply making the system more reliable.
5. Multilayered and multiplex storage system, storing the heat at different temperatures for different applications and for different periods such as diurnal or seasonal.
6. Use of heat pump along with the collectors operating at lower temperature difference and thereby increasing the efficiency.
7. A device for exhausting the surplus heat avoiding the boiling of water.
8. A suitable liquid-to-air heat exchanger or pipe work or panels in the load loop for dissipating heat to the space required for heating.

These eight additional components and many other components along with the main five subcomponents discussed above make a solar heating system quite complex. Therefore, an understanding of each of these components and their optimization is required to make a system cost effective.

Passive Heating of Buildings

Passive systems are generally more efficient and less costly than equivalent active systems and just about all systems are supplemented by passive heating. Passive systems contain five basic components:

1. Collector: Windows, water ponds, dark walls.
2. Storage: Walls, water ponds, large interior
                  thermal masses irradiated by sunlight.
3. Distribution Radiation conduction, free convection,
    systems: simple circulation fans.

| 4. | Controls: | Moving insulation panels to control building or collector heat loss, vents and windows. |
| 5. | Backup systems: | Any non-solar heating system. |

The design of a passive system requires the strategic placement of windows, storage masses and occupied spaces. There are many factors (Bansal et al., 1994) involved in passive building design: type of building (such as single storey and multi-storey, compact design, clustering of buildings, etc.); design of building such as orientation, thickness of wall, area of wall and roof, berming, overhangs, insulation materials used, single or double glazing, etc.); placement of living, sleeping, storage areas etc.; placement of glazing for the admission of solar radiation; placement of vents and windows etc.; berming and excavations; selection of building materials (such as dark materials absorb more heat, insulation reduces heat flow, hollow black walls filled with some insulation are better, heavier construction materials store more heat, emissivity of surfaces, etc.). These are all very important factors which should be seriously considered for designing a building. Passive solar buildings are classified as direct gain, thermal storage wall, attached sunspace, thermal storage roof and convective roof. All these concepts are shown schematically in Figure 17.10.

The simplest passive solar heating concept is the direct gain system (Figure 17.10 (a)) in which a double-glazed window facing south is used, through which direct radiation enters in winter and strikes the floor, walls, or other objects in the room. An appropriately sized overhang above the window is needed which shades the window during summer. In this system the floor and/or walls are of a massive construction to increase the thermal mass which helps to store the heat during the day and release heat during the night. Sometimes thermal insulation is used to cover the windows during the night time.

The temperature oscillation in the room, which takes place in case of the direct gain system, is considerably reduced by using a thermal storage wall (Figure 17.10 (b)) between the double glazing (facing south) and the room. In this concept of the thermal storage wall, the entire south facing wall is covered by one or two sheets of glass or plastic with some air gap between the wall and the inner glazing. In the air gap the hot air moves from bottom to top generally due to natural convection. The thermal storage wall is usually blackened, made of masonry or concrete at the outer side and facing the sun. The hot air in the gap moves up and goes through the upper vent into the room while the room air enters the gap through the bottom vent. This circulation continues till the wall goes on heating the air. This concept is also known as the trombe wall. In some cases the wall is made of drums or barrels or other suitable containers full of water (Figure 17.10 (c)) stacked on top of each other which collect, store, and distribute the heat. Then it is termed the water wall or drum wall.

In the concept of the attached greenhouse (Figure 17.10 (d)) both the concepts of direct gain and thermal storage wall are used. In this concept there is a sun space (Zone 1) on the extreme south facing the side of the house which is covered with a single or double layer of glass or plastic sheets. So it becomes a greenhouse that can be used either for raising vege-

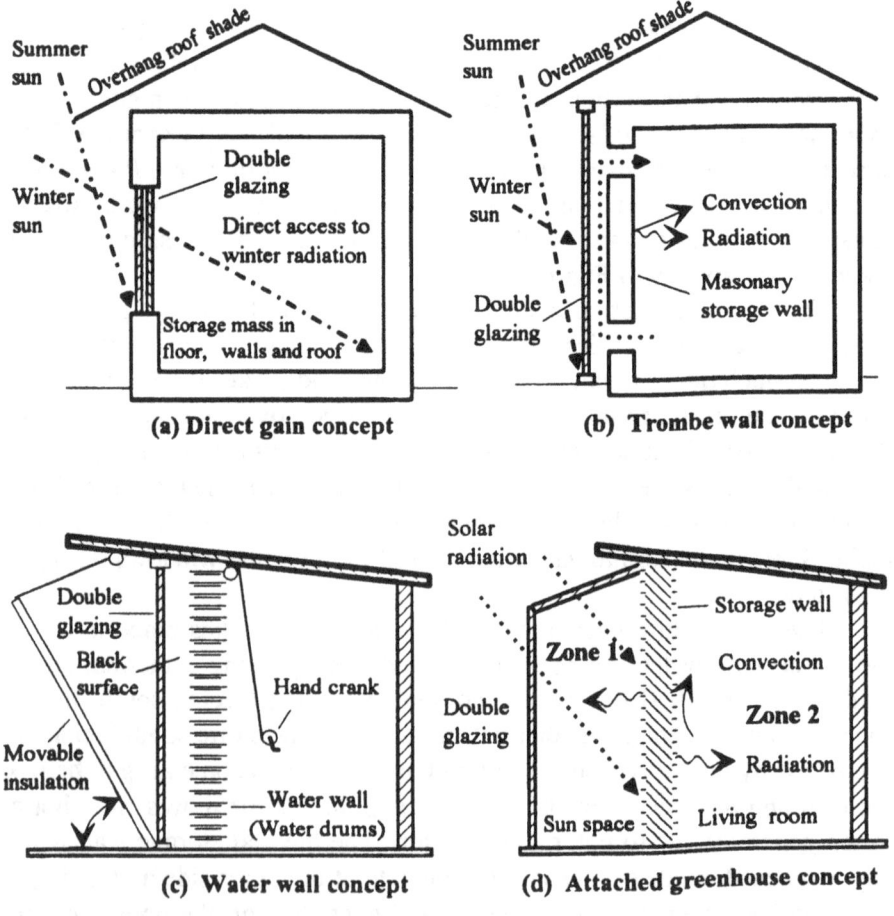

(a) Direct gain concept   (b) Trombe wall concept

(c) Water wall concept   (d) Attached greenhouse concept

Figure 17.10 (a-d) Passive heating concepts

tables or flowers or as a sunny space for living. There is also a thermal storage wall facing south between the room (Zone 2) and the greenhouse (sun space). This thermal storage wall is heated by direct absorption of solar radiation coming through the greenhouse transparent cover and the living room is heated through convection and radiation heat loss from the thermal wall.

The concept of the thermal storage roof (Figure 17.10 (e)) is more or less similar to the thermal storage wall except that the interposed thermal storage mass is placed on the roof instead of covering a wall. In the thermal storage roof system, a metal roof is used over which water bags made of

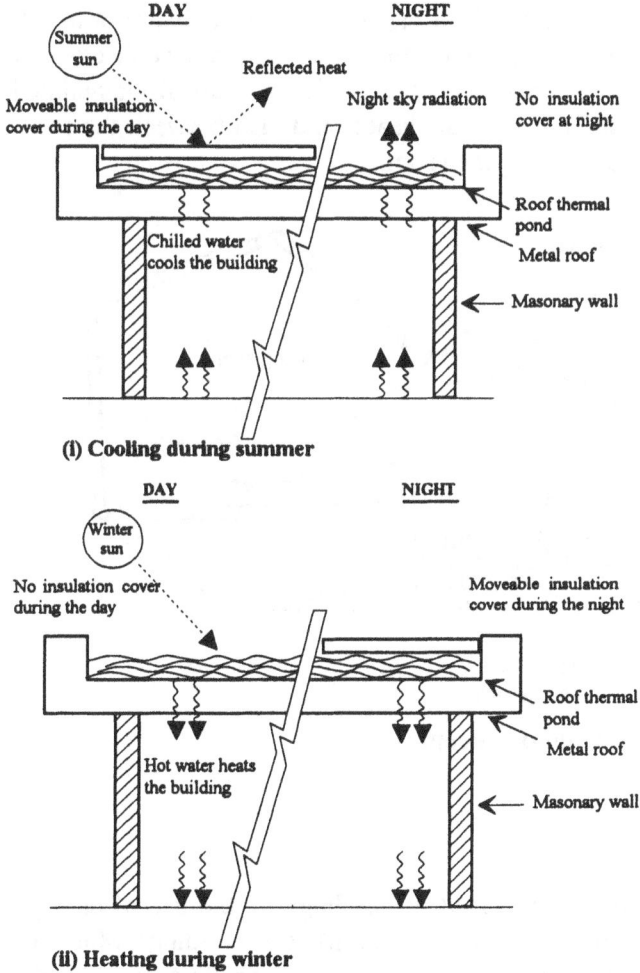

Figure 17.10 (e)　　　**Roof pond concept**

transparent or black plastic sheets filled with water are arranged. A moveable insulation covers the entire roof when required. In winter when heating is required the water in the bags is heated directly by the sun and enables a heat transfer directly to the room through the metal roof. During the night time the insulation covers the water bags. In summer the process is reversed, i. e. during the day time the water bags remain covered with the insulation layer and during the night time the insulation layer is removed, thereby allowing cooling of water bags and roof by thermal radiation heat loss to the outside resulting in a cooling of the room.

In the convective loop system (Figure 17.10 (f)) a liquid or air solar heating flat-plate collector is used to heat the fluid, generally water or air. A pebble bed storage system is placed above the level of the solar collector but below the level of the room in such a way that air is automatically circulated between the storage bed and the solar air heater and also between the room and the storage unit thereby heating the room.

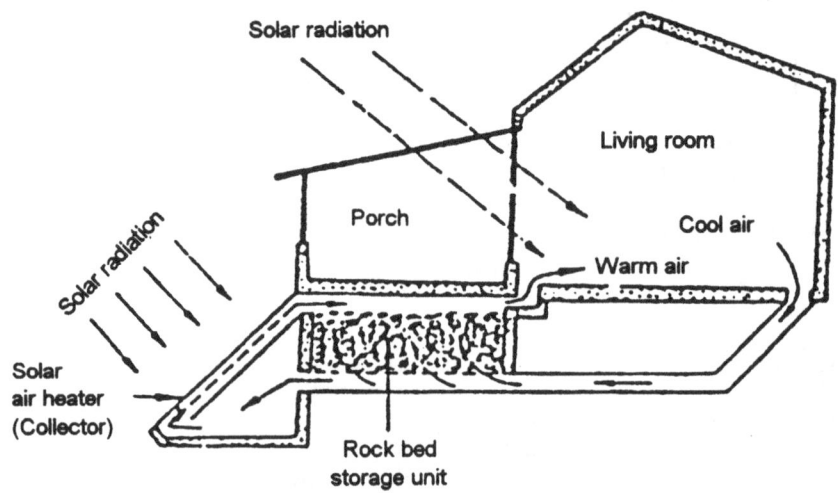

Figure 17.10 (f) Convective loop concept

Rational Energy Use

A large amount of energy can be saved in buildings by the use of daylight and/or energy-efficient compact fluorescent lamps. For buildings which are kept heated and/or cooled large energy savings are possible through architecture with methods like orientation, shading devices, cavity walls, use of insulation and others like natural ventilation, outside wind management, landscaping etc. In order to quantify some of these effects, we consider a typical building, the plans for which are given in Figure 17.11.

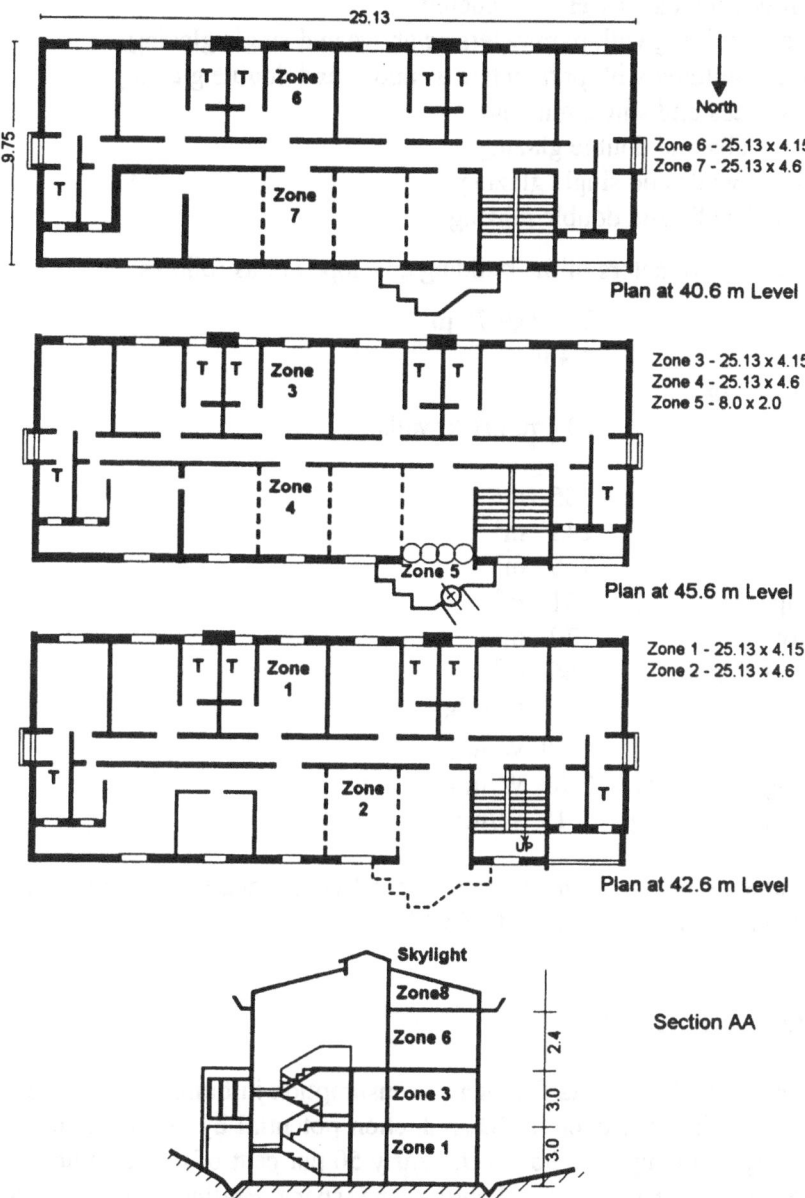

Zone 6 - 25.13 x 4.15
Zone 7 - 25.13 x 4.6

Plan at 40.6 m Level

Zone 3 - 25.13 x 4.15
Zone 4 - 25.13 x 4.6
Zone 5 - 8.0 x 2.0

Plan at 45.6 m Level

Zone 1 - 25.13 x 4.15
Zone 2 - 25.13 x 4.6

Plan at 42.6 m Level

Section AA

Figure 17.11   Plan and section of RIREPD building

The calculations were performed by using a sophisticated computer software SUNCODE capable of calculating hourly values for heating and cooling energy demand and then the sum over the entire month and year.

The following cases were considered:
1. Original building with parameters as above and single glazing.
2. Original building with parameters as above and double glazing.
3. Cavity walls and single glazing.
4. Cavity walls and double glazing.
5. Insulated walls and single glazing.
6. Insulated walls and double glazing.

The basic parameters of the building envelope are as follows:

Floor area	25.13x9.75 m
Height	8.4 m
Number of floors	3
Walls	23 cm, brick walls
Total area	
Wall	586 m²
Roof	245 m²
Floor	735 m²
Envelope	831 m²
Window	220 m²
Opaque brick wall	366 m²
U_{walls}	2.1 W/m²K
U_{roof}	1.48 W/m²K
$U_{building}$ (single glazing)	2.89 W/m²K
$U_{building}$ (double glazing)	2.15 W/m²K

The annual energy consumption for different locations representing various climatic zones is given in Table 17.7.

CO₂ Reduction Potential

In the absence of reliable data for energy consumption in buildings, it is very difficult to calculate the overall CO_2-reduction potential by energy efficient building designs. In any case however, nearly 50 per cent of the rural households depend on electricity for lighting and space heating/cooling while 100 per cent of the urban households use electricity for this purpose and

Table 17.7 Annual energy consumption for heating and cooling of the building (MWh/yr)

	Location	Leh	Shillong	New Delhi	Madras	Jodhpur	Bangalor
1.	Heating	155	22.0	9.6	-	-	-
	Cooling		48.0	169.9	210.5	205.8	125.8
2.	Heating	133	22.0	7.5	-	-	-
	Cooling	-	45.5	154.2	191.4	187.4	115.8
3.	Heating	106	17	5.8	-	-	-
	Cooling		44.4	136.1	167.2	165.3	103.8
4.	Heating	85	13	3.9	-	-	-
	Cooling	-	41.9	120.2	147.7	146.8	93.8
5.	Heating	63	10.5	4.1	-	-	-
	Cooling	-	43.6	104.7	124.4	125.8	82.0
6.	Heating	44	6.6	2.1	-	-	-
	Cooling	-	41.1	88.3	104.8	106.9	71.7

nearly 5 per cent of the electricity is used for households only, whereas in the whole building sector, about 20 per cent of the electricity is used. This amounts to about 80 billion kWh of electricity every year resulting in nearly 56 million tonnes of CO_2 released annually into the atmosphere. Use of insulation and other techniques can reduce these emissions by at least 30 per cent according to conservative estimates. Measures of energy conservation in buildings are therefore not only beneficial from an individual point of view but also from the point of view of national interest. Use of solar energy for water heating and other purposes can similarly contribute substantially to a greenhouse gas reduction programme.

References

Bansal, N. K., Hauser, G. and Minke, G. (1994): "Passive Building Design", Elsevier Science, Amsterdam.

Garg, H. P. (1987): "Advance in Solar Energy Technology", Vol. 1: *Collection and Storage Systems*, D. Reidel Publishing Co., The Netherlands.

Garg, H. P. (1987): "Advances in Solar Energy Technology", Vol. 2: *Industrial Applications of Solar Energy*, D. Reidel Publishing Co., The Netherlands.

Garg, H. P. (1987): "Advances in Solar Energy Technology", Vol. 3: *Heating, Agricultural and Photovoltaic Applications of Solar Energy*, D. Reidel Publishing Co., The Netherlands.

Garg. H. P. (1986): "Solar Water Heating Systems", D. Reidel Publishing Co., The Netherlands.

Garg, H. P. (1982): "Treatise on Solar Energy", John Wiley and Sons, UK.

Malik, M. A. S., Tiwari, G. N., Kumar, A. and Sodha, M. S. (1992): "Solar Distillation", Pergamon Press, Inc.

18 Analysis of a Residential Building in India Through Modelling Techniques

MAHABIR SINGH BHANDARI

Introduction

Buildings consume nearly 30 per cent of the total energy in the urban household, making them one of the largest consumers of energy. Most of this energy is used for space heating and cooling. Energy consumption in buildings can be reduced by designing energy-efficient buildings. Studies on possible energy savings in the building sector show that the energy-efficient design of new buildings could result in a 50 per cent reduction in energy consumption and renovations/retrofitting in the existing stock of buildings could yield energy reductions of 25 per cent (Clarke and Maver, 1991). In a large number of cases this approach can extend the level of building thermal comfort.

But how does one tackle this integrated complex scenario related to design decision making or renovation? The entire design process starting from client-designer dealings, concept drawings to final working drawings for construction involves a number of repetitive steps for the final outcome. Appropriate design intervention is possible with the aid of various design tools. These tools aid the analysis of the energy performance of the building.

General Design Tools

Currently available design tools fall into four broad categories (IEA, 1990):
1. Physical Modelling and Graphic Devices: These are used primarily for site analysis to assess solar access and site shading patterns; this category includes design tools for graphically plotting the path of the sun at different times during the year vis-à-vis objects on the site or on the adjacent sites.
2. Design Guidelines: This category includes quantitative and qualitative rules of thumb and similar sources of design guidelines based on local

climatic data. Specific recommendations for additional features such as insulation level and the sizing of glazing and thermal mass are given therein. Design guidelines provide a starting point for an energy-efficient house design.

3. Handbooks: Design manuals and handbooks generally contain recommended procedures for designing energy-efficient buildings. Manual calculation procedures are usually provided for determining the energy efficiency of small-scale solar houses. The calculations are also extended for determining the energy and economic performance of different energy-saving strategies. The nomograph and psychometric chart are examples of this category.

4. Computer Programmes: The proliferation of design tools based on computer programmes has been dramatic, corresponding to the growth of microcomputer use in architectural and engineering offices. These tools are especially relevant in the later stages of the design process, as design details are available. These models also enable the designer to determine the effect of varying one or more components of the buildings, thus allowing the energy performance of the building to be optimized.

With the onset of large computation facilities, especially PCs becoming a household good, the 4th tool is one of the most viable tools in terms of time and detail analytical study.

Basic Heat Flows in Buildings

Generally speaking, the energy analysis of buildings calls for an in-depth knowledge of the basic heat flows in the buildings. The building heat-flow path system is shown in Figure 18.1 (Clarke, 1985).

The heat flow into the building takes place through conduction, convection and radiation. This can be expressed in terms of mathematical equations. From a mathematical standpoint several complex equation types are required to accurately represent such a system. Since these equations represent heat transfer processes which are highly interrelated, it is necessary to apply simultaneous solution techniques if the performance prediction is to be accurate and the spatial and temporal integrity of the thermodynamic system is to be preserved. Various possibilities exist for analysing the thermal performance of a proposed building. These range from full-scale field experiments to laboratory tests, but simulation models are widely used because of

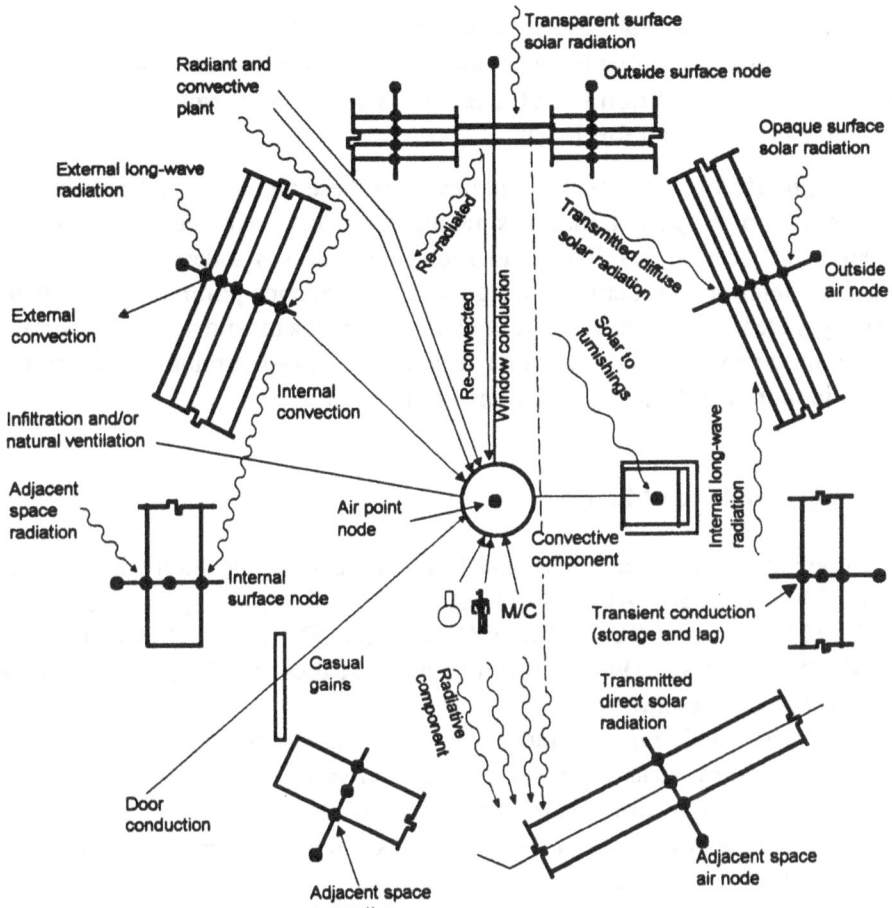

Figure 18.1 Building energy flow paths

the high costs of the other methods and their restrictive nature. A simulation model can be used to answer such questions as (Clarke and Maver, 1991):

- What is the maximum demand for heating, cooling and illumination and where and when does it occur? What are the causal factors?
- What will be the effect of a particular design strategy, such as using "superinsulation", a glazing system or other passive techniques?
- What is the effect of various orientation options on building performance?
- What will the performance of a building be if the choice of building materials is changed?
- How will infiltration or temperature stratification be affected by a par-

ticular management strategy and will condensation become a problem? How will the occupants' behaviour affect the infiltration rate?

- What is the contribution of a passive feature to energy saving and its impact on the comfort level?

In an effort to address the complexity of these questions and provide effective design support, building simulation models have received growing attention in recent years. The simulation model allows a designer to understand the interrelation between design and performance parameters and then identify potential problem areas, and thus implement and test appropriate design modifications. The resultant design is energy-conscious with efforts to attain more comfortable conditions in the interior.

Building Simulation Models

The commonly used computer models for simulating the thermal performance of buildings are: ACCESS, BLAST, DOE-2, EMPSS, F-Chart, HISPER, SHASP, TRNSYS, TWO-ZONE, UWENSOL, SUNCODE and TSBI3 (Sodha et al., 1986). From the study of these models, the following conclusions can be drawn:

1. There is a wide range of theories and programme types in use,
2. the degree of variation in results between various programmes is high - the degree of accuracy is largely unknown,
3. there is no evidence that more complex engineering models give more accurate results and
4. there are not many publications on a comparative study of these codes enabling someone to conclude which model is suitable for what type of analysis etc.

The main difference between the models is the way of solving heat transfer equations involved. For example, TRNSYS uses the response factor method, SUNCODE uses the finite difference method, DOE2 uses the weighting factor method, TSBI3 uses the lumped capacity model and IKARUS-ADMIT uses the steady-state as well as the periodic solution method. Based on the requirements and the type of analysis to be carried out, one can choose the appropriate model.

The usefulness of a simulation model as a design tool to predict the thermal performance of a building can be ascertained by comparing the predictions with the experimental results from existing buildings. The validation methodology uses three different kinds of tests: (1) analytical verification, (2) empirical validation, and (3) code-to-code comparisons. Standard codes like SUNCODE have been validated for a range of buildings and climate types represented by the test cases. These validated codes can be used for the validation of the other models. Some general features of the commonly used building simulation models are given in Table 18.1.

Table 18.1 Commonly used building simulation models

Characteristic	TRNSYS	SUNCODE	TSB13	DOE	IKARUS-ADMIT
Developer	Solar Energy Laboratory Wisconsin, Madison	Ecotope Corporation	Danish Building Research Institute	Lawrence Berkeley Laboratory	STE, Research Centre Juelich and CES, IIT[1] Delhi
Mathematical technique	Response factor method	Finite difference method	Steady state with lumped capacity method	ASHRAE method and weighting factor	Steady state and periodic solution metho
No. of zones	25	10	No limit	No limit	No limit
Input format	Text	Text	Graphical	Text	Graphical
User friendly	No	No	Yes	No	Yes
Daylighting	No	No	Yes	Yes	No
Equipment sizing	No	No	No	Yes	No
Data base	Building material	Building material	Building material	Building material	Building material

[1] Centre for Energy Studies, Indian Institute of Technology, New Delhi

Simulation Procedure

To begin with, the building design is simplified in a manner suitable for simulations. The process depends on the objectives of the analysis. For example, a complex building with many offsets may be simplified with fewer projections, or rooms where similar temperatures are desired may be grouped together. Although there is no hard and fast rule, it is usually sufficient to preserve surface areas, aspects and contained volume so that the heat conduction, thermal capacity and the dominant spatial relationship are preserved.

The next step is to organize the data defining the problem in the format dictated by the application and to determine the type of climatic influences to which the building will be subjected. This forms a base case of the problem.

The programmes are run for the base case and the results obtained are analysed for the potential energy-saving measures. Different aspects have to be kept in mind before applying any measure. For example, if the direct heat gain into the building has to be reduced, windows become an important feature and thus parameters like day-lighting come into the picture. Window sizing should be such that it reduces heat gain but at the same time does not affect adequate day lighting.

To exemplify the use of simulation models, a case study is illustrated below.

Case Studies

Rental Housing Shoghi, Shimla

Shimla lies in the cold and cloudy climatic zone. It is characterized by low solar radiation in winter but a high percentage of diffuse radiation. The diurnal temperature swing, which is the difference between daytime high and night-time low, ranges from 5-20 °C. Precipitation in the form of snow and rain is distributed throughout the year with maximum rainfall during the months of July and August. The total precipitation is around 1,400 mm.

Building Description The building is designed as a 4-storeyed block with a built-up area of approximately 360 m². The construction is basically of a RCC (reinforced concrete) frame structure with 230 mm thick external walls and 115 mm thick internal walls. CGI sheets are used for the roof. The whole building is divided into four zones for the simulation (Figure 18.2).

Results and Discussion

The annual heating demand of the building for different energy-conserving measures is shown in Table 18.2.

From Table 18.2, it is clear that replacement of single-glazed by double-glazed windows can reduce the annual heating demand by 13 per cent. By providing cavity walls the demand is reduced by 15 per cent for the original design. After applying different energy conservation measures, it is found that the building with insulated walls/roof and double-glazed windows gives the best performance and the heating energy demand is reduced from

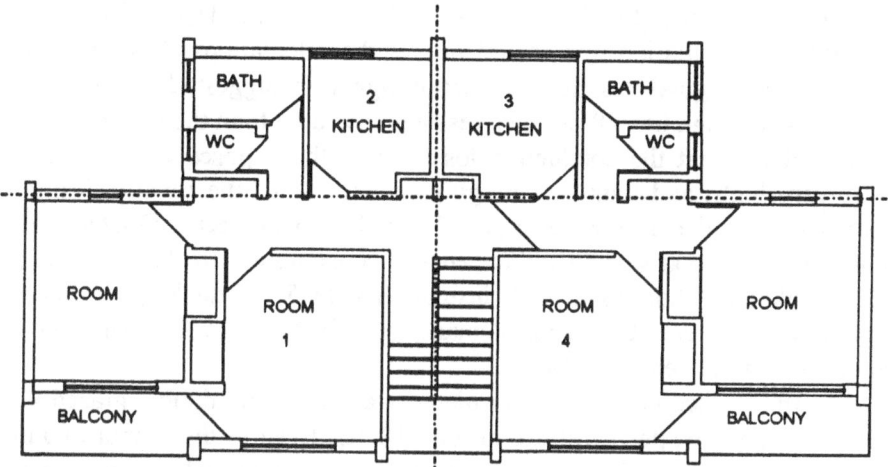

Figure 18.2 Rental housing, Shoghi, original design, typical floor plan

Table 18.2 Annual heating demand of the building for different energy-conserving measures (base temperatures 20 °C)

Design	Annual heating demand (MWh)	
	Original design	Revised design
1 No wall insulation, single-glazed	76	41
2 No wall insulation, double-glazed	66	36
3 Cavity walls, single-glazed	65	40
4 Cavity walls, double-glazed	56	37
5 With wall insulation, single-glazed	19	13
6 With wall insulation, double-glazed	12	9
7 Cavity on south wall, rest insulated, single-glazed	-	17
8 Cavity on south wall, rest insulated, double-glazed	-	13
9 Trombe wall on south wall, rest insulated, single-glazed	-	18
10 Trombe wall on south wall, rest insulated, double-glazed	-	14

76 MWh (base case) to 12 MWh, i. e. by 85 per cent. A layer of 5 cm thick mineral wool insulation was considered for the calculations. After a detailed study of the original design, a revised design was suggested (Figure 18.3). The revised design has 28 per cent less exposed area than the original design (it was found that the conduction losses from the exposed opaque surface were very high) and thus the energy consumption of the revised design in comparison to the original design is lower by 45 per cent. Double-glazed windows with good sealing reduce energy consumption by 12 per cent (no wall insulation). Additional wall insulation with 5 cm thick glass wool or mineral wool reduces the energy demand from 36 MWh to 9 MWh, which is equal to a 75 per cent reduction.

In the revised design with insulated walls/roof and double-glazed windows the room temperatures are around 18 °C. Even in the month of January, without the use of any conventional energy, the annual heating demand remains only 9 MWh. The monthly demands are presented in Figures 18.4 to 18.7. Figure 18.8 shows the annual demand.

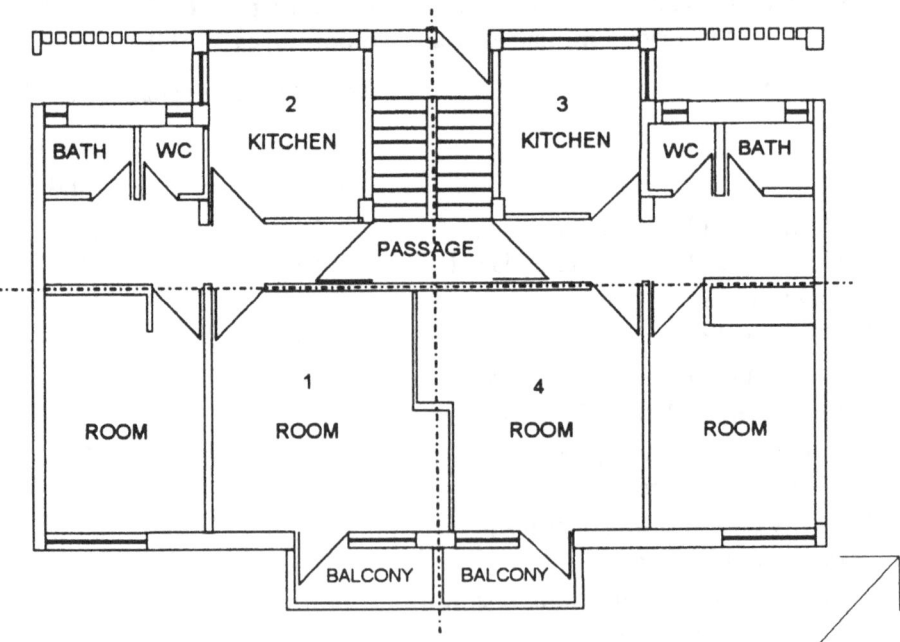

Figure 18.3 Rental housing, Shoghi, revised design, typical floor plan

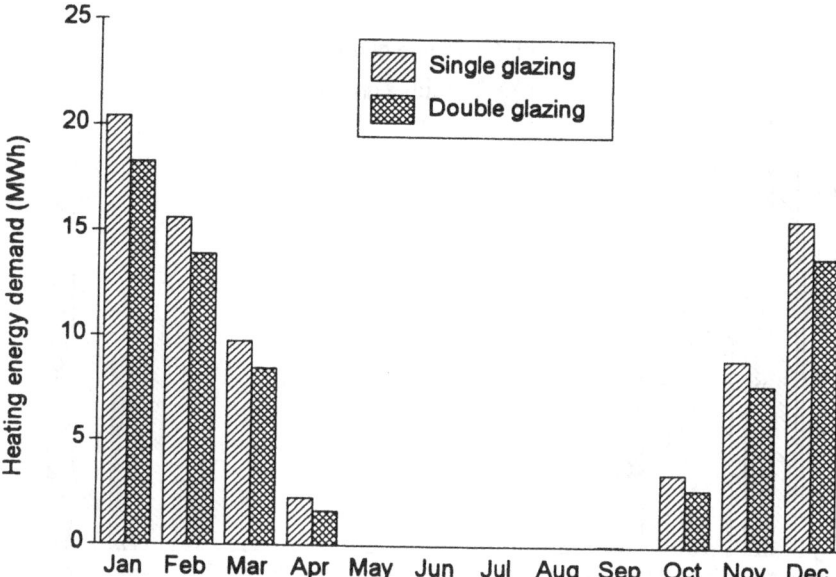

Figure 18.4 Heating energy demand for rental housing, Shoghi, original design, no insulation

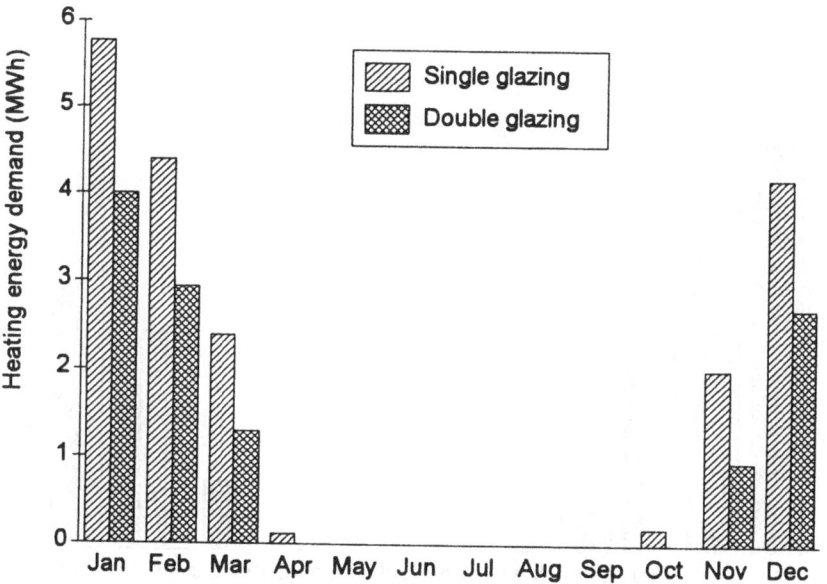

Figure 18.5 Heating energy demand for rental housing, Shoghi, original design, with insulation

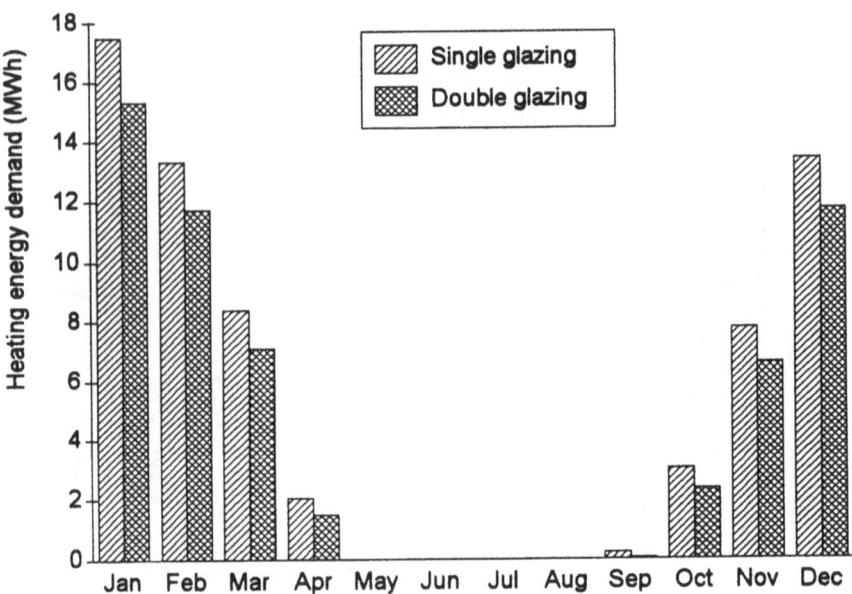

Figure 18.6 Heating energy demand for rental housing, Shoghi, original design, cavity walls

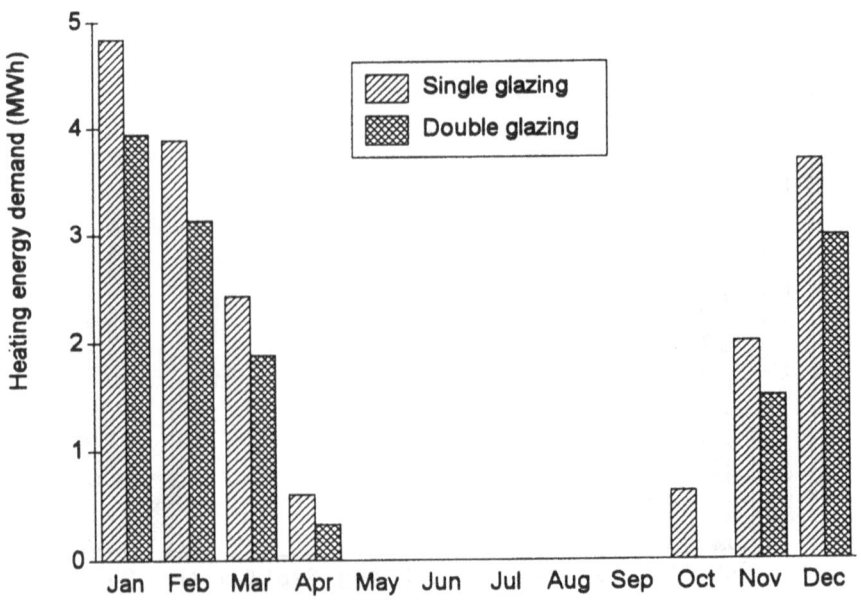

Figure 18.7 Heating energy demand for rental housing, Shoghi, revised design, with wall insulation

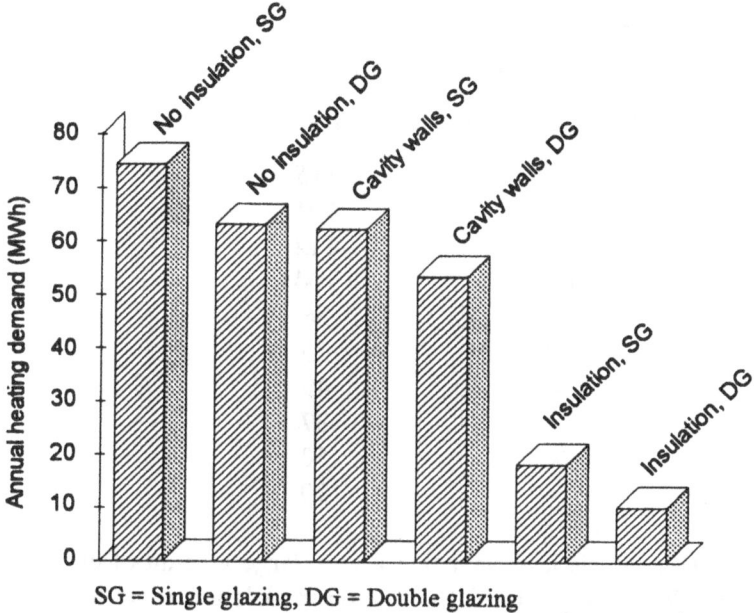

SG = Single glazing, DG = Double glazing

Figure 18.8 Annual heating demand for rental housing, Shoghi, original design

Conclusions

Energy-efficient buildings are quantified in terms of energy consumption per unit floor area per annum required to keep the inside space temperatures at the desired comfort level. Keeping the relative humidity at fifty percent, the acceptable indoor air temperatures are 18 °C and 24 °C in the winter and summer months respectively. In the 1980s, the energy consumption per unit floor area per annum for domestic buildings in Europe was more than 200 kWh/m²yr. As a result of various energy-saving measures enforced through appropriate legislation, this energy consumption is being reduced to 100 kWh/m²yr, thus setting up an energy performance index (EPI), hitherto missing for buildings in the Indian energy scene.

In colder regions, the main energy consumption results on account of space heating and there are no quantifiable measures available to determine the energy performance index.

The energy performance index EPI of the building in different cases turns out in Table 18.3 to be as follows :

Table 18.3 Energy performance index

Construction	E P I kWh/m²yr	
Type	*Original design*	*Revised design*
1	212	115
2	185	101
3	182	112
4	157	104
5	53	36
6	34	25
7	-	49
8	-	37
9	-	50
10	-	39

From the analysis it is clear that a very large amount of energy can be saved at the design stage itself. Simulation models are basic tools to determine the energy-efficient design of a building and hence they can help to reduce greenhouse gas emissions.

References

Clarke, J. A. (1985): "Energy Simulation in Building Design", Hilger, Bristol.

Clarke, J. A. and Maver, T.W. (1991): "Advanced Design Tools for Energy Conscious Building Design: Development and Dissemination", *Building and Environment*, Vol. 26(1), pp. 25-39.

IEA (July 1990): Solar Heating and Cooling Programme, Task VIII, Design Guidelines: An International Summary (3).

Nadel Sreven, Kothari, V., and Gopinath, S. (November 1991): "Opportunities for Improving End Use Efficiency in India", Prepared for World Bank, USAID.

Sodha, M. S., Bansal, N. K., Kumar, A., Bansal, P. K. and Malik, M. A. S. (1986): "Solar Passive Buildings", *Science and Design*, Pergamon Press.

19 Modelling Energy Savings and CO_2 Mitigation in the Residential Sector in India

SUJATA GUPTA, RITU MATHUR
AND LEENA SRIVASTAVA

Introduction

There are widespread discussions on the contribution by different countries to the emissions of greenhouse gases and strategies for reducing these emissions. For developing countries, the focus is on efficiency improvements and the increased share of renewable energy technologies in meeting the increasing energy requirements. A realistic assessment of carbon abatement options is necessary and this section evaluates these for the residential sector.

Sub-section 2 briefly discusses the energy scenario in India and the pattern of energy consumption in the residential sector. The modelling approach used, the options available for carbon dioxide reduction and future projections for energy consumption by households are presented in sub-section 3. The final sub-section discusses the limitations of CO_2 mitigation strategies.

Energy Scenario

Primary energy can be classified as commercial energy and traditional energy. The term commercial energy is used for energy forms that are bought and sold, i. e. coal, oil, natural gas, hydroelectricity and nuclear power. Traditional energy sources are firewood, animal dung and crop or agricultural waste, which are mostly non-traded forms of energy being by-products of agricultural and allied activities. In India, traditional sources of primary energy are significant contributors to the total energy supply and are estimated to currently account for 40 to 55 per cent of total primary energy consumption (for example Hall, 1991 and Government of India, 1991). Although traditional energy sources are important, data on their use are difficult to compile. Therefore, most energy analyses relate to commercial energy only.

Between 1985 and 1995, commercial energy consumption increased at an average rate of 5.8 per cent per year (British Petroleum, 1996). Coal accounts for more than 55 per cent of commercial energy consumption. The share of natural gas has increased and that of oil has fluctuated around 30 per cent and seems to decline from 1989 onwards. The share of non-fossil commercial energy, that is hydro and nuclear power, is declining (TERI, 1996).

The average per capita income for India was $ 300 in 1993 compared with the world average of US$ 4,420 (World Bank, 1995). Per capita commercial energy consumption was 242 kgoe for India and the global average was 1,421 kgoe in 1993 (World Bank, 1995). The low levels for per capita incomes and energy consumption in India (Figure 19.1) suggest that these will increase in future. Beyond a certain level of per capita income, production techniques become efficient, but changes in lifestyle dominate the growth in energy. In India in the next 2-3 decades, these changes will be manifested in an increase in energy demand by the residential sector.

Of non-commercial energy, 80-90 per cent is consumed by the domestic sector, which in addition accounts for 10 per cent of commercial energy consumption. The share of this sector is thus 40-50 per cent of the total energy

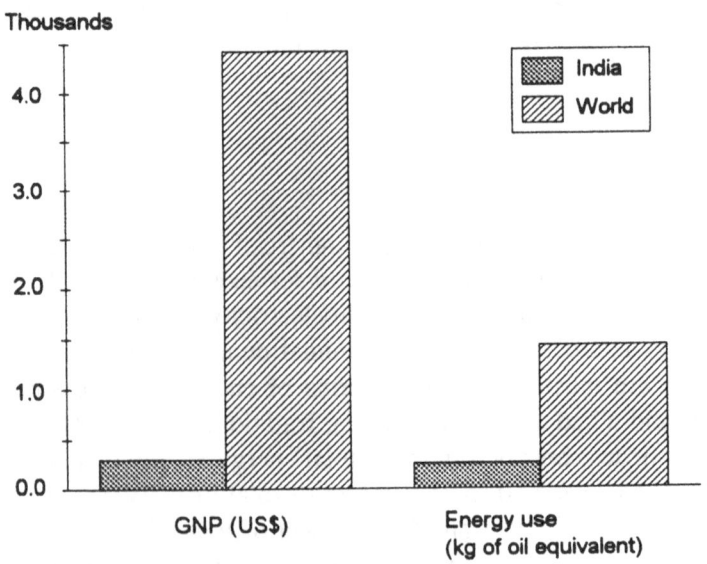

Figure 19.1 GNP per capita and energy use (1993)

consumed. In future, commercial energy consumption by the residential sector will increase due to the following reasons. Firstly, increasing per capita incomes will induce a switch on the "fuel ladder" where biomass and other traditional fuels (solid fuels) are replaced by commercial fuels (liquid and gaseous fuels). Secondly, availability of non-commercial energy sources have reached a level of saturation whereas energy demand continues to increase with an increase in population. This switch is brought about by the affordability of these fuels at higher per capita incomes and the convenience of using these fuels. Thirdly, the increasing level of urbanization will change the composition of the fuels consumed by households due to the limited availability of traditional fuels in urban areas and the differences in the energy end uses in urban areas.

Annual growth rates for consumption of LPG, kerosene and electricity by households were 14.4 per cent, 5.5 per cent and 12 per cent, respectively, over the period 1984-1990 (TERI, 1996). Data on ownership of energy-consuming devices also support the increasing trend in energy use by this sector (Rao, 1996) (Figures 19.2 and 19.3). Data collected by Rao also show that the ownership of these devices is much higher in urban households. Cross-sectional survey data for urban households reveal that, as income levels increase, useful energy consumption increases and the share of

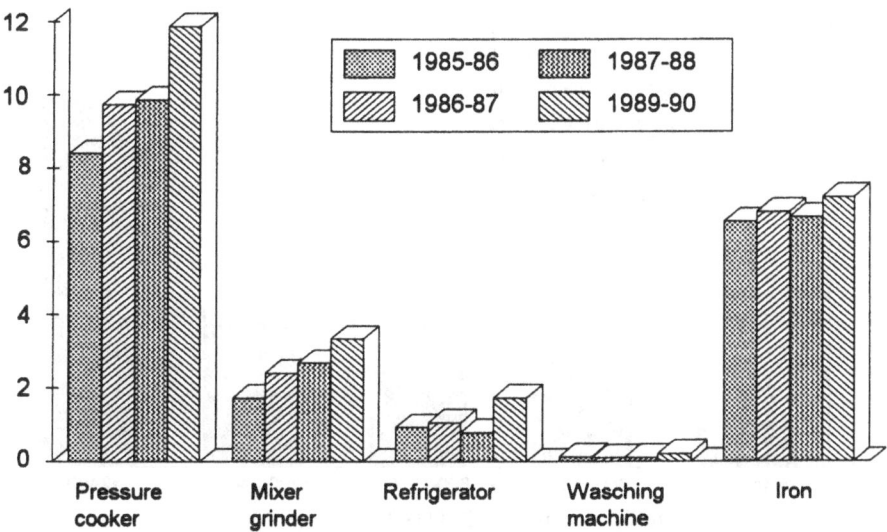

Figure 19.2 Number of electric appliances in rural areas (number per thousand households)

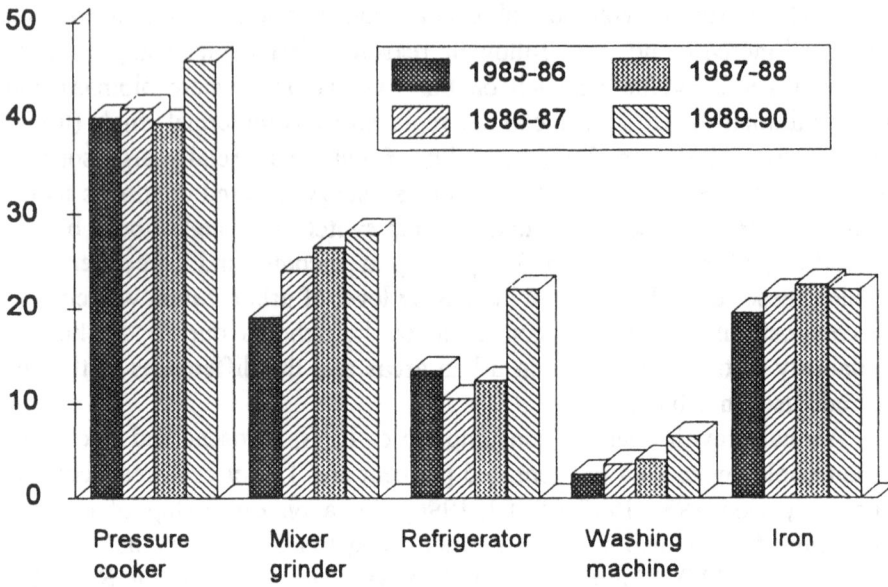

Figure 19.3 Number of electric appliances in urban areas (number per thousand households)

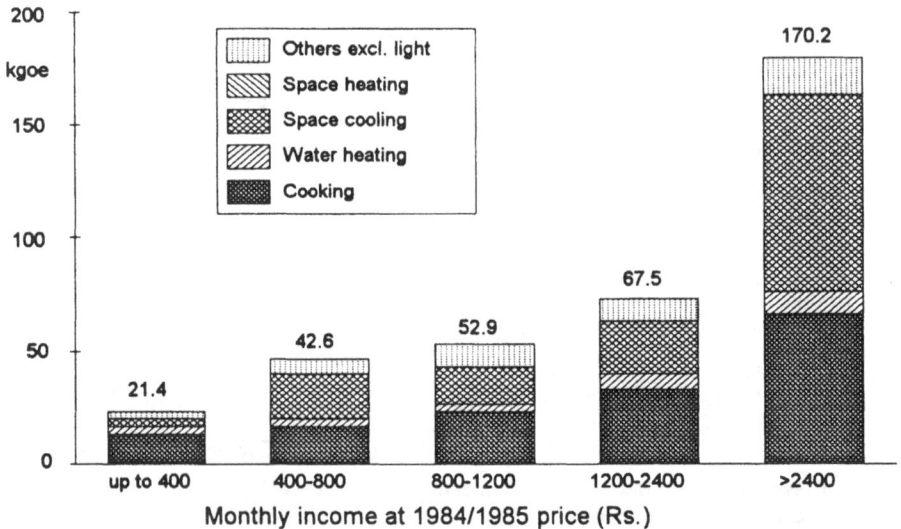

Figure 19.4 Annual per capita useful energy consumption for different end-uses

cooking- and water-heating (the main energy end-uses in the low income categories) declines from 75 per cent to less than 40 per cent (Figure 19.4) (TERI, 1996). Figure 19.5 shows that there exists substantial potential for growth in the ownership of essential energy-consuming devices. Of the 160 million households, only 60 million own a fan which is a basic requirement in an almost tropical country.

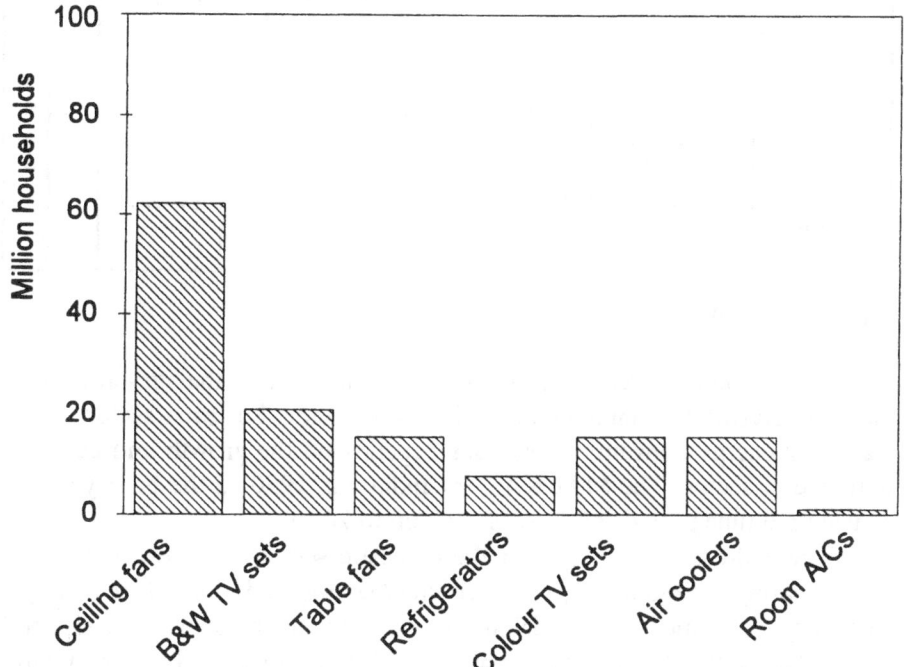

Figure 19.5 Appliance stock (in millions)

Strategies for Carbon Abatement in the Residential Sector

Model

The MARKAL model, a dynamic linear optimization framework, has been adopted to study CO_2 mitigation options in the different sectors. The model traces the flow of energy from extraction through conversion and distribution to the final consumption stages (Figure 19.6). The objective function is the minimization of the cost of energy supply and use. An end-use approach is taken which enables the model to consider the use of different devices to meet a particular end-use demand. This approach facilitates the assessment of demand-side management options.

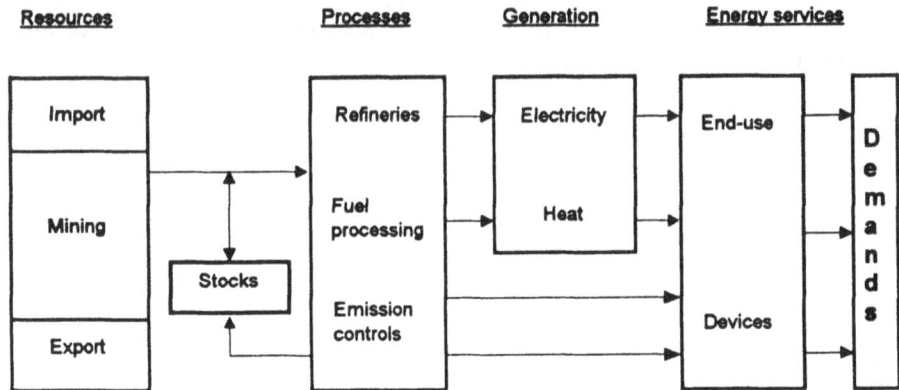

Figure 19.6 MARKAL building blocks

The model is driven by the demand for energy from the agricultural, industrial, transport, commercial and domestic sector. For each sector the demand for energy consuming end-uses depends on the growth and composition of that sector. The MARKAL for India has 1990 as the base year and considers 9 time periods of 5 years each up to 2030.

The end-uses considered for the domestic sector are lighting, cooking, water heating, refrigeration, space cooling/heating and others (for example, electricity consumed by televisions, irons, washing machines, radio, etc.). Given that demand and supply options differ for rural and urban populations, these are considered separately. Besides the growth in total population and the rural-urban mix, the demand for these end-uses also depends on the growth in per capita incomes and the distribution of the population across different income categories.

Mitigation Options

Mitigation options in the residential sector can be classified as fuel switching opportunities (from high carbon to low carbon fuels), efficiency improvement measures and the use of renewable energy technologies. Specific options considered in this section are the increased penetration of compact fluorescent lamps, fluorescent tube lights, efficient refrigerators and air-conditioners, improved cookstoves, solar water heating, photovoltaic home systems and solar cookers and the increased use of biogas. The rest of this sub-section discusses these options.

For cooking in urban areas, solar cookers are one of the options considered. Use of a solar cooker can help to save conventional fuel. It is estimated that the use of a solar cooker saves one LPG cylinder per year (Kishore, 1993a). Other studies (Philip et al., 1987) have estimated annual energy savings by the use of a solar cooker at two cylinders of LPG.

Biogas from a family-sized plant is an option for rural households for providing the energy for cooking and water heating. In this analysis KVIC biogas plants of 2 m³ operating for 250 days in a year (Kishore and Raman, 1993 and Kishore, 1993b) have been assumed.

The National Programme for Improved Cookstoves (or chulhas) has gained momentum in the country and fiscal incentives are being provided to beneficiaries as well as to the implementing agencies. In this study two types of improved chulhas were evaluated - the mud-clad, pottery-lined fixed chulha and the portable metal-clad ceramic-lined chulha. The non-subsidized costs of these are 100 rupees and 150 rupees, respectively (Mittal, 1993). Fixed and portable chulhas are reported to be 1.4 and 1.5 times more efficient than the traditional chulhas. Mittal (1993) quotes studies reporting that the actual usage of the improved chulhas ranges from 60 per cent to 86 per cent of those installed. Over the last ten years more than 12.5 million improved cookstoves have been installed. While evaluating this technology it should be kept in mind that these devices have a short life span (3 years for the fixed chulha and 5 years for the portable one) and cumulative numbers do not indicate the current population of these improved cookstoves.

Photovoltaic home systems were considered for rural households to meet their power requirements. Typically an entire system consists of 2-3 compact fluorescent lamps, a photovoltaic module of 35 W$_p$ and a storage battery. The annual electricity output is around 26.3 kWh (personal communications: Dr. B. D. Sharma and Dr. N. S. Prasad, TERI). The life of the system is 20-25 years. This option does not have very promising economics.

In urban areas solar water heaters are considered for providing hot water at 60 °C. A 100-litre-per-day system costing about 16,000 rupees (personal communications: Mr. Dilip Singh and Mr. Rakesh Kumar, TERI) is not economical over the other options of using kerosene or LPG or electricity to heat the water.

Two significant mitigation options in the urban domestic sector include efficiency improvements in domestic refrigerators and air-conditioners (AC). The most common refrigerator used in Indian households is the 165-litre unit (which had 90 per cent of the market in 1990). We have therefore considered these units as the basis for looking at mitigation options. In 1991, the population of domestic refrigerators was estimated at 8.3 million units. The Indian refrigerator market had a growth rate of about 21 per cent in the period 1986-1990 (Sand et al., 1994). The improved refrigerator unit has modifications in door design and compressor unit and uses 20 per cent less energy. Indian households generally use the 1.5 tonne air-conditioner. The efficient AC unit using improved EER (Electronic Equipment Regulation) compressors instead of the normal compressors uses 10 per cent less energy for the same service level and cost.

Lighting consumes 8-17 per cent of the total electricity produced in industrialized countries (McGowan, 1989). Its share in developing countries is probably even larger. Electric lamps may be incandescent, fluorescent, and compact fluorescent lamps (CFLs). Incandescent lamps (GLS) are used mostly in the residential sector. Fluorescent tube lights (FTLs) are used mainly in offices though some are used in houses and industry. Incandescent lighting is estimated to account for about 10 per cent of the total electricity sales and FTL about 6 per cent of total sales (Gadgil and Jannuzzi, 1989). The FTL system usually consists of a 40-watt lamp, a ballast for controlling the lamp, a starter, and a luminaire to hold the lamp. CFLs were initially introduced in the early 1980s. Many produce a warm light that is similar to that from incandescent bulbs. Some can also be screwed into GLS lamp sockets. CFLs have a long life (rated at 9,000 hours or more) and they do not have to be replaced frequently. Producing the same amount of light as GLS lamps, CFLs consume a quarter as much or even less electricity. A CFL that consumes only 16 watts has the same rated light output as a 75-watt incandescent.

Incandescent lamps are the most inefficient but continue to be widely used in the country, especially in the residential sector. Since the introduction of fluorescent tube lights in the 1930s, many offices and industries have switched to these, though the penetration is still quite small due to higher capital cost, more complicated installation and poorer light quality. With voltage fluctuations and the low level of voltage frequent in most parts of India (specially in towns/villages), FTLs often flicker and do not start. Electricity use in incandescent lamps is best reduced by replacing high-usage lamps with CFLs and low-usage lamps with FTLs (given that the quality of electricity is available).

The energy cost of an incandescent lamp exceeds the purchase price for lamps which are on for several hours a day. In such a case, the CFL is found to be cost-effective at electricity prices in many countries (ADB).

Base Case Results

The MARKAL model was run with a constrained supply of firewood and biomass and other restrictions such as an upper bound on the penetration of fluorescent tube lights. Figure 19.7 shows the preliminary base case results for the residential sector with minimum constraints imposed on the model, specially on the demand side.

The results indicate that the gross energy demanded by this sector will decrease by 11 per cent over a forty-year period. This result is due to the replacement of old technologies by efficient ones, more so when the resource availability is restricted in the later periods (for example, that of firewood). Consumption of kerosene increases in the future. In the initial time periods it is used for meeting a large percentage of rural lighting demand, but after 2005 there is sufficient electricity available to meet lighting requirements. Then kerosene is used for cooking and water heating. Animal wastes, which in the initial periods are burnt in inefficient stoves, are in the later time periods converted to biogas. This conversion increases the useful energy from the same quantity of animal waste by 45 per cent. This improvement is at a cost and is adopted after 2000 due to the constrained availability of fuels. The total useful energy consumption of the residential sector increases by 2.8 per cent per annum, despite a reduction in final energy consumption. This growth rate is above the population growth rate.

For the viable carbon abatement option there are several other barriers which prevent the penetration of these options. There exists a large unexploited potential for renewable energy technologies and there are optimistic cost projections for most abatement options. However, a realistic assessment of these options requires the recognition of certain limiting forces which exist in the real world. The results indicate that some of the options with higher efficiencies are more economical. An examination of the achievement for various renewable energy technologies and their potential indicates that there is substantial scope to increase the diffusion of these technologies. Restriction on the fuel availability of some fuels like firewood make some additional options economically viable.

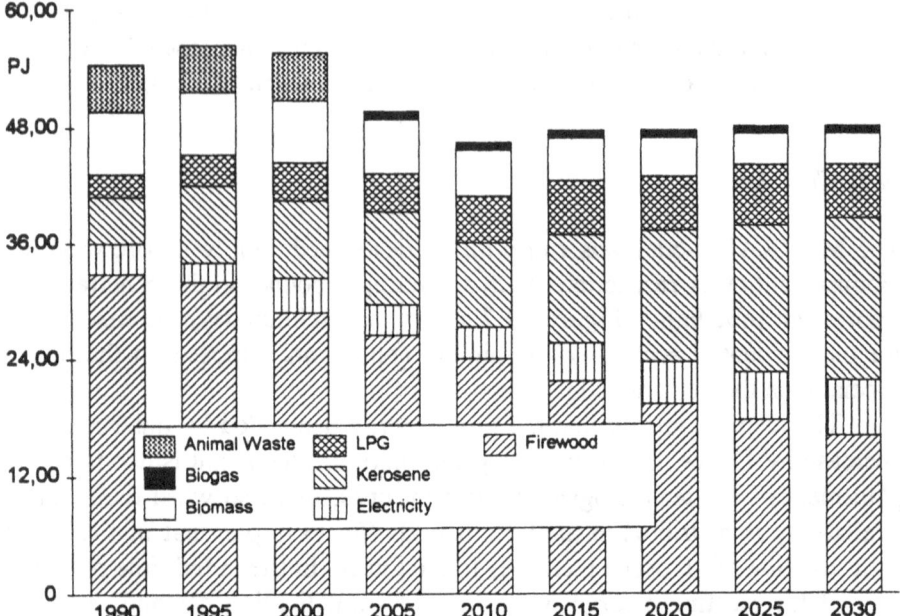

Figure 19.7 Development of energy consumption in the domestic sector (TERI results from MARKAL, 01/97)

Barriers

The level of dissemination of some of the renewable energy technologies has not achieved significant savings. It is estimated that 2.2 million biogas plants and 20 million improved chulhas have together resulted in 5 per cent savings in firewood and have covered only 9 per cent of households.

There are numerous barriers which are preventing these technologies from achieving their full potential despite the favourable economics indicated. Firstly, the assumption of perfect information for consumers is not entirely true. It is not common for individuals to carry out a complete cost-benefit analysis or do a life-cycle costing exercise of the options available. Often, they do not have the complete data or the expertise to evaluate the options. Secondly, there is a difference in the discount rates used by the economic analysis and those used by individuals, who have much higher rates. Often in developing countries, very high rates of interest are charged for personal credit, or the lending rates are high due to lack of credit and the higher risk associated with lending to individuals and for renewable energy technologies which are in the initial stages of technological development. Also, the investor may be a different party than the person who actually uses the device and pays the energy costs. An example of this would be the investments made in energy-saving construction in the building sector.

The other factor which is not reflected in a pure economic analysis is the acceptability of the option in terms of convenience of use. Economically viable options will be adopted if they are desirable. Other factors which affect the acceptance of a technology are the level of reliability and its operation in the real world. The Indian power supply is a major constraint in improving the EER of Indian compressors. In the case of air conditioners, compressors in India are designed to operate under a wide voltage range (150-260 V). According to some compressor manufacturers, a 150-260 V compressor consumes 10 per cent more power than a 190-260 V compressor. The cost for both options are comparable. Similarly, Indian compressors for refrigerators are oversized to withstand the poor quality of power which ranges from 125 to 270 volts at a frequency of 50 Hz. Working conditions are not expected to improve in the short term and so it is important to investigate efficiency improvements in this context. Surveys have revealed that the energy consumption of a refrigerator does not figure as a prominent attribute that consumers consider while making a purchase.

Many technologies underperform due to lack of support systems. In addition, there are transactional costs associated with many new technologies, which are not considered while undertaking an economic analysis. Further, there are institutional and policy barriers (for example, the Indian standard for energy consumption of 730 kWh/yr for a 165-litre model is not sufficiently rigorous to encourage innovations by manufacturers) which obstruct or discourage the adoption of efficient technologies.

In conclusion, it can be said that many social and institutional and a few economic factors are not incorporated in a model. Model results provide useful policy implications, however, these are directional and indicative. There exists scope for international financing of not only the various energy saving options but also of activities which would help to remove some of the barriers identified and to facilitate the propagation of economically viable and hence sustainable energy-saving options.

The authors would like to acknowledge their colleagues Dr. B. D. Sharma, Dr. N. S. Prasad, Mr. Dilip Singh, Mr. Rakesh Kumar and Ms. R. Uma for providing useful information.

References

Asian Development Bank (ADB): "Energy End Use - An Environmentally Sound Development Pathway", Manilla, Phillipines.

British Petroleum Company (1996): "BP Statistical Review of World Energy".

Gadgil, A. and Jannuzzi, G. (1989): "Conservation Potential of Compact Fluorescent Lamps in India and Brazil", Lawrence Berkeley Laboratory Report LB.-27210, University of California, Berkeley, CA.

Government of India (1991): "Sectoral Energy Demand in India", Planning Commission, New Delhi.

Hall, D.O. (1991): "Biomass Energy" in: Energy Policy, October, pp. 711-737.

Kishore, V.V.N. (1993a): "Cooking Energy Systems: a Comparative Study" in: Renewable Energy Utilization - Scope, Economics and Perspective, Edited by V.V.N. Kishore, Tata Energy Research Institute, New Delhi.

Kishore, V.V.N. (1993b): "Biogas Technology: Potential, Problems and Research Needs", in: Renewable Energy Utilization - Scope, Economics and Perspective, Edited by V.V.N. Kishore, Tata Energy Research Institute, New Delhi.

Kishore, V.V.N. and Raman, P. (1993): "The Biogas System for Cooking Energy Production: Is It More Efficient?" in: *Renewable Energy Utilization - Scope, Economics and Perspective*, Edited by V.V.N. Kishore, Tata Energy Research Institute, New Delhi.

McGown, T. (1989): "Energy Efficient Lighting" in: Johansson et al. (Edited) *Electricity: Efficient End-Use and New Generating Technologies*, Lund University Press, Sweden.

Mittal, D. K. (1993): "Improved Chulha Programme: Alleviating Fuel Crisis and Uplifting Quality of Rural Life", Urja Bharati, Ministry of Non-conventional Energy Sources, March, Vol. 3, No. 3, pp. 25-27.

Philip, S. K., Makwana, H. M. and Singhal, A. K. (1987): "Monitoring and Servicing of Subsidized Solar Cookers in Gujarat - a Case Study" in: *SESI Journal*, No. 1, pp. 37-46.

Rao, S. L. (1996): "Consumer Demographics in India", National Council for Applied Economic Research, New Delhi.

Sand, J. R., Vineyard, E., Bohman, R. H. (1994): "Improving the Energy Efficiency of Refrigerators in India", ORNL.

TERI (1996): "TERI Energy Data Directory Yearbook (TEDDY)", Tata Energy Research Institute, New Delhi.

World Bank (1995): *World Development Report*, The World Bank, Washington D. C.

Summary and Conclusions

NARENDRA BANSAL AND MANFRED KLEEMANN

The Purpose of the Joint Workshop

Human-induced climate change influenced by greenhouse gas emissions into the atmosphere is not a fiction. The evidence has established that the global mean surface temperature has increased by about 0.5 °C since the late 19th century. Global sea levels have risen by about 10 to 25 cm over the past 100 years. One of the major contributors to these phenomena is the use of fossil fuels by mankind all over the world.

Over the last 10 years, scientists have been pointing to the grave danger posed by increasing greenhouse gas emissions to the climate as well as to the global economy. In accordance with scientists from all over the world the UN Intergovernmental Panel on Climate Change decided that the use of fossil fuels has to be reduced to achieve a stabilization effect of greenhouse gases in the earth's atmosphere. Each country is obliged to take strategic steps to honour its commitment to this social cause. Developing countries face a dilemma because the fossil fuel consumption in these countries is still rising due to the developing economy as well as to the population growth. But on the other side, the per capita emission is still significantly lower in developing countries compared to industrialized countries.

Especially in India, increasing energy supply is a necessary condition for the economic growth to which the country is committed. Energy sources capable of meeting a certain demand and at the same time keeping the environment free from pollutants, represent a very challenging task for which data, analysis and technological selection are needed. A joint discussion between German and Indian groups on these aspects is warmly welcomed.

Therefore the Systems Analysis and Technology Evaluation Group (STE) of the Research Centre Juelich and the Centre for Energy Studies (CES) of the Indian Institute of Technology (IIT) Delhi held a joint workshop on "Strategies and Technologies for Greenhouse Gas Mitigation" in New Delhi in December 1996.

This seminar was organized in order to discuss concrete efforts which Germany and India, as developed and developing economies, are considering to reduce climate-relevant emissions. Various speakers, drawn from a list of leading experts in this field from both countries, discussed the political goals, measures undertaken for climate protection, role and potential of renewable energy sources and rational energy use especially in the residential sector.

The seminar started with an inaugural address where the Secretary of State of the Ministry of Environment and Forest, Government of India, and His Excellency the German Ambassador emphasized that the widest possible co-operation between industrialized and developing countries is necessary to protect the climate system for the benefit of present and future generations.

The deliberations during the seminar on "Strategies and Technologies for Greenhouse Gas Mitigation" were grouped into three broad areas, namely:

I.   National Strategies and Programmes,
II. Renewable Energies for Climate Protection,
III. Reduction Options in the Residential Sector.

The contributions cover German and Indian scenarios for greenhouse gas mitigation strategies, reduction measures, renewable energy utilization, and energy saving in the residential sector presenting German and Indian views and technological developments in both countries.

The papers and discussions at the workshop and the material subsequently submitted form the basis for this book. The rationale behind the book is to compare the environmental policy and the achieved state of the art for environmentally compatible technologies in a typical industrialized country and in a typical developing country. Although the book describes two country-specific studies, it has a broader scope. The purpose is to contribute to global thinking and to encourage better international co-operation in the field of climate protection between developing and industrialized countries.

Strategies and Reduction Measure Programmes in Germany

The first paper describes the political situation in Germany which is characterized by reunification, European integration and globalization of the economy and environment. Recent developments of the gross national product, population, energy consumption and the resulting greenhouse gas emissions are outlined. In 1990, the German Government pledged itself to make an ambitious 25 per cent reduction in national CO_2 emissions by 2005 relative to 1990 emissions. A general outlook is given in the paper which refers to reduction measures and future emissions. The projections are based on the results of the national energy supply optimization model IKARUS (Instruments for Greenhouse Gas Reduction).

Finally the paper presents briefly the European perspective. A comparison of basic demographic, economic and environmental data provides insights into the European context. The energy policy of the EC is briefly outlined as well as the consequences for future CO_2 emissions.

The second German contribution discusses a comprehensive programme of concrete CO_2 reduction measures to reach the 25 per cent reduction goal. A package of 115 reduction measures in all sectors of the energy economy has been implemented step by step since 1990. The policy measures include regulations, standards, subsidies, pollution taxes, infrastructure funding, R&D and information programmes etc. The technical measures are fuel switch, energy conservation, efficient technologies, CO_2-free technologies and demand-side management. With these measures a reduction of approximately 17 per cent could be achieved by 2005. Further efforts will be necessary to reach the 25 per cent reduction goal. But there are various constraints which make it very difficult to realize the necessary additional measures.

Emission Situation and "No Regret" Measures in India

The first Indian paper identifies the various CO_2 emission sources in the country and quantifies sectoral emission inventories. The emissions of coal, oil and natural gas utilization in industry, transport and power generation are analysed in detail. The historical figures show the rapid increase of emissions due to economic and population growth. Moreover, the figures for carbon dioxide emissions from various forest-related activities are provided. The projections for Indian CO_2 releases into the atmosphere give reason to expect a further strong increase in the future.

The next paper includes important aspects of anthropogenic emissions, the related human activities and the direct and indirect radiative effects from the viewpoint of atmospheric science. The second part of this paper deals with options for greenhouse gas reduction in India. Here the author looks especially at so-called "no regret" measures, which are compatible with the situation of a developing country like India. A quantification of the measures is not yet possible.

Renewable Energies for Climate Protection in Germany

The first two contributions deal with overall strategic aspects whereas the last three papers are more technology oriented. They focus on photovoltaic, wind and biomass utilization.

The first paper examines the contribution of renewable energies to the total energy supply in Germany and explores issues of the state of the art. The potentials of the various sources of renewable energy are estimated. Environmental effects and economic aspects are discussed finally. The paper points out that the contribution of renewable energies to the total German energy supply will remain relatively low.

The second paper analyses the contribution of renewable energy to power generation under changing conditions in Germany. The analysis was performed with the support of the national energy supply optimization model IKARUS (Instruments for Greenhouse Gas Reduction Strategies).

The shares of renewables in electricity production are expected to increase both under the changed boundary conditions of CO_2 reduction and in the reference developments and forecasts. The strongest increase is to be observed for wind and biomass, whose contributions will be many times higher in 2020 than today. In all reference developments and forecasts, however, the percentage of electricity production from renewables remains far behind the optimistic expectations. Although electricity production from renewables furnishes a contribution to CO_2 reduction, major saving potentials will be achieved by other measures (e.g. increased use of natural gas, thermal insulation, more efficient passenger cars etc.), which are often less expensive.

The first of the three following technological papers deals with photovoltaics in Germany. After an introduction into the physics of the photovoltaic effect, silicon is discussed in detail as the most important semiconductor material for solar cells. Other solar cell materials are briefly addressed. Two strategies are analysed in order to lower the system costs and to make solar cell technology economically acceptable. Finally, predicted cost developments and the possible role of photovoltaics in future energy scenarios are investigated. The authors present a more optimistic view of photovoltaics and demand stronger support for this technology.

Since the early nineties the capacity of the installed wind power plants in Germany has doubled nearly every year. This increase is mainly due to the "Act on the Sale of Electricity to the Public Grid" which took effect in 1991. It guarantees a minimum payment level for electricity generated from renewable energy. Presently, about 20 manufacturers are producing wind turbines in Germany. The characteristics of commercial plants are capacity ratings between 1 and 1,500 kW and rotor diameters between 4 and 60 m. Wind turbines are grid-connected and operate mainly in so-called "wind parks". Despite the progress achieved, the utilization of wind power is still limited by several financial and ecological constraints. The maximum future potential estimated for CO_2-avoidance in Germany is about 3 per cent.

Next to hydropower, biomass is by far the most widely used option in Germany today. Biomass can be used by a variety of different technologies and processes. The options differ substantially according to the type of biomass used (e.g. liquid manure, sewage sludge, forest waste wood, rape seed, wheat) and according to the desired form of useful or final energy (e.g. heat, electricity, ethanol, motor fuel, pyrolysis oil). For this reason, the current state of the art regarding the various possibilities for using biomass is analysed in the last chapters. Subsequently, the technical biomass potential (8 per cent of the total supply) is assessed and its current utilization (0.8 per cent) within the German energy system described. This is followed by an analysis of the supply costs for final and useful energy. Based on this, the possible reduction of CO_2 equivalents due to current and still conceivable biomass utilization – determined over the entire life cycle – and the associated reduction costs are calculated and discussed.

Renewable Energies for Climate Protection in India

The first Indian paper provides an overview of the CO_2 reduction potential through renewable energy and rational energy use. The estimated technical potential for electricity generation is at least double the total existing generation capacity in India. Out of the possible options the following technologies have reached the highest level of utilization: hydropower plants, wind generators, biogas plants and improved cooking stoves. The paper presents a comparative analysis assessment and considers costs and emissions of various heat- and electricity-producing technologies based on renewable sources of energy. Finally, general aspects of rational energy use are considered.

The following two papers deal with the state of the art of photovoltaic cells and with promotion programmes for photovoltaics in India. The first paper describes manufacturing processes for solar cells and various rural, remote and urban applications. Then an overview of photovoltaic cell production in India is given, and the numbers of installed units for various applications are provided. The second paper discusses the Indian photovoltaic programme, which was initiated in the seventies with emphasis on indigenous technologies. Demonstration programmes, especially for lighting and water pumping, were initiated in the eighties. With the growing demand quite soon seven manufacturers of solar cells and 12 photovoltaic module manufacturers emerged in the Indian market. The main issues involved with photovoltaic electricity are the high initial costs, commercially viable production levels, technology upgrading, storage distribution and service network, market development and financing.

The next paper points out that recent studies identified a tremendous wind energy potential in India. The total installed capacity reached 900 MW in 1995 and the wind resource assessment programme includes several even more promising sites. A few problems arose in the early demonstration projects, but with the adaptation of wind turbine equipment to Indian conditions as well as better planning and service the performance improved considerably. During the Eighth Plan, the Ministry of Non-conventional Energy Sources (MNES) has consolidated and strengthened technology development and commercialization by providing market orientation and creating a favourable policy environment. After the presentation of costs and environmental benefits the author then draws an optimistic picture of the future development of wind energy utilization in India.

The last contribution in this section supplies a description of the attractiveness of biomass utilization in general and especially in India. After the estimation of the energy potential of biomass, Indian technological capabilities, government programmes, policies and incentives are discussed. The current state of the art and future expectations for the most promising technologies are presented.

Reduction Options in the German Residential Sector

With the help of three scenarios the energy saving potential and the scope for political measures in the German building sector are identified. Substantial savings can be achieved by the installation of more centralized systems, high-efficiency heaters, and especially by retrofitting old buildings to meet current thermal insulation standards. The paper discusses scenarios for the improvement of old buildings and recommends various technical and political measures. This includes improved insulation standards for buildings, public information and motivation programmes, energy tax and financial assistance programmes. Finally a policy strategy is proposed for an effective application of these instruments.

The second paper describes a space heating model which was developed by the Research Centre Juelich for strategic analyses. The space heating model calculates the annual heating energy demand of a building or a set of buildings using the European EN 832 norms as the mathematical basis. The model further calculates the corresponding emissions for various types of buildings in the Federal Republic of Germany. Buildings are classified according to their physical size, age, building use and heating technology applied.

The modelling approach used to evaluate the energy demand of existing and new residential buildings, to estimate their impact on the CO_2 emissions and to forecast the trends of subsequent measures required to reduce these emissions is discussed in this paper.

Reduction Options in the Indian Residential Sector

The first paper mainly focuses on the energy consumption pattern of the residential sector and distinguishes between urban and rural households, but also concentrates on the respective technologies for cooling, heating and cooking. Special emphasis is put on solar energy utilization. Solar equipment, like collectors, cookers and distillation units, is considered. Two separate paragraphs deal with active and passive solar heating of buildings.

The last two papers discuss energy and CO_2-saving options based on model calculations. The first contribution describes a simulation model for energy analysis in buildings and presents a case study for a single house in a cold climatic zone of India. The paper discusses various improvements of the design in order to achieve a higher energy efficiency of the house.

In contrast to the above paper, the final contribution presents a scenario for the whole residential sector by using the MARKAL (market allocation) optimization model which is based on linear programming.

Mitigation options considered in the study are fuel switching opportunities, efficiency improvement and use of renewable energy technologies. Since the level of dissemination of renewable energy technologies has not achieved significant savings yet, the paper discusses the barriers to the propagation of renewable energy technologies.